MISS MANNERS® RESCUES CIVILIZATION

OTHER WORKS BY JUDITH MARTIN

Miss Manners®
RESCUES CIVILIZATION

From Sexual Harassment,
Frivolous Lawsuits,
Dissing and
Other Lapses in Civility

JUDITH MARTIN

Illustrations by Daniel Mark Duffy

Crown Publishers, Inc.   New York

Copyright © 1996 by Judith Martin
Illustrations copyright © 1996 by Daniel Mark Duffy

Published by Crown Publishers, Inc., 201 East 50th Street, New York, New York, 10022.
Member of the Crown Publishing Group.

Random House, Inc.   New York, Toronto, London, Sydney, Auckland

CROWN is a trademark of Crown Publishers, Inc.

Printed in the United States of America

Design by June Bennett-Tantillo

Library of Congress Cataloging-in-Publication Data
Martin, Judith
    Miss Manners rescues civilization : from sexual harrassment,
frivolous lawsuits, dissing, and other lapses in civility / Judith
Martin.—1st. ed.
    Includes index.
    1. Etiquette—United States.   I. Title.
BJ1853.M297   1996
395—dc20   96–1939

ISBN: 0-517-70164-2

10 9 8 7 6 5 4 3 2 1

First Edition

For Nicholas and Jacobina; Penelope, Deborah, Marc, Sarah and Jacob; David, Justin, Daniel, Alexandra and Noevie; Benjamin, Julia and Joshua; David and Aron; Samuel, Noah, Emma, Suzannah and Eliot; Sarah, Benjamin and Alexander; Helen and Mott; Nicholas and Daniel; Jordan, Evan

. . . and their children and their children's children

Acknowledgments

Miss Manners expects everyone to pitch in and help her rescue civilization, but the mission would be impossible without the generous and wise support of David Hendin, Ann Hughey, Gunther Stent, Linda Bosson, George Hughey, Lucinda Williams—and Lord Manners.

Contents

MISS MANNERS® RESCUES CIVILIZATION

THE CASE AGAINST
ETIQUETTE

o you have to use that word? It's not the idea that turns people off, so much as the word. Can't you think of a better way to put it?"

Miss Manners clapped her hand over her little rosebud mouth. What offensive word had slipped out? Had the standards of the times gotten to her without her realizing it? Was it time for her to bite the soap?

Etiquette. Strong men and women are frightened of the word "etiquette." Miss Manners would refer to them as ladies and gentlemen, as it is her habit to encourage gentle behavior, but she doesn't want to scare them even more.

Those who have complained to Miss Manners about her vocabulary are not advocates of rudeness. On the contrary, they are the very people who have come to agree with her about the rudeness crisis, because they also are painfully aware of the difficulties caused in modern society by the way people routinely treat one another. Some are working actively to encourage better behavior in their professional societies, their schools, their government. Others just go around deploring everything in sight, which Miss Manners supposes is also a contribution.

Yet they never mention the E word except to disavow etiquette, which they are careful to do explicitly. What they say they want is civility, decency, consideration for others, common sense, making others feel comfortable, good sportsmanship, tact, collegiality, congeniality, respect, fairness—"but of course, not etiquette."

Biting her lip to keep from bursting into tears, Miss Manners tries to find out why they want to disassociate themselves from her cause, when we all seem to be working for the same goal. Why not etiquette?

1

The Founding Fathers lay the foundations of egalitarian etiquette. Although the results are not as widely known as the Declaration of Independence and the Constitution, Thomas Jefferson, George Washington and other early patriots also wrote about etiquette. Their successors in the noble cause of using etiquette to express equality, individual freedom, social mobility and the dignity of labor have included Ralph Waldo Emerson, Harriet Beecher Stowe, Eleanor Roosevelt and your own Miss Manners.

Because it's artificial! It's elitist! It's old-fashioned! It's arbitrary! It's stuffy! It's prudish! It represses people from expressing their true feelings! It inhibits little children! It's hypocritical! It's dishonest! And—*it uses forks!*

The charge that etiquette is only about forks is a shorthand way of saying that etiquette is snobbishly picayune—the hobby of otherwise useless scoundrels who, being in possession of some pointless information, set vicious traps for the fun of catching good-hearted folk who are only trying to live out their honest lives in peace. To such dastardly behavior they give the name that belongs to polite and considerate behavior. There is a vocabulary problem here all right, but Miss Manners doesn't think it is hers.

Familiar as this charge is to her, Miss Manners has never ceased to be puzzled by it. Everybody eats. Every society has rules about that most basic ritual, mealtime. Our own rules are extremely simple, compared with the short, infamous late Victorian period of table-tool specialization, an era when silver was relatively cheap and plentiful, and there were no discount computer stores to supply the great human need for gadgets to do simple tasks in a complicated and expensive fashion. Anyway, between the food critics (*"Eeewwww, how can you eat that stuff?"*) and the naturalists (*"Who cares how you eat?"*), Miss Manners is in danger of losing her zest for debating the etiquette of eating. It is difficult to explain the beauty of ritual to people who don't even agree that they should learn to take sustenance without revolting or insulting anyone trying to do the same in their vicinity.

It is true that any tool, even the eager-to-please fork whose sole aim in life is to nurture everyone, can be misused. There was more going on than innocent silver collecting in that little matter of the social aftermath of the Industrial Revolution, Miss Manners admits. With shifting fortunes, working-class people who suddenly got rich developed fancier table manners to distinguish themselves from their former peers. So leisure-class people, who had turned correspondingly land-poor, made a point of maintaining rigidly simple manners (as opposed to the lackadaisically simple manners of the working class), to distinguish themselves from their new peers—right up until any opportunity arose to marry their children off to the newly rich and declare them charming after all.

People always use periods of social unrest to play class identification games with toys. Silverware was the Victorians' weapon of choice (a notable exception to the rule that the less industrialized the society, the more complicated are its eating rituals), and now the weapons are status cars and clothes. Has that given a bad name to driving and dressing?

No, it gives etiquette a bad name. Miss Manners' head is spinning. To sacrifice the principles of manners, which require compassion and respect, and bat people over the head with their ignorance of etiquette rules they cannot be expected to know is both bad manners and poor etiquette. That social climbers and twits have misused etiquette throughout history should not be used as an argument for doing away with it. Worse villains have misused the law to promote injustice, but the majesty of the law manages to survive. You don't judge a system by the people who abuse it.

Nevertheless, those great fork trials of a century ago were apparently so traumatic that a fear of forks has survived into an era when a fear of plastic forks, which break off in the food, would be more to the point. Miss Manners is here to comfort those who are still frightened by assuring them that most of those scary forks have long since been melted down for their silver content. The supernaturally powerful society matrons of their nightmares are no longer hovering over the dinner table; they're running multinational corporations and wolfing carryout food at their oversized desks. It is time for everyone to move on.

Miss Manners knows what is really rankling today's children of nature. Table manners, even ones as streamlined as ours now are, are particularly onerous because they are examples of etiquette that must be learned by rote. You can't just figure out the best way to approach an artichoke. (Warily.) You can't make these rules up for yourself. Miss Manners concedes that memorizing rules isn't as exciting as exercising freedom, although she does wonder whether it is all that exciting to figure out how you might want to approach your muffin every morning.

Be that as it may, she gently suggests that people making up their own rules and deciding which courtesies they want to observe, and which they don't, is exactly the problem that has been identified as incivility and lack of consideration. Given the choice, people will naturally drop the courtesies they find inconvenient or incomprehensible without regard to other points of view and without exploring possible social consequences. The opportunities for misinterpreting the motivations of others become rampant, and even the most kindly intentioned find that they may inadvertently cause offense. Activities as basic to the society as the classroom, the meeting and the athletic contest cannot proceed unless everybody knows and agrees to obey the same specific etiquette rules that provide orderliness and fairness.

Just tell people to be more considerate and they growl back that of course they are already being that. Insist that they follow the rules of etiquette and they at least understand what is required of them. This is why Miss Manners insists on the E word. With a bit of practice, one can even get used to saying it without blushing.

CHARGED: THAT ETIQUETTE IS NO FUN

DEAR MISS MANNERS,

Too many manners just might mean too little fun. With this in mind, I would like to ask you if you have:

1. eaten a pizza with bare fingers?
2. been to a bowling alley (of your own free will)?
3. drank a six-pack of beer?
4. called a man a "hunk"?
5. ever not worn underwear on a hot day?
6. eaten fried chicken straight from the bucket?
7. ever gone on a date in a pickup truck?
8. kept wearing tennis shoes with holes in them, just because they were comfortable?

If you answer no to more than three questions, I recommend you immediately start watching re-runs of *Laverne and Shirley* on T.V.

GENTLE READER,

Have you ever:

1. been shocked by Miss Manners?
You are about to be. Prepare yourself.

No, she is not going to plead for your cultural approval by claiming that her recreational tastes are identical to yours. The prospect of riding in the back of a pickup truck with six cans of beer sloshing around in her stomach and no underwear is not, as you have astutely guessed, her idea of a rollicking good time. But she has no objection to its being yours. The shocking news—are you sure you are ready for this?—is that none of the things you mention is intrinsically rude.

Sure, you could make them into bad manners by dragging them into the wrong context—drinking your six-pack during your father's funeral service, for example. For that matter, you could make them into illegal behavior by dragging them into the wrong context—drinking your six-pack while driving. Table manners are especially context-dependent. Eating fried chicken or pizza with the hands is correct at picnics and fast-food restaurants but not at formal dinners. This is why bucket-chicken and pizza tend not to be served at formal dinners, which are not, incidentally, given as eating-etiquette tests for the unwary. Contrary to what you may imagine, people give and attend formal dinners because that is *their* idea of fun.

What you are really trying to say is that manners apply only to formal behavior, and that the opposite of manners is informality and fun. Wrong, gentle buddy, wrong.

Do you imagine that there is not an etiquette for bowling? Try showing up with the wrong shoes, or going out of turn, or carrying on so that it breaks another player's concentration. Now it is Miss Manners who has to ask: Have you ever been to a bowling alley? To count bowling as an unmannerly activity is incorrect. To label fun as automatically unmannerly is also dour. To chastise people for having different pleasures from your own is snobbish. Snobbery, in whichever direction it may choose to direct its sneer is, Miss Manners is sorry to tell you, rude.

CHARGED: THAT ETIQUETTE IS ELITIST

Miss Manners admits that most of those common charges against etiquette are true, and she promises more confessions to come. Etiquette not only uses forks, but it is artificial, which is to say civilized; it inhibits little children, but only if their parents are very, very persistent and patient; it tries its best to repress the expression of true feelings within earshot of people who don't want to hear them; it strives to be hypocritical when it's feeling surly; it is our folklore, if that makes it old-fashioned, even though its biggest tasks are sorting out the present and developing guidelines for the future. Also, Miss Manners is decidedly stuffy. Somebody has to offer a jaded world some novelty. She's prudish, too, but that is hardly anything to brag about these days, when that category includes everybody who might hesitate to disrobe on television.

The charge that etiquette is elitist is something else. That hurts. Etiquette is the great equalizer. It applies equally to everyone, and it's equally available to everyone— free. The etiquette-less rule of behavior used by those with power toward those without power is a natural and logical one: Might makes right. Get out of my way or I'll blast you into next week. There is also a more refined version, which is: Go ahead, sue me—and may the most expensive lawyer win. When society refuses to obey the rules of etiquette, rudeness becomes much more of a burden to the poor than to the rich, who can often pay for special treatment and buy their way out of any trouble caused by their own rude behavior.

It takes quaint old manners to come up with such an unnatural and illogical concept as noblesse oblige. A mainstay of etiquette, this requires the powerful not only to avoid taking easy advantage of the weak, but to behave even more politely to those whom they could buy and sell than to those to whom they might find it advantageous to flatter. Etiquette condemns all rudeness, but it secretly recognizes that being rude to a superior at least has a bit of reckless glamour to it. (Caution: This should not be interpreted to mean that Miss Manners is fair game.) Being rude to a subordinate, such as an employee, who is not in a position to respond in kind is one of the most heinous crimes known to etiquette. Who dares call that elitist?

EAST LANSING, MICH.—**"Almost every American has some experience with this—a rude tax collector, an arbitrary regulator, an insensitive social worker, an abusive law officer," said the President following the bombing of the Federal Building in Oklahoma City, adding that no one has a right to respond with violence.**

Moving Down

DEAR MISS MANNERS,

Is it rude to discuss class or even use the word?

It is my experience that people who insist that we don't have classes in America, just "cultural differences," are class conscious hypocrites. The more they protest their egalitarian classlessness, the more they despise poor people in general and their own background in particular. They are also snobs who crave to impress people with appearances of wealth and other class status, and to hobnob with upper-class people.

I bring all this up because class consciousness and class snobbery involve dress codes. Humans advertise their class identity with dress and they express class bigotry by despising the way lower classes dress. Open class discrimination is outlawed here, so dress codes are used to discourage lower-class people from social events.

I am of working class stock and occupation and not ashamed of it. Generally speaking, working class men do not wear neckties. Indeed, to not do so is basic to our identity. Neckties are a class badge that distinguish upper and middle class men from working class men.

A very, very important reason why working class men don't like neckties and don't want to wear them, even at weddings and funerals, is because this class badge misrepresents their identity. Honest working men don't like to pretend to be what they are not. We are not bankers or executives or rich people. Pretentiousness, which feels good to middle class people (and may well be vital to their economic survival) is painful to us.

GENTLE READER,

Oh-oh. Just when Miss Manners was about to deliver one of those class denials you despise, she picked up a telling clue about you.

Nobody who observed and understood the people you claim to represent would foist upon them that European idea of a proletariat class identity. The working people of America have never had the mind-set you describe: "We know our place, and we don't aspire to imitate our betters."

Rather, there is the properly egalitarian attitude of "We deserve the best." America has economic classes, to be sure, but not social classes sealed off from one another by the circumstances of birth. So yes, it would be rude to suggest that there is such a permanent identity.

Funny that you should mention dress. For several decades now, Miss Manners has noticed, the rich have aspired to imitate the casual styles of working people. Whatever started out as cheap and utilitarian clothing has been copied in expensive versions.

Yet high formality, in the form of fanciful elaborations of the comparatively plain late 19th and 20th century tradition, is more common at weddings at the lower end of the financial scale than at the higher. The funerals of poor African-Americans tend to be models of dignity, where every mourner is properly dressed, while the funerals of the rich are increasingly slovenly.

Miss Manners does have to agree with you that there is an unfortunate amount of snobbery present in the society. She would only add that not all of it is by people pretending to be richer than they are.

Moving Up

DEAR MISS MANNERS,

I have always been a small-town girl, and have married "big money." I do not know how to communicate with a lot of these types of people. I have always been in a "servant's" position and now may have one myself! How can I learn to walk and live the life comfortably?

GENTLE READER,

You have the perfect background for behaving properly.

Miss Manners assures you that there is nothing like having been on the receiving end of the behavior of the rich to make one understand what is pleasant and unpleasant about them. Keeping this in mind, you will surely have less of a problem talking to servants than anyone else you are likely to meet, and probably also to your husband's friends and colleagues as well.

Of course, anyone making a change of social environment has to learn new surface etiquette rules—the range of how people dress, how they entertain, what they like to talk about and what they consider off limits, and so on. Miss Manners would have been happy to supply the particulars if you had told her more about your new circle. Are they the rich who find it rude to talk about money, or the kind that find it puzzling to talk about anything else?

In any case, this is not as great a leap as you think. Every child who moves to a new school and every person who takes a new job knows how to observe and ask discreet questions to become oriented. It is made easier by realizing that you are only changing surface manifestations of the same underlying principles, such as (Miss Manners hopes) respect for others and for tradition.

Miss Manners only worries about one error. Once you begin to get the hang of it, you will be tempted to brag about your working class origins. She asks you at least to disguise this, as it is rude to suggest to other people that their antecedents lack interest.

Attacking Elitism Politely

DEAR MISS MANNERS,

As a gentleman, I refrain from bringing attention to the seemingly incorrect behavior of others; however, lately I have found myself confronted with a situation in which I do not wish to remain acquiescent. This is the unsolicited reference to some lost wealth, or the manner in which a friend or acquaintance has previously benefited from the generosity of some person of considerable financial means:

"Oh, last summer, David Whozit and I went to the Bahamas for a month on his private yacht."

"Of course I grew up on a large estate, so any apartment is a matchbox to me."

"In the old days, I wouldn't have thought of going out to dine with less than three hundred dollars."

Grandeur of this nature, especially when obviously untrue, seems so petty. To compound this nuisance, the people prone to make these statements are usually repeat offenders. Am I being a bit too fussy? How does one tactfully let it be known that hearing such nouveau riche prattle, especially when unprompted and unsubstantiated, is wholly undesirable and nearly unbearable?

GENTLE READER,

Miss Manners does not mean to be fussy either, but she must tactfully let it be known that the phenomenon you observe is not nouveau riche prattle. Quite the opposite. It is prattle known as "Before the Revolution, my family used to own all this." Rather than being irritated, Miss Manners suggests you learn to have fun with it. This is done by looking impressed and questioning the braggart with naive persistence: "On a yacht! Imagine that. Where did you stop? How many were in the crew? Who's David Whozit? Does your family still live on the estate? Three hundred dollars for dinner? What did you eat? Does that include the tips?"

The beauty of this approach is that it is faultlessly polite, only taking up matters that the person has already offered for conversation. If it does not put a stop to the offensive conversation, it provides material for future conversation with more amusing and sophisticated partners.

Getting Too Personal

DEAR MISS MANNERS,

Isn't it a sign of excessive pride to refer to oneself in the third person? You seem to do this quite frequently.

GENTLE READER,

Does she? Oh-oh.

CHARGED: THAT ETIQUETTE IS TRIVIAL

Etiquette? Trivial? Miss Manners is flabbergasted.

It isn't only the scoffers—Nature's ladies and gentlemen who claim we don't need etiquette, as they attempt to run us off the highway of life—who make the charge.

Perfectly charming and polite people, while they are in the very act of inquiring about a point of etiquette, are given to apologizing, on the grounds that what they want to know really isn't very important: "I know this is trivial, but . . ." "Of course it doesn't matter, but I was just wondering . . ." "Not that it makes any difference, but . . ."

Miss Manners wonders why they just don't just spit it out, as it were. They seem to feel the need to make it clear to Miss Manners herself that even though there is an etiquette point of passing interest to them, they still subscribe to the notion that etiquette is too trivial for intelligent people to bother with—although, of course, they hasten to add, they understand that it *is* important to Miss Manners. The more tolerant will concede that etiquette might actually be useful in connection with activities that don't really matter, such as eating or getting married, as long as it is not allowed to impede the serious business of the world.

Miss Manners is willing to overlook the personal implications. But she finds the charge of triviality annoying, even when it is made in connection with surface questions that really are minor points of etiquette. The tiniest custom may offer a glimpse into how a mannerly concept, such as fairness, has been translated into behavior. In addition, it may offer a tip on how to avoid annoying others, which is no small contribution in an edgy world.

Trivial? Compared to what? World Hunger? Yes, the little customs of society are less important than that. So is just about anything else. It is only once people are able to manage physical survival that manners become crucial. Then tradition is what gives a society meaning and the rules by which it lives are what make it work. We call that civilization. Miss Manners will not countenance having the foundations of civilization classified as trivial.

A Deep Question

DEAR MISS MANNERS,

I have been perplexed for over a year now about finding the appropriate term for the man I have been dating. He is 44, and I am 39; we are certainly too old to be referred to as boyfriend and girlfriend. When we introduce each other, I could just say, "This is Ed," but it helps to have a label to clarify that we are not married, engaged or otherwise related. I acknowledge that this is of minor consequence when one takes into consideration the rest of the world's problems, but hey, we are all entitled to retreat to the inconsequential once in a while.

GENTLE READER,

Inconsequential? This problem, which affects not only everyone who is part of such a couple but everyone who knows any such couples—virtually the entire population—arises from a profound change in the way we live. A generation or two ago, the assumption was that teenagers "went steady" (a peculiar term for such a rocky state), but all grown-ups got married and stayed married. Society could giggle when it noticed that middle-aged people were "keeping company," and it could tisk-tisk over gays or married people having such dear friends, but it didn't need a respectable term for them as a couple. Officially, there was no such thing as an adult unmarried couple.

You've only been perplexed for a year, but Miss Manners is still not satisfied after working on this one for more than a decade, with the help of countless well-meaning and hard-working Gentle Readers. By all means, use the gentleman's name when introducing him. When it is necessary to point out that you are a social unit, the best that Miss Manners has come up with so far is that you add, "We are a couple." She's still accepting suggestions **(rules on page 485)**.

CHARGED: THAT ETIQUETTE IS INSINCERE, HYPOCRITICAL, WEAK, PRETENTIOUS, STUFFY . . .

Those who pride themselves on being etiquette-free have a special glossary of unpleasant terms for attacking anyone they catch trying to be polite:

Insincere: Going around being pleasant to everyone, without apparent regard to the consequences for one's advancement in life.

Unassertive: Refusing to start a fight, especially with those whose favor one doesn't need to court, such as people one spots in the express checkout line with more than nine items.

Weak: Being considerate of those one is in a position to hurt, such as underlings at work.

Apple-polishing (that is not really the modern term, but Miss Manners trusts that everyone knows what that term is): Being nice to people who outrank one, such as a teacher or boss. Also being nice to those who have no influence over one's life, as when a young person talks to, and perhaps even offers to help, the parents of a host while the other children pretend parents don't exist.

There is another vocabulary for people who don't volunteer everything there is to know about their lives and even resist nosy questioning:

Inhibited: Not answering questions about one's love life.

Defensive: Not encouraging personal criticism.

Ashamed: Not disclosing serious illnesses, addictions, financial and marital difficulties to whoever will listen.

Secretive: Declining to tell other people's secrets—what was wrong with a friend's former spouse or why a colleague got fired.

There are several terms for those who like to live in an aesthetically pleasing manner. This does not necessarily mean having an expensive household, which is admired, but taking some trouble rather than always doing things in the easiest possible way:

Stuffy: Eating in the dining room instead of the kitchen, using cloth napkins instead of paper ones, putting out guest towels that need ironing, and not bragging about being casual.

Show-offy: Dressing according to the occasion.

Inconsiderate: Drying one's hands with the guest towel.

Finally, there are two all-purpose terms for anyone who may not commit the above crimes but has the irritating habit of not having been caught in the common rudenesses:

Insecure: Having a mild manner and a modest life.

Hypocritical: Always being polite.

CHARGED: THAT ETIQUETTE IS ARTIFICIAL

Let us presume, for the sake of argument and a good laugh, that you have nothing but the kindest of emotions and motivations toward everyone else in the world, every minute of your life. So does everyone you know. Why, then, would you need etiquette?

Constant and universal altruism is necessarily the premise on which the most common challenge to etiquette is posed by those who have noticed that etiquette is artificial. Rather than allowing free expression, they note disdainfully, etiquette puts a sly spin, if not a dizzying turnabout, on truly harbored emotions to make people simulate emotions that are considered socially acceptable.

For the moment, let us ignore the perhaps faulty research that led to this touching faith in human nature. Miss Manners needs that moment anyway, to be helped up off the floor, having been overcome with hilarity at the idea that normal people's emotions are reliably presentable. Even if it were true that no one ever felt a flicker of feeling that required a polite cover-up lest it cause mayhem, etiquette would have a mighty peacekeeping job to do. It would still have to make up for our disgracefully bad sense of timing.

Presuming you always have all the right emotions (why, good for you), you are not likely to have them all at the right time. Let us suppose that you are sitting at an important meeting, or you are attending religious services, or you are hearing at length about some tragedy elsewhere in the world. You notice that the person who is presiding has a spot of whipped cream from lunch right at nose-tip. What is more, it seems to move slightly when that person talks most vehemently. To giggle is to mark yourself as someone who has no interest in the work at hand, no respect for the services, or no compassion for the tragedy. This would be a false impression. You are nothing but hardworking, respectful and compassionate. You just also happen to be convulsed. Etiquette is what admonishes you to fish out your handkerchief (etiquette having admonished you to carry a handkerchief in the first place, as it can cover a multitude of social sins) and cover your face so you can pretend you are sneezing. Sneezing may not be socially desirable, but it is at least acceptable.

NEW JERSEY—Discussing the sense of alienation Marines feel from civilian life, one young Marine told the *Wall Street Journal* of attending a street fair: "It was crowded. Trash everywhere. People were drinking, getting into fights, no politeness whatsoever."

Or someone does you an enormous favor, which happens to be the wrong favor, thereby creating even more trouble for you than the trouble it was intended to relieve. Or gives you a present that you hate and that will be particularly annoying to return or bury in the backyard. Truly, you are glad to know people who want to please you. The last thing you want to do is to discourage anyone from trying. But the honest reaction, no matter how good-natured one is, would be "Can't you get anything right?" Etiquette is what tells you to address yourself to the effort rather than the disappointment. It knows that there is nothing spontaneous about a rush of gratitude, even by the truly grateful, toward someone who has bungled.

Perhaps someone you really deeply love is in a sentimental mood, while you are in a sour one. There you are, working on income tax figures that don't add up, and the person whose accounting skills may well be responsible for the problem puts a hand in your hair and asks winningly, "Do you still feel the same about me as you used to?" Etiquette is what whispers, "Say yes. What you don't feel now, you will later, only it will be too late to say so. Besides, saying no will only lead to more conversation."

And so it goes. Nobody has ever felt a happy emotion upon appearing with no advance grooming among a roomful of people who leap out and shout congratulations. But on reflection, even later that same evening, a person in that position may be thrilled to have so many good friends. So without etiquette there could be no surprise parties. Now, there is a really trouncing argument that Miss Manners' opponents seem to have missed.

Con-Artistry

DEAR MISS MANNERS,

I am being held hostage by family, friends and neighbors expressing aberrations of behavior in terms of obscenity of language and behavior, a lack of table manners, common politeness, all under the guise of individual identity.

Where does an individual's rights end and those of serving the greater society begin? I have thought of running away, but everyone that I know who possesses good manners is a con artist.

GENTLE READER,

Don't run away—please! Miss Manners would be left alone with all those people you describe.

They are your circle, so she assumes there is also good in them. Possibly, their goal is not to grab all they can at everyone else's expense, which is nevertheless the result of assuming that individual rights leave no room for societal ones. They have probably just fallen for the seductive idea that there is something immoral about checking any of their impulses, even those that might be troublesome to others.

Meanwhile, as you noticed, the really mean people get the advantage of practicing ingratiating behavior. So please stick around. Miss Manners needs your help in persuading the con artists to be more sincere and the sincere to develop more con-artistry.

CHARGED: THAT ETIQUETTE IS LETHAL

It's all etiquette's fault. Miss Manners is used to hearing this charge. Ever the naive goody-goody, she knows she is a tempting target for anyone interested in placing blame for trouble. Naughtiness gets a winning gleam in its eye, points at prissy etiquette sitting there docilely in starched ruffles and clean shoes, and announces, "She started it!"

But accustomed as she is to this ploy (and the depressing fact that it almost always works), Miss Manners was stunned when she read who was responsible for the tragic fate of the two young children who drowned when their mother strapped them into car seats and pushed the car into a lake.

Manners were responsible. An excess of etiquette caused this crime. Oh, perhaps not alone, but anyway as an instigating force. Miss Manners should probably not say anything until she confers with her lawyer.

The argument behind such accusations is unfortunately familiar to her. People seeking causes for wrongdoing often explain that, because the restraints of etiquette in our society are so rigorous and unnatural, those who submit to them will eventually be catapulted into violent reactions. Given that we all have wicked impulses (no argument here), the safe outlet people have when they can indulge in everyday acts expressing their dissatisfactions is a protection against suppressing bad feelings until they explode in one outrageous act. So here's the choice: People can either be constantly but more or less benignly rude, or they can be polite most of the time but sporadically vicious.

Even Miss Manners would rather be shoved than shot. And she has to admit that following etiquette does indeed prevent people from daily enjoying the satisfaction of annoying others in small ways. However, she does not quite follow the part about why it therefore stands to reason that by restraining obnoxious behavior, etiquette causes evil behavior.

The injustice of being targeted as antisocial for harboring socially conscious ideas would render Miss Manners speechless if she weren't inured to its success. People of good will who are interested in understanding and discouraging wrongdoing are peculiarly susceptible to this implication that the habit of considering other people's feelings and welfare, and not only one's own, is dangerous to society.

Thus it was that the director of the Center for the Study of Southern Culture at the University of Mississippi told a *Washington Post* reporter analyzing the Susan

Smith case: "We have been taught manners, we have been taught a code of etiquette and behavior, a kind of politeness and chivalry and formality that does not allow emotion to surface, that does not allow the frank and open discussion needed for resolution. . . . You often have powerful forces that are not brought out until they explode in tragic fashion."

The article then showed that the murderer, although leading a wild and tortured private life, had maintained a surface demeanor that was usually considerate, friendly and cheerful. This was characterized by the reporter as "poisonous denial and odd formality."

Hampered as Miss Manners is by being so polite, she too would like to alleviate suffering and reduce crime. So instead of just trying to beat the rap here, she would like to explore the accusation to find if etiquette does indeed bear any culpability.

Here is what she can't understand:

Nowhere in all of the literature and tradition of etiquette is there a rule against seeking help for problems. (In the Smith case, a teacher, social workers and hospital workers had all been consulted.) The nearest thing Miss Manners can find that might inhibit the disclosure of suffering is that it would not be polite to do so to acquaintances at the dinner table. Is that a threat to mental health?

Does the ability to drop one's own troubles, if only occasionally, and contribute to the comfort or happiness of others actually exacerbate the feelings that prompt crime? Miss Manners had the impression that the consensus —from folk wisdom's injunction to "stop focusing on yourself" to the justice system's use of community service to make wrongdoers understand the effect they have on others—held the opposite conclusion.

Is there, in fact, a correlation between politeness and crime? Is the typical child abuser or murderer characterized by an interest in etiquette? It is possible, but Miss Manners gets a different impression from the many horrifying stories about parents who have turned on their own children.

And by the way, where is this society that claims such rigid adherence to formal etiquette? Miss Manners does not know of such a place, and she has been on the lookout for some time. Even if the required manners of our time were not infinitely less formal than those of previous eras, they are more laxly enforced and less likely to be observed.

Lastly, if you are looking for a reason that people do not control their ugliest behavior so as not to make the innocent suffer, why pick on etiquette, whose mission it is to teach people the habit of controlling ugly behavior so as not to make the innocent suffer?

Miss Manners apologizes for the note of hysteria that has crept into her voice. Naturally, she is expected to run amok.

CHARGED: THAT ETIQUETTE IS NOT AS LOVABLE AS IGNORANCE

People are always claiming their ignorance of etiquette as an asset. It's the fork fetish again—used, this time, to suggest that nobility of soul is incompatible with the ability to wield table implements.

That odd but frequently heard statement, "I can never remember which fork to use," is intended, Miss Manners gathers, to be endearing. (Point of information: There is a rule of etiquette against setting a place at the table with more than three forks. If more are needed, in the case of an absolute pig-out, these are brought in with the additional courses. Use the fork farthest to your left, and hold it as you would a pencil. How long did that take to learn? Five seconds?) This confession of ineptitude is not made by people who have been forced to forage for food under primitive conditions. It is the boast of the privileged, engaged in the pursuit of modesty.

Who could not love someone who is befuddled by forks? Or fail to be wary of someone who is not? Bad news not just for Miss Manners but for the millions of people who eat successfully every day, even several times a day.

The phenomenon of know-nothingism is not limited to forks, Miss Manners acknowledges. Before the existence of spelling checkers on computers, not being able to spell was a popular way of establishing intellectual credentials. She also remembers when ladies routinely bragged that they were unable to balance their checkbooks, and gentlemen that they wouldn't know how to boil an egg. How this would enhance the attractiveness of either was something she was never able to figure out. If there still exist gentlemen who are excited by the idea of capturing a lady who would wreak havoc with their accounts, or ladies whose hearts would be softened by knowing that a gentleman would starve if not served all his meals, Miss Manners hopes they will be spared the consequences of getting what they wish. There is enough marital discord available without having to find out what it means to live with willful ineptitude.

Although it is true that people are often judged on their manners—it being more difficult to peer into the depths of the human heart to evaluate the soul—it is not the small technicalities that form the basis of this test. Someone who is obviously endeavoring to get along with others, rather than forever tweaking and annoying them, will be deemed courteous in spite of small lapses. Etiquette is far more lenient than its reputation suggests in accepting excuses for inability to comply with its regulations. Being new to local practices—if, say, one is a foreigner or a novice to a subgroup of the society—buys tolerance and time. Infirmity, when known, engenders sympathy, as when one finds it painful to shake hands or less difficult to type than to write.

Defiance is another matter. Proud ignorance—the old How-was-I-to-know-that-Grandma-expected-to-be-thanked-for-the-check routine—is inexcusable. Also, it isn't lovable. If it is rude to brag about what you know, it is ridiculous to brag about what you don't know.

CHARGED: THAT ETIQUETTE IS MEAN

Dear Miss Manners,

I would like you to tone down the moral imperative that I hear you attach to your advice. A person who does not show what the majority of us perceive to be proper manners is not bad, nor should in any way be made to feel inadequate. Labeling a person as unmannered or anything less because of a lack of manners is the greatest breach of social etiquette I know.

I become so embarrassed when I commit any kind of social faux pas, and I think the most gracious display of manners comes from those who witness my inadequacies but react with even more gracious and benevolent kindness. I writhe under criticism but feel a vicarious shame that makes me think the public keeper of my manners is the least mannered of us all.

How can the purpose of manners be to make the world a nicer place, if the rule-makers are demanding or demeaning in the process of keeping the rules for others?

Gentle Reader,

How can Miss Manners stop moralizing, when she wants to endorse what you have said? She couldn't agree with you more that using knowledge of etiquette to correct, embarrass, or demean others is the height of rudeness. This is one of Miss Manners' very favorite moral imperatives.

But you puzzle her when you say that people who lack manners are not unmannerly. Sure they are, by definition. Whether this is bad is another matter. If you use Miss Manners' definition of manners as the moral underpinnings of etiquette, such as graciousness and kindness, unmannerliness *is* bad. It means not caring how your behavior affects other people.

This is the opposite of the way you describe yourself—as making mistakes when you are understandably unacquainted with the particular rules of etiquette of a place or situation new to you. Everyone who gets around has the experience sometime of feeling at a disadvantage through temporary ignorance (a word Miss Manners is not using pejoratively, by the way), and the polite person treats any error with the graciousness you recommend.

CHARGED: THAT MISS MANNERS RUNS A BOARDING SCHOOL

DEAR MISS MANNERS,

When my sister and I misbehaved, as young children, our mother threatened to send us to Miss Manners' boarding school on the East Coast. Does this school, in fact, exist?

GENTLE READER,

Only in your mother's mind. And now yours and your sister's, evidently. Not that Miss Manners has any objection to being used to frighten small children. Teaching children manners is not a popularity-enhancing part of child-rearing, and she often worries that the difficulties involved put a burden on the otherwise idyllic parent-child bond. Conversely, those whose bonds are not otherwise idyllic sometimes displace their anger onto innocent etiquette. Your mother and Miss Manners have a lot in common, and if she can be of any help, she would consider it an honor.

Miss Manners also realizes that there is a lot of remedial work to be done with children whose parents don't get the job done, for one reason or another. Unfortunately, the etiquette schools she keeps hearing about concentrate more on

Sports Illustrated **reported a severe degeneration in the quality of abuse being hurled at athletes by critical fans, with ugly epithets and obscenity becoming commonplace. "It has become a little more personal, a little more profane, a little more vulgar, and sometimes it's just plain sick," one Philadelphia Phillies outfielder told the magazine.**

manners for snobbish restaurants than those for food courts. Rather than opening a school of her own, Miss Manners is trying to turn the entire world into an etiquette school. How's that for frightening?

CHARGED: THAT ETIQUETTE IS RUDE

There must be a racier way to get a bad reputation than to take up good manners. Or so Miss Manners would have thought, until she went into the etiquette trade. That was when she discovered that people known to be devoted to mannerliness are automatically assumed to be inflexible, self-righteous, intrusive, condescending, and a general pain in the neck. In other words—rude.

Dear, dear. Then what do they say about people who devote themselves to rudeness? Oh. They give them the benefit of the doubt.

That is all very well, but Miss Manners wishes the same charity would be afforded to the polite. How did politeness come to be defined as, of all things, rudeness? Isn't it etiquette itself that most fiercely condemns the behavior that others seem to think it practices?

That the opposite is widely believed is made clear to her in small but telling ways, directed at Miss Manners herself—not personally but as a champion of good manners. By way of being complimentary, people are always telling her that they were afraid to meet her because they expected her to snub or criticize them, and that they are surprised to find that she behaves pleasantly. That's only what they say to her face. Goodness knows what they say behind her back.

To perform all of the alleged etiquette violations, Miss Manners would only have to do what people admit they suspect is her chief recreation—peer into other people's plates while they are eating, in the hope of catching them in some little slip she can then use to hold them up to censure and ridicule. What a life they must think she leads. However, if that were what Miss Manners did, instead of eating with others for the pleasure of concentrating on their conversation, she would put herself in danger of committing an enormous violation of dining etiquette: she would soon be gently resting her head in her own plate, as she succumbed to the boredom of watching other people lifting their forks up and down, up and down.

What disturbs Miss Manners is not the personal implications—if no one wants anything to do with her, she will be content to wait by her own fireside for dear Henri Beyle to send her a new novel—but the underlying assumptions about etiquette that are thus revealed. Polite people don't go around monitoring others, not only because they may have better things to do, but precisely because they are too polite. They offer etiquette advice only if they are asked. If you should happen to run into such a person, please be polite.

OLD-FASHIONED OBJECTIONS TO ETIQUETTE

It is with nostalgia (curiously untainted by affection) that Miss Manners recalls how people used to feel about etiquette in the dear bygone days. They wished it would go away. Why, they would charmingly inquire, couldn't we just be free and natural, doing as the spirit moves us, unhampered by the stuffy restrictions of the past? Instead of following artificial and inhibiting dictates, why couldn't people just act on their feelings and say what they really meant? The Victorians were particularly shameless at this sort of yearning and moping. They were always babbling on about how important it was to be sincere.

The luxury of holding this sweet attitude, with its endearing optimism about the human spirit, is affordable only when etiquette does, in fact, prevail. One is then deliciously free to imagine how beautifully people would behave if they were left to improvise their behavior as each saw fit. It is that innocence for which Miss Manners is nostalgic.

What drives her to ladylike distraction is that people still harbor such fantasies. Pay attention to the world around you, Gentle Readers: we have now found out how people see fit to behave when they are uncontaminated by etiquette.

We experience it every day with the shoves, shouts and fingers offered by those who feel free to talk and behave as their uninhibited impulses suggest. We hear it in the nosiness and bossiness of those who air their curiosity, opinions and advice without such hypocritical restraints as those ancient rules about minding your own business, not insulting people to their faces, and pretending that you know less about how to run other people's lives than they do. We observe it when trying to follow such basic social practices as offering hospitality and giving presents, only to find that the responsive half of each practice—answering invitations, showing up when promised, offering thanks, reciprocating—is not, after all, a natural reaction to generosity.

What seems to be natural is a selfishness that, now unbridled, is turning births, weddings and even deaths into fund-raisers, and religious holidays into occasions for self-pity over loneliness or the quality and number of presents received. It turns out that dear old hypocrisy, inhibitions and artificiality, daintily wrapped in a package called etiquette, were protecting us from forms of natural behavior that even the most vehement opponents of etiquette find intolerable.

If everyone were happy with etiquette-free living, Miss Manners would cheerfully acknowledge defeat and retire to her porch swing with a split of champagne and a teacup to drink it from so as to avoid scandalizing the neighbors. Oddly enough, the very people who are proudest to be free of those tiresome rules are loudest in denouncing rudeness directed toward themselves. That dispensing with etiquette means becoming a victim, as well as a perpetrator, of rudeness does not seem to have occurred to them. Being rude is fun only when you're the only one doing it.

Caught, these people have tried to fight back without using the spurned concept of etiquette. Finally abandoning the idea that all we need do to improve the quality of life is to bring out truly unsocialized human nature (a theory that presumes we are all infinitely agreeable and tolerable), they find themselves with three weapons: counter-rudeness, violence and (for the fastidious and deep-pocketed) lawsuits.

That these methods have not been satisfactory in making life peaceful and pleasant should be evident by now. Rudeness in retaliation sets off a chain of further rudeness. Violence does often silence the original offender forever, but rarely ends the conflict. The law settles the conflict, but prolongs the animosity.

"Treating everybody with respect is the first line of Self Defense!"—advertisement for the U.S. Martial Arts Association.

Miss Manners is therefore apt to be very short (a reaction barely on this side of politeness) with those who still harbor the notion that we can get along without etiquette, as valiantly as many have tried. That idea is guilty of what etiquette itself is often accused of—being hopelessly old-fashioned.

THE VERY LATEST OBJECTIONS TO ETIQUETTE

A curious lament has arisen in connection with such truly obnoxious behavior as grabbing ladies without their permission, blowing smoke in people's faces, littering the landscape and insulting segments of the population wholesale: "How was I to know they'd mind? When I was brought up, this was perfectly okay. They keep changing the rules."

Miss Manners runs for an ear trumpet; she cannot have heard that right. The public domain used to be considered the proper place for everyone to throw trash and garbage? Nonsmokers used to be perfectly happy to find themselves in smoke-filled rooms? It used to be taken as good-natured fun when one's disability, race, or sexual orientation was ridiculed? It used to be gentlemanly to reach out for whatever body part was handy when a lady happened to pass by? Or, as one person claimed, a lady used not to mind when you surprised her by pulling her head down by the hair and sticking your tongue into her mouth?

People did such things, of course. People still do rude things, if you can believe it, even after Miss Manners has told them to cut it out this very minute. Rudeness that was practiced freely in the past, because its victims protested less loudly or successfully than they do now, was nonetheless improper.

What is now called hate speech was always considered hateful by civilized people. Bigotry toward groups and nastiness toward individuals were, and are, the highest (or lowest) sins of etiquette.

Children who failed to pick up after themselves never used to be given lectures on how they were ruining the ecology, but they were scolded for being inconsiderate of others. Telling them to respect the environment is a wordy way of putting the old injunction against such public slobbiness as littering.

The concept of respect for other people's lifestyles is an even trendier way of putting the rule that it is not anybody else's business how others conduct their private lives, so long as they don't conduct the most private parts in public.

The current lament offers a revisionist account of recent etiquette history, as well. According to this version, a few people with no sense of fun got together one grim day and managed to get all the rules changed without bothering to obtain general approval or provide intelligible guidelines. From then on, simple, well-meaning folks were always being caught in minuscule slips that unaccountably got them into major trouble. For a long time, these good folks tried to behave themselves, but they got dizzy trying to follow the rapid and whimsical changes of a society that couldn't make up its silly mind. Finally goaded to exasperation (and realizing that the over-finicky group making all that fuss is itself the cause of our present troubles), people of fairness, sense and wit have triumphantly claimed the privilege of being as rude as they please.

Miss Manners would like to welcome these people out of the etiquette business. They have as little knowledge of what was acceptable in the past as they do of how to behave in the present.

What they really mean, of course, is that it used to be easier to get away with certain forms of bad behavior. Not that they weren't aware that this was bad behavior. Their mothers taught them that they should respect ladies. Their fathers introduced them to public back rooms and private studies where they were welcome to smoke. The target groups of their jokes were glowering at them instead of beaming with shared amusement.

What they really mean by "perfectly all right" is that they got away with behaving badly. They never got sued. These things were not against the law. They were only against every tenet of—etiquette. Oh. Only poor old defenseless etiquette. Well, then, no need to worry.

Their laughing claim of "Who's going to make me?" finally got on everyone else's nerves. It has now been answered by using something stronger than etiquette, namely law.

ST. LOUIS—Traffic researchers reported that nearly 84 percent of automobile accidents in Missouri are caused by rude behavior, such as tailgating, not paying attention, making improper turns and failing to yield. "When we're in a hurry to go somewhere and we're thwarted, the result is aggression," a researcher told the St. Louis *Post-Dispatch*.

When the result of behaving offensively was not that they had a good chuckle at others' expense but that they lost money or jobs, they started paying attention. That is also when all this whining about change started. Miss Manners is not moved by it. Etiquette does change, and it allows generous time for learning new rules. But no matter what anyone claims to remember, there never was a time in history when etiquette approved of boorishness and callousness.

The Would-Be Gentleman

DEAR MISS MANNERS,

I'm a white, heterosexual, able-bodied male, in my twenties, and am finding it very difficult to remain polite in these politically correct, anti-male times. Because of the sub-group I belong to (which IS a minority, incidentally), I, like others, am being singled out as the villain by every interest group in the world. This is unfortunate and though it is unpleasant, I can handle it—most of the time.

Being a gentleman, I try to be courteous, chivalrous and kind to all people—but they're making it increasingly difficult. I hold a door open for a woman, and she gives me a dressing down, asking me if I think she is too weak to open the door for herself. I help a child who has injured herself, only to find her mother running toward me, screaming for me to get my @#$%& hands off her baby. I try to carry on a pleasant conversation with an African-American male, only to have him blame me—me, personally—for 400 years of oppression, which I try to remind him politely I wasn't responsible for.

I could list examples all day long. I'm hopelessly confused and frustrated! I don't want to be confrontational, but I don't want to be anybody's doormat, either. I usually just walk away. How should a gentleman handle these and similar situations?

Gentle Reader,

Now, now, now. Calm down. Here's a nice lady to help you, and you mustn't take it amiss. Miss Manners dislikes all bigotry, whether it is against gentlemen or against those who are branded as politically correct for fighting prejudice and requiring respect.

She also condemns people who treat obvious politeness with anger. In all of the incidents you describe, the other person was intensely rude. Interpreting obviously well-meant gestures as political assaults is an unfortunately prevalent rudeness nowadays. Just please try to keep in mind that you are dealing with rude persons, not rude groups who need to be punished collectively by more rudeness or more provocative discrimination.

A Reply

Dear Miss Manners,

All the complaints cited by the man who wrote you about the travails of being a '90s white male are decades-old stereotypes. (Well, maybe the stereotype of the distraught mother who was angry because he tried to rescue her child is only a few years old.) I was sucked into that sort of thing in 1917 or '18 and stopped in revulsion. I could see what I was doing to others, but that was not what bothered me. What was happening to me was what I was not going to allow. And since then, I have opposed all forms of exploitation and oppression. Including such stereotyping.

The only confrontational African-American I encountered was about 1970, a time when there was a strong racist counterattack. If I treat a person as an equal, I find I'm accepted with equal courtesy. The confrontational woman who doesn't want the door held is also one I've never met. Though I've always had a reply ready ("I do it for men, too"), I've never had to use it. Some women have complimented me on my old-fashioned courtesy, so rare these days.

I think the stories are excuses for his own confrontational attitudes and feelings of persecution. Indeed, we are all victims, but not of what he claims. What he wants is a return to the sort of power he thinks men of his sort used to have, to harass the "girls" and "darkies." The travails of being a '90s white male simply consist in continuing to be a victim of social and economic stratification, while being denied the formerly available scapegoats.

The Would-Be Politician

Dear Miss Manners,

A group of women was giving testimony before a congressional committee regarding an issue of serious concern to them. When it came his turn to question them, a certain southern Senator said, "Mr. Chairman, we've got a lovely group of ladies here. We thank you for your presence. I have no questions." The Senator surely thought he was being gentlemanly, but the women felt they were being patronized and did not hide their displeasure at being referred to as "lovely ladies."

Is it ever correct for a government official—or anyone for that matter—to make such remarks? If not, what would be the proper response to discourage such offenses from being recommitted? This sort of thing seems to occur frequently. Was the Senator rude, or were the women overly sensitive?

Gentle Reader,

Yes.

The Senator was rude, but not in the purposeful sense of delivering an insult. The manners he used once passed for all-purpose graciousness, although they are now widely recognized to suggest, when employed in a clearly nonsocial context, that the chief function of ladies is to be decorative.

There is a grandfather clause, by which elderly people who are obviously unaware of changes are not fined for mild offenses that are well meant, but Miss Manners is thinking of closing this loophole. There has now been ample time for the grandfathers to understand changes that began more than a quarter of a century ago. In any case, politicians usually do not wish to avail themselves of the excuse that they are unaware of what is going on in the modern world.

You did not tell Miss Manners which Senator it was, so she will kindly presume that he was not being wily. Let us hope he had not thought of trivializing the witnesses' appearance in such a way that they would appear ill-tempered by bristling. It would have been better to reply graciously, "How kind of you, Senator; we gather this means that you fully support what we are saying."

Chapter Two

A BRIEF DEFINITION
OF ETIQUETTE

Miss Manners hates to be difficult when kind people express their sympathy with her mission "because after all," they explain, "etiquette is just plain common sense" or "always making others feel comfortable." Sternly, she reminds herself that it is ungracious to quibble with supporters.

Not that Miss Manners has anything against common sense or making others feel comfortable. They are both charming attributes, and indispensable tools for the skill of dealing with etiquette problems in real life, where rules and circumstances have to be weighed intelligently as well as compassionately. One rule may conflict with another, and situations rarely come in exactly the form for which a rule may have been devised, so both good sense and good will are required.

Of course, if that were all it took, a polite person in America would behave no differently from a polite person in Japan, and anyone from the 20th century could figure out how polite people behaved in the eighteenth century without looking it up. Or the second century, for that matter. Miss Manners wouldn't have to do a thing except, with a languid wave of her hand, urge people to be sensible and kind.

The discouraging fact is that with all the good will in the world, etiquette cannot be deduced from first principles. It has to be learned. Miss Manners is sorry about that. Perhaps if got she got herself out of the hammock and defined her terms, people would understand why and listen to her plea that the system is worth that trouble.

Miss Manners uses the word "manners" to refer to the principles underlying any system of etiquette, and "etiquette" to refer to the particular rules used to express these principles. All societies—along with a great many subgroups organized according to such factors as time, place, family, age, gender, interests or occupation—have etiquette rules. Although these rules may differ widely, they all come from the same mannerly principles.

Because etiquette rules are fashioned to pertain to a particular time and social setting, they are subject to development and change. However, the principles of manners from which they derive their authority remain constant and universal. Even directly contradictory rules of etiquette prevailing in different societies at the same time, or at different times in the same society, may derive their authority from the same principle of manners.

For example, a universal principle is "Show respect in a house of worship." Here are two rules to turn this into action, equally valid under the appropriate circumstances, but directly opposite to each other:

1. A gentleman must take off his hat (or baseball cap) in church.
2. A gentleman must wear a hat in a synagogue (well, all right, unless it is a reform synagogue).

Let's try another principle: Guests must show respect for their hosts, and hosts must show honor to their guests. However:

1. Failing to take off one's shoes when arriving at a dinner party in Japan would show a lack of respect for the hosts, while seating guests with their backs to the most decorative part of the room is understood to honor them by having these objects serve as their background.
2. Taking off one's shoes upon arriving at an American dinner party would be a demonstration of disrespect, while an American host who asks guests to remove their shoes in order to preserve the state of the floors is disrespectful to the guests, by showing more honor to his possessions than to them.

The next question (Miss Manners is ignoring the outcry from the infuriated owners of expensive flooring) is bound to be: If I promise to use those nice principles of manners, why can't I make up my own etiquette?

How creative we all feel, even if we weren't born that way. Personally, Miss Manners, with all her vast experience in the subject, doesn't want to have to get up every morning and invent ways of acknowledging the presence of others at the breakfast table, eating her grapefruit without spraying them, and deciding whether it would be more fun to wear what are now classified as evening clothes during the day, or a bathing costume to work.

Even if that idea didn't send her back to bed with a bad case of ennui, it would create chaos. A society in which everyone improvises an individual set of etiquette rules wouldn't work any better than a society in which people followed only those laws they personally invented or endorsed. A mutually intelligible code of behavior is designed to prevent misinterpretations, which is exactly what a variety of different codes operating in the same place would be bound to cause. (Besides, Miss Manners doesn't trust people to make up their own etiquette rules, because she has seen what they come up with. "Cash gifts preferred" is the current favorite.)

It is true that etiquette can, should and does change over time to fit new ideas, habits and technology. But these changes usually develop sedately, because of the strength of tradition. Remember how long it took for people to go from being angry at friends who use telephone answering machines ("I hate talking to machines, and they're probably home screening their calls") to being angry at people who don't ("They're wasting my time by making me keep calling back because I can't even leave a message")?

Miss Manners' chief task is to sort out the suggestions and possibilities, and to chronicle and guide the legitimate changes. Etiquette rules change when Miss Manners says it is all right for them to do so.

It should be clear by now that it is no use asking "What if I don't know the rules?" or "What if I don't feel like following them?" because Miss Manners will again trot out her comparison with the law. Etiquette is more lenient than the law about making allowances for strangers who haven't yet learned the rules of the situation they are in, but it is not safe to presume on Miss Manners' good nature by offering such insolent excuses as "I just don't feel comfortable with that." Etiquette cannot be unilaterally abandoned in the name of individual freedom, honesty or creativity, much less comfort, without social consequences.

This, of course, suggests the rather hostile question concerning consequences: Who's going to make me? (Usually rendered as: Oh, yeah? Who's going to make me?)

Obviously, etiquette does not have the enforcement power of the law. It's more like international law in that it keeps begging sovereign entities to behave themselves but uses disapproval instead of bombs to terrorize them. Tame as this sounds (although there are severe forms of showing disapproval, such as boycotts, shunning and ostracism), it has a higher rate of success than the more dramatic alternatives. Miss Manners' look of disapproval has been known to sizzle bacon.

A Reply

DEAR MISS MANNERS,

Since manners were made for man, and man was not made for manners, why is it important that such things as whether a woman does or does not cut the loops from her dresses before wearing them become "the rule of good behavior"?

Why is it important to thank the hosts for the dinner? They may have wondered if I appreciated the dinner, if it perhaps was something that my allergies could not stand, if I ate it only to be polite, etc. Why is it important, when being served soup, which way I maneuver the spoon, towards myself or away?

Obviously if I value the friendship of any person, I will try to be aware of any hang-ups they have and do my best not to tread on these whether I think them to be of value or not. Even if they are not my friends, it would be of the very poorest of manners to do or say anything needlessly to indicate that they had a silly hang-up.

Where do these things get started that it is necessary to do some certain thing that doesn't otherwise matter? Aren't the rules of good manners only important to help each of us get along and enjoy each other's company? Without causing any discomfort of others?

GENTLE READER,

Do not fear, your lady friends may keep the loops on their dresses. Those threads were sewn there to hold the belt in place while the dress was being rattled around on the racks in the store, and fastidious people don't much care for the look, but there is no etiquette rule one way or the other. It is not rude to be loopy.

Miss Manners does have a stake in those other questions, as well as in the cause of harmony to which you also subscribe. Here's how These Things—the rules of etiquette—get started.

Someone who wants to avoid other people's hang-ups gets tired of constantly trying to figure out what each person's hang-ups are in regard to every step of life. One person hates it when greeted in the morning, on the grounds that he isn't fully awake yet; another hates it when not greeted, on the grounds that it is an insult to ignore someone; a third feels that she should always go first in deciding whether or not to greet, and so on. Rather than keep a notebook of everyone's different hang-ups, and risk mixing them up and annoying strangers, people decide to agree on conventional actions with set interpretations.

People often choose to ignore these nowadays and set their own interpretations on the details of others' behavior. In that case, Miss Manners might have stopped at your opening statement and cried, "Manners made for man? *Made for man?* Why you dreadful thing you, what makes you think that manners were not made for woman?" Instead, she calmly digs into her experience with society's conventions and recognizes that you are using the old-fashioned form denoting all humankind, in approximation of a quotation, and don't mean any harm.

Excessive, idiosyncratic interpretation of petty acts is not only tiresome but mean-spirited, in that it attributes ill will when none may have been intended. How much simpler it is merely to do ordinary things in ordinary ways and save one's imagination and critical faculties for the complexities of life or the glories of art.

Many of the rules of etiquette are almost entirely arbitrary. Miss Manners is not prepared to argue that it is more polite to slosh soup away from yourself, possibly onto the table-cloth, than toward yourself, possibly hitting others. It is just the way we do it. Other rules have deeper than sur-face meanings. To thank someone for hospitality is to recognize the generous intent, whether or not the steak was burned and the conversation deadly.

A Census Bureau survey found that the biggest problem in most neighborhoods—bigger than crime, traffic or litter—was nasty neighbors. "Hate-thy-neighbor feuds consume so much police and court time that most local jurisdictions have mediation programs to cool things down," the *Washington Post* reported.

You would be surprised at how much such soothing details contribute to our shared goal of getting along with one another.

A Basic Rule

There is a rule of etiquette that the same people sometimes find extremely easy and sometimes extremely difficult to follow. It all depends on who and what. The rule is that who has precedence over what.

What? People are more important than objects.

Miss Manners is sure that all kindly folks who think of themselves as humanistic (or, in current baby talk, people-people), would agree with that. People have hearts and feelings and all that good stuff, and objects are just objects.

Unless, of course, they are your objects. Your new white rug, your car, your CD collection, your scissors, your antique table, your box of chocolates, your sweatshirt, your favorite rocking chair, your stash of groceries, your new magazine, or your delicate guest towels. Do you have to let other people use them? Do you have to stand by and watch other people destroy or devour them?

Well, yes, to a certain extent you do, if you have any pretensions about being polite to your guests. If you also have a new white rug, then you have to let your guests walk on it without making them take off their shoes, wash their feet, tie fresh dust-rags over them, and then teeter around the outside edge. If you have a box of chocolates around, you have to offer them to everyone, even taking the risk that they will pick off the squishy ones you like best and were saving for last. (Deafening cry of *"I don't wanna! It's minnnnnne!"*)

Now what is your definition of "heartless"? Miss Manners, no doubt, who is peddling that insistence on sharing that you hated in your childhood and don't much care for now, in spite of those wonderful sentiments you had expressed.

You should also have learned some wily tricks since childhood, and if you promise to appear to be generous with your guests, Miss Manners will show you how to protect your goods. One way out is that what is not seen need not be offered. Hide the chocolates until everyone has gone to the video store, and then cram them all in your mouth at once, wash your face, and pretend in front of the guests that the chocolates never existed. Don't leave your new magazine around where anyone might pick it up in an idle moment, and especially don't do so after reading that person something interesting or funny from it.

Of course, this means rolling up the rug and putting it in storage if you don't want people to walk on it. Or better yet, not buying something that is obviously made for general use if you will be unhappy when people use it.

Another way is to show concern for a guest's comfort and safety, at the expense of the reputation of your treasured object: "Here, don't sit on that chair; it's a bit rickety. I think you'll be more comfortable over there." This is particularly good with children of guests who aren't paying attention. "No, no, don't play with that—I'm afraid it might smash and cut you, and I'd feel terrible." (It is not necessary to specify which aspect of this calamity would make you feel terrible.)

Although the household goods must reasonably seem to be at the service of guests, it is within the bounds of politeness to decline lending things, even without an excuse beyond that of having a general policy. "I'm so sorry, I never lend my CDs"— or desk supplies or clothes. While one must always seem to share with guests, the arrangement with members of your own household can be up for negotiation: "You know it drives me crazy to have anyone else using my desk things. If you're really in a bind, please ask."

Miss Manners cautions against instructing the family not to use the guest towels. It is the only etiquette injunction that you may be sure they will obey, but for the rest of their lives, polite people whose houses they have visited will be ever so slightly put off upon discovering that even though they used the bathroom, they do not appear to have washed their hands.

Damages Assessment

Dear Miss Manners,

For my hope chest, I will have to choose between a large quantity of stoneware dishes or a smaller set of fine china. I would prefer the china, but cannot afford to constantly replace broken or chipped pieces.

Is there a graceful way to force one's guests to replace what they'd mar, while still retaining their friendship?

Gentle Reader,

You have another choice to make in planning your trousseau. Now that you have decided that you prefer china to stoneware, you must decide whether you prefer china to guests.

Evidently, you do.

Guests are human beings who cause a certain amount of wear and tear to the items they use. Miss Manners would not suggest entertaining people who are known to toss their dinnerware over their shoulders when they finish dinner, but now and again someone may accidentally chip or even break a plate.

The polite guest then falls all over the place apologizing, taking care not to hit another fragile item in the process. He or she should also offer to replace what is broken, although a better method is simply to do it without asking.

A hostess, in contrast, is obliged to protest that it doesn't matter, even if her heart is sinking and she allows herself reluctantly to accept the replacement "if it will make you feel better." That is because hostesses are supposed to value the feelings of their guests over the welfare of their possessions, however emotionally unlikely that may be.

Making clear the opposite (were you thinking of putting a sign in the dining room: You Break It, You Pay for It?) will mean that your set of friends will dwindle rapidly. If you prefer china, this may be a convenience, as it will give you more time at home to enjoy your collection undisturbed.

THE THREE SUBDIVISIONS OF ETIQUETTE

Reasonable people may finally agree, after Miss Manners has worn them out, that we need some specific rules to keep from upsetting one another unnecessarily. Some will even go so far as to acknowledge that they really should learn and follow such rules, as they learn and follow the law, rather than depend on everyone's having an endless supply of good will, tact and tolerance.

At this point, Miss Manners would love to head back to the porch hammock. Unfortunately, she knows what is coming next. Some gentleman will remove his tie and wave it at her, demanding, "Why do I have to wear this silly thing? It doesn't serve any purpose, and I don't hurt anyone but myself if I don't wear it—or if I do, too bad, because what I choose to wear is not anybody else's concern." (Ladies think along the same lines, but because of mechanical difficulties they don't remove and start waving their panty stockings in public.) Miss Manners then remembers that it is not enough to have tossed in a quick point about the tie's being symbolic. People who are being held hostage by their own clothing are upset, and they deserve a more thorough explanation.

Is there any of that nice juice left, and could there perhaps be a splash of champagne in it? Thank you.

Within any etiquette system, there are three sets of rules governing three functions: the regulative, the symbolic, and the ritual.

REGULATIVE ETIQUETTE

This is the please-be-nice stuff that makes some sort of logical sense:

Don't do that because it drives your father bananas.

If people don't let us know whether they're coming, we might not have enough food, or we might get stuck with too much.

We never hear from them except when they want something, so I don't see why I should run over every time their computer crashes.

Because regulative etiquette can be understood functionally, has an obvious practical purpose and resembles the law, it is the least troublesome type of etiquette to the literal-minded. It restricts freedom of expression more than law does because its function is to prevent conflict or settle it before it gets serious enough for the law to have to deal with it.

It is within every citizen's legal right to tell you that you are ugly, or that your baby is, but it is proscribed by etiquette because exercising this right may turn things really ugly. Then the law will have to step in. But for all its strictness, etiquette is much more flexible and less threatening than law, and therefore more suitable for gently regulating ordinary life.

Regulative Rules

Taking Turns

Dear Miss Manners,

While waiting at the center of a long checkout line, I have a bad habit of rehearsing my acceptance speech were I to be notified that I am the grand prize winner in a million-dollar lottery. Thus, I often fail to notice that a clerk is about to open another line next to mine, and the person behind me steps to the head of the new line, while those behind him join the stampede. I belatedly do likewise, and find myself behind the people who were behind me. I have always accepted it with grace.

However, at the supermarket recently, I did read the signs with more alacrity than usual and promptly stepped to the head of the new line. Whereupon the man who was ahead of me at Line No. 1 pushed past me, saying, "Let me in, please. I was ahead of you."

Not wishing to sully my (nearly) perfect record of impeccable social behavior, I refrained from shouting, "This one's mine, you big oaf," and docilely fell in behind him. However, when I later saw this man sitting on a bench in the front of the store counting up his money, I inferred that his wife was not waiting in the car for him to drive her to the delivery room, and the firemen were not waiting for him to bring them the key to his house so they could extinguish a blaze therein.

Of course, if one stays in his original line, there is no problem and one can feel superior to the Johnny-come-lately who chooses to join that line. However, when there is a $100 basket ahead waiting to be checked through, it is human nature to want to improve one's lot if the opportunity arises.

GENTLE READER,

Miss Manners appreciates your having restrained yourself from attempting to enforce, through rudeness of your own, the rules that you have unilaterally invented, and that you use to condemn others who may be operating by a different system of fairness. However, she does not authorize your rules. They only enforce a chaotic state in which those who stampede to a newly opened line are confirmed in their illegitimate priority.

The rest of the world recognizes that the etiquette of lines requires people to be served in the order in which they arrived. You needn't point out that this system is not always followed, because rude people seize any opportunity to push ahead. Miss Manners is sadly aware of that fact.

The situation you describe ought to be regulated by the checkout clerks. The simple call of "Who's next?" is the proper announcement of a newly available counter.

BETHESDA, MD.—A young man was beaten and stabbed in a suburban grocery store by two men after he complained that they had cut in front of him in the checkout line, the *Washington Post* **reported.**

A truly polite person in line would gently awaken a daydreamer with priority by saying, "Do you want to move over there?"

The gentleman who asked to take his rightful place ahead of you was not rude—assuming that he didn't literally push you or shout. By your own account, he did say please. He did not need to claim an emergency to assume the priority he had from having arrived in line ahead of you. While Miss Manners supposes we always have to throw in the possibility that rules be suspended in dire situations, she doubts that this has much application in the situation you describe. People rarely stop for groceries on their way to the maternity ward or to call the fire department.

Not Overstaying Visits I

DEAR MISS MANNERS,

A close friend of mine has been in and out of hospitals for several years, fighting cancer. I know that all her visitors have been well-meaning, yet I've been amazed at what they've done. A friend of the patient's mother, whom the patient had not seen in ten years, stopped by and for over two hours recited the ups and downs of her own and her grown-up children's lives. The woman had traveled an hour or more, so I suppose she wanted to stay long enough to make it feel worth her while. An old college friend, again someone who had been virtually out of her life for many years, bragged endlessly about her success, showed pictures of her children, her husband, and all the traveling she'd been doing.

Strangers dropped by to see her—"a friend of a friend." I can't imagine anyone who is sick wanting to be visited by someone they don't know. When in the uncomfortable position of being abed, I think a sick person would rather visit only with relatives or close friends. (I realize I could be wrong there.) One such lady came and stayed when my friend's sister was there, so that the sisters could not have the kind of personal chat they would have liked. Surely the stranger should check with family members first, or keep the visit very short unless it seems to be going very well. Since my friend was in the hospital so long, it was a help to her and her family to be able to schedule visitors, to provide some respite for family members who don't like her to go long periods of time without visitors.

Like so many of us, my friend is not a very assertive individual, and has felt like a captive audience. While it's true that she could be more gracious—they do have the best of intentions—I feel she should be able to use all her energy for getting well, not putting up with thoughtless visitors. Not all patients are alike. Some may delight in having visitors; others may much prefer cards and phone calls. Some people just have a hard time putting aside their hospitableness even when their energies are needed for the more urgent task of healing.

GENTLE READER,

Visiting the sick is supposed to exhibit such great virtue that there are some people determined to do it whether the sick like it or not. Like your friend, Miss Manners sometimes just doesn't feel up to pointing out to well-meaning people how tiresome they can be.

Etiquette rules require calling ahead for permission to visit a patient and limiting the stay to twenty minutes tops, unless a robust patient begs to prolong it. All visitors everywhere are supposed to make plans to depart if they observe their hosts visibly wilting or in pain, but this is especially true at hospitals.

The skill of being an interesting conversationalist under trying circumstances is a rare one. Hospital visitors who at least realize that they are not supposed to ask distressing questions, or offer amateur medical advice, or volunteer harrowing stories about their own or other people's illnesses to amuse the patient, often fall back on reciting their own news as being less dangerous. This does not make their doings and their children's any more interesting than under normal conversational conditions, of course.

If your friend cannot defend herself by saying, "You're so sweet to come—but forgive me, I need to rest now," her intimates should see to it that she is protected.

Not Overstaying Visits II

DEAR MISS MANNERS,

As a result of a major storm, many homes in my town were damaged, flooded or destroyed, including one belonging to an acquaintance of mine. She contacted me for advice (I'm a general contractor) and, in the course of conversation, asked if I would allow her to use my guest room while her house was repaired. (I am not doing the work.)

This was over seven weeks ago! Her house had only six inches of water! The repairs could have been completed and the house livable in less than one week. But my guest is taking this opportunity to do major renovations, and is not planning to return home until it is complete—eleven weeks!

When I assumed that her stay would be two weeks or less, I did not request rent or utilities. In the ensuing weeks, she has offered once to contribute to the heating bill, and I politely declined. She has made herself at home in every way—behavior I would expect from a guest, but not a "storm victim" who has overstayed her welcome. She has been part of my home entertaining, used my laundry supplies and some food staples, and generally invaded my lifestyle.

Miss Manners, I am a generous person and happy to share my good fortune. Under the circumstances, I feel uncomfortable withdrawing my hospitality or asking for a contribution to the household expenses. I will probably suffer in silence, but feel abused and used. My "guest" is financially well off and has been given a generous insurance settlement for the storm damage. She has a very good job and is probably more financially comfortable than I am. We are both single and live alone. Before this, we were casual friends who saw each other socially two or three times a year. What are my responsibilities as host, and hers as guest?

Gentle Reader,

Hers is to go home or to a hotel. But as she shows no inclination to do either, yours is to get your house back. Do this by saying, "I was glad to be of service to you and I enjoyed having you, but I'm afraid I can't keep you here any longer. Please make some other arrangements by Sunday, at the latest." You need not—and should not—offer any excuse. An act of generosity does not get wiped off the slate if it does not continue forever. Miss Manners does not want you suffering in silence. She only wants you, as a building contractor, to remember how much damage can be caused by unmet deadlines.

Keeping Appointments

Dear Miss Manners,

A friend of mine called to say she was "getting a group together" to hear a lecture of a psychologist whose methods we all admire. The fee was $20 a person, and we would all be responsible for our own transportation. I asked her to order a ticket for me, promising to mail the cost plus an additional handling fee as soon as she informed me of the total.

The next day, she called again to say that the "whole thing got out of hand" and she had decided to attend the event with the first person she had invited, and that person only. She claimed that this was an important step in her "development"—that she was learning to "take care of herself." Miss Manners, am I crazy? Does "taking care of oneself" include the right to be rude and to disappoint your friends? I'm confused and angry. Please help me put this in perspective.

Gentle Reader,

Miss Manners is not so disturbed by the crime of which you complain. Having allowed less than a day to elapse between suggesting the excursion and abdicating from acquiring your ticket, your friend has not seriously inconvenienced you. But she shares your abhorrence of the excuse. It is disgusting enough for people to brag about their own development, without them making the point that they are happy to ignore your convenience in the process.

Acknowledging Presents

DEAR MISS MANNERS,

Is there a statute of limitations on thank you notes? About six months ago, I left a foreign country where I had been living for several years, and returned to the United States. I found myself the recipient of numerous going-away presents from close friends, casual acquaintances and a range of well-wishers in between.

Writing so many thank you notes all at once would be a very time consuming task, especially since a number would have to be in a language upon which my grip is rather shaky. Therefore, I put it off until the more urgent tasks involved in my international move and accompanying career change were completed. At last I find myself settled into my new life, with the time I need to acknowledge the generosity I was shown in my last one. However, so many months have gone by that I fear that any thank you notes I send out now might draw more attention to my prior negligence than to my continuing gratitude.

GENTLE READER,

Wish on. Miss Manners does not absolve you of your obligations if you only neglect to fulfill them long enough. Just because you put at the bottom of your list the necessity of thanking generous friends for their kindness does not mean that they have ceased wondering what happened to you. The only statute of limitations of which Miss Manners is aware is that when it becomes obvious how indifferent you are, they may cease to care.

The fact is, the obligation to express gratitude deepens with procrastination. The longer you wait, the more effusive must be the thanks. The way to write a tardy thank you letter is not to explain that you had more important things to do, such as locating a good video store. This is not charming to people who spent their time and imagination getting you a present instead of doing something for themselves. Rather, what you must do is to write rhapsodically of how often you think of each friend, as you enjoy the present he or she gave you.

Acknowledging Lifesaving

DEAR MISS MANNERS,

At a dinner party for my niece's engagement, my mother choked on some food, turned totally blue, and collapsed. Our family all stood mesmerized in horror.

Fortunately, the groom-to-be's mother, a nurse, and another of his relatives, a police officer trained in CPR, went into immediate action. Through use of the Heimlich maneuver and other methods (which included physically reaching down her throat), they were able to dislodge the food and save her life. Emergency paramedics had been called, but they would never have arrived in time.

Of course members of the family thanked the two rescuers immediately after. I also feel that as a follow-up, to show appreciation for all they did, the members of our family should send flowers, a box of fine cookies or candy to each of the people who saved Mom's life, with a written note of thanks. Some agree that it would be a gracious gesture, but others feel that it would embarrass and humiliate them to receive such a gift for doing an act of humanitarianism.

GENTLE READER,

What is the embarrassment argument? That it would be more gracious to ignore your debt? Or that cookies are an insufficient exchange for your mother's life?

If it is the latter, please explain to them that the key part of your gesture is the written expressions of extreme gratitude—effusive statements about how fortunate you all are to be connected to these people, with an acknowledgment that you can never hope to repay their kindness. The treat is merely an accompanying token.

If it is the former, however, please introduce Miss Manners to the rescuers quickly. Just thinking about such an attitude would make her turn blue and collapse.

SYMBOLIC ETIQUETTE

Symbolic rules of etiquette are totally arbitrary, which is why people often assume they can be violated with impunity. This is a mistake. Everybody scrutinizes such things as clothing, nomenclature and gesture for symbolic content all the time:

I can't wear that to school. They'll all think I'm a nerd.
I don't read my in-laws' letters when they address me as "Mrs." They must think their son now owns me.

We can't hire him—he's not serious. All during the interview, he had his feet up on my coffee table.

If regulative etiquette can't be figured out logically, symbolic etiquette *really* can't be. There is a whole new set of rules to go with practically every culture, and others with subcultures. Once these rules are learned, however, they provide people with a tremendous fund of nonverbal knowledge about one another, helping them to deal with a wide range of social situations and relationships.

Forms of greeting, dressing, eating and restraining (or exaggerating) bodily functions can all be read as symbols of degrees of friendliness or hostility, respect or contempt, solidarity with the community or alienation from it. It is safe to assume that a person who advances on you with an outstretched hand is symbolizing an intent to treat you better than one who spits.

It doesn't matter how arbitrary any of the violated rules may be—ignoring them is interpreted as defiance of, indifference to, or antagonism toward the interests of the person or community whose standard is being ignored. If you wear jeans to a formal wedding, or a business suit to a casual party, you may protest all you like about your choice being only an expression of your personal style, budget, or comfort. Miss Manners guarantees that everyone present will interpret it as disdain.

Following the conventions of the society is taken as a measure of respect for it. No one, not even those who are most vehement in claiming to have sartorial freedom from symbolism, would hire a trial lawyer who wore pajamas (which would serve the practical function of covering the body as well as a suit) to court, or submit to an operation by a brain surgeon who wore a Dracula sweatshirt in his consulting room. Don't even think about flouting symbolic

"In the courtroom, you always want to put your best foot forward and your best foot should have the same color sock as your other foot," a Columbia Law School vice dean told the *New York Times* in a story on the importance to jurors and clients of what lawyers wear. A bright young law student couldn't get a job because she dressed "like a whore," the dean said, adding, **"Some Legal Aid people believe they should be 'of the people' and dress down for political reasons. It's patronizing. The clients don't want that. They feel they should get real lawyers."**

dress conventions if you want a career in the law, the military, diplomacy, the church or athletics. All of these professions have particularly strict etiquette rules, and compliance is taken to symbolize adherence to the particular values that these professions require: fairness, obedience, respect, piety or valor.

SYMBOLIC RULES: DRESS

Hats

A major etiquette battle is raging these days over the propriety of wearing hats, and it is not being fought by the likes of Miss Manners.

Many ladies would love to comply with etiquette's suggestion that they wear hats on formal occasions, but are prevented from doing so by raging timidity. The undaunted Miss Manners is made aware of this every time she shows up properly hatted at a wedding, funeral, graduation, religious service, tea party, garden party or grand luncheon. Ladies of all ages come up to her, one after another, and say, "Oh, I had a hat I wanted to wear, but I didn't dare." Miss Manners is too polite to notice that some of them had no qualms about appearing almost without skirts. She considers it kind of them to offer her the opportunity to outdo them in daring.

The actual current hat controversy is among those who do dare and those whom they offend: elementary and high school pupils who insist upon wearing baseball caps to school, which their teachers hate, and grown-up gentlemen who refuse to take off their caps or cowboy hats indoors, which seriously annoys their female contemporaries.

The younger parties to this dispute are ignorant of the traditional rules about head coverings and innocent of the very concept of clothing being symbolic. They can't even imagine why hats should be subject to regulations other than those dictated by comfort or fashion. The older people, both those who are fighting the offense and those who are committing it, are skeptical or uncertain about how the old rules should be applied under modern conditions.

Miss Manners has been inundated with letters on this subject, some of them from entire classrooms, with an appeal by the teacher enclosed. They are asking:

Can currently worn headgear be properly defined as hats?
Why should hat-wearing have special rules at all, rather than being a matter of each individual's taste?

Weren't there separate rules for male and female, and should that distinction still be made?

If there are different rules for indoors and out, which apply in a shopping mall?

If rules apply only in a formal setting, how could that include cafeterias, movie theaters, bars, convention centers and friends' living rooms?

Miss Manners will issue updated rulings, but first some background:

Hats are hats, and so are caps. The Gentle Reader who claimed that "cowboys never take off their hats" in the presence of ladies must not have seen any classic westerns. They also called ladies "Ma'am." Head coverings have always been fraught with symbolism, which is why many religions specify showing respect in terms of hats and veils and why royalty is crowned. Cowboyhood and a devotion to baseball are not, for this purpose, deemed to be religions.

For those who think that hat symbolism has disappeared from everyday life, Miss Manners passes on a report kindly sent to her by a Gentle Reader from Chicago: "If a young man wears his hat tilted in a certain way here, he is in danger of being beaten up or killed. He could also be wearing his baseball cap tilted in a certain way to threaten or challenge others. Certain 'gangbangers' wear hats which represent the colors of their gangs, and tilt the hats to the left, right, or in another position which identifies them as members of a certain gang. Someone who isn't a gangbanger and happens to wear the 'wrong' colors or tilts his hat the 'wrong' way may be in danger."

Among ladies, as opposed to gangbangers, the traditional everyday rule was that a lady never went out in daylight without a hat, and she kept it on indoors, except in her own house. But a gentleman who failed to remove his hat indoors, or even to "lift" it ("tipping" a hat being too jaunty a phrase to be approved by etiquette) outdoors if he stopped to talk to a lady, was insulting everyone who saw him, even strangers across the room. This distinction of genders has been used to support the argument that girls, but not boys, could keep on their cap indoors.

Now the rulings:

A mall is "outdoors," because it is, for all intents and purposes, a street.

Bars, movie theaters and cafeterias are indoors, as are schools, houses of worship and private houses.

Gentlemen, even very young ones, must still remove their hats indoors as a sign of respect.

A lady who is wearing the sort of formal daytime clothes that are the female equivalent of the male suit with tie may keep her hat on indoors. This distinction does not apply with unisex clothing, but if the young ladies in the classroom are wearing dresses and gloves (pearls optional), they may properly keep their hats on.

Baseball Caps

Dear Miss Manners,

My daughter, who is 20, attended a basketball game and did not remove her baseball cap during the National Anthem. Some young men in the group criticized her for this. I don't recall seeing women take off their hats or caps at any sports events I've attended. I've never taught my daughter to do this. Have I been in error?

Gentle Reader,

It is an excusable error, because you are of a generation to whom the question of ladies wearing baseball caps for social events other than softball practice did not arise. Of course, that might then excuse your daughter, who is of the baseball cap generation, from not practicing cap etiquette, as you did not teach it to her.

Pretty soon, Miss Manners would be excusing the entire stadium. There would go civilization as we know it. In fact (Miss Manners has just looked out the window, at all those people brandishing their etiquette excuses), there it goes now.

Instead of adding to the excuses, she will give you the rule now, quick, so you can pass it on to your daughter. A lady's hat is indeed worn as a sign of respect but a baseball cap is not a lady's hat. It is a unisex item of male origin, and therefore is subject to the removal-for-respect rule, even when worn by a lady.

Heads

Dear Miss Manners,

Would you kindly find out for me the background and reason why hats should not be worn by males in a room of people, e.g., a classroom. Since I teach law, I've had to relax the rule, as students would like a reason for it.

GENTLE READER,

Miss Manners knows those law students. God bless them, they want a practical justification for every rule. There isn't one. Hats are as symbolic as the judge's robes they hope one day to wear.

White Shoes

Miss Manners would have thought that the annual excitement of getting those white summer shoes out of the closet after the deprivation of a cold winter (or a warm one) to symbolize the change of seasons was a treat well worth the waiting. Heaven knows there are few satisfying arbitrary rules left, and the one about wearing white shoes only between Memorial Day and Labor Day is so mild. Propriety used to require people to wear stiff collars and jackets, or long skirts and petticoats, no matter what the temperature.

Nevertheless, an ungrateful populace wants to make an argument of it and claim that choosing shoes is a matter of comfort, taste, or color coordination, any of which they know how to judge themselves. Never mind that it is too hot to argue, thus making the whole fuss a violation of the rebels' case that weather should dictate behavior.

All right. Let's take up the issues that have been raised. Let's make a metaphysical battle out of a sweet little folk practice. Miss Manners' Gentle Readers have attacked on many fronts.

> *The Historical Argument:* "In the days of horse and buggy and many unpaved streets, women's winter clothes were mostly dark colors that wouldn't readily show mud spatters. Light colors were saved for dry summer months. Now white, off-white, light and bright colors are worn all year. If clothing color styles change, why shouldn't shoes?"
>
> *The Discrimination Argument* (divisions of both Wealth and Health): "Dictating the color of one's shoes seems rather presumptuous and picky, and smacks of snobbery by the wealthy, who can afford a closet full of shoes. Not everyone can afford shoes to go with every outfit. Some of us have foot problems or feet that are hard to fit, limiting the range of selections. Sometimes trying to find a comfortable, affordable dress shoe in a suitable style and color becomes 'mission impossible.' "

The Multi-Cultural Argument: "Queen E II wore white shoes on a visit here when it wasn't summer. How does the rule apply to Her Majesty?"

The Weather Argument: "Setting style by a date on the calendar, regardless of weather or climate, seems impractical and somewhat ridiculous. If the weather is 90 degrees in April or October and one wants to wear a summery pastel print on white, I should think white shoes would look better than black or brown, or is a summer dress also taboo?"

Just when Miss Manners had decided she had had enough, a Gentle Reader caught her with, "Please don't throw this into your 'Oh, Stop It' pile yet. I assiduously adhere to your White Shoe Edict. Are spectator pumps considered to be white shoes? I wasn't too concerned about it until I came into possession of a spectacular pair of spectators. I don't want to make a mistake."

This is so obligingly phrased that Miss Manners regrets exceedingly that tradition compels her to admit that spectator pumps are considered summer shoes. Dark shoes may be worn at any time of the year; white sneakers, bridal shoes and baby shoes are exempted from the summer-only rule; saddle shoes, which are white shoes with brown trim across the middle, are considered year-round shoes.

NEW CITY, N.Y.—When a college student accused in a carjacking and murder case appeared on the witness stand in a blue blazer with a handkerchief in his breast pocket, the prosecution asked him at least twice during the trial to change into the black sweatshirt, jeans and boots he wore when he was arrested "to persuade the jury that he was a more intimidating figure than the blue blazer would make him appear," the *New York Times* reported.

But spectator shoes, which have brown heels and toes, are considered summer shoes. Symbolic etiquette is not required to make sense.

Ribbons, Buttons and Jewels

Why, what a charming little brooch you are wearing. What is it trying to tell us?

The possibility that a personal ornament, such as a piece of jewelry or a ribbon, could carry a specific symbolic meaning is not new to Miss Manners, who has nevertheless always been careful not to lean too close to anyone's lapel to hear what is on its mind. Coded baubles existed long before the idea of turning clothes into form-fitting sandwich boards, so that people could broadcast their beliefs wherever they went, without troubling to open their mouths or to engage others in conversation.

Colors have long been worn to symbolize political and other causes, and jewelry has not always been luxuriously above the fray. Late 19th and early 20th century necklaces and brooches made of emeralds, amethysts, and pearls were intended to be read as Green, Violet, White, or Give Votes to Women, and the colors have been retained among feminists with a sense of history. Rings containing, in this order, a ruby, emerald, garnet, amethyst, another ruby, and a diamond were the gifts of admirers who trusted it to be understood that the stones spelled out their REGARD. But then, love always seems to have found its way into jewelry, from the wedding ring to the wearable eye portrait (a miniature depiction of an illicit lover's eye, to thrill the wearer without the danger of giving away the loved one's identity) on brooch or ring.

Codes for causes were most prominently revived in recent years with the yellow ribbons in support of hostages, red ribbons in sympathy with AIDS sufferers, pink in sympathy for breast cancer, and so on. Miss Manners is thinking of wrapping herself in a rainbow to signify that she opposes all diseases and kidnappings.

She refrains only because she is not crazy about wearing advertisements, no matter how noble their cause. Nevertheless, she is delighted to see an alternative to expression of emotion through self-inflicted graffiti. Bumper stickers on automobiles may possibly be excusable, on the grounds that they reach those whom one would not be able to engage in conversation anyway. When previously unacquainted motorists meet face to face, it is less likely to be for the exchange of ideas than for the exchange of addresses and insurance companies.

When the bumper is a human chest, on which written statements clearly bark out orders to Save This or Nuke That, the effect is to preclude conversation in a not very polite way. The implied tone is not "I thought you might want to know how I feel about an issue to which I have given much thought," but "This is the way it ought to be—want to make something of it?"

A certain delicacy is required in the matter of announcing one's beliefs to people who didn't inquire. The subtlety of a symbol is that the option of using it as a conversation piece is the observer's. It is hard to pretend not to understand a statement in huge letters, spread out in front of you on someone's chest, but an ornament may be remarked upon or not. Its message may also be absorbed at leisure, without the necessity of arguing with its bearer.

Even those who thoroughly agree with the written material on someone else's costume may be put off by the way its preemptive announcement smacks of moral superiority. Those who disagree are not likely to hang around unless they are spoiling for a fight. Neither reaction should be desirable to anyone who wishes to influence the thinking of others. Nor do they serve Miss Manners' favorite cause.

BALTIMORE, MD.—A high school tried to stop a boy from wearing an anti-abortion T-shirt depicting a bloodied, dismembered fetus to a home economics class for fear it would upset other students, including a pregnant girl, according to the *Wall Street Journal*. The school then found itself embroiled in a lawsuit over freedom of speech, the *Journal* reported.

Artists' Uniforms

Dear Miss Manners,

I am a young artist. To fill in the gaps, I've worked as a fashion model and I've come to enjoy wearing beautiful clothes, most of which I make myself. I was raised in a family which believes that gracious manners are meant to put everyone at ease. But when I get dressed up, I wonder if anyone will take me seriously as an artist.

All the young artists I know show up at formal affairs wearing torn paint-splattered jeans. It's the badge of a "real" artist. Of course, the idea is to be a revolutionary, and artists have been doing it for a long time. Do you think it is too shocking of me to dress in beautiful, fashionable clothes, and use the manners I've been taught? It sounds funny to ask, but I'm quite serious.

Gentle Reader,

What Miss Manners finds shocking is the rigid conventionality of the artist-revolutionaries you describe. She thought artists' clothes were supposed to symbolize their defiance of convention. Alas, Miss Manners has come to realize that people who most vehemently champion originality and flair are scandalized at anything unusual. They have been after Miss Manners and her little white gloves for years.

Let us not hear any more nonsense about artists only being real when they have the superficial proof of wearing studio work clothes. Miss Manners reminds you that the great painters of history were only too delighted to apply their visual sense to their own persons. As for your manners, of course you should use them. If rudeness were an indication of artistry, this would be the Renaissance.

Nudity: Hosts

Every summer, Miss Manners starts looking nervously over her shoulder for naked ladies and gentlemen on the attack.

These are not potential criminals out to do unspeakable things. All they want to violate is social custom. They simply appear naked on certain social occasions and refuse to understand why there should be any legitimately recognized objections.

The certain occasions are perhaps not the ones that first spring to mind. Having refused to complicate her life by noticing the private practices of consenting adults, Miss Manners does not concern herself with the emotionally active, so long as they frolic peaceably among themselves. Nor does she wish to disturb nudists, sunbathers, swimmers, or tub-bathers who agree upon their dress codes.

Such people are generally too preoccupied to consult her, anyway. Those who come after her, or whose victims come to her for shelter, practice nakedness among the nonconsenting. They can be recognized, if one doesn't wish to stare, by the words, "Oh, come on . . ." delivered in a long-suffering tone of voice, as if it is too tiresome to imagine that there are people left on earth so stuffy as to insist upon dress. They then offer the following justifications: It's cooler. The human body is beautiful. It's natural. It's comfortable. People have a right to decide the dress in their own houses. It makes less laundry. Everybody ought to loosen up. Nobody is going to see anything that hasn't been seen before. Or for anyone who hasn't, it's high time. Only evil-minded people would find this objectionable. Those who don't like it should worry about their own hang-ups.

Notice the mixture here of feigned innocence and sincere meanness. The first line of attack is to claim that everyone else admits that their practice is reasonable, and the second is to ridicule anyone who doesn't. Miss Manners hardly knows which she dislikes more, the false naïveté or the bullying.

She hardly believes that our naked friends are in genuine need of being taught that every society establishes certain codes of dress whose symbolic significance may be unrelated to the amount of skin displayed. You can equally upset people by showing too little of the body, according to the customs of the society you are in, or too much. Think of the shock Americans feel at the mandated, nearly total, covering of ladies in some cultures.

Naked hosts do need a lesson in how to treat their guests. Failure to warn guests of even the nuances of dress expected is rude; failure to warn them that the society's normal practice will be suspended—and then trying to bully them into believing that there is nothing odd about it—is unconscionable.

Nudity: Guests

Dear Miss Manners,

My college roommate visited me for three days, along with her husband of two years and his daughters from a previous marriage, aged ten and fourteen. My friends are nudists. I knew this, and of course I have no objection to their pursuit of this interest in their own home or in an appropriate place, such as a nudist camp. I was surprised, however, when my friend's husband and his elder daughter began to strip practically as soon as they entered my home. The girl, who is well into adolescence, had her blouse over her head before she said, "This doesn't bother you, does it? Because it doesn't bother me." (She did change into another blouse eventually.)

I was so surprised that I really couldn't summon up an honest, assertive response. I just muttered, with some embarrassment, that if she was

> **"Dressing down" in the name of increased productivity is just as silly as "power-dressing" in the name of increased productivity, according to a story by a Brandeis University researcher on the *Wall Street Journal* editorial page. "Dress codes were never intended to fatten a company's bottom line. Rather, they reinforce the concept that part of self-respect is showing at least the same level of respect for others and one's endeavors."**

comfortable, it didn't matter to me. She and her father apparently took this as an invitation to parade around naked for the next three days.

In retrospect, I'm rather annoyed by the whole matter. My friend's husband at one point joked that I wasn't seeing anything I hadn't seen before. And although he was right, I don't think that was the point. These folks were guests in my house, and I don't think it's asking too much for them to conduct themselves there pretty much as I would. Is it appropriate for me to raise the issue with my friend (who did not run around nude, nor did the younger girl) and let her know that the behavior of her husband and stepdaughter made me uncomfortable, or should I simply let it go? These folks no doubt will be back to visit me. My friends are also members of several social groups for the super-intelligent, and they seem to regard nudism as a badge of some sort of superiority. I'm not prudish about nakedness, but good grief, aren't there limits?

Gentle Reader,

Yes, but you didn't set them. Admittedly, the girl should have asked your permission before she had her blouse over her head—such an awkward position in which to speak, anyway. But once she did, in not the most charming way, you granted it.

Miss Manners understands that being flabbergasted, you popped out the nearest cliché, which you didn't mean. She also understands that you were somewhat bullied by their tone, and feel called upon to defend yourself from accusations of prudishness. You should have said pleasantly that yes, it did bother you. Failing that, you could have gently said later, "You know, I find it does bother me after all."

They know perfectly well that nudism is not appropriate everywhere. The policeman on your beat has seen it all, too, but they didn't attempt to show it to him by approaching your house nude. There is no point now in telling guests that you are annoyed that they behaved as you specifically told them they could. When you invite them again, however, you should take care to specify that "We will be dressing for dinner."

Symbolic Rules: First Names

What is symbolized by assuming the use of someone's first name? Friendliness, love, intimacy and good will toward everyone, according to the friendship squads who insist on the practice regardless of age, acquaintanceship, or the preference of the person being addressed. If so, there must be a lot more love of humanity out there than Miss Manners would have suspected from looking out the window.

Although decidedly stuffy, Miss Manners is strongly in favor of friendship and warmth. She only opposes pretending that these states exist when they obviously couldn't.

Strangers don't feel warm toward one another, at least in the establishments Miss Manners patronizes. There is nothing that ages an adult so much as the claim of not really feeling grown-up and thus not wanting to be addressed as such. Instructing a young person, "Don't call me that; you make me feel old," inevitably engenders the worry that the speaker is not only old but probably, not realizing it, demented as well.

We Americans have always prided ourselves on showing to everyone the respect that people in other nations save for their betters (because we don't have betters), and on a demeanor of cheerfulness, helpfulness and openness. We have also always scorned and satirized phony behavior, of which social pretense—the kind of kissy-poo intimacy of people who want to seem more closely connected than they are—is, Miss Manners would think, an excellent example.

In any case, the symbolism that some profess to find in the use of first names is by no means universally benign. Other, sinister, meanings spring to many minds. When the United States Postal Service used the first name of one of the honorees in its Black Heritage stamp series (the biographical note on Jan E. Matzeliger read: "Jan invented and patented a shoe-lasting machine"), an African-American history scholar cited the racist tradition of addressing blacks by their first names. "By using 'Mr.' or 'Mrs.,' the speaker acknowledges that the black is an adult, and the use of first names is a sign of a certain power relationship, that the black is kept subservient," said Ethelbert Miller, who was quoted by the *New York Times*.

To one of Miss Manners' Gentle Readers, the unauthorized use of his first name symbolizes disrespect for his age, if not insinuations about his competency: "I am an old man. Fortunately, so far as I can tell, I have most of my marbles, but the people in the health care business may change all this. I don't mean to be chauvinistic, but the worst offenders are women. They almost universally treat me as if I were a lovable but mentally deficient child. They practically never address me as 'Mister.' Instead, they call me by my first name (William) with a stress and intonation that clearly indicates that they are making a special emphasis on their doing so. In many cases, they call me 'Bill'—thank God, there have been only a couple of occasions when I was called 'Billy.' "

Another Gentle Reader questions whether this symbolizes disrespect by gender: "Now that I work in a professional setting, I find I often have to call people who are strangers. Generally, I use their last name, and generally, they respond with my first name. I am a woman lawyer, and many of these people are male lawyers. When they use my first name after I have already addressed them by their last, I feel foolish and unsure whether they simply have a different set of manners from myself, or if they are showing a lack of respect."

Many Gentle Readers find it a sign of disregarding their wishes: "I prefer that my given name be reserved for use by family and friends, not by sales people whom I have just met. When I tell someone that my name is "Mrs. _____" I resent being asked, 'What is your first name?' If I wanted to be called by my first name, I would introduce myself in that manner."

"After seeing my name on my charge card or check, waiters, salesclerks and bank tellers have addressed me by my first name. Now, I've never been a very formal person, but I am startled, and feel rather insulted."

Miss Manners does not really believe that any of these misuses were intended as insult, but she does not easily forgive people who claim to be ignorant of long-standing symbolism commonly used in their own societies. The Post Office reply mentioned that some of the writers it employs "might feel uncomfortable" using "Mr." That is no excuse for causing discomfort to people they profess to be honoring.

Honorifics

DEAR MISS MANNERS,

What can I do to get my (university) students to call me Ms. Harlowe? Or, failing that, Dr. Harlowe? Is there any way in which I can safely get away with calling them Mr. Lovelace and Ms. Howe (as I would prefer to do), rather than Richard and Anna?

All of my attempts to use the title–last name formula have been rewarded with abysmal instructor evaluations, with students adducing my preferred mode of address as evidence that I am hostile, cold and unhelpful—despite the counterevidence of hours spent working on their papers and exercises, writing comments designed to enable them to do better, a classroom attitude that encouraged participation and questions, and even more hours spent in private tutoring for students with problems.

I should add that I need good student evaluations to continue in my present (marginal) employment. Students become bellicose if I do not refer to myself as either "Clarissa" or "Dr. Harlowe." (I was indoctrinated with the "reverse snobbery" that required that all college instructors be addressed as "Mr. Belford" or "Mrs. Sinclair," the idea being that they would of course be possessed of the Ph.D., and that "Dr." indicated a medical doctor or irretrievable lack of sophistication.) Students see in my preferred form either dishonesty ("If you have a Ph.D., why don't you call yourself 'Doctor'?") or incompetence ("You don't even have your doctorate!") or, the worst crime, "unfriendliness."

If I simply put "Clarissa Harlowe" on my syllabus, leaving it up to them, most call me "Clarissa"! If I use "C. Harlowe," they ask what my first name is, and call me by it anyway. I am certainly not young enough for them to regard me as a peer! "Professor Harlowe" is not an option. I am not a professor, but a lowly lecturer. Do you have any solution that will allow me to remain both (a) dignified, and (b) employed?

GENTLE READER,

Yes, indeed. It is called education. Miss Manners does not expect you to teach manners to university students. However, as you are in the English Department (how did Miss Manners manage to guess that?) it is part of the job to teach them about the symbolism and forms of speech, as well as about how usage changes, depending not only on country and period, but on the people talking and the activity in which they are engaged.

After they learn why Mrs. Bennet calls her husband "My dear Mr. Bennet," even though they know each other well enough to have five daughters in common, you will astonish them by explaining that in our very own time, grown-ups make distinctions between formal and informal situations, between friendship and professional life, and use different language accordingly. The example that will drive this lesson home will be that of the formal, professional relationship between students and their teachers.

SYMBOLIC RULES: PRESENTS

DEAR MISS MANNERS,

I called my girlfriend and told her we didn't drink tea, and I'd like to return the teapot she gave me for a shower gift, and get something I can use. I didn't think she'd mind when I asked her where she bought it, and she didn't seem upset when she told me. She sent a check for the wedding, but she and her boyfriend did not attend. I've called her on their answering service, but she has not called back. We used to talk all the time. Do you think she is mad at me for having returned her gift? I thought she'd understand.

GENTLE READER,

What your friend understands is that you considered her present only for its practical value as a trade-in, and not as a symbol of her affection. Miss Manners presumes that that is why she decided to hand over the money instead of choosing a wedding present for you, while withholding the affection that you treated as being of so little account.

What you failed to understand is that you could have had it both ways. You need only have thanked her for her thoughtfulness instead of making it clear that you considered the present to have been a thoughtless one. Then you could have made other use of the teapot—tracking down the store on your own, or giving it away, donating it to charity, or using it to water plants.

Symbolic Rules: Behavior

Dear Miss Manners,

I am, unfortunately, a "resident" in the county jail and I am criticized by fellow residents for comporting myself in a manner befitting the outside world. I have not forgotten my basic manners and I do not wish to abandon them as so many others have done here. My question is simply: Is being in jail sufficient reason for abandoning one's manners?

Gentle Reader,

Miss Manners trusts that you are only too familiar with the concept of "Time off for good behavior." In preparation for your trial, your lawyer should have pointed out that good manners, while always an asset, are crucial to anyone in trouble, because they symbolize respect for the rules of the community.

Nowhere, including jail, do good manners include emphasizing one's superiority to others. Rather, living among strangers usually requires learning to adapt to prevailing practices that do not conflict with one's morality. Far from believing that being jailed is reason for abandoning manners, Miss Manners believes it to offer an incentive for practicing them.

Symbolism Run Amok

You don't often catch Miss Manners going around advising people to lighten up. On the contrary (she said darkly). It seems to her that there are far too many lightweights among us already. Merrily taking a light view of etiquette, they make life heavier going for the rest of us by claiming that our customs and courtesies are flighty.

But even Miss Manners' august patience is occasionally strained when people start etiquette battles over the trivial, the irrelevant and, often, the illegitimate. These would-be defenders of manners have the gall to declare their idiosyncratic practices to be standard etiquette (only Miss Manners can do that) and then violate the principles of manners by picking quarrels with innocent people over these unauthorized rules.

It was the satin hangers that drove her over the brink this time. A Gentle Reader confessed: "I had given a man and wife gifts of padded satin-bound clothes hangers, pink for the wife and olive green for the man. I was told that no one would give padded satin-bound clothes hangers to a man. Please tell me if it's true. I'd like to know if I was incorrect."

This is clearly a question of symbolism. Does one insult a gentleman by the present of padded satin hangers? The Etiquette Council, not known for its careless disregard of details, has nevertheless never met on the subject of gender in clothes hangers. The closest Miss Manners ever came to considering the matter was to endorse—actually, to join, with some urgency—the cause of traveling ladies whose skirts kept slipping to the floor of hotel closets because they had not been provided with proper hangers. Since there is no clear tradition for deciding this case, one must fathom intention. Miss Manners hereby decrees that padded hangers being items useful to both gentlemen and ladies, neither can claim that such a present was made with malicious intent.

When Miss Manners thought she had recovered, she heard from another Gentle Reader, who was experiencing "a mild case of shock at seeing American women, upon a first date, ordering a glass of beer, which they seem to regard as a political statement in defiance of the 'artificial refinement' of a glass of wine. Am I correct in regarding such women as lacking in aesthetic development?"

No, sir. A beer is still a beer, not a symbolic manifestation of political principle. Perhaps Miss Manners ought to go have one.

Just Stop It

DEAR MISS MANNERS,

I would like to know where you stand on feminist issues.

Is calling oneself Ms. improper? Is not shaving legs and underarms and not wearing make-up or a bra improper?

Also, please tell me if women are to keep their legs crossed or knees together while sitting.

GENTLE READER,

Feminist issues?

Shaving? Make-up? Underwear? Using a sensible and standard honorific that one happens to prefer for oneself?

Why is it that if gentlemen start wearing earrings, it becomes merely a fashion, while ladies' grooming and underwear are considered open for political interpretation and criticism?

Your examples strike Miss Manners as being Mind Your Own Business issues. As a feminist, she believes ladies' opinions are learned from listening to what they say, rather than snooping into their clothing. Perhaps this is why it is proper for them to cross their ankles, rather than their knees.

RITUAL ETIQUETTE

Appreciation for ritual strikes rarely in casual modern life, but when it does, it is powerful enough to knock over anyone in its way:

> *I don't care if you haven't spoken to Daddy in twenty years—you have to dance together or you'll spoil my whole wedding that I've planned since I was a little girl.*
> *Open presents the night before? That's the whole trouble with your family right there. Everybody knows you're supposed to open presents on Christmas Day.*
> *No! You have to read me the story the same way you always read it! And my lambie goes on this side, not that side! I can't sleep if it's not right!*

Ritual etiquette, which governs the ceremonies of life, both momentous and daily, is not supposed to be a weapon for destroying families. Its set, well-known patterns provide an aesthetically pleasing and emotionally reassuring sense of social belonging. As anyone knows who attends weddings at which the couple write their own ceremonies, traditional ritual, smoothed by time, is far more satisfying than any behavior that can be improvised under emotionally complicated circumstances. Miss Manners just wishes that the emotion wouldn't drive the participants in rituals so far out of control that they get hysterical about details, often on points so trivial that even etiquette has never deigned to fool with them.

We abandon ritual at our peril. Although the most etiquette-resistant people do not maintain that it would be more practical to put corpses down the garbage disposal, funerary ritual has been truncated at great emotional cost. We now have celebrations (Miss Manners being the only person who still hopes that when she dies her friends will not all celebrate), and then it's back to the normal routine. Not only are the bereaved unprotected from social demands by customs of seclusion and symbols of vulnerability, but they are encouraged to act as if nothing had happened, only to be deemed heartless if they actually succeed.

RITUAL RULES

The Jolly Funeral

DEAR MISS MANNERS,

As I entered the funeral home for the funeral of someone very close to me, I was in shock. Before I opened the door, I could hear this very loud laughing. It would give you the impression you were entering a cocktail bar.

There were four relatives carrying on, one show-off in her late sixties and the rest not too far behind. To me, that was acting uncivilized. The undertaker was in shock. When I asked for them to lower their voices, I was told you go to a funeral to cheer people up, not to have a long face, like me. There was another funeral across the hall, all elderly people, and I'm sure the carrying on must have hurt them as well as myself.

GENTLE READER,

No, it is not the purpose of a funeral to cheer up the bereaved. What a shocking idea. That is what the whiskey and condolence visits are for, later. The purpose of a funeral is to pay honor to the departed. No matter how many people are prepared to swear that the deceased would not have wanted anyone to grieve, Miss Manners has never yet met anyone who would want his or her death to have left intimates emotionally indifferent.

Solemnity

"Whatever happened to solemnity?" inquired a gentleman of Miss Manners' acquaintance.

"You must be kidding," she would have responded, were she not too polite.

As the gentleman was pointing out, occasions that used to be considered solemn are no longer approached in that spirit. People of all ages broadcast, through their conversation, dress and behavior, that they do not take such things seriously.

Is a religious service worth the trouble of changing out of the sweat clothes one plans to wear for the rest of the day's activities? Does a graduation require the graduate to sit still and listen, and to wear those rented robes as intended rather than using them as a background for jokes and slogans? Is being invited to a wedding important enough to elicit a serious commitment, first to answer the invitation, and then to attend? Should a funeral subdue sociability, so that those attending do not call out cheerily to one another, "Hey! Great to see you!" and move around to catch up on gossip?

Is there anything worth getting all that serious about? Aren't we better off taking life as a joke? Miss Manners thinks she hears a resounding chorus of "No!" to the first question, and "Yes!" to the second.

Perhaps that is why those responsible for the planning of such occasions often accept the idea they must keep everything entertaining and undemanding to attract people at all. Or perhaps it is the common adoption of so lackadaisical a style that has convinced participants not to consider them anything special.

Why, then, Miss Manners wonders, has ritual survived at all in modern society? It is true that she has noticed that occasions that have assumed new importance—formerly casual events such as bridal and baby showers, anniversaries, and birthday parties—are invariably connected with getting presents. This makes her highly suspicious of the sheer appreciation of ceremony. Nevertheless, even these lightweight rituals would surely have died out if ritual did not still have a hold on people.

Somebody finds it worth bothering about. It seems reasonable to assume that someone must be taking ritual seriously. In some cases, that might be only the person on whom it is focused. The bride and bridegroom may take the wedding seriously, and the deceased would presumably take the funeral seriously, if that were possible. People attending may be dismissing these occasions as of little importance because they are not happening for their benefit, and because they do not have the imagination to go along with the tone, in the hope that when their turns do come, others will reciprocate.

Conflicting Rituals

DEAR MISS MANNERS,

To someone raised on the modified European eating style (tines down for spearing such as meat, then flopped over for nasty items like peas), the sight of endless American-style switching seems idiotic on principle. Few can be so bereft of motor skills that they cannot, throughout a meal, skillfully and gracefully use one implement per hand. Neither forking nor knifing is all that difficult.

If you still think the American style is superior, please bear in mind that an American agent was captured and executed by the Gestapo (in *13 Rue Madeleine*) because he made the mistake of eating this way in a French café.

Why, then, the absolute insanity of calling a place setting "proper" when the fork is at the left, the knife at the right? This makes sense only if the typical diner picks up and uses the implements without having to switch them immediately. For a recent dinner party, over my wife's objections, I put the knife left, the fork right. When our guests stared in incomprehension and disbelief at this dreadful breach, and I got them to admit it made sense, they could only reply, "Yes, but . . ." This suggests that you might ponder the question of whether the tradition should be defended when, despite its antiquity, it makes no sense at all.

Whenever I wonder whether I am being a bit unmannerly, I take comfort in the fact that the dress code, as adhered to by fancy restaurants, must be a code, for more and more of my fellow Americans seem unable to understand it. As when a couple in running suits (!) raises hell with the fellow who refuses to seat them among those wearing leather shoes and clothes requiring dry cleaning. "Elitist!" is the word they hurl into the faces of those harried souls who can still distinguish, though only dimly, between democracy and anarchy.

Gentle Reader,

You have a powerful argument there: Eat the European way or be picked up by the Gestapo. Perverse patriot that she is, Miss Manners is afraid that such a threat makes her more attached, not less, to the American way.

The utilitarian argument you make has less force, she is afraid, because you undermine it by arguing for ceremony and tradition in regard to dress. Those people in running suits could as easily use your reasoning to show that their clothes, serving the purpose of keeping their bodies decently covered and being more comfortable than yours, make more practical sense.

Miss Manners is not on their side. Nobody knows better than she that "elitist" is a charge hurled at anyone who cares about maintaining the rituals of our own—and their own—society. She certainly would not want to add to your discomfort by suggesting that you are perhaps overeager to dump our society's in favor of other people's.

EXTRA CREDIT: SYMBOLISM AND RITUAL IN GOVERNMENT

America has never settled its presidential etiquette problem. As Miss Manners recalls, this was put on the agenda in anticipation of the Washington Administration and we're still working on it. The question is: How should a President of the United States comport himself and conduct state functions in order to maintain the dignity of the office and of the country, without acting like a silly fool who seems to think he's king?

Every new President of the United States has been expected to work this out for himself and after an amazingly short while we let him know that he's getting it wrong. We call this The American Way. If he forgets he won office as a man of the people and starts behaving like a big shot, we ridicule him. If he is too good at showing us how ordinary he is, we complain that he doesn't seem presidential. (At that, he gets off easier than his wife, to whom we traditionally assign ceremonial tasks so we can scorn her for being frivolous—when we're not complaining that she has no business interesting herself in substantive state matters because nobody elected her to office.)

Consider the symbolism of clothing. What would you think if you saw a President being inaugurated in a cutaway and high silk hat? That he cherished comically doomed pretensions? That he was harboring dangerous ambitions to establish a ruling aristocracy? That we had elected a hoofer? A nitwit?

Both General Eisenhower and Senator Kennedy, neither of whom was perceived as haughty or silly, dressed this way at their presidential inaugurations, at a time when the high formality of morning clothes was already rare in private life. Since then, the idea that any kind of formal clothing symbolizes political rapaciousness has taken increasing hold. The last such attempt was Governor Reagan's. His suggestion that he be inaugurated in a sack coat, a milder degree of formality than his predecessors', was greeted with ridicule, featuring lots of low hilarity about how female officials would look in this outfit. (The ladies' equivalent is a dress, for goodness' sake, preferably worn with hat and gloves.)

Now, what did you used to think when you saw dignitaries from Communist or Eastern Bloc countries show up at White House black tie dinners or other international formal occasions in double-breasted suits (inevitably described in the Western press as "ill-fitting")? That they were pathetic? Prisoners of a dreary state? Plutocrats in hypocritical disguise?

To the former Soviets, formal clothes, even the low-key, comfortable modern dinner jackets, symbolized capitalism, with perhaps a reminder also of Russian aristocrats who kept ballet girls and who considered dinner jackets much too infor-mal. Miss Manners was fascinated by the transitional shift when Mikhail Gorbachev, ousted as President of the USSR and out fund-raising, suddenly appeared in black tie at formal dinners, while Russian President Boris Yeltsin stuck to the Communist tra-dition and wore a black business suit with a dark red print four-in-hand tie to a White House state dinner. As neither was any more a member of the my-clothes-are-really-me school than . . . well, than Miss Manners herself, that change was full of symbolic meaning. It was not that former President Gorbachev had been liberated to indulge upper class tastes he had presumably always harbored. The point is that good fellow-ship, rather than defiance, is the symbolic statement one wants to make when one is trying to raise money. He was simply continuing to dress symbolically by wearing clothes whose meaning corresponded to his change of career.

The symbolism of political clothing can be even more complicated than that. The American diplomat Charles Thayer wrote that although Kremlin leaders followed the post-Revolutionary order to wear business suits to black tie events, they actually gave black tie events in Moscow, and were "visibly miffed" when "several foreign am-bassadors decided collectively that if their hosts were not going to bother to change for dinner, they would not, either" and wore business suits like their hosts'.

People who defy dress standards—even standards they have chosen to set—are always inordinately proud of themselves, precisely because they feel they assume greater dignity than conventionally dressed people, whatever the prevailing conven-tion of the occasion happens to be. This stratagem fails utterly if everyone else goes along with the change. Don't those other people know that they are supposed to feel discomfited and aghast?

In recent years, a number of state visitors to Washington sent word that they would not be wearing the stipulated dress to black tie White House dinners, but would appear in business suits, no matter what everyone else wore. The White House could have responded by saying, "Okay, you don't like to dress up, and the truth is that many of us aren't crazy about it, either. So we'll just give you a blue jeans party, unlike the formal ones we give for other world leaders." It would have been considered an insult.

All revolutionaries like to fool with etiquette, and they particularly enjoy mess-ing around in the costume department. The diplomatic tradition of balking at formal clothes is, in the modern era, originally an American one. Benjamin Franklin came up with the idea of making plainness stand out in a fancy crowd for political rea-sons. As American Minister to the court of Louis XVI, that worthy went to Versailles wearing his bare head (of course he wore his head; Miss Manners knew that; but wigs were also required for court appearances) and carrying a crabapple cane. The symbolism intended was that, as he represented a country where everyone was of equal dignity, he could not wear court dress, with its symbolic deference to the sovereign.

If anyone could have gotten away with it, it was Dr. Franklin, whom the French considered a dear old sexpot, but he soon found it wasn't worth it and changed to gold-embroidered blue and slapped on a wig. It is always easier to do business when you do not look as if you disapprove of those from whom you want treaties and loans.

Nonetheless, the idea of Americans' not dressing up on the international scene kept resurfacing, and in 1867, Congress passed a joint resolution against American diplomats' wearing any but authorized (i.e., military) uniforms. The alternative was plain black evening clothes, a costume that made it easy to pick out the American ambassadors, along with the waiters, at a time when other countries sent their representatives forth in fancy diplomatic uniforms. Foreign service lore contains the story of the American envoy who was asked by a grand lady at a party whether he was the butler, and who snapped back, "No, madam; are you the chambermaid?" And the one about the American ambassador in London who, upon departing a grand party, was ordered by another guest to call him a cab. "You are a cab, Sir," he is said to have replied, adding, "At least you didn't ask me to call you a hansom cab."

The era of diplomatic uniforms is over, anyway, but the symbolic problem remains unsolved. Which should it be, dignified formality or egalitarian simplicity?

Over the centuries, Miss Manners has argued with equal fervor for both less and more ceremony at the White House. Without disrespect to the gentlemen involved, she was as shocked when Mr. Jefferson received dignitaries at the White House while wearing his house slippers as when Senator Nixon wore a business suit on the beach. Nevertheless, she has maintained the consistent position that the American official style must be both simple *and* dignified. These are not mutually exclusive concepts. "Ceremony" is not another word for "frivolity." "Informal" is not another word for "warm and caring," but it can mean *not* caring when it involves ignoring the forms of respect and national ceremony that are symbolic of egalitarianism.

Any whiff of imperiousness is, of course, symbolically wrong. We get a good chuckle out of anyone who tries it, right before we merrily consider pitching him out of office. Free people do not like their leaders to seem to hold themselves to be in a class above them. Politicians tempted to dismiss the formal trappings altogether, in the hope of ingratiating themselves with the voters, should not interpret this to mean

Benjamin Franklin dresses down for his job as Minister to the Court of Louis XVI.
Originally going for simplicity and comfort in his court wardrobe (here shown in period and updated versions), the ever-practical Dr. Franklin finally decided that observing the court dress code made his mission more effective. He even clapped a wig on his sage brow when he realized that was what it took to show that he meant business.

that we belittle dignity, and can allow ourselves no formal national occasions or meaningful rituals. Attempts to display an aggressively unassuming style, so to speak, have not gone over with the public.

When we decided to eschew fancy titles in favor of calling our leader "Mr. President," and his wife just "Mrs." with her surname (after a false start in which one heard "Lady Washington" and witnessed undemocratic curtsies), it was because we decided that the best titles were formal, but granted to all. When we rejected dangling ermine tails, it didn't mean we would have no way of showing respect for an occasion by changing out of our work clothes.

Miss Manners has never been willing to concede that America has a class system in which formality is a prerogative of the rich, and ordinary people should suffer public disapproval if they ever attempt anything finer than the sturdy daily peasant costume of sweat clothes and jeans. She thinks that work clothes and dress clothes should be worn according to the occasion, not the station of the individual.

It has been a while since we have had any but the lowest degree of formality at an inauguration, or since we have had the highest, which would be white tie, at a state function. If Miss Manners were to see a president being inaugurated in morning clothes, she would think that the gentleman was taking the occasion seriously. One dresses differently on a momentous occasion from a day when nothing special is happening.

For all that, Miss Manners recognizes that in this century there has been a general decline in the use of formal clothing and formal manners in the society, and she doesn't necessarily deplore it. If she never has to wear a bustle again, it will be too soon. Increased public exposure has accustomed us to seeing presidents under properly informal circumstances, as well as on state occasions. If killing formality were the price of doing away with ostentation, Miss Manners would consider it a bargain. Unfortunately, the decline of the City of Washington's tradition of modest and serviceable formality (in what other city do ladies yearn for evening dresses that are durable and inconspicuous?) had no discouraging effect on vulgarity.

But for its most formal events, the White House has slipped into practices below the standards that are still in effect for the most formal occasions in which most citizens participate—their weddings. According to current practice, there are three degrees of formality above silliness at the weddings of ordinary citizens: suits and ties for gentlemen and daytime suits or dresses for ladies; the sack coat (day) and black tie (evening), with afternoon and dinner dresses respectively; and morning dress (day) and white tie (evening), with dressy dresses and hats, and ball dresses with above-the-elbow gloves.

Most people expect written answers to their formal wedding invitations; the White House ceased requiring any but mere telephone calls years ago. About the same time, the rule that one never refused a White House invitation except for dire reasons fell into disuse, and entertainers and others bragged publicly that they were too busy to accept what ought to have been treated as a high honor.

Miss Manners is afraid that abandoning standards is not a sign of character. The fact is that there are two types of pretentiousness: acting so grand that you require constant splendor, and acting so grand that you need not take seriously ceremonies and events that ordinary citizens revere, and customs that they choose to practice.

Former Presidents

DEAR MISS MANNERS,

Politics completely aside, I am very upset by the casual way the media refer to the President and former Presidents of the United States with just the title of "Mr."—Mr. Clinton, Mr. Bush, Mr. Reagan, Mr. Ford, Mr. Carter, and even Jimmy! Please, Miss Manners, what is the correct method of addressing or referring to the President, former Presidents, and also Presidents who have resigned?

GENTLE READER,

Modern politics should certainly be cast aside in this matter, but you can't so easily dismiss the work of earlier politicians. Allow Miss Manners to remind you that the first United States Congress had itself a rousing time debating this very matter, before the inauguration of General Washington—as he was called then and would be again if he were alive today.

Washington, D.C.—"You just wonder where is their sense of manners? Where's their sense of courtesy?"—The Speaker of the House of Representatives characterizing the President and the Executive Branch of government in the winter of 1995.

The debate came down to whether "Mr.," the term of respect for all male citizens, was fancy enough for our elected leader. Other suggestions included "Elective Majesty," "Serene Highness," and versions of "High Mightiness" that were shot down by the Speaker of the House on the screamingly funny grounds (well, it doubled over everyone except the unfortunate person used as an example) that a short man might someday be elected.

Miss Manners considers the selection of "Mr. President" to be a ringing endorsement of the dignity of the ordinary term and a lesson in the folly of trying to improve upon it. While the President is correctly so addressed to his face, it is no insult, by our laudably egalitarian standards, to refer to him as "Mr." with his surname. His wife is correctly addressed and referred to as "Mrs.," there being no such silly official title as "First Lady." A lady holding the office would be "Madam President" and her husband "Mr." with his surname.

Another rule is that there is only one President of the United States at a time. Former presidents do not hold the title. They are—correctly and respectfully—called "Mr.," or they may revert to an earlier title, such as "General" or "Governor." Thus, we now have Governor or Mr. Reagan, Governor or Mr. Carter, Mr. Ford (the title "Representative" is not retained), and the late Senator or Mr. Nixon. Mr. Jefferson had a whole slew of titles to choose from after he left office, but remained, as he still does to his many admirers, Mr. Jefferson.

Don't worry that their feelings are hurt by this. By the time you become President of the United States, you can safely figure that everyone knows about it. When the full name but no other title is used (on envelopes and for formal introductions), former presidents are styled "Honorable." This has nothing to do with how they left office or what you thought of them when they held it.

Current or past presidents are not correctly called by their nicknames (Miss Manners means the nicknames they themselves use, although those their opponents might have fashioned for them are not correct, either) even though, as Miss Manners would like to point out without mentioning names, much less nicknames, certain presidents actively encourage being so addressed, with the thought that this endears them to the public. She agrees with you in rejecting this, overruling the rule about addressing people as they prefer with the more compelling rule that citizens must respect their elected leader, whether he personally encourages it or not.

Unpretentiousness is not the same thing as chumminess. In fact it is the pseudo-chumminess of this that she finds pretentious. She would have thought that any seasoned politician would know that familiarity does not necessarily breed admiration.

High Level Kissing

An increasing number of world leaders seem to believe, in the face of all evidence about where the political primrose path leads, that physical, not to mention photogenic, warmth promotes the cause of world peace.

Many statesmen woke up after the world upheavals of these last years wishing they hadn't been so promiscuous. Those who have dallied in the public embrace of Yasir Arafat of the Palestine Liberation Organization at various stages in his career suffer periodic regrets. Those who did so with such out-of-favor huggers as Erich Honecker, the former East German leader, are wondering what they ever saw in him, as are their constituents and opponents.

Just about anyone who came within range of Iraqi President Saddam Hussein before the Persian Gulf War found out that, as they say in divorce court, one picture is a dreadful liability. At an Islamic Conference Organization conference, the Crown Prince of Saudi Arabia was reduced to exclaiming, "No kissing, please!" and extending a defensive arm when his former enemies bore down on him with a gleam in their eyes.

Miss Manners understands that no one can forecast all the turns of the kaleidoscope of world affairs. She is not suggesting that statesmen should be more prophetic about whom they allow to kiss them. She is certainly not suggesting that they show more sincere feelings, which would be a disaster. Statesmanship largely consists of preventing competing nations from expressing their feelings in the most sincere way possible. Miss Manners is only suggesting that they stop kissing other statesmen altogether—that they practice safe protocol.

WASHINGTON, D.C.—Tactics such as calling the President by his first name on the floor of the U.S. Senate have stirred debate over proper manners in the traditionally decorous chamber, the *Washington Post* reported. Critics complain that it is disrespectful and contributes to the coarsening of political debate in the country. Defenders maintain that they must be provocative in order to effectively pursue their political goals.

It is true that chiefs of state and heads of government symbolize the countries they represent, which is why they must be treated with dignity, unless an affront is intended to their peoples as a challenge or a response to one. It has also long been the habit for them to discuss alliances in terms of friendship and even parenthood—our good friends, the mother country, and so on. This is a legacy from when the world was ruled by all-powerful monarchs who were likely to be related to one another, if not by blood or marriage, then even more strongly by a shared belief in the divine right of guess who. These people were occasionally known to put family interests ahead of the bonds they had with their own subjects, which has a bit to do with why they are now either in exile or busily earning their keep by keeping their countries entertained.

Colonialism, with its assumption of permanent and uneven ties between nations, has also passed out of fashion. That a country should remain bound by affection to one that had conquered it militarily is no longer a popular notion. Miss Manners finds it odd that recent decades, when these changes were most apparent, nevertheless witnessed the return of the smooching chiefs of state. Hugs and kisses are more common than handshakes now, among leaders whose countries are not obviously on the brink of war.

She suspects this has less to do with a revival of the international brotherhood of royalty by its less colorful substitutes than with the happy-go-lucky belief of the same period that all of the world's problems would be solved if only everyone learned to love everyone else. No doubt this is true, and the fact that it has never happened in the history of the world should not discourage people from trying.

Still, this should not begin with world leaders' behaving as if their dealings, on behalf of their citizens, with the chiefs of other countries were personal relationships which would remain unaffected by national interests or political events. Symbolically, they are better off treating one another with cordial formality. Not only does this demonstrate that they are acting as representatives of their peoples, rather than as a privileged international interest group of their own, but it leaves no embarrassing traces.

PROTECTING THE FLAG

In judging how best to protect the sanctity of the American flag, the United States Supreme Court awarded custody to etiquette. Miss Manners concurs. The United States Congress keeps begging to differ.

Probably not everyone who reads (or wrote) the *Texas v. Johnson* decision, which declared unconstitutional the state laws proscribing flag desecration, would summarize the disposition of that case as Miss Manners has done. Few other people—even, or perhaps especially, few members of the legal profession—seem to realize that symbolism properly comes under the jurisdiction of etiquette. In its periodic consideration of amending the Constitution to make disrespectful uses of the flag illegal, Congress does not debate the etiquette angle. But passing this amendment would advance the takeover of etiquette by law, and thereby weaken the complicated regulative structure under which we live. This is a trend that Miss Manners finds scary, as should other freedom-loving citizens. (What do you mean, you didn't think of Miss Manners as freedom-loving? Cut that out—she won't stand for that kind of talk.)

Failing to understand that etiquette has any power at all, many people have erroneously concluded that the flag is left totally unprotected if the rights of its potential desecrators remain protected. If the law does not prohibit flag-burning, they ask indignantly or sorrowfully, what will? Anyone will be able to trash the national symbol with impunity. Miss Manners begs to differ. A flag protected by etiquette is not defenseless.

Jurisdiction over such a crucial question of taste must remain under the control of a more suitable (and no less majestic) authority than law, one with a long and successful history in mandating respect for venerated symbols. Etiquette's record in achieving the proper show of respect is not perfect, attacking an institution by degrading its symbol being a common revolutionary gesture throughout history, in all cultures, no matter how draconian. But neither is the law's record for achieving respect, for all of the penalties at its disposal.

The fear of offending public sensibility by flouting etiquette is not, Miss Manners maintains, a negligible deterrent: The amount of voluntary restraint etiquette inspires is incalculable. Every day, civilized people hold back from expressing a wide range of urges to avoid disgusting or antagonizing others; even the most vehement proponents of acting naturally don't claim the right to cough into other people's faces. Whether this self-restraint is attributable to respect for the rules of etiquette or the desire to avoid the social censure that is etiquette's punishment, Miss Manners does not inquire, any more than the law distinguishes between those kept honest by morality or by fear of punishment.

What of people who do not care about whether they offend others, or who deliberately set out to do so? No one ever burns a flag publicly in ignorance of the fact that other people might not approve. Those other people are right there in the street surrounding the flag burner. Is their disapproval, if not expressed in violence, strong enough to handle determined offenders?

The task by then is no longer to deter offensive behavior, but to punish it. Etiquette's usual plea, after all, is only "I wonder if you would mind not doing that; a number of us find it offensive." Shouldn't those who reply "So what?" be told, by the law, "So we'll throw you in jail"?

Miss Manners does not scare so easily as to rush for help at the first sign of disobedience. Symbolism being one of the domains of etiquette, she is familiar with the darker side of using symbols—abusing them in anger against that which they symbolize. Engagement rings are flung back (except by rude ladies who prefer diamonds to symbolism), wedding rings tossed in the trash, and medals and other awards coldly returned.

Etiquette is hardly interested in encouraging provocative acts. Yet in its very capacity as peacekeeper it recognizes the value of exchanging hostilities on a symbolic level, in place of the alternative methods of dispute. Diplomacy, not war.

The abuse of revered symbols is repulsive to those who love them. They should nevertheless appreciate that assigning responsibility over these acts to etiquette means keeping them at a nonviolent level.

Miss Manners is by no means condoning kicking around symbolic objects as a way of expressing hostility. Flag-burning, in particular, is repugnant to her. So it is to most people, and their condemnation and wrath are the proper response. Those who discharge their negative feelings on cherished symbols had better be prepared to encounter correspondingly negative feelings directed toward themselves and their causes. The punishments of etiquette—public disapproval and political condemnation—are not only psychologically harsh but also more fitting for dealing with transgressions involving symbolism than are fines or jail.

A Reply

WASHINGTON, D.C.—During a congressional debate over a Constitutional amendment to prevent desecration of the American flag, one committee chairman said the measure was in part "a popular protest against the vulgarization of our society." Another congressman said the amendment was unnecessary because "the flag and the principles for which it stands do not need protection from an occasional imbecile who does not understand that he is burning the symbol of his right to protest."

Dear Miss Manners,

The removement of one's hat or cap during the National Anthem is only a custom. You have the RIGHT not to remove your hat. If you look up the definition of custom and right, you will see the difference.

In this free country, which I fought a war for and received the Purple Heart and other awards and medals, I have the right to not remove my hat or cap during the national anthem.

I do give respect, but I do it in my way, not your way or their way. Now they are trying to change the Bill of Rights to make burning the flag a crime and against the Constitution. When does it stop?

I agree with you on most things, but on this topic I totally disagree with you. But in this great country of ours, we both have the right to disagree.

GENTLE READER,

We even have the right to agree for reasons on which we disagree. And to tell each other to look up the meanings of words before we use them carelessly, annoying as that habit is.

Miss Manners not only agrees that removing a hat or cap during the National Anthem is a voluntarily practiced custom not mandated by law, but joins you in opposing enforcing the customs of respect by law—as the proposed amendment prohibiting flag-burning would do. Our freedoms are better served if these matters are mandated by manners.

Here's how it works. Manners kindly provide society with a collection of customs to demonstrate certain attitudes, such as respect. These gestures are only arbitrary symbols—as your medals are only arbitrary symbols of your country's gratitude for your valor—but everybody knows and recognizes them. You don't have to follow these customs, but it is reasonable for everyone to interpret violating them as indicative of disrespect.

Where you err is in assuming that each person can unilaterally make up a different vocabulary of gestures and expect to have these understood, or at least not misunderstood. Should you be overflowing with respect for the flag, but nevertheless decide that your personal way of showing this is to thumb your nose at it, people would not take it kindly. You have the legal right to do this, but you must be prepared for the right of others to express their disapproval in this great country of ours.

ETIQUETTE'S PEDIGREE AND CREDENTIALS

A BRIEF HISTORY OF ETIQUETTE
(WITH APOLOGIES FOR NAME-DROPPING)

Society cannot exist without etiquette, Miss Manners must overcome her modesty to admit. It never has, and until our own century, everybody knew that.

Evidence of the prehistoric practice of manners (in archaeological findings indicating communal eating and ceremonial burying of the dead) serves to define human social existence in its earliest manifestations. Not yet blessed with etiquette books, hunter-gatherers were nevertheless on to the idea that forms the philosophical basis of society and, not coincidentally, that of manners: that people must agree to restrain their impulses and follow a common language of behavior in order to avoid making communal life abrasive, unpleasant and explosive. This has its personal drawbacks, of course, but it is considered worth the advantage of living among people who aren't perpetually furious.

In small communities, where everyone knows everyone else who lives in the cave, the rules and customs of social behavior are easily communicated without Miss Manners' assistance. But when the blessings of specialized labor, trade, travel and dreaming about falling in love with a stranger began to appear, as a result of such good ideas as agriculture and animal husbandry some ten thousand years ago, the manners situation became more complex. To provide predictability, coherence, cultural identity and bloodless recreation in this more interesting world, codified etiquette was needed.

Miss Manners is not sure when her earliest avatar swept grandly onto the scene, but etiquette rules were around when Hammurabi was a mere slip of a boy, and things started to move quickly. Secular law soon shared manners' commitment to regulating human conduct and drew on its etiquette injunctions. All major religions, most explicitly Confucianism and Buddhism, deal with the regulation of social conduct as an indispensable part of the virtuous life. The Bible and the Koran are packed with etiquette injunctions given theological authority—higher even than Miss Manners'.

Back down at her level, Socrates ran around making others feel uncomfortable with his troublesome question of how one should live. Erasmus wrote a popular etiquette book suggesting that the Renaissance would be more attractive if people didn't belch and pick their noses in public. (Modern academics who scoff at etiquette might note that Erasmus' stated objective was to teach etiquette to young intellectuals, so that they would be influential in powerful circles and thus able to translate their theories into political action.)

Eventually, the world's upper classes began to suffer from a severe case of etiquette excess. Miss Manners sometimes harbors the strange thought that had she been living at Versailles when the word "etiquette" came into its own—to denote the "ticket" of rapidly changing rules-for-the-sake-of-rules required at court—she would have entertained revolutionary fantasies.

Founders of the United States of America, notably Mr. Jefferson, Dr. Franklin, and General Washington, did not, as more hotheaded revolutionaries are wont to do, try to overthrow the rule of manners. Accepting its principles, they went to work—not only as political theorists but as practical arbiters of rules, the same job Miss Manners is called upon to do these days—redesigning court etiquette to fit republican society. They did a masterful job, and America has been the chief influence on international etiquette ever since. Only Mr. Jefferson's directive to Congress entitled "Etiquette," which abolished recognition of diplomatic, as well as personal rank, went too far and had to be jettisoned, but Miss Manners loves him for trying.

The framers of the Constitution took it for granted that a system of etiquette was permanently in place that would make people voluntarily temper the exercise of their Constitutional rights so they wouldn't spend all of their time and energy suing one another. So did prominent Americans who continued refining egalitarian etiquette: Ralph Waldo Emerson wrote an essay "On Manners," and Harriet Beecher Stowe, Eleanor Roosevelt, and Millicent Fenwick all wrote etiquette books. The regulation and interpretation of social behavior is a subject that has always drawn the interest of extremely serious people, even if Miss Manners occasionally forgets herself and turns giddy.

MODERN HISTORY

After all that honorable history, there persists a widespread belief that etiquette was newborn from the desire of Victorian killjoys to ruin private pleasures, to quash the freedoms achieved during the Enlightenment, and to enhance the power of rich snobs over the proletariat. Not satisfied with continuing the refinement of etiquette, for the purpose of making the mannerly concepts of respect and dignity available to those who had been excluded from them, modern revisionists have set out to murder manners.

When she finally hunted down and captured the arch-criminal, Miss Manners went into shock. To her horror, it turned out to be—idealism! How can anyone, least of all your gentle champion of politeness, think of prosecuting idealism?

Idealism was not the obvious suspect. People whose daily lives include being shoved on the sidewalk and cut off on the road, ignored by service people or insulted by customers, addressed as equals or inferiors by juniors and as intimates by strangers, and cursed, if not shot, by anyone who is simply feeling surly and finds them a convenient target, tend to blame only those immediately responsible. Miss Manners doesn't much care for bullies, cads, slobs and criminals either, and is far from absolving them of personal responsibility. But however much trouble they cause, they are not the brains behind the rudeness crisis.

It was during the 1960s that idealistic social theorists (who, like everyone else, are always willing to put more thought and energy into getting out of social duties than into simply performing them) came up with the following astounding revelations:

1. Good surface behavior is not a truth-in-packaging guarantee of a virtuous heart inside.
2. Teaching children manners inhibits them from behaving as their natural impulses may prompt them.
3. Many conventions of etiquette are arbitrary and cannot be functionally justified. For example, the necktie does not do the sort of valiant and obviously useful job a belt does.

4. Among our inherited etiquette traditions are patterns of behavior apparently based on ideas that we now find repugnant, such as that ladies are weaker than gentlemen and must therefore be given protective treatment.

5. Anyway, people are now practical, and so mere tradition has no emotional hold on them.

6. Specialized forms of etiquette practiced by a particular social subgroup—the prime example being rich people who use peculiar silverware to baffle and embarrass the uninitiated—serve to distinguish those people from outsiders and may therefore encourage them to feel superior.

7. Etiquette being a practice of complex societies, it would be a relief to get away from its pressures and live in a more spontaneous society.

Yes, my dears, Miss Manners replies to these discoveries. One must then go beyond them to realize that:

1. It is not therefore true that a virtuous heart excuses surface behavior that inadvertently inconveniences, antagonizes or disgusts others. What is more, an evil heart that is constrained by the demands of politeness is less of a public menace than one freer to follow its evil impulses.

2. The children who are most paralyzed—and by perfectly natural inhibitions—turn out to be the ones who are thrown into the complications of life without being sufficiently instructed in etiquette to know what behavior is expected of them in situations they are likely to encounter, or warned how their actions will be interpreted.

3. Etiquette sometimes employs symbolism, and symbolism is, by definition, arbitrary, although this does not prevent it from being useful. A tie symbolizes respect and seriousness, as T-shirts or bare chests with gold chains, no matter how much more comfortable, washable and alluring, do not.

4. Because etiquette is based on tradition, and people often have affection for the traditions of their youth, its customs tend to lag behind developing sociological thought. Yet etiquette can, should and

does change over time to accommodate new ways of living. "Ladies first" was never a permanent rule of etiquette, having replaced the ancient rule of "Ladies never." It is now gradually yielding to a precedence system based on age (and it was always improper, although commonly violated, in the work place where rank, not gender, is what counts).

5. Even people who carefully eschew etiquette in the rest of their lives often go into an etiquette tailspin in connection with momentous events. A bride who has been supporting her bridegroom for years in their shared household will ask their own toddler to "give her away," out of emotional attachment to a ritual developed to mark the transfer of a young lady from her father's support and protection to her husband's. (Meanwhile, the intent of the ritual, which is to make the union of the couple part of a wider commitment involving family and the community, may be abandoned with the typical battle cry of the bridal couple, "Well, it's our wedding, so we get to do whatever we want"—and they don't have to alter their plans if they conflict with the wishes and comfort of relatives and other guests.)

6. The people who swagger most with their insiders' rules about clothing, forms of greeting and social hierarchy—distinctions to which the rich have become increasingly indifferent—are teenage gangs. Anyway, when knowledge of special forms moves from cultural identification to delight in humiliating others, the practice is reclassified as bad manners.

7. Where would that be? Etiquette exists in primitive societies as much as in industrialized societies, often in more rigid forms. Romantics who pronounce their own heritages stultifying, yet wax sentimental over the folklore of societies they regard as more authentic, just haven't studied comparative etiquette—or don't care about anthropology, so long as they can get a rise out of their parents.

Miss Manners doesn't want to attack idealism. When good people gather, she wants to persuade them to add the virtues of manners to the other causes for which they fight, and to convince them that their fights will be better fought if they do.

MODERN MORALITY'S DIM VIEW OF ETIQUETTE

Miss Manners did not expect to live to see the day when a polite public demeanor would have a whiff of immorality arising from it. Lately, however, she has noticed that calmness and tolerance in a debate about serious issues are interpreted as signs of not caring.

This leaves only two approved postures for modern moral discourse: Indignation to the Point of Outrage, and Just Kidding. It is usually possible to tell them apart.

In times when people generally agree about what comprises morality, even though they may differ strongly about how to achieve or maintain it, quiet types like Miss Manners don't come under suspicion because everyone uses the tone of outrage sparingly. If it is barely possible to believe that respectable people may honorably disagree with oneself about particular issues, an attitude of patience and kindness, with just a dash of pity, is more appropriate for thrashing out differences than spluttering.

Historically, when there is one great explosive moral question dividing a society, or when, as now, everybody concentrates on a different pet issue to the extent of being driven berserk by the failure of others to choose the same one, outrage thrives. Consider how the Morality of the Menu is now able to get its believers worked into a frenzy when condemning food groups that fail to meet their particular ethical, healthful or culinary standards. (Nutrition is a worthy discipline, but doesn't Miss Manners recall that, for years, it practically served to define "boring"?) The other posture, Just Kidding, is the only currently respectable way out of all that self-righteousness.

What does not seem acceptable, to Miss Manners' great sorrow, is sullying moral argument with etiquette. Debating politely, respecting the feelings and dignity of one's opponent, tempering the display of contempt, and generally mixing in namby-pamby old etiquette are considered to show a deplorable lack of fervor. The arguments she hears against manners in the service of morality are, in descending order of politeness:

1. If we didn't have anything else to worry about, practicing etiquette would be fine, but people who are concerned with making life better for others simply do not have the time to slow down and be polite.
2. To those who are working on issues of vital concern to humanity, following the dictates of etiquette that require sparing the sensibilities of others would demonstrate lack of zealousness, and thus constitute a betrayal of the cause.

Thus, by a neat argument, rudeness becomes an indicator of fine feelings. Compared with being polite, Just Kidding appears to be glowingly idealistic.

Miss Manners, who has some fervor of her own, will not stand still for that. She is trying not to stamp her little foot, but she considers the claim that it is easier to persuade people to change by using rudeness than by politeness to be a fraudulent excuse. Or, as she would put it if she had to argue this matter face to face with an opponent:

That's an interesting view, but have you perhaps considered how defensive people get when they are embarrassed or insulted? Don't they tend to dig in and stop listening? If you have a good argument to make, don't you want them to hear it with open minds? Are they not more receptive to new ideas when they don't feel they have to defend themselves from personal attack? Isn't it more effective to offer them a graceful and face-saving way to change their minds and behavior? Isn't diplomacy, artificial as it necessarily is, preferable to the frankness of war?

Oh, dear. Miss Manners is gasping, and not just from letting out all that rhetoric. In putting her case this way, she has compromised one of her own moral quirks. Not by being polite, of course—in a reverse of popular ethics, she considers politeness right, but bribery wrong. That is why she tries not to urge people to behave well on the promise that this will enable them to get what they want (which may be love or money, rather than a moral triumph), and that is just what she has gone and done.

True, the polite approach usually does work better than the rude one when the goal is to change people's minds, but Miss Manners can't guarantee it. She is only too aware of the number of people who regularly fall in love with cads and demagogues, no matter how many times they promise their exasperated confidantes that they've learned their lesson. Even if she could make that guarantee, though, Miss Manners wouldn't want to bribe people to be polite. She believes they should be polite simply because it is the right thing to do. She believes it is the moral choice.

Oh-oh, now she's said it. No one else would dare to dispute the proposition that morals are more important than mere manners, or the assertion that etiquette can and should be jettisoned for a higher good.

Morality dictates (or so it is claimed) that people run around insulting the fat; snatching foods out of the hands of those who are about to eat something that might be bad for them, even if they happen to be strangers in restaurants; pointing out whose pathetic body would improve through exercise; dispensing anecdotal medical advice; and generally offering their wisdom to other people who didn't ask for it and are embarrassed by being singled out for attention.

"You can't do that!" Miss Manners wails. There are etiquette rules proscribing causing humiliation and embarrassment, and requiring people to mind their own business.

"But I'm concerned about people's health," is the reply. "I'm a caring person." It would be ungracious to object to being vilified by a caring person.

Caring amateurs also deliver mental health care to involuntary patients. Volunteers who practice without a license give themselves license, not just to offer opinions and advice, but to collect clinical evidence. In the interests of science, they refuse to be held back by etiquette-based doubts, such as: Maybe it's not nice just to march up to people and ask them what's wrong and start hazarding guesses, because maybe nothing is wrong and they always look that way, or maybe it's something that can't be helped by discussion, or maybe it's something they want to keep to themselves.

Other caring persons take to screaming, cursing and vandalizing property to perform good works. "This is more important," activists declare when called upon to defend hurling ridicule or invectives at passersby who appear not to endorse their causes. The moral worth on behalf of, for example, animals or the environment is seen as overriding the etiquette injunction against attacking people.

Caring activists argue that such tactics have made people more aware of issues they were previously able to ignore, which Miss Manners believes to be true. She only questions whether this constitutes winning hearts and minds to the cause. People who have been ambushed by rudeness are frightfully aware of who is doing this to them for what reason. Even if they temporarily alter their behavior in order to get out of the way of humiliation, they are likely to regroup and fight back, escalating the conflict from one of etiquette to one of law. Miss Manners believes that those who outrage the feelings of society will ultimately alienate people from their causes. We have too much trouble thinking of those who don't care whether they hurt us as our moral leaders. More importantly, she would like to point out that even if they win politically, they lose morally.

Principle in the Men's Room

DEAR MISS MANNERS,

I believe myself to be a civilized sort who is sensitive to, and respectful of, the sensibilities of other people. However, I am becoming sensitive to what I perceive as the devastating and unconscionable and decidedly ill-mannered way in which we human beings are destroying the Earth's (and thereby our own) natural environment.

I am taking some political action—an activity which I customarily confine to an appropriate public arena. However, I firmly believe that the wasteful habits of Americans are a large part of the problem, and increasingly I find myself tempted to let my political feelings intrude into my personal relations. For example, after dining with friends at a nice restaurant after the theater, I was washing up in the men's room with a member of my party. As is my wont, I used only one of the paper towels provided to dry my hands, although the task would have been much easier with two. I told myself I was saving trees.

Imagine my disappointment to see my friend use not two, but three paper towels to dry his hands. I very much wanted to say something, to make him aware of my conviction that even in that seemingly small way, he was contributing to ecological degradation. Constrained, however, by a life time of good manners, I refrained. Yet I have not been able to stop thinking about the situation, and anticipating the recurrence of similar circumstances. Is there any polite way that I could have told my friend my thoughts and feelings? Can I do it now, after the fact? Could I communicate my views to a stranger?

Do you foresee any point at which the preservation of good manners could give way in face of the necessity of preserving a civilization in which there are apt not to be any manners at all?

In response to an article about People for the Ethical Treatment of Animals, a letter to the editor of the *Washington Post* objected to the use of adjectives in the story such as "rude," "obnoxious," "hostile" and "immoderate," asking, "Since when has it been rude to speak out against cruelty? Was it rude to fight slavery? Was it rude to condemn the Holocaust? Is it rude to stand up to child abuse? If that's rude, throw out the etiquette book and sign me up." Another letter stated, "PETA's most dangerous trait is its willingness to take any action to advance the cause," noting that a PETA member "says that she opposes violence but she clearly endorses harassment, threat and intimidation."

GENTLE READER,

Miss Manners congratulates you on your new sensitivity, but suggests that you hang on to the old one as well. This is not a zero sum game in which your consideration for the planet should destroy your consideration for its inhabitants.

Showing respect for human beings, which includes refraining from haranguing sovereign individuals for not practicing your favorite virtue, is not, itself, a frivolous virtue. It is essential to peace and harmony. Surely you do not want to save civilization by abandoning civilized behavior. The proper way to attempt to change behavior is through the public arenas you mention, not by embarrassing people one at a time in the men's room. Humiliation is a terrible teaching tool. The likelihood of your friend thanking you for criticizing how he washes his hands is less than that of his dumping you in the nearest receptacle.

Citizen's Arrest

DEAR MISS MANNERS,

What, if anything, should I do when I witness someone who is obviously not handicapped and does not have a handicapped plate or sticker, park in a handicapped parking space in a public place? While I am aware that in the strictest sense, this is none of my business, I also have noticed that nobody in authority ever responds to these situations. I feel the public would be the most likely to be able to remedy the matter.

GENTLE READER,

It is never easy to make a citizen's etiquette arrest, and Miss Manners is sorry to hear your report of unresponsiveness on the part of the authorities. Such abuses must be corrected.

The proper way of doing this is always to assume that the offender has made a mistake. Not only does this allow that person to retreat gracefully from what may actually have been a purposeful error, but it covers you in case you are in error—for example, if the supposed offender turns out to have a qualifying but not-obviously-apparent disability. The proper remark is not "Don't you know better?" but "Excuse me! Do you mean to be in a handicapped space? I think there are some free spaces along the edges, if you look."

Emergency Measures

In case of disaster, reach first for—etiquette.

Miss Manners is well aware that no one on earth would agree with her about this emergency directive. If there is a highly dangerous situation—a flood, an earthquake, a bombing—serious behavior is mandatory, and surely the first thing to cast aside would be the troublesome luxury of etiquette. That there would be no time for frills seems so obvious that the very question of maintaining etiquette wouldn't even be considered, at least by anyone not so totally besotted with the idea of proper behavior as your own Miss Manners.

Only, yes, it would be. It nearly always is—in practice although not in theory. Miss Manners may be used to a certain loneliness in her devotion to etiquette as the basic force of civilization, but when a disaster occurs, she has plenty of company. The same people who would continue to deny Miss Manners' theory of the importance of etiquette nevertheless instantly switch to a standard of etiquette vastly above that, if any, which they practice in their ordinary lives.

When disaster strikes, either as a major blow to an entire community or to individuals whose plight arouses community sympathy, Miss Manners can almost always find evidence of a rallying to the principles of manners and the observance of specific etiquette rules. After the bombing of the federal office building in Oklahoma City, large and small acts of consideration, thoughtfulness and kindness abounded. In the evacuation after the World Trade Center was bombed, people not only proceeded in an orderly fashion down the smoke-filled stairways, rather than pushing themselves forward, but they yielded to those more obviously in need of assistance, such as a pregnant woman. The etiquette rules of going in turn and of offering precedence to the weak were observed by a vast crowd who were given excessive provocation, which they resisted, to collapse into panic and selfishness.

This mannerly response occurs not just in the heartland but also in New York City, among people who are known throughout the world for their ability to cut one another off viciously in such ordinary activities as driving, walking and shopping. Would that same pregnant woman—even if she were in the final throes of labor—have been offered a seat in a subway?

Well, maybe. Miss Manners is not interested in the national pastime of New York–bashing, and has even been known to argue that some of what is taken for rudeness there by out-of-towners is actually local sport, understood by the participants to be without rancor. (This optimistic position has been increasingly undermined by the number of such altercations that advance to not-very-sporting gunfire, but that could be explained by the presence of newcomers who don't understand rough but good-natured fun.) What she wants to point out is that the standard urban excuse for rudeness is stress. Bad conditions create and perhaps even justify bad behavior, it is commonly argued. Yet bad as New York traffic might be, Miss Manners doubts that even cabdrivers would argue that being in it is more stressful than being bombed.

In natural disasters, too, one hears of exemplary behavior. It is heartbreakingly true that hurricanes and earthquakes also bring out looters and profiteers, but generally Miss Manners has been heartened and impressed with how well people have behaved. And a good thing it is for them, too. Behaving with restraint, rather than giving in to the natural tendency to go crazy or to save oneself at any cost, often saves lives. Had those New Yorkers behaved, as they went down the endless staircases, as they might have behaved in crossing an ordinary street on an ordinary day, most of them might now be dead. It is etiquette that turns these so-called instincts or allegedly justifiable reactions to stress into civilized behavior that serves the good of the community as well as, ultimately, the individual.

PRINCIPLED REFUSALS TO COMMIT ETIQUETTE

In the Name of the Environment

DEAR MISS MANNERS,

I am a member of an adult-education foreign language class, where twelve students meet for two hours once a week, and the teacher has introduced the charming custom of having a coffee break after the first hour. When I first joined the class, Styrofoam cups were stacked beside the coffeemaker. Since I had an oversupply of these much maligned cups at home, I brought a stack to class. One lady member has gotten so enthusiastically into environmentalism that, when she saw me putting the dreaded cups on the table, she gave me a severe lecture on the subject of landfills, disposable diapers and other unpleasantries.

"Oh!" she mourned, "if only some way could be discovered to make those cups biodegradable!"

I said, "Why don't you think of a way?"

She said she wanted everyone to bring a ceramic mug from home. It was like an order to do so. I told her I didn't want to bother lugging a mug to class every week, along with textbooks and notebooks. But since she was obviously upset, I searched out a variety store (which wasn't easy) that stocks those paper hot cups that used to be so readily available.

LOS ANGELES, CALIF.—In the aftermath of the earthquake here, the *New York Times* reported, "the mood of the day was civility throughout a region that has experienced more troubles than Job in recent years. Shoppers with no cash because teller machines were inoperative asked politely if merchants would take checks, and mostly they did. Virtually no one pushed and shoved in the long lines to buy food, gasoline or newspapers. And people using pay telephones to reassure friends and relatives cut conversations short in deference to others, lent each other quarters and inquired about the well-being of strangers.

Nowhere was that civility more essential than at major intersections, most of them without traffic signals throughout the day because of power failures."

Unfortunately, the only kind the store had were decorated with patriotic red, white and blue stripes and stars. I didn't think the artwork mattered, but when the environmental lady saw me stacking them beside the coffee maker, she said, "Why don't you take those things back home and save them for the Fourth of July?" She then launched into another lecture on the subject of everyone bringing a mug from home—obviously failing to take into consideration the amount of energy it takes to produce just one ceramic mug.

About half the class bring their own mugs; the other half have been wantonly using my gaudy, too patriotic paper hot cups. I can tell from the grim expression on the environmental lady's face that she is not pleased. I had also bought some little red plastic spoons to go with the cups, since the class had been stirring their coffee with knives, and probably they aren't biodegradable, either. I realize I'm being anti-environmental, but am I also rude, out of line, ill mannered?

Gentle Reader,

Somebody is being rude, out of line and ill mannered in this situation. Miss Manners considers you a model of politeness for having refrained from pouring your coffee on this lady's head.

Self-righteousness, even when the cause is good, does not excuse the intrusion of supervising other people's ordinary lives. Also, it seems to be habit-forming. When you kindly met the environmentalist's first requirement, she moved on to issuing what Miss Manners presumes are orders against colors that clash with the indoor environment, since she did not claim that your new coffee cups desecrate the flag.

Perhaps Miss Manners should not be giving her ideas. Perhaps it is time to announce politely that you are doing the best you can, but prefer to take your coffee break in peace.

In the Name of Feminism

Dear Miss Manners,

I was riding a bus and when it became full, I offered my seat to a lady. After taking my seat, she proceeded to read me the riot act for my chauvinistic behavior. This went on for fifteen minutes until she got off the bus. Most of the men at the office said they have had similar experiences, if only in the form of glares.

I will still give up my seat to the elderly or anyone who obviously needs a seat. I allow women to go first and hold the door for them. But this one woman has changed my being willing to give up my seat to able-bodied women. I would suggest that if you want the men to be gentlemen, the women must be ladies.

Gentle Reader,

She berated you for offering her your seat while she was sitting in it and you were jostling awkwardly in the aisle? Miss Manners is almost forced to admire her nerve.

Almost, but not quite. People who rudely reject obviously kind offers in the name of abstract justice are bad enough. Those who take advantage of such offers and then are rude to their benefactors prove they have no sense of justice at all. Allowing such incidents to discourage you from being polite only adds another rude person to the population.

In the Name of Peace

Dear Miss Manners,

My nephew was killed in the Gulf War. After some chitchat on the telephone with a friend, she asked me how I was and I told her what had happened. A strong opponent of the war, she called his death "senseless" and said that the government hid from us the true number of casualties, which she believed to be much higher than reported. Three times she tried to tell me that I had no idea how disturbed she was by the war, that she couldn't watch the news, that America was wrong, etc.

I told her that she and I had some fundamental disagreements about the merits of that war. She kept forcing the issue, so the fourth time, in an attempt to stop the pain she was inflicting on me, I told her, "I don't care what you think!" to which she said, "I think you are very insensitive to say that." We concluded the call shortly thereafter. I feel now that I don't ever want to speak to this insensitive clod again. Am I being too hard on her? Obviously, she was disturbed by the war, but, on the other hand, I don't need to have someone force down my throat that all this was a big conspiracy and that my nephew died in vain. How do I explain to our mutual friends that I really want nothing to do with her, without compromising her friendships with them? This hurts.

GENTLE READER,

As Miss Manners understands it, this lady believes you are insensitive for taking your nephew's death personally rather than politically, as a humanitarian such as herself is doing.

Although it is Miss Manners' mission in life to soften antagonisms to keep them from festering and spreading, she finds that she has even less tolerance than you for someone who would use a friend's bereavement as a platform to air her views. The point your friend was pressing would have resulted, had she convinced you, in increasing your suffering. Miss Manners agrees that you must cut her off. A friend is someone you believe you could count on if you needed her, and you can no longer have such an illusion about this person.

NEW YORK, N.Y.—A group of women calling itself "Titi Liberation" rode the city's subways bare-breasted "to smash mammophobia" and prove that toplessness is a civil liberty. Transit police chose not to make arrests although the Mayor reportedly urged them to do so.

It is considerate of you not to wish to prejudice her other friendships, and Miss Manners approves of your not discussing the matter with others. All you need to say, should an occasion arise in which you might be expected to socialize with her, is a quiet "I don't care to meet her" to the hostess, adding, "It's not something I care to discuss," if pressed for details. Your former friend will then be asked, and may, if she wishes, tell her version of the story.

In the Name of Friendship

DEAR MISS MANNERS,

Two weeks ago, my mother, who is in her early seventies and who has always been healthy and active, suffered an unexpected heart attack. (She is recovering very nicely, although she now has to modify her energetic lifestyle and watch her diet.) She and my Dad have had a happy marriage of over fifty years, and are devoted to each other. Today, Mother came to me with tears in her eyes. Since her heart attack, she has been asked, on different occasions:

1. Has your husband started looking for another wife yet?
2. Have you found your husband your replacement yet?
3. Have you and your husband discussed how long he should wait before he remarries?

Bear in mind that my mother is a proper, genteel southern lady who, in the 41 years I've known her, has never said a strong curse word or even uttered a derogatory statement about anyone. Can you advise her how she should respond to such inquiries?

GENTLE READER,

Miss Manners, who was healthy and active when she read this report, is now clutching her heart. It would finish her off to hear these people justify themselves with the claim that they are only performing a duty by bringing up a situation that your mother might like to contemplate.

Obviously, they can contemplate it with equanimity, which disqualifies them, right there, from being counted as your mother's friends, or your family's. No one is required to respond to someone who is looking forward to her death. Your mother should simply walk away from people who have so cruelly demonstrated that they have overstepped the bounds of human decency. She might also tell your father, who could in a gentlemanly but forceful way let these people know that he wants nothing further to do with them or their grisly predictions.

Outdoing Mahatma Gandhi and Dr. King

Dear Miss Manners,

To what extent does engaging in civil disobedience grant one a license to inconvenience and act rudely toward others? I recall what my mother used to say about having any opinion I could defend, but to keep a civil tongue in my head. How is one supposed to do that, faced with indifference, bigotry and discrimination?

I put forward the non-violent protest model of King and Gandhi, but admit that progress with such forms of protest is slow at best. What about the methods of such groups as Act Up and Queer Nation? If people are literally dying in the streets and time is critical, how far can a person go? It is easy to ask this question and it can't be easily answered.

Gentle Reader,

True, so perhaps you will be kind enough to allow Miss Manners to ask you some other questions. These concern ideas that you seem to take for granted, but which are not quite so obvious to slow Miss Manners.

Do you believe that you can do better than Dr. King and Mahatma Gandhi, each of whom radically changed his entire society and altered forever the way human beings think and behave? Do you believe that they could have accomplished this in a fraction of the time, or won over more people, if they had behaved rudely or violently instead? Do you believe that you will have more success if you humiliate and threaten people? Have you noticed that public intimidation, which admittedly has dramatic impact in the short run, makes people share the kind of vision that produces long term change?

THE OBNOXIOUS VIRTUES

HONESTY

Miss Manners remembers when there was a wide variety of virtues, most of them still pristine in their boxes. Honesty was certainly one of them, but it had to take its chances against competing virtues, which often won. Even the little mannerly virtues—kindness, consideration, loyalty, modesty, discretion—were often judged more important than honesty. The virtue of informing people honestly just how appalling they looked used to lose out to the virtue of sparing their feelings. The virtue of explaining what was privately undesirable about one's spouse, parent or child would lose out to the virtues of loyalty and discretion.

Suddenly honesty turned into a bully and knocked all the other virtues out of the ring. Smart people now duck when they hear the dread announcement, "I'm going to be perfectly honest with you." To the question, "Don't you want me to level with you?" Miss Manners recommends the answer, "Oh, no, please, but thank you so much just the same."

On the single-virtue system, whatever fiery sins one may commit, confessing to them with earth-scorching candor cancels them. Miss Manners has watched with dismay as some major sinners are absolved for "being honest enough to admit it," while others are condemned not for sinning—heavens, no—but for trying to cover it up.

Well, etiquette doesn't work that way. Admitting to wrongdoing when cornered doesn't suffice to clear the record, much less win congratulations for honesty. Along with the admission must come an expression of sorrow and, when it is possible, atonement. "I broke your window" isn't enough; it has to be accompanied by "I'm terribly sorry; I feel just awful about it," and "I got an advance on my allowance so that I can replace it right away." A person who realizes that she has neglected to do something she was supposed to do, such as sending a wedding present, has to go out and do it. If it is too late to do what was supposed to be done, such as making a call when necessary, the apologist is supposed to blame himself, not the victim. "I can't think what possessed me—I must have been out of my mind" is a just barely sufficient excuse. Suggesting that it is the other person's fault for being so forgettable is not. Under the rules of etiquette, truth is no defense.

Playing Defense

DEAR MISS MANNERS,

I am perplexed by people who believe they have the right to point out "imperfections," making the recipients think that they have done them a favor by "enlightening" them as to this "fact." These rude people are more likely to make cracks about children than adults. They'll inform children that they are too tall, too short, too thin, too fat; have acne outbreaks, moles, birthmarks; wear heavy eyeglasses, hearing aids, braces.

A person with any of the above-mentioned "imperfections" is already painfully aware of it, and usually cannot change it. Therefore, the comment is not constructive, and can only make one more self-conscious. Anyway, too many Americans are obsessed with appearance, which has nothing to do with the worth of a person. What is the proper height, weight and appearance? What gives these self proclaimed experts the right to judge?

Our two-year-old son is an adorable, cheerful, outgoing child who happens to be extra tall, large-boned and very muscular in comparison to other children his age. He will likely be as tall, if not taller, than his father, who is 6 feet 4 inches. My child's doctor has told me that his growth is above the average curve, but is proportionate.

In public, we regularly hear: "Wow, is he big for his age!" "He's going to be a football player (linebacker, fullback, etc.)," "What do you feed that kid?!" "It looks like your parents never feed you!" and "Look at how fat he is!" My husband and I fear that these comments will damage our son when he is old enough to understand. What should we say or do when someone makes such a nonconstructive remark? I'd like to know how the parents of Refrigerator Perry, Hulk Hogan, André the Giant, etc., responded to insensitive people.

Gentle Reader,

Miss Manners cannot enlighten you there, but she hopes the answer is "More sensitively than they deserve." It is a cruel world, but she is sure you do not want to teach your child to be cruel in return.

That said, Miss Manners wishes to state her emphatic agreement with your argument. She would only wish to remove from it the idea of personal criticism being "constructive" or "nonconstructive." Addressing insulting remarks to matters that can be changed—choice of clothing, for example—does not make them any less intrusive. As you so eloquently state, these are opinions, not facts, and on a subject, appearance, which should not be open for discussion.

In your particular case, oddly enough, the offenders actually wish to compliment your son. Being large is considered a desirable trait in a gentleman, and they mean their comments to be flattering teasing. Nevertheless, the comments do fall into the category of Remarking Upon the Obvious, which ought to be stopped. Those people may well be apt to point out to another child that he is what they consider small. The polite way to respond to unwanted personal remarks, which you can now do on your son's behalf, is "Do you think so?" The child's version, for when he is old enough, is "Really? Thank you for telling me."

Disdaining Discretion

DEAR MISS MANNERS,

My husband, who is in his 50's, has had little to do with his mother since he was a child. She is emotionally unstable, and her behavior is so vicious that all family members have virtually banished her from their lives and homes. After years of trying to be a friend and encouraging her to get psychiatric care, I, too, have decided it is best to have nothing to do with her.

We are now planning a large family party for our daughter, and my husband and I agree his mother should not be invited because of the disruptions she is certain to cause. There is also a slight danger that she would hurt herself or someone else, since she often makes dire threats. I have told family members of our party and I have asked them not to mention it to my husband's mother, in case she calls them. My husband thinks that this is an unfair burden to place on others and is dishonest besides. He wants to tell his mother about the party and explain to her that she will not be invited because of her years of insulting and threatening behavior.

I think it is cruel to tell her about the party, particularly when there is little chance of her finding out. She lives many states away from us and other family members and seldom (but admittedly sometimes) talks to them.

GENTLE READER,

Oh, dear. Must every argument be framed in terms of brute honesty? Miss Manners blesses you for challenging your husband in terms of the mannerly concept of refraining from hurting feelings.

It is hurtful to announce a party to anyone whom one is not inviting, even someone whom one has had to ostracize. Nor is it right to involve other people, even other relatives, in the mechanics of a family problem outside their immediate concern. This makes the solution amazingly simple, you will be relieved to hear.

BISMARCK, N.D.—A restraining order was issued by state courts to keep a 17-year-old boy from, among other things, calling a 14-year-old boy "Dumbo" because of his large ears, the Associated Press reported.

Just go ahead and give the party. Explanations will be necessary only if your mother-in-law both hears of the party and taxes your husband with excluding her. In the meantime, you might point out to him that silence is more eloquent than denunciation. Does he really want to engage her in argument?

POLITE FICTION

Perhaps Miss Manners ought to define the term Polite Fiction before she starts trying to revive the concept. She does not want to risk bringing back the sort of literature that gentlemen used to believe suitable for ladies because it was too stupid for themselves.

Nor is Polite Fiction quite the same thing as what is called, often with misplaced disdain, the Little White Lie. That concept ought to be revived, too, as there are now many people who self-righteously refuse to avoid insulting others whenever they possibly can. The moral superiority of substituting "You look awful" and "I find your parties such a drag that I'd rather stay home and do nothing" for such sinful untruths as "How nice to see you" and "Oh, I'm so sorry, I'm busy then," is not apparent to Miss Manners.

Polite Fiction is a different sort of benign falsification—one that is aimed inward. It requires that one school oneself not to see, hear or notice certain things. By not acknowledging that material for possible etiquette disasters actually exists, one renders awkward or awful reactions to them unnecessary. No reaction at all is required when something didn't happen, not even an apology or a statement of forgiveness.

The classic example of a fact of life that cannot be commented upon in any edifying way is the unfortunate and involuntary minor physical manifestation. Does Miss Manners make herself clear? One reason she doesn't mention it by name is that she is offering this as an example of the unmentionable. Another is that she has been astonished to discover, from the reports she receives from the offended, that there is apparently no limit to the body's imagination in producing unwelcome manifestations. Besides registering disgust, the complainers want to know what they should say or do (other than their own vulgar suggestions about running for cover), or what the offender should have done (after what, in the best of worlds, that person should not have done). The answer is: nothing. There exists a Polite Fiction that such a thing never happened.

Believers in Polite Fiction have trouble hearing things that were not intended for their ears (or, for just as much credit, have learned to eavesdrop while looking steadfastly in the opposite direction). That is why they look so puzzled when they suddenly appear in a room where other people have been talking about them. They never jump into conversations that strangers are having in public places, not even after saying, "I couldn't help hearing what you were saying . . ."

Polite Fiction also affects the eyesight, although selectively. Practitioners are able to spot a present they gave only when the recipient is wearing or displaying it; they would never be able to spot its absence, and therefore to inquire crossly whether it was actually appreciated. They can see that other people look well, but cannot see any detail that would account for this. Therefore, their compliments are in the nature of, "You look wonderful," not "You've finally lost that weight" or "I see you got your nose fixed." They have terrible trouble seeing anything wrong. On the rare occasions when they do, their eyesight is good enough to spot the remedy at the same time.

Finally, Polite Fiction sometimes interferes with their memories. The polite person who talked over a friend's romantic prospect never remembers any crucial part of the conversation—damaging information, harsh opinions—if the friend marries. Expressions of doubt about prospective children—that the parent-to-be has doubts about wanting a child, or has a preference for one gender—should never be made in the first place, but no harm is done if everyone observes the Polite Fiction that they never were.

The strange thing is that people who suffer from the symptoms of Polite Fiction—deafness, blindness and amnesia—tend to be especially beloved for their debilities.

Polite Fiction Dines Out: Seeing No Evil

Dear Miss Manners,

My husband and I recently accepted a good friend's invitation to sup at a highly acclaimed French restaurant. As we greeted our friend and his date, who had already been seated, we gasped as we focused on the next table. The couple there seemed innocent enough until we spotted the full side view of the young woman's breasts! She was seated across from her date—we had the side view. Without straining, one could see literally down to her navel. At times, she would try to cover up, due to the obvious chatter from neighboring tables. Other times, she would sit back and arch her back, so all was shown. She knew what she was doing.

Our friends sat with their backs to her, but were aware of the situation. Whenever we would converse with them, the woman's breasts were in full view. An otherwise wonderful evening should not be subjected to this sort of poor exposure. What if anything could have been done to change this situation? Must we sit and pretend that she's only a loud, barking dog?

GENTLE READER,

Miss Manners supposes you could have thrown a tablecloth over her, but begs to know why you are so excited. The offense was not comparable to that of a barking dog; a sight at a neighboring table is more easily avoided than a loud noise emanating from it. It is not polite to stare at other diners, for whatever reason. However, if you could not take your eyes off this sight, you could have solved the problem by quietly asking to change tables.

Polite Fiction Dines Out: Hearing No Evil

DEAR MISS MANNERS,

My aunt and I lunched in a crowded restaurant, where the men next to us were talking animatedly. Half-way through the meal, one of them leaned over and said, "So you're interested in [the topic of their conversation], huh?" It was obvious from his tone that this wasn't a line, but a jocular, matey acknowledgment of the fact that (as he supposed) we'd been listening.

When my aunt smiled and told him we couldn't help overhearing a little, he replied that it was a free flow of conversation, and otherwise made himself friendly. But it's the assumption that we'd been eavesdropping I object to.

After they left, I said, "That was one of the rudest people I ever met!"

My aunt said, "It's only natural. He's middle-aged, successful and male—of course, he assumes everyone is interested in what he's saying. I wasn't offended."

Did I take offense unduly? Is this just an old-guard versus the 90s thing? Or would it have been a breach of etiquette in any era?

GENTLE READER,

Would you be offended if a sweet little old modest lady asked you a question? Weren't you eavesdropping?

It sure sounds that way to Miss Manners, who failed to catch the distinction between that and listening to the conversation of strangers. Eavesdropping—or, rather, being caught eavesdropping, which is what seems to have happened to you—has always been considered a breach of etiquette. Insinuating that it was the talkers' fault for being too loud is not new, either. (It is a better defense for the apprehended eaves-dropper to look puzzled and say, "I beg your pardon?" as if having been startled out of a reverie.)

What is very 90s is the rude assumption that rudeness naturally goes with being middle-aged, male and successful. In the 80s, reports of rudeness were often prefaced with the remark that the offender was "a professional" and therefore ought to know better. Before that, the middle-aged were supposed to refrain from rudeness because they were "old enough to know better." Way back in the distant past, there was sur-prise that males did not always behave as gentlemen.

Miss Manners does not think the reprimand, which was at least offered in a jolly manner, the rudest thing she ever heard—even that she heard today. You would be better advised to concentrate on teaching yourself to look in the opposite direction from anyone on whom you happen to be eavesdropping.

Polite Fiction Dines Out: Speaking No Evil

DEAR MISS MANNERS,

Coming out of a local restaurant, I noticed a couple of people sitting in their car, involved in a romantic scene. As I walked closer on the way to my own car, I saw them more clearly. Those people I saw, to my shock, were the wife of someone I know and her Romeo. I must have paled in disbelief as I stood there for a few seconds, watch-ing. I think I was not noticed, or she did not remember my face. It was getting dark, anyway.

I see the husband every day and I cannot help feeling sorry for him. I know lit-tle about his personal life and less about his marriage. I am finding it difficult to get to sleep after seeing that outrageous scene. I think I should not intrude in someone else's life, but I wonder if he knows about his wife's love affair. Should I tell him, or try to ignore this sin?

GENTLE READER,

The conflict between the manners injunction against interfering in other peo-ple's business and what some consider to be the duty, or the pleasure, of exposing sin is a classic one. Not surprisingly, Miss Manners tends to come down on the side of manners.

Admittedly, it is hard to think of an innocent explanation for what you saw, but while Miss Manners is optimistically trying, she would like to remind you how difficult it is for an outsider to imagine the complications of any marriage. Do not forget that if you informed the husband of what you saw, you would be conveying two pieces of information—not only that the situation occurred, but that you had witnessed it. So in addition to learning of the betrayal, which he may or may not already suspect, the husband would have to deal with the fact that it was now public.

If you decide to tell him, please allow Miss Manners to persuade you to do this in a way that is face-saving for the gentleman you already pity. If you merely say in a neutral way that you ran into his wife and that man, giving the time and the place, you allow him to suspect the nature of the encounter without letting on that you do, and to follow up the inquiry without feeling pressured by you to do so.

OPENNESS

Since the happy day when Miss Manners took fond leave of her senses and entered her present peculiar profession, sensitive but indignant souls have been complaining to her about their disgusting fellow citizens. By every mail, she receives reports on who is sickening whom by doing what. These are not altogether pleasant to read.

Duty is duty, however, and Miss Manners gives proper attention to each unappetizing description of nose blowings, burps and worse. She then urges restraint on all sides, figuring that if she can encourage one group to employ the polite fiction of not noticing and the other to carry clean handkerchiefs, she will have done something to alleviate the problem.

Lately it seems to Miss Manners that the situation has worsened. There has been a decided drop in the quality, so to speak, of disgusting things being done in public. No longer are the offenses simply inadvertent physical phenomena, undesired and often unanticipated by their performers. There seems to have been a conscious decision made by some—to the disgust of others—to liberate from private confines the common routines that were traditionally performed out of view. It constitutes a coming out, as it were, not of the closet but of the bathroom, which has long been considered the proper place for grooming and other bodily housekeeping activities. A few examples reported to Miss Manners by her Gentle Readers:

- "I find it totally obnoxious to work in an office with the smell of fingernail polish, but I have seen secretaries, as well as professional women, polish their nails in the office. I suppose the last straw was a few weeks ago, at a first-class live theater. During the intermission, a woman in front of me had the audacity to take out her fingernail polish and paint her nails. I glanced around me and others were taking a quick look at her in disbelief, also."

- "While waiting in a supermarket checkout line, my husband called my attention to a man sitting on the window ledge, cleaning out, of all things, his dentures or partial plate. I couldn't look at that too long! What is this world coming to?"

- "I belong to a respectable racquet and fitness club, where the members average forty-something, with incomes well above that mark. On the whole, it's a clean club, but there are things I simply can't ignore: women shaving their bodies in the steam room, where others will sit or recline; women and men who wear permeating scents in the exercise areas; people who not only trash the facilities we all must use, but leave their very personal trash all about; and the recent, repugnant, sight of a woman obviously peppering the locker room floor, where we all walk barefoot, with her toenail trimmings."

- "A co-worker insists upon clipping her toenails at her desk."

- "The last thing I need on my long trek to the office on public transportation, is to hear that endless click-click-click of the clippers, knowing that pieces of someone else's dirty fingernails are flying all over the place and could end up in my lap or, even worse, my eye. Why can't these people conduct their personal grooming at home?"

These are extensions of the once common etiquette violation of ladies' wearing curlers in public, a matter that Miss Manners thought solved by the marvels of technology. Before portable hair dryers and hot curlers, when it took a day for a lady to be ready for an evening, the less fastidious allowed themselves to appear before their families and neighbors (although not, if they had office jobs, their colleagues) in the primitive and unappealing gadgets used to effect the transformation.

This was correctly interpreted by inadvertent onlookers as insulting them. Miss Manners cannot remember whether a lady's appearing at breakfast in curlers constituted legal cause for her husband to divorce her, but sympathy would have run in his favor. However utilitarian, the presence of curlers clearly said: "You are not the one whose opinion I value; you're not even someone I want to avoid offending while I get ready for someone who does count."

The utilitarian argument has grown, and the number of people who count has correspondingly shrunk. When Miss Manners attempts to stuff current offenders back into their bathrooms and close the doors on them, they argue that they have no time to consider the sensibilities of others. Their lives are too busy, their time too precious, to allow them to retreat from public view merely to do unattractive things to make themselves attractive to others.

Miss Manners notices a little paradox in there somewhere. For whom, exactly, are they preparing themselves? Anyway, she does not accept such excuses. If your life is too full to allow going to the bathroom, there is something wrong with your life, not with the concept of bathrooms.

So the offenders go on to argue that as these activities are common, some of them ubiquitous, to humanity, the fastidiousness of hiding them is ridiculous. As the natural extension of this point of view, large cities are increasingly reporting problems with public urination. Although the defense of this cites the reasonable complaint of a scarcity of public bathrooms, turning public space into one big bathroom is not, Miss Manners would think, a palatable solution.

She considers the existence of a backstage area, in which one prepares oneself to go on public view, to be as necessary for the dignity of each person's public persona as it is for the sensibilities of the audience. Many routines performed in order to increase human attractiveness are themselves unsightly. Seen in one's own bathroom mirror, these practices are at least softened through a sympathy and love that one cannot expect even of one's intimates, let alone the general public.

The Open Bathroom Door I

DEAR MISS MANNERS,

I have noticed a revolting behavior trend exhibited by males of all ages, classes, races, etc.: spitting on the sidewalks. I understand that in an earlier era, public spittoons were available, but I am under the impression that they were used for chewing-tobacco, not phlegm. Where do men pick up this gross habit? What can I do about it? I vent my anger by muttering "Disgusting!" under my breath, but I resent the fact that I must look down as I walk to avoid stepping in spittle.

GENTLE READER,

As thoroughly as Miss Manners agrees with your distaste for this behavior, she cannot recommend that you spit words back at people who are better armed.

The Open Bathroom Door II

DEAR MISS MANNERS,

Last week, while riding the Metro to work, I happened to sit next to a woman who began to put on her make-up. I am not speaking of a little lipstick. This particular woman, and I have seen others like her, pulled out her mirror and proceeded to pluck her eyebrows, put on foundation, mascara, blush, eye shadow and whatever else came from her little bag. I was horrified. Is this proper? I was taught that things dealing with appearance and hygiene should be kept to the privacy of the powder room.

GENTLE READER,

When etiquette foolishly condoned "a little lipstick" and a furtive look in the mirror to indicate where the hand could smooth the hair, it should have guessed what was coming. Should Miss Manners condone what you describe, you would soon see people gargling on the subway and spitting in the aisles. The rule that grooming must be done in private remains in effect, no matter how busy and important you may think you are.

The Open Bathroom Door III

DEAR MISS MANNERS,

I have been a flight attendant for two years and, while most passengers are polite and considerate of their neighbors, I have seen passengers clip their or their children's toenails, pluck eyebrows, floss teeth, whistle, play loud video games or allow their children to play toy instruments. I have no problem telling them to refrain from disturbing others with loud noises but what can I say about toenail clipping? I'd also like to remind people that snapping fingers or saying, "Hey, you!" is no way to get anyone's attention. How about trying, "Excuse me, Miss/Sir?"

GENTLE READER,

Miss Manners supposes that the captain does not want to make an announcement that "Passengers are kindly requested to refrain from doing their personal toilet routines in plain sight for the duration of the flight." But you may offer to be of assistance to the passengers. Inquire pleasantly, "Would you like me to check if the bathroom is available, so you can do that in private?" or whether "Hey, you" was a reference to you.

The Open Bathroom Door IV

DEAR MISS MANNERS,

A war of sorts began between my husband and me over the point of his blowing his nose, snorting, blubbering and honking to his heart's content in front of guests, and the question of whether it is excusable to pass wind in the presence of one's spouse. The result for us of the breakdown in simple etiquette within the family is that I feel I am falling out of love. It is difficult to remain starry-eyed with someone who stands right in front of your face and flosses his teeth while conversing with you. Nevertheless, I am dedicated and determined to remain a family solidly glued by love and duty, if not good manners, till the day one of us dies.

GENTLE READER,

Miss Manners is blubbering herself, but only because she cannot bear to have a love story end like this. Please, can't you and she together appeal to your husband on the importance not just of manners but of his not deliberately making himself unappetizing to you? Miss Manners is afraid that his attitude—that politeness is for strangers, not family or friends—has killed many a romance and, when it involves those less stalwart than you, many a marriage.

COMFORT

People seem to have an inordinate amount of interest nowadays in their own feelings. This does not strike Miss Manners as quite decent. First they put an enormous effort into examining themselves, in the hope of discovering what their feelings actually are. This seems to be an operation of exquisite delicacy. They are forever murmuring, "I have to be sure how I feel about that." Then they act on those feelings. This requires no thought at all.

All of this puzzles Miss Manners, who always knows exactly how she feels but considers the question of how and when to express or to act upon one's feelings to be a highly complex subject—namely, etiquette. Miss Manners has nevertheless been so impressed by the introspective excavations in which everybody else is engaged that she expects fascinating results. Such a difficult quest should surely reveal a range of emotional subtleties unsuspected by the likes of her.

But no, there are only two announced results: Comfortable and Uncomfortable. Sort of like On and Off, or Hot and Cold, with nothing in between. Miss Manners has noticed that the bearers consider these to be the only normal possibilities. Other feelings that still crop up with distressing frequency, such as guilt, embarrassment and shame, are considered abnormal or, as we say now, inappropriate, and one works on getting rid of them.

The declaration "I'm comfortable with that" is used to describe every feeling from not objecting to renting a videotape for the evening to being willing to get married. A variation, "I'm fine," can cover anything from "I don't want any more pie" to "You can't make me budge." The negative version, "I'm not comfortable with that," has a range from "We don't have a deal" to "I can't stand having your parents visit."

Not visiting the dying or attending funerals, and not sending

"Individuality, self-expression, artistic freedom, civil liberties, sex, diet, personal success and political awareness have all served as justifications for boorish behavior," stated a writer in *Vogue* magazine. "A woman I know once slugged a man who had presumed to open a door for her, thus striking a blow for feminism."

thank you letters in return for hospitality, favor or presents, were once perceived as evidence of rudeness, presumably prompted by selfishness or sloth. Now the declarations of discomfort, sometimes with explanations attached ("I want to remember him as he was," "Funerals give me the creeps," "I hate to write letters," "People should do things just because they want to, not because they expect to be thanked"), imply that there is virtue in the act of refusing to let the expectations of etiquette prevail over personal comfort. We seem to have reached a point where anyone who expects us to overcome discomfort for the duties of etiquette is seen as exhibiting a lack of compassion and respect, and Miss Manners can unfortunately guess who that is.

A virtue of the old system that made people uncomfortable was that it allowed a huge range of feelings, not only charming ones but also such blunt ones as lust, greed and sloth, which make today's discomforts seem hardly worth mentioning. Rather than merely missing one's expected comfort, one could be racked by passions of all kinds. Such feelings were not so tame that one had to puzzle and fret before one could manage to identify them.

However, one wasn't allowed to express all these feelings as they happened to occur. There was a gap between feeling and saying or doing during which one was supposed to guess not at one's own feelings but at the probable feelings of others should one's feelings surface. (Too much feeling—Miss Manners needs to go lie down now.) Would people on the receiving end feel insulted, hurt, disgusted or otherwise adversely affected? If so, the gap became indefinite.

No one thought you would damage your own emotional health by sparing the feelings of others. On the contrary, there existed an interior mechanism that ravaged your feelings if you caused undue damage. Instead of a Comfort Scale, one had a Conscience. The conscience was activated when one did something wrong, however sincerely the desire to do it was felt. It could never be satisfied by merely relieving the symptom of discomfort. The conscience had to be appeased by making amends for whatever wrong was done.

Miss Manners is sometimes asked whether she is ever rude, and she is forced to admit that no, she never is. Incredulous questioners have then been known to press, "But aren't you ever tempted to be rude?" Certainly. Would you trust a minister who had never felt a desire to sin?

Discomfort

DEAR MISS MANNERS,

When I first married, my father-in-law invited me to call him Dad or whatever I felt comfortable in calling him. I called him Dad. My mother-in-law I called Mom, although I was not invited to do so. That was five years ago. Dave and I have had so many problems with his parents since then that we have decided to move out of their area.

Do I have to continue to call them Mom and Dad, and if not, do I have to inform them that I will no longer do so? I'm sure that would cause more problems, but I believe that they are as uncomfortable with it as I am. Can I just call them by their first names the next time I have contact with them?

GENTLE READER,

Somehow, Miss Manners just cannot get as worked up as everyone else over the possibility of minor social discomfort. Now that the threat of nuclear extinction seems to have subsided a bit, feeling uncomfortable seems to be the society's greatest dread.

In Miss Manners' opinion, there are worse states than feeling uncomfortable. One of them is open warfare, which is what you would be declaring by advising your parents-in-law that you no longer wish to address them as members of your family, or even by simply ceasing to do so. Especially as you are moving away from their area, Miss Manners cannot see that addressing them as parents in the occasional letter or telephone call will produce overwhelming discomfort. If it does, why don't you just call them "Ummmm," as most people address their in-laws?

SENSITIVITY

Are you ready for an attack on sensitivity? Miss Manners, who ought to count herself as part of the burgeoning sensitivity industry, is starting to hate the word. Perhaps that is because sensitivity, once such a sweet and modest attribute, now goes swaggering crudely about, bragging about itself and bludgeoning others: I'm so sensitive. You're insensitive. Everyone needs sensitivity training. And on and on.

Couldn't all you sensitive people get a grip on yourselves and show a little consideration for others? That, in fact, is what sensitivity was all about, back when Miss Manners was crazy about it. The sensitive person was one who was interested in, and good at, picking up feedback from others and adjusting accordingly.

This is essential to the practice of good manners. As important as the rules and conventions of etiquette are, they cannot be practiced by rote but must constantly be fitted to particular circumstances and checked against the reactions they provoke to make sure that the desired effects are achieved. For example, compliments, apologies, invitations and expressions of gratitude are all polite forms, encouraged and often mandated by etiquette. But to persist in offering them when the target is obviously becoming embarrassed—to keep inviting people who keep refusing or to compliment people in ways they seem to find too personal—would be impolite.

To know when that is happening, one has to be able to distinguish between reactions of polite protest and those that indicate true discomfort. Is your hostess begging you to stop apologizing for breaking the lamp because she never liked it anyway? Or is she doing so because your carrying on is spoiling the evening? Does the guest who declines another helping wish to be urged, or is he annoyed at being pressured? Skill at interpreting clues to such feelings, often in situations where these clues are by necessity subtle, was always a requirement of etiquette. It was called sensitivity.

The therapy model has changed the definitions. To call another person "insensitive" no longer suggests an unfortunate but involuntary absence of that ability to read and react to others. It now means that the person is deliberately evil, most likely harboring despicable bigotry. Oddly enough, to call another person "sensitive" is also likely to be pejorative. "You're being sensitive" or "oversensitive" or "too sensitive" is the new way of saying, "If you feel insulted when I insult you, it's your own fault. A normal person would love it."

Another use of the word "sensitive" is to point out that someone who is nice is nevertheless unattractive. When a lady says a gentlemen is very sensitive she sometimes means he's wimpy. When a gentleman says it of a lady he means she's pathetic. People also call themselves sensitive to denounce others. "Perhaps I'm just being oversensitive," they will begin when embarking upon a narrative clearly designed to show that they were reacting only too mildly to extreme provocation.

Then there is "sensitivity" as in "sensitivity training," a concept that Miss Manners, of all people, ought to endorse. So she would, with all her heart, if it only meant teaching people to watch for the reactions they inadvertently produce in others. Now it can just as easily mean characterizing individuals by assumptions drawn not from them but from their race or ethnic background. Or it can mean declaring that one should not expect members of one group or another to live up to the standards of the society. Before that was called "sensitivity," it was known as "prejudice."

While true sensitivity is enhanced by a sophisticated knowledge of different cultures, it particularly mandates reacting to each person as an individual. Manners have always required making allowances for those who could not be expected to know the particular rules of an unfamiliar society. But they also demand treating everyone with the respectful assumption of intelligence and capability.

Modern sensitivity is supposed to go beyond surface behavior, to deal with people on the basis of their ancestry, their economic and cultural status—with particular attention to disabilities and disadvantages they may be presumed to have.

Miss Manners would hate to discourage anyone from making an effort to help those who might benefit from assistance. She would only like to point out that it is an etiquette disaster to skip over examining surface behavior for clues about how an individual wishes to present himself or herself and to be treated. To ignore people's behavior and deal only with their presumed insides—especially as gleaned from a cursory knowledge of generalities about their background—is rude. To be sensitive to someone as a representative of a group, but not as an individual, only because one is interested in that person's own good is not something Miss Manners would now call insensitive. She prefers the old-fashioned term—"patronizing."

Oversensitivity

Dear Miss Manners,

Trying to keep the conversation going at a family dinner, I decided to look at people's hands. I remarked that one grandson and also his wife had beautiful hands. However when I came to my other grandson's hands, well, they were huge and I didn't really have much time to think, so I said, "Your hands would be slimmer if they weren't so fat."

Well, that obviously was the wrong thing to say, as he is overweight, although truthfully, I wasn't thinking of that. He was furious! My daughter-in-law said, "That's your grandmother for you," and he said, "We don't have to take that!" So everyone looked at me, and I felt like crawling under the table.

Is it normal for anyone to be that sensitive? I really didn't intend to hurt his feelings, but I do feel that most people would have just flubbed it off and said, "Thanks a lot," or something. I am eighty years old, and I just feel that he was not respectful. Or am I wrong? Isn't there such a thing as being overly sensitive?

Gentle Reader,

You know who is beginning to get over-sensitive about such claims? Your very own Miss Manners. She is far too polite to exhibit fury, but she is really exasperated with the common double whammy you describe:

First you deliver an obvious, standard insult to an unsuspecting person, and then, when he feels insulted by it, you hit him again, with the coy insult of being over-sensitive.

It is not that Miss Manners fails to realize that people can say perfectly stupid things they don't mean. That is why we have the fine old institution of the apology. As you immediately realized your error, you should have started groveling: "I can't believe I said that! That's not what I meant at all! You have beautiful hands; I've always thought so. Whatever idiotic joke I thought I was attempting, it came out all wrong. Will you ever forgive me? I hate myself for being such a fool. . . ."

Had you done this, and had your nephew not finally interrupted you by muttering, "Oh, that's all right, forget it. I know you didn't mean it," Miss Manners would now be on your side. Instead, you allowed the insult to stand, thus allowing him to believe that you did mean to insult him. Now you want to act insulted by him because he felt insulted that you insulted him. That strikes Miss Manners as under-sensitive.

SELF-EXPRESSION: THOUGHTS

One day when Miss Manners wasn't paying careful attention, perhaps because the breezes were stirring the flowers, a new virtue was announced. Added to the standard list of virtues, such as charity, chastity and working out, was, of all things, The Virtue of Self-Expression.

This new virtue does not necessarily consist of expressing kindly feelings or useful thoughts. It gives full credit simply for the act of bringing to the surface anything rumbling away in that mess we all keep sloshing around inside. That things may be expressed that are unattractive or hurtful to other people does not seem to detract from the value of expressing them. Here are the new cries of the virtuous:

You know I'm not the only person who thinks that; I just have the guts to say it.
Anyhow, that's the way I feel.
I don't really care what anybody else thinks of me.

Ever pleased to hear of more goodness appearing in the world, which would cut down her work load, Miss Manners made a special effort to fit the impulse that prompts these statements into the catalogue of ancient virtues. It seemed to have something to do with the historic courage with which our heroes stood up for their most cherished beliefs against wicked social and political pressure. What a fine thing that is.

But wait. This isn't exactly the way the new virtue is being practiced. Those statements are as likely to preface expressions of frank bigotry, criticisms in the form of insults, and assorted declarations that are known to be widely offensive. Wasn't the idea supposed to be that it was a virtue not to be shaken from other virtues? Can courage be defined as a willingness to indulge self-expression at the expense of others?

Supposing that she must have misunderstood, Miss Manners next tried matching the new virtue with our appreciation of individuality. Teaching children to think for themselves, even if this is unaccompanied by anything to think about, is, after all, the stated objective of our form of education. As she recalls, the sort of individuality that has always been admired was also in the service of others. The person who invents new ways of improving the world is celebrated for originality. At least until the contemporary art world got hold of it, originality wasn't actually required to be antisocial. Surely there must be a difference between always thinking for oneself and always thinking about oneself.

Miss Manners can't quite see herself running around congratulating people for airing ugly thoughts. Self-expression is getting to sound too much like lack of self-control, a common trait, but one that will have to remain uncelebrated by her.

Impugning All Feelings

DEAR MISS MANNERS,

What does one do about those who judge others by their own behavior, i.e., "What's in it for me?" We offer our concern for others, often to have our efforts on someone else's behalf—not theirs—questioned as to the purity of our intentions. Since the questioning is by innuendo, one does not recognize it verbally, but the implication is disconcerting.

GENTLE READER,

Self-interest is one of the great discoveries of high school philosophers. Along about tenth grade, Miss Manners has noticed, bright and audacious teenagers always attempt to prove that, for example, a mother who starves herself in order to feed her baby is only yielding to her own selfish desire to think of herself as being self-sacrificing. The actual mothers of those teenagers, being bright too, merely reply "Yes, dear," in the hope that someday their young philosophers will understand more about life.

The first thing to understand is that by such a definition, "self-interest" becomes meaningless. If it is the only motivation for voluntary behavior, then some other distinction has to be made to explain why some people do virtuous deeds and others don't. The second is that the decent person does, indeed, have wishes based on the interests of what one might call a wider self—child, family, community, humanity. It is too bad that people who have not experienced such love do not understand it, but Miss Manners hopes that will not discourage those who do.

SELF-EXPRESSION: CURIOSITY

"If there is anything you want to know, don't hesitate to ask" sounds like such a polite way of saying "I will be glad to be available if you have any questions" that Miss Manners had a hard time figuring out why it made her nervous. A gentleman of her acquaintance tried to argue that it puts the person who uses it in a superior position by suggesting that the other person is cowering with unnecessary fear at approaching him, but needn't be, as he plans to be gracious. That wasn't it. Miss Manners doesn't believe in examining conventional wording too closely. What frightens her is that the idea that not hesitating before asking questions is being more generally applied. Of course you should hesitate. It should be a pause long enough to ask yourself, "Is this any of my business? Could this question hurt the other person's feelings? Could it seem to suggest something offensive about that person?"

A Nevada-based business offers get-even gifts and will send anonymous insulting gift cards and letters for customers. One example cited by Gannett News Services of the company's merchandise is a card that says: "Deep down inside you must hate yourself because all the rest of us do." Another is a witch's broom with a label that says, "So you will never be without transportation—Witch!"

She realizes this goes against current usage, by which the admission of curiosity is thought to cancel the etiquette rule against nosiness. When people who ask personal questions are taxed with invasion of privacy, they merely point out that they were "wondering" or "interested in" what you paid for your house, why you use a wheelchair, or whether you are planning to get a divorce. The victims of this non-hesitation are reporting in:

"There is a unanimously shared opinion among my single friends that questions such as *Are you still single? Are you dating anybody? Is there anyone special in your life?* and *How's your love life?* are unwelcome, whether they come from smug acquaintances or well-meaning friends. If the aim is to find out if the single person is interested in meeting a specific person, that is best stated explicitly."

"I am often assaulted by persons who boldly seize me by the arm to remark brightly, *I wish I had your lovely brown skin* (emphasis on the brown) and go on to ask, *You must come from somewhere else—where?* When I reply that I am Canadian, just Canadian, I am asked where my parents come from, and when I say, Canada, I'm asked about my grandparents. Once I replied, *Isn't that funny? We native people are accustomed to thinking of the fair-skinned people as the immigrants and foreigners, but, as you point out, many of them are unaccustomed to thinking of themselves in that way, wherever they happen to find themselves."*

"Our children are 14, 11 and three years of age. We give this information when requested, but are then at a loss when we're asked if the three-year-old was an 'accident' or a 'surprise.' "

"I am an artist with a knack for color and style in my wardrobe, and what you would call a bargain shopper with an eye for quality. I must constantly deal with *Oh, another new outfit!* or *It must be nice having so much money to spend on clothes,* when, in fact, it may be about clothes I've had for a long time but have found new ways to put together."

"I know there are people who take *Have you lost weight?* as a great compliment and go into a proud dissertation on how many pounds they have lost and how they did it, but I believe this implies that the person was a fat pig before and it was about time they did something. One of the responses I'm considering is, *Why? Has someone found some?*"

"I am frequently asked, *How old are you, anyway?* by younger men I have just met, and some of whom I have, until this question is posed, found attractive. When I respond, *Why do you need to know?* they say, *What are you afraid of?*"

"My family is prone to prematurely grey hair, and I have dark hair with a grey streak. Acquaintances seem compelled to say, pointing, *Is that grey? Are you thinking of coloring that?* On occasion, I have answered, *No, I've been painting the ceiling and I can't get the paint out,* or *I'm 53 years old; I CAN have grey hair.*"

"As a Southerner born and raised, living in the north for the past 25 years, I never fail to be annoyed by, *Where is your accent?* The best reply I can muster is, *I don't know.*"

"When I was always being asked, *When do you plan to retire?* I used to answer with, *Every morning when the alarm goes off.*"

Miss Manners is grateful that all of these Gentle Readers seem to have politely hesitated before making the obvious (but unfortunately rude) reply.

The Really Personal Question

DEAR MISS MANNERS,

It often occurs that people ask me:

"Are those your real nails?"

"Is that your natural hair color?"

"Is your hair really that long?"

"Are those your eyes or contacts?"

I can't imagine that someone would consider that information any of his/her business. I am usually so shocked by the question and the way that it is asked, that I respond without making it evident that I'm upset. I'd like to say something that would let the questioner know that I'm offended, without making too much of a big deal out of it. I've considered many responses, but I don't want to say anything rude.

GENTLE READER,

Miss Manners was herself dumbfounded to be asked, at a gala social event, "Is that your own skin?" She didn't even understand the question (which seemed to be directed more at her décolletage than her countenance). Supposing that she did want to wear someone else's skin—how would she go about it?

In the silence that followed, the inquirer identified himself as being in the film business, and went on to explain that apparently some ladies among his colleagues were now in the habit of simulating a look that, on Miss Manners, represented nothing more glamorous than old-fashioned parasol pallor. Miss Manners' stunned silence was not planned, but she recommends that you duplicate it. This would probably involve nothing more than projecting the shock you already feel. What, after all, can one say? One cannot exactly go around cataloguing one's natural endowments.

A Reply

DEAR MISS MANNERS,

I was shocked at your answer. Some people who ask these questions are most curious or envious of people who are able to grow long fingernails or have beautiful, vibrant hair, or even a smooth, beautiful complexion, or an unusual, pretty color of eyes. Unless you are embarrassed or ashamed of trying to make the best of your personal appearance, there is really nothing to worry about.

The Ultimate Personal Question

DEAR MISS MANNERS,

My husband died of AIDS. I am sick to death of people asking me how he contracted this disease. It is none of their business and just plain rude.

I have responded in many and various ways, sometimes making up stories, telling the truth, or whatever suits my mood at the moment, depending on what I perceive to be the motive of the questioner.

I have also prefaced my disclosure by saying, "My husband died of AIDS and you would be amazed at how many people are so rude as to ask how he contracted this disease." This method works, but requires the right mood and sense of outrage on my part to pull it off successfully.

I am just plain tired of having to do this. It's bad enough that he died—must I have to suffer further with this? Please help me come up with some response that is not too evasive or rude.

GENTLE READER,

The reply you occasionally use is so apt that Miss Manners doesn't understand why you need work yourself up into outrage in order to deliver it.

It seems to her it would be much more effectively conveyed with merely an amazed look. The politeness of the statement is ensured by the mere fact of your sharing it—thus establishing the presumption (to which people are forced to live up) that your interlocutor would not be capable of this offense.

SELF-EXPRESSION: FOOD

How do we describe someone who is intensely aware of the composition and consequences of every bit of food he or she eats and who takes pains not to ingest anything offensive? A sensible eater? A sensitive person? A gourmet? A nutritionist? How about a food fuss?

Miss Manners is not unsympathetic to the current interest in food from dietary, aesthetic and political standpoints. She has always appreciated the traditional religious and ceremonial considerations. She understands about allergies, scruples and preferences. But enough is enough. She can no longer tolerate people talking when their mouths ought to be full.

The pretense of being grateful for whatever refreshment is offered has disappeared into a self-righteous demand for menu control that is ruining modern social life. Guests are announcing what they want and what they disapprove of. Those who consider themselves polite do it beforehand, kindly allowing the hosts time to fill their orders. Those who don't care do it right at the table. Hosts are being advised to be extra careful not to offend their guests by serving . . . well, any of the major or minor food groups. There isn't anything that someone isn't allergic to, or against. The list of common objections includes alcoholic beverages, animal fats, veal, shellfish, nuts, saturated fats, pork, eggs, fried foods, game, sugar, heavy sauces, red meat, butter, starches, organ meats, heavy desserts and caffeine. Kind of simplifies your dinner planning, doesn't it?

Miss Manners suggests that hosts put their energy into fighting back against the food fusses. We all agree that everybody does not eat everything. That is not the issue. There are polite rules for avoiding what you don't want:

1. If you are serving yourself, from a tray or a buffet table, don't take it. Take what you can eat and leave the rest.
2. If you have no choice but are given something you don't eat, mess up the plate a bit (sure, you know how—Miss Manners saw you hiding your vegetables under your potatoes when you were a mere toddler).
3. If your list of things you don't eat covers most of what is served at a normal meal, then eat before you go. Take a minimum amount for messing up purposes. We don't want to waste food, but we don't want to waste the hosts' energies, either, by making them rush around trying to find something to please you.
4. If you are worried about truly hidden ingredients—ubiquitous foodstuffs that are not easily detected, but to which you have a serious reaction—you are allowed one whispered word to the hosts, or a reminder in advance to those with whom you dine often. Other than that, follow rules one through three.
5. Don't discuss food. (If Miss Manners weren't so polite, she would say, "For heaven's sake, shut up about it.") Nobody is interested in hearing about what you don't eat. Don't announce it, and refuse to be led into any discussions about it. If prodded, just smile happily and decline what is offered, refusing to supply an explanation.

Miss Manners is fighting this battle for the sake of beleaguered hosts, so she feels she can make requests of them, too:

1. Use service that allows people to choose what they want to eat. The most proper dinner service is the formal presentation of a tray or the informal family-style service, in which the host looks inquisitively at the guest he is about to serve, allowing for that person to say, "I prefer dark meat," or "No meat for me, please."
2. Have available generous amounts of the foods most people are likely to eat—salads, vegetables and fruits.
3. Pretend not to notice what your guests are eating. If Miss Manners can get them to be quiet about it, that is the least you can do. It has always been the height of rudeness to monitor what your guests choose to put in their mouths.

Impolite Pressure

DEAR MISS MANNERS,

At the family Easter gathering, once again, my husband and I, who are vegetarians, must endure relatives who lecture, interrogate and plead with us to have a bit of meat or gravy. We became vegetarians for ethical reasons. It is not simply a "diet" that we can "cheat on."

The same people who would never dream of asking a Jewish friend to eat a piece of ham "for a special occasion" will pressure vegetarian guests to try "just a bite" of the Easter ham. We are constantly pressured "to be polite," because Mom worked all day in the kitchen.

When guests stay in a vegetarian home, they often ask the host to prepare them some meat—although they would never ask a Catholic host to prepare a steak during Lent. We do not allow meat in our home, but we have had a weekend house guest insist on bringing meat so he could have bacon and eggs for breakfast and cold cuts for lunch. People who interrogate us about our diets would never quiz an overweight friend. In other words, people act as though our diet is an affectation, rather than a moral choice. We are endlessly questioned by co-workers and clients when we go out for lunch—often crude, silly questions. I do try to be gracious, but I am forever forced to be on the defensive. Help!

GENTLE READER,

Not that she is on the defensive herself, but it worries Miss Manners when people offer examples of rudenesses they claim no one would dream of committing.

Oh, yes, they would. People constantly harangue those they consider to be overweight. If they haven't yet practiced the other rudenesses you use for comparison, it's only because they haven't thought of them.

In any case, this is a good time to learn passive defensiveness. The key is denying people the opportunity to start an argument. Keep saying, "No, thank you," no matter how much wheedling they do. It is perfectly polite, but with repetition—however much is necessary to answer each little affront—it can wear people down:

Oh, come on, just one bite.
No, thank you.
Once won't hurt you.
No, thank you.
Why can't you try some just this once?
No, thank you.
But Mom worked all day.
No, thank you.

Never mind that this statement does not always answer the argument put forth. It is your object to discourage them from questioning your beliefs and practices, and an unrelieved dose of automatic politeness eventually gives people the idea that they are making no progress.

SELF-EXPRESSION: VACUUM

Miss Manners has identified a social blight that is not quite nosiness or meanness, although it has the same appearance and result. She calls it blather. It occurs when people without malicious intent say thoughtless things because, in a situation where they feel they have to say something, they are . . . well, not thinking.

The person who asks you if you have any marriage prospects may not be truly possessed by a desire to know the details of your love life; the question may have been just something that seemed relevant in talking to a single person. The one who observes that you have put on weight and suggests a way of getting it off may not actually be a proselytizer of thinness; it may have just been an observation that came to mind, either on seeing you, or perhaps only because of a weight problem of that person's own. Of course, this blathering is rude, and, intended or not, Miss Manners holds these offenders strictly to account for the etiquette crime of insulting innocent people. Nevertheless, she has hope for improvement. Having come up with a diagnosis, she can now offer a cure.

Blather happens because there seems to be a need to say something. Miss Manners is sorry to report that the first thing that comes to a lot of so-called minds is disastrous (so as not to say stupid). She has a desk full of examples of people who have been hurt by these thoughts. The fact is that there often isn't any need to say anything at all. It is not necessary (read: it is rude) to comment at all on the appearance of strangers, nor on minor alterations in the appearance of acquaintances. Such remarks as "Smile!" or "How much did those new shoes set you back?" only fill a void that was intended to be void. Rather than straining the mind to come up with something fitting, the polite person only needs to consider whether this is a situation in which the mouth can be kept shut and, if not, to reach for the conventional statement and concentrate on delivering it with the appropriate expression.

Street Blather

DEAR MISS MANNERS,

My beautiful daughter, age three, happens to be of a different race than I. Every so often, a stranger will approach us and the following conversation will ensue:

"Is this your daughter?"

"Yes."

"She's Oriental."

So far, I have held my tongue, but I have been tempted to yell, "Oh, my God! She wasn't when we left the house this morning."

Instead, out of respect and concern for my daughter, and not manners, I have quietly said, "Yes, I know." If trapped with the inquisitor, I might add after further questioning that yes, she is adopted. Then the questions become even more ignorant: "Couldn't you have any children of your own? Does she speak English? Does she have your last name? What happened to her 'real' parents?" I suppose these conversations are inevitable. With my daughter's privacy and feelings as the foremost considerations, how do I respond?

Gentle Reader,

Once, it might have been safely assumed that people who inquired, "Is that your daughter?" were planning to continue with, "She's just the most adorable thing I ever saw in my life." That was before the concept of open expression came to confer a false respectability on impertinence.

The streets are no longer safe from rudeness. While Miss Manners agrees that your daughter's privacy and feelings are paramount, you surely want to teach her not to cooperate with strangers. It is best not to answer even a first question from strangers, other than "Am I anywhere near Elm Street?" It's easier to explain a policy of not engaging in conversation on the streets before your daughter has to listen to questions about herself.

You will, of course, do it politely. Whether you are concerned with manners or not, you want your daughter to have the advantage of knowing them. Although you should smile your thanks to anyone who offers a stray compliment, it is not rude to refrain from gossiping with strangers. Simply smile vaguely at the first question, and go back to chatting privately with your daughter, or just look absently elsewhere. If you are in a situation where you do get caught—for example, when the person is not a stranger but an acquaintance—you might say brightly, "Oh, you'll have to wait until she's finished writing her autobiography."

Office Blather

Dear Miss Manners,

Both my boss, the vice president of a bank, and I, her administrative assistant, enjoy fresh flowers and often have arrangements on our desks. My desk is outside of her office in a well-traveled hallway and I have been the recipient of the following questions:

"Who sent these to you?"
"Someone sure thinks you're special, huh?"
"Did you send these to yourself?"
"What's the special occasion?"
"Are they real?"
"Are they yours?"
"Are they your boss's?"
"Did your boss let you keep her flowers on your desk?"

I am dismayed at such personal and illogical questions—who else's flowers would they be, and is it anyone else's business why or from whom I have flowers?

I adopted the tactic of making a series of positive remarks in response to inappropriate questions:

"Aren't they pretty?"
"They certainly do brighten up the area."
"They smell so fresh!"

But I began to feel uneasy about such blatant rudeness in ignoring pointed questions. I have even been forced to explain that I would never answer one man's questions because I did not believe that I would ever feel that it was any of his business. I do not like to be so blunt.

I have considered not having flowers at work, but I don't think that I should be penalized because of the vulgarity of others. Flowers can be such a bright spot in an often humdrum work day. I don't understand why people can't just enjoy them and stay out of my personal business.

Gentle Reader,

Just a minute here. Miss Manners is one of the most stalwart warriors against the forces of nosiness and she will uphold to the death (well, not quite—but at least to the point of risking a headache) your right not to answer intrusive questions. But do you really think that your visitors are burning with curiosity to know the provenance of your flowers?

What you are encountering is a form of social speech Miss Manners has identified as Blather. People engage in blather when they want to say something merely for the sake of sociability and reach for the first thing that comes to mind.

Admittedly, that first thing is usually stupid and invariably obvious. For example, people love to tell the tall that they are tall, and short people that they are short. As soon as they learn someone's occupation, they produce a cliché about it. If a name can possibly be made into a joke, most of the people the bearer of that name meets will make that joke.

These are all etiquette violations and Miss Manners is not excusing them. But they are not the result of evil intentions. The motivation is not to probe, insult or ridicule, but only to start a mild sociable exchange.

Unfortunately, they believe the best method is to say something they fondly conceive to be "original," instead of drawing on the conventional statements etiquette produces for this very purpose—such as "Strange weather we're having for this time of year" or "How you doing?" Thus they manage to be not only spectacularly boring, but often offensive.

All this sounds as if Miss Manners is working her way up to helping you declare war on them. Not a bit. Rather, she is suggesting that once you recognize this for what it is, you will be able to deal with it without rancor. These people are attempting to brighten the hallway with conversation, just as you are brightening it with flowers, only their efforts are dying on the vine.

The non sequiturs you sometimes practice are perfectly polite, provided you deliver them cheerfully. Except under subpoena, no one has to answer a question just because it was asked.

Or you could just develop a standard response ("Actually, they grow here—the vase has a false bottom and the desk hides my garden plot") indicating that you accept their sociability, if not their idea of conversation.

MANNERS ASSERTS ITSELF AND EXPRESSES
ITS TRUE FEELINGS

Watch out. Miss Manners is now going to argue that manners, far from being a weak and optional virtue, much less a nuisance in the way of morality, is the oldest social virtue and an indispensable partner of morality. Rather than being an optional luxury, a sort of a hobby virtue, this is a key virtue—one that can hold its own with the biggies—and civilization's first necessity.

She cannot claim to be the first to offer this argument, just the first to offer it in this century. Throughout recorded history, theologians and philosophers, in both Western and Far Eastern civilizations, have taken etiquette seriously (which is far from the same thing as saying they all behaved well), in the correct belief that manners are a virtue akin to morality. In the 20th century, moral philosophers came to regard manners as a dispensable frill, at best. Even among those who now profess to value civility, it is conceded that the decline of etiquette is a problem to be dealt with only after the entire panoply of serious social problems has been solved.

But what if the decline of etiquette IS one of the most serious social problems, from which other serious social problems devolve? What if the lack of etiquette is not just a modern daily irritant but a flaw that could prove fatal to moral society?

Miss Manners has never understood why two such lovely concepts as morals and manners are considered to be in conflict. Together they preside over the fundamental beliefs and needs that we hold because we are rational agents blessed with practical reason. Morality includes the concept of the sacredness of the person, for example, while manners includes the dignity of the person. So committing murder, which violates the sacredness of the person, is immoral, while causing humiliation, which violates the dignity of the person, is unmannerly. Morals and manners share such concepts as compassion, respect and toleration.

A few of manners' other principles are:

Respect, other than at gun point or for celebrities whose full biographies are not yet known—for example, respect for age, position or simple humanity.

Reticence and Privacy, those twin gateposts preventing the casual offering of and probing for statistics, startling details and complaints.

Modesty, which requires decently covering one's midriff and one's achievements when not among intimates who find them exciting.

Discretion, a warning system to prevent one from doing or saying that which is unnecessarily offensive, on the mere grounds of its being . . . well, offensive.

Where conflicts arise between ethics (which derives its authority from morals) and etiquette (which derives its authority from manners), giving precedence to etiquette may be the more virtuous choice. The likelihood of bringing about a higher good by humiliation and forced confrontational consideration of moral issues is small, while the likelihood that morally righteous rudeness will cause evils that manners seek to forestall is enormous.

Believing in restraint by law alone necessitates redefining simple transgressions of etiquette—insult as slander or libel; meanness as mental cruelty; tobacco smoke and noise as health hazards—so that these will be treated as moral problems and controlled by law. Unfortunately, however, the law does not do a good job of regulating, policing and judging petty disputes, and is seriously overburdened from the attempt. It cannot assert its authority in private life without being ludicrously, and dangerously, intrusive. You can't solve the problem of kids' picking on one another by declaring name-calling defamation of character and cliquishness mental cruelty, and turn their playground disputes over to lawyers. You can't call the police to stop an uncle from lighting up in the living room or a teenager from playing the radio too loud.

Miss Manners wants the niceties of everyday life returned to the rule of etiquette. This is not the same as saying that one should pay less attention to them. On the contrary, it requires elevating the dictates of manners to equal status with the dictates of morals, and considering when they are in conflict.

It would be honest to tell friends how much they have aged since you last saw them, but would it be kind? It would be open not to hide the fact that one cleans one's nose, but could it possibly be unpleasing to others? It would be true to self to tell people how stupid they are, but would it be respectful?

Conflicts may arise not only between morals and manners, but also within etiquette itself: Should patients show respect for their doctor by addressing him or her by title and surname if the doctor is calling them by their first names? Is the doctor doing this because he lacks respect for his patients or because he believes that the manners of personal friendship put patients more at ease? Suppose the patients are offended, rather than put at their ease, by this inequity. Should they ignore it to spare the doctor embarrassment, or object to it on the grounds that they owe this to their own dignity or that they owe it to the doctor to let her or him know that the effect produced is opposite from that intended?

Has a boss who calls women employees "honey" given evidence of evil intent, in which case he should be properly chastised, or is he of good will but ignorant of social conventions? How long after customs have changed is such ignorance excusable?

Complex judgment—wisdom—is required in order to decide on a course of action that best serves the ends of manners, either alone or in connection with morals. Miss Manners never said it was easy to be good. She only promises that when manners are allowed to help morals, instead of being roughly pushed aside when social behavior is being considered, things will get easier.

Enlightening Friends

DEAR MISS MANNERS,

My husband and I hold long-standing philosophical objections to television and to the Disney Corporation, although we do not totally boycott either one. As the parents of a small child, we are bringing him up with minimal exposure to TV, videos or the commoner franchised characters. (Interestingly, he nevertheless recognizes Mickey, Barney and Big Bird.)

Our son is outgoing, active and loves books. In conversation with other parents, I will occasionally make such remarks as "I'm afraid my son doesn't know that show; he doesn't watch TV," or "Actually, we're anti-Disney in our household." These comments often spark defensive or even hostile reactions, and lead to awkward moments.

Is expressing a minority opinion intrinsically rude? Is it impolite of me to make my sentiments known? Believe me, I neither criticize nor attempt to proselytize others. Yet I feel that remaining completely silent implies acceptance of some cultural norms with which I disagree. I compare myself to the vegetarian who, when the subject of hamburgers arises, comments that he doesn't eat red meat.

GENTLE READER,

Without throwing you to the vegetarians, Miss Manners doubts your assumption that anyone's dissension from what you call cultural norms passes without adverse comment these days, no matter how tactfully it is phrased. One way of looking at it is that everyone loves a good philosophical debate. Another is that everyone feels free to comment rudely on other people's habits.

But wait a minute—you are explaining yourself as wanting everyone to know that you dissent from the cultural norms. And since your listeners *are* the cultural norms, what did you expect? Humble thanks?

Miss Manners is delighted to hear that parental restrictions on television-watching have led your son to enjoy reading. There is nothing wrong with discussing your opinions, provided you put forth the topic as a conversation, in which you are interested in hearing other people's views as well as stating your own. The same restriction applies to a discussion of the effect of television on children, or on what television limits parents should set. Merely to mention your principles in passing gives them a tone of "I'm doing the right thing," to which your listeners have no trouble adding the provocative implication of, "and you're not."

Enlightening Family

DEAR MISS MANNERS,

Among the values that my husband and I have made a concerted effort to instill in our four-year-old daughter are an abhorrence of violence and concern for the environment. Occasionally, we have visited friends while their children were watching violent television programs or using products we consider wasteful. My daughter invariably requests, in the presence of other parents, that we rent that video or buy those juice boxes. How do we respond in a way that is consistent with our values, without offending our hosts or sounding self-righteous?

Gentle Reader,

Your concern about sparing your friends' feelings is not only polite but wise. People get a lot of entertainment value out of seeing the self-righteous humbled by their own children.

The response called for here is a firm "We'll discuss that later." Whether or not they agree with your rules, Miss Manners assures you that all the other parents will be in sympathy with your predicament. Two of the points for that discussion, which will take place out of earshot of your friends, should be recognizing that different families make different choices, and refraining from embarrassing parents in front of their friends.

Embarrassing Friends

Dear Miss Manners,

I have a friend of otherwise impeccable taste and tact who persists in carrying her political sentiments on her sleeve, so to speak. The intent is to announce to the world, "I am a good person." (Does this imply that those of us who don't wear buttons are not good persons?) I enjoy her company, but I am embarrassed when she meets me for lunch wearing a large, conspicuous button with the slogan *du jour:* DON'T EAT ANIMALS, WAR IS NOT THE ANSWER, SUPPORT YOUR LOCAL POLICE.

It is beside the point that I may not have agreed with her sentiments, which she has every right to express. But is a social occasion the proper time to express them? In public, she attracts attention and engages in conversations with total strangers who comment (favorably, of course) on the button she is wearing. This turns a pleasant social occasion into a sort of rally. When we went to the theater together, we were surrounded at intermission by quite a circle of playgoers who wanted to endorse her sentiments and congratulate her on her courage for wearing the button in public. (There was also an outer ring of onlookers wearing expressions ranging from curiosity to outrage.)

How does one handle this without alienating a friend? Accept invitations to meet for lunch with a proviso? Would it be appropriate to say, "I'd love to see you—if we can agree not to wear our campaign buttons"?

GENTLE READER,

As much as Miss Manners sympathizes with your distaste for going about town with a walking billboard, regardless of the sentiments posted on it, she despairs of being able to make your friend understand why. Attempting to do so will only result in an outrage based on the erroneous conviction that it is her politics that offend you. The likelihood of your friendship surviving that is small.

Entertaining a valued friend of embarrassing public habits is best done in private. If she questions why you prefer not to meet her in public, you might gently say that you do not wish to share her attention with her many admirers while she is out politicking.

Being Politely Political

DEAR MISS MANNERS,

When sitting next to a known fascist, does one have to make polite conversation? I was eating dinner in a university cafeteria with some people who live in my dorm. One of them invited his acquaintance to eat with us. This new guy is an infamous campus figure with professed homophobic and fascist views. He sat down next to me.

I made polite conversation so as not to insult him or my friend or embarrass myself. My roommate, who was also at the table, thinks it was "morally reprehensible" to even acknowledge the politico's presence. When I said that ignoring him would have been rude, my roommate replied that in cases like this, politeness takes a backseat to integrity. The politico's views disgust me, but I feel that ignoring him would serve no purpose.

GENTLE READER,

One does not have to choose between being polite and being political. You can meet the minimum requirements for politeness without chatting up someone of whom you disapprove as if you were charmed by him.

As the person in question has publicly identified himself with views you find highly offensive, he knows that he has acquired political enemies. At the same time, Miss Manners presumes that he is not such an example of evil incarnate that civilized people would cut him rather than acknowledge his humanity.

The correct posture for such a situation is coolness. You do not ignore him, but you nod unsmilingly as a greeting, pass the salt when asked, and murmur a noncommittal "Ummmm" before turning away if he tries to open a conversation. Miss Manners is trusting you not to abuse this technique. She would prefer to have students argue their differences in a polite and restrained fashion, instead of treating one another as permanently embodying a particular view.

Being Politically Impolite

DEAR MISS MANNERS,

My best friend was one of a five percent minority who objected to a decision by an organization of which my husband and I are also members. She was incensed that we did not share her views, and she unsuccessfully campaigned to force the governing board to resign.

MANCHESTER, N.H.—Following a polite one-hour public dialogue with the President, the Speaker of the House of Representatives was forced to defend himself against charges from fellow conservatives that he had been too cordial to the more liberal President, behaving, as one newspaper editorial put it, like "a shaggy lap dog grateful for the privilege of being in his master's presence."

"Conciliation in tone is not the same as compromise in principle," the Speaker told the *Washington Post*.

She now refuses to speak to me. I had tried to reconcile our differences both in person and by letter, but she adamantly refused to consider an opinion that differed from her own. She turns her back whenever she sees me, if she possibly can. When I approach a group where she is standing and exchange pleasantries with others, she stares through me as though I didn't exist. If I address her by name, she ignores me. This is embarrassing not only to me, but to those who observe her behavior.

It is impossible for me to avoid her completely. We have many mutual friends and share many social and community activities. What is protocol when someone won't return your greeting? Do I continue to speak to The Wall, or do I ignore her presence whenever I greet others? I do not wish to be perceived as refusing to speak to her. Frankly, I thought this behavior existed only in third rate novels, but I assure you this is real life.

GENTLE READER,

Miss Manners hopes your friend is not planning a career in politics. Holding public grudges is the worst possible way to persuade people to be on your side, no matter what their views. Even people who previously agreed on an issue have been known to switch to avoid being on the same side with such a person.

You therefore want to make sure people do not think that you behave that way. If you also cease speaking, they will soon forget who started the feud and assume that you are equally responsible. It would be within the realm of correctness to cease speaking to someone who has behaved vilely toward you, but Miss Manners does not advise it. Try to make a point of greeting her by name, whether or not she replies. If there are awkward silences, you can say gently, "I'm so sorry you're still angry that I disagreed with you on the zoning vote."

Being Rudely Provoked

DEAR MISS MANNERS,

I am vehemently opposed to the wearing of fur, the fur industry, trapping, etc. I have supported groups who share my view by contributing funds and long hours of volunteer work. Two of my sisters-in-law received fur coats as holiday gifts. We socialize together quite a bit, and in all honesty and integrity, I cannot congratulate or praise their newly acquired attire. I can't be hypocritical and yet I don't want to offend. What can I say to them when we are together?

GENTLE READER,

Miss Manners so much admires your restraint in not wishing to make your principles into an annoyance to others that she is delighted to be able to release you from your etiquette qualms. Contrary to popular opinion, it is by no means obligatory to admire the expensive acquisitions of others. Although occasional compliments are pleasant, it strikes Miss Manners that there is altogether too much social notice being given to other people's dry goods.

For you to pretend to admire fur coats would be ludicrous. The greatest kindness you can do your sisters-in-law is to say nothing. Should they be so foolish as to prompt you for an opinion, Miss Manners would think you more than justified in saying quietly, "You know I can't approve."

Being Confused

DEAR MISS MANNERS,

I do not wear fur. In fact, I am a strict vegetarian and also deeply concerned about wildlife. So I do not use "exotic" accessories, like snakeskin or alligator, nor do I wear ordinary cowhide-type leathers, as they are by-products of the meat industry. My husband shares my views and habits.

I currently use an elegant embroidered shawl as an evening wrap, but that just won't do in the cold climate to which we are moving. Could Miss Manners please make some suggestions for appropriate formal wraps and accessories for people who might be concerned about the use of animal products? Please understand that I am not asking for advice on fashion trends. But for example, what would be more appropriate for a formal dinner or party—a fake fur, or an elegant velvet cape? Are elegant fabric purses acceptable for evening wear? What about tasteful fabric pumps?

"Resentment, testiness, and rudeness have become so pervasive that they have even soured discourse among political allies," the *New York Times* reported in a story with the headline: "Government Service Gets Nasty."

GENTLE READER,

You may be sure that Miss Manners is not the place to go for trendiness. She can tell you with tremendous authority that a velvet cape is highly proper for evening wear, and so are fabric evening shoes and bags, while cow-hide or reptile accessories are actually traditionally incorrect with evening clothes. She hastens to assure you that these rules were not, as you are, motivated by principle. Or rather that the principle involved is that one really must change one's things for evening, right down to the tippy-toes. This is why the leather goods that are proper during daytime are not so at night.

Both your principles and Miss Manners', since you kindly asked about them, should prevent you from wearing fake fur. Etiquette frowns on passing anything off as something it is not, preferring the less pretentious and real to the ersatz luxury item. The concept that it is wrong to use animal products but right to pretend to do so is one that leaves Miss Manners morally baffled.

The Mannerly Expression of Morality

DEAR MISS MANNERS,

I've heard that more unborn babies were killed in abortions than people in the Civil Revolutionary, and also the World Wars I & II. Isn't that awful? Even though I'm only in ninth grade, I'm all against abortion. I even want to have six kids when I grow up! Our class will have to watch an abortion on T.V. this year. I'm all against abortion. I know some people won't agree with me, but I'm really strong on this opinion. How can I say this without getting a mortal enemy?

GENTLE READER,

By treating with respect those who disagree with you, and presenting your argument calmly and politely. Of course, this would make you one of the few people of any age and on either side of this issue who aren't just hurling insults, or worse. But as none of them is convincing anybody who didn't already agree, theirs is not a method worth emulating.

Miss Manners doesn't care for your school's method, either. Requiring ninth graders to watch a televised abortion is not an appeal to examine their moral sense, but a way of shocking them instead of making them think. Were you required to watch a birth, you might be equally horrified by the idea of having children. If the school is trying to teach you to be moral, it should train your mind, not play on your unexamined emotions. (It might also clear up that matter of the Civil Revolutionary for you.) You will need a sharp mind to deal with those six children.

Whether abortion should be legally permitted is an issue on which deeply moral people can strongly disagree. Miss Manners doesn't want to frame your argument for you, but it seems to her that the key question is whether humanity begins at conception or at birth. If you believe it begins at conception, you can maintain that the state has the right to protect a person's life. You must also recognize that those who disagree with you, and believe that humanity begins at birth, can then maintain that the state has no right to interfere with a woman's decision about whether to have a child.

The Mannerly Expression of Immorality

DEAR MISS MANNERS,

Although this question is purely hypothetical, I have been troubled about it for years. If a lady or gentleman were a bank robber, should he or she use conventions of etiquette such as "please" and "thank you" in plying his or her trade? I hope no one will need this information, but for the sake of curiosity, I must ask.

GENTLE READER,

All right, all right, Miss Manners believes you. She thinks. The fact that she gripped her hand over the clasp of her pocketbook when you approached is purely coincidental.

If your question is whether politeness would help a bank robber advance in his or her profession, the answer is probably no (although it might well be of assistance to a jewel thief, embezzler or anyone else whose doings are made easier by charm and trust). As far as conveying deference is concerned, there is just not that much difference between "Stick 'em up" and "Stick 'em up, please."

The more interesting question, which is the one Miss Manners hopes you are asking, is whether a person who has no morals should also do without manners for the sake of some kind of pseudo-honorable consistency. Because astute people have noticed that a person can have manners without having morals, they condemn manners for being misleading.

It is also, of course, possible to have morals without manners. We have quite a few people like that nowadays, who go around rudely making other people feel terrible for not measuring up to their standards, in everything from body weight to what they consider moral weightiness.

Obviously, it is better to have both morals and manners. Miss Manners does not deny that morality is the more serious requirement, but wishes to point out that the two are related. The chief premise of manners is a readiness to temper one's selfish wishes for the communal good, which is not a bad place to start building morality. So the worst case is to have neither manners nor morals. A bank robber who follows the forms of consideration toward others may, sooner or later, come to understand that robbing banks is a violation of that principle.

THE FIFTH FREEDOM:
FREEDOM FROM ETIQUETTE

*N*obody ever picks Miss Manners to play Miss Liberty on the Fourth of July. It is apparently not obvious that someone who spends her life telling others how to behave is the very personification of freedom.

Naturally, she does not define freedom as including the right to disagree with her. Aside from that small restriction, however, Miss Manners advocates a system—the regulation of everyday life by the rules of etiquette—that she believes offers more freedom than any other we have tried.

The entire society, she is well aware, has been galloping in the opposite direction. In private life, the practices of etiquette have been increasingly abandoned. In public life, rules that were taken for granted as the proper way to behave in such institutions as schools, legislatures or theaters are being challenged. Most people concede that we cannot have total freedom because the more ghastly crimes have to be forbidden by law. But to throw off the yoke of mere etiquette—*there's* an exhilarating prospect. Just think:

Not to have to show respect, whether for peers, elders, umpires or civic officials, when it is not felt.

Not to have to dress up to meet anybody else's expectations—a boss's, a host's, or other people's—at religious or ceremonial occasions, if one doesn't feel like it.

Not to have to shut up just because a class is being conducted or a movie is being shown.

Not to have to refrain from chewing gum or listening to music or using dirty words or smoking because someone claims to be annoyed by it.

Not to . . .

Wait a second. Smoking?

Miss Manners threw that one in to see if anyone would screech to a halt. Far from tolerating lapses of smoking etiquette, the society has slammed down the heavy hand of the law to stub out smoking.

The one about watching movies quietly shouldn't have slipped by either. Miss Manners has noticed that the staunchest advocates of killing off etiquette in the name of freedom turn vicious when other people's etiquette-free behavior takes place during their own favorite entertainment—movie, concert or ball game. Ask them if they don't want a law passed against coughing at concerts or male shirtlessness in stadiums. The only people who will demur, other than the offenders, will be the ones who would prefer to have offenders shot on the spot.

There does seem to be this small problem with all that wonderful freedom. Exercising it goads other people into a frenzy if it interferes with their self-respect or their comfort or their favorite activities. So they turn around and smash the offenders, or they pass new laws against behavior that annoys them. One way or the other, the whole mess ends up in the legal system. Miss Manners ought to be relieved. When the law goes on duty to handle day-to-day conflicts, she can go off duty. The law can compel where Miss Manners can only wheedle. It can mete out punishments that make more of an impression than etiquette's severest frown of disapproval.

But weren't we talking about achieving more freedom rather than less? Unless people follow the rules that prevent society-wide irritation and the sabotage of its institutions, they will—as is already happening—see the law take etiquette's place.

A less harsh but still etiquette-free approach—namely, that bad behavior is only a symptom of personal unhappiness and that, therefore, relieving unhappiness would solve the problem of achieving an orderly yet free society more effectively than will punishing offenders—is waning in popularity. Miss Manners would have been satisfied if that had worked—she is all in favor of society's relieving unhappiness. It's just that no one who has done etiquette field work could believe this is a solution to the crisis. If happiness ensured, or even inspired, consideration of others, bridal couples would be frantic worrying whether their wedding plans will please their guests, rather than whether their dearest friends are going to ante up what they want in the way of wedding presents.

By pointing out that etiquette cannot be enforced, but arguing that if it is not obeyed, someone will call the police, Miss Manners realizes she opens herself to that frighteningly simple question: What's the difference? The difference is that minimizing and resolving problems through law, rather than through etiquette, has its cost in money, time, money, public resources, money, social atmosphere and money. It requires expending the energies of hordes of people, from police to juries, to settle trivial matters. Even then, it exacerbates anger by giving formal attention and dignity to petty differences.

The conventional expression of sympathy for misfortune has already changed, Miss Manners has noticed. In more innocent days, if you stumbled or spilled something all over yourself, kindly onlookers used to ask, "Are you all right?" Now it's "Aren't you going to sue?" The only painful accident Miss Manners can think of that no one has yet suggested as the basis for a lawsuit is biting one's own tongue, and then only because of the disadvantages of testifying against oneself, especially when it hurts.

Under the reign of etiquette, people are responsible for policing themselves just enough to make life bearable for others. Etiquette rules, being more flexible and less cumbersome than law, allow for more actual freedom. So you see, Miss Manners IS in favor of freedom. Most dictators are, provided they get to define freedom, with no back talk.

Back Talk

DEAR MISS MANNERS,

I have to say that I find your position on manners, specifically politeness, to be narrow-minded and absurd. How can you expect everyone on earth to conform to your views on etiquette? Why should we? Why should we have to alter our personalities and our behavior to suit you? You are just one person and I don't believe that the rest of us should have to value your opinions any more than our own.

GENTLE READER,

Oh, stop flattering Miss Manners. You'll spoil her. Only in her dreams could she make anyone, let alone everyone, conform to her personal views. Not that it wouldn't make for a better world if they did.

What she actually does is to teach, cite and encourage the society's own concept of behavior—the respect and consideration that all of you agree everyone else ought to exhibit toward you, but that you ought to be free from having to exhibit to those pesky other people. The rules and patterns by which these concepts are expressed have been slowly developed until they may be considered our folkloric tradition, although they keep changing to meet changing social conditions. Miss Manners has undertaken the mission of sorting this all out and assisting people to apply it fairly. Isn't this a noble thing to do? Wouldn't you rather help out than snarl?

FREEDOM THROUGH ETIQUETTE

Does everyone except Miss Manners believe that we must choose between a free society and a livable one? That the only way to preserve human rights is to give up on humane behavior? Miss Manners sadly holds that this amounts to an admission that to achieve freedom, we have to renounce civilization.

BROOKLYN, N.Y.—A youth was shot to death in an argument that began when he "dissed"— showed disrespect for—another boy by refusing to slap hands in a high five, police told the *New York Times.*

Yet Miss Manners hears people on both sides of current issues of behavior arguing from this assumption. Whenever the flaunting of obscenity, bigotry and personal or symbolic disrespect (such as flag-burning) is discussed, it is with the underlying presumption that there ought to be nothing whatsoever to restrain any individual's impulsive acts, no matter how damaging or outrageous they may be, other than the full force of the law. Nobody seems to question this; at issue is only whether we ought to try to outlaw all behavior we don't like, or to tolerate a daily dosage of disgust.

"Lock 'em up," says one side.

"Let 'em sue," says the other.

This is not a proper choice. We seem to have a national crisis that calls for— Miss Manners!

Miss Manners starts from the assumption that everyone wants to get through the day without being too seriously affronted. When she says everyone, she includes those whose chief goal in life is to offend others, because it is impossible to be outrageous unless there is a minimal expectation of civility to violate. You can't shock someone who doesn't have any standards. Yet she also assumes that every American recoils from the idea of compromising freedom of speech and other liberties. Even people driven to distraction when others exercise their rights don't want to give up their own. They just want their own standards, which they choose in freedom, to be universally compulsory.

The difference between Miss Manners and all these other people who want it both ways is that she knows a system for restraining offensive behavior that does not interfere with our Constitutional rights, because it is not a part of our legal system. What ought to stop people from shouting epithets, flaunting obscenity, desecrating national symbols and otherwise upsetting their fellow citizens is etiquette.

True, it doesn't always work. Even Miss Manners has noticed that—especially Miss Manners, in fact. Being a voluntary system, etiquette cannot, by definition, be forced upon others, which is why Miss Manners is pleading for reason instead. She would appreciate her fellow citizens' help, although not by the methods they usually use. Miss Manners sometimes despairs of achieving a better world, because such nastiness is so often the first thought of those who profess to be on the side of manners.

The approved methods for enforcing etiquette are:

Self-restraint. You do not have to do everything disagreeable that you have a right to do. Nor do you have to bring everything you do to public attention. Controlling yourself to avoid causing unnecessary jolts to others is the trade-off we make to live in communities.

Child-rearing. Contrary to the theory behind the great experiment of the last few decades, allowing children to rely totally on their own judgment or that of their peers has not resulted in the children's becoming happy and/or artistic. Kindly discipline seems to be as necessary for happiness as it is for creativity.

House rules. Athletics seems to be the only remaining area in which it is taken for granted that anyone who wants to play the game must abide by the rules—although the sports news is beginning to make Miss Manners worry that things may be slipping here, too. The fact is that you cannot run anything—a class, a dinner party, a town meeting, a club, a household, a ceremony, a courtship—unless everyone involved agrees to abide by certain standards of behavior, and those who do not accept the terms are banned.

Social consequences. Much as Miss Manners admires tolerance, the effort to show people who outrage society that society is unshockable and uninsultable has gone too far. In the public arena, miscreants should not be protected from reasonable social disapproval.

Bringing in the Law

DEAR MISS MANNERS,

Last June, we received a four-page typed "pre-invitation" to a friend's second wedding ceremony. The length and advance notice, with information about hotel accommodations, golfing and wine country tours, were a courtesy to out-of-town guests. We sent in our acceptance on time.

Later that summer, we spent a day with the gentleman's children and his ex-wife, whose second wedding we had also attended. We were friends of hers since before her first marriage, and our children get along famously. I left a message on the gentleman's answering machine, saying that we had just seen his children, and telling him how much we enjoyed them. I presumed he would be pleased. I also complimented his "pre-invitation" (it was humorously done) and told him we were looking forward to meeting his new wife.

Within a few days, my husband received a phone call at work un-inviting us to his wedding. Upon the advice of his lawyer (!), he had stated, it was inadvisable to have anyone there who still had contact with his ex-wife. He ended the conversation with the hope that this would not affect our friendship. I believe the divorced couple was having child support disputes. Did the intended couple think we were going to spy on their financial resources? I consider the reneging of the wedding invitation most rude and tacky.

GENTLE READER,

Please do not attempt to talk to your friend about this directly. You don't know what kind of trouble you could stumble into from attempting to conduct a friendship without professional advice. What were you thinking? As your etiquette adviser, Miss Manners will inform his lawyer that you have been advised to award his former wife exclusive custody of your friendship.

WHO (BESIDES MISS MANNERS) CARES ABOUT ETIQUETTE?

One of the leading causes of modern crime, Miss Manners gathers from paying attention to the news reports, is senselessness. "Another senseless shooting," they keep announcing. "A senseless stabbing . . . a senseless murder . . ." We used to have such sensible crime. Miss Manners can't help wondering what went wrong.

Sensible crimes were ones committed for love or money. When neither revenge nor revenue is involved, modern crime naturally strikes people as unreasonable. However, Miss Manners has also been paying attention to what the criminals themselves give as their motivations, and they make a certain deplorable sense to her. People are now killing over—you're going to have a hard time believing this one—etiquette.

One of the leading causes of murder is a perceived lack of respect. Respect is a basic concept of manners, an institution that features such principles as dignity and compassion, rather than strict justice, which it leaves to the law. Being treated respectfully is not one of our Constitutional rights, nor is treating others respectfully a legal obligation. Only manners require it. Yet dissin'—showing real or apparent disrespect—is cited as the motive in an amazing number of murders. As a Washington, D.C., high school football player said when discussing the shooting toll among members of his team for a single summer—one dead, three wounded—"the biggest thing everybody is looking for is respect in the streets. It isn't money. They are just trying to make sure you respect them. People are just pushing each other to the maximum to get respect. And the maximum is death."

Remember what all those 18th century Frenchmen in lace cuffs did when they got fussed about people looking at them cross-eyed? The chief difference with today's custom is that the duel, like air travel, has dispensed with the frills. There are no more gloves, seconds or instructions about when to shoot. In keeping with modern practicality, the idea caught on that it is more effective to shoot when your opponent isn't looking. Yet everybody claims that etiquette is irrelevant to the serious problems of modern society. (Small pause while Miss Manners sighs.)

All right, let us continue. Failure to provide road courtesies is given as the motivating incident in accounts of the contemporary sport of car-to-car shootings. Law is supposed to regulate the highway, but traffic law does not mandate such courtesies as letting others pass, not playing a car radio so loudly that it frazzles people in other cars, and not observing the speed limit in a fast lane. So highway assassins explain themselves, in terms somewhat more forceful than Miss Manners might use, as teachers of Drivers' Etq.

Another believer in manners was caught running around midtown Manhattan stabbing people. In itself, this action was not startling; what attracted attention was that he was not robbing anybody. New Yorkers, who thought they'd seen everything, were flabbergasted. He eventually explained to police that he was punishing people who had bumped into him on crowded sidewalks and failed to say "Excuse me."

In a posh suburb, two men broke into a checkout line at a grocery store, not to hold up the store, but just to get their potato chips and soapsuds lawfully checked out. Unlike the rest of us, who have nothing better to do all day than wait in line, they were in a hurry. Although fairness is a concept that manners shares with law, only etiquette requires it in such informal situations as waiting in line: *First come, first served* is only a rule of etiquette. The other people in this line wished to uphold this etiquette rule. Again, somebody ended up getting stabbed.

WASHINGTON, D.C.—A cycle of violence and death was touched off when a gang member who "didn't like the way [a] rival gang member was looking at him" and later may have shot at him, ended up being killed himself, shot execution style in a car stopped at a red light, the *Washington Post* reported.

"If you dis' someone and make him look bad in front of his crew, he's got to take some kind of action to show his people he's not a punk," a detective who tracks street gangs told the *Post*.

Two brothers in Queens, both New York City policemen, got into an argument over the arrangements for one brother's wedding, at which the other was supposed to be best man. The best man offered to withdraw from the ceremony, and in return, the bridegroom offered to punch him. Noticing that he had a gun in his waistband, the bridegroom offered the taunt, "Go ahead, shoot me!" which, in fact, the best man did. The wedding was called off.

Three little boys in High Bridge, New Jersey—two thirteen-year-olds and an eleven-year-old—got into an argument, and one of the older boys demanded that the other apologize to the younger boy, which the offender did. However, the eleven-year-old refused to accept the apology, even when the peacemaker said he must do so or die. He died. The peacemaker shot and killed him.

These stories were on the front pages of newspapers. This sort of thing is going on every day, as the Gentle Reader will see from the accounts provided throughout this book, all gleaned from newspaper reports. People are stabbing and shooting and beating up one another and running cars off the road in the hope of—as they sometimes even put it—"teaching them some manners." Which, of course, makes it sound as if they work for Miss Manners.

It is true that when you stab rude people often enough, they tend not to misbehave again. Nevertheless, rude retaliation is not a response of which she approves. It does not accomplish her objective—which they all also state as their own objective—of lessening the amount of rudeness in the world.

Miss Manners wants it noted that she makes a strict division between the jurisdictions of law and of etiquette. Crime is not merely lethal rudeness. Without even squabbling, she and Miss Justice have managed to divide the task of regulating social behavior, so that tough Miss Justice, with her fierce sanctions, agrees to punish behavior that is seriously threatening to life, limb or property, while gentle Miss Manners tries to persuade people to avoid the kind of behavior that leads to such unpleasantness, and to settle things politely when it does.

It is always a humiliating defeat for her when people so consistently refuse to curb their rudeness that the law has to take over matters that used to be under the jurisdiction of manners, such as smoking and, Miss Manners blushes to say, sex. Asking the law to regulate what ought to be private conduct runs the risk of its trespassing on our basic rights—yet allowing individual impulses to go totally unrestrained leads to mayhem.

Her point about etiquette-motivated crime is that when there is no recognition of the need to observe courtesies, everyone finds life unbearable. And speaking of unbearable behavior that pushes people to the brink—please stop telling Miss Manners that no one else cares about etiquette anymore. Outlaws will not stand for rudeness.

The Natural Reaction

DEAR MISS MANNERS,

Even as I write this, I am listening to the melodic litany of complaints of an alarm on a car parked a few blocks away. Each time a bus, truck or motorcycle passes, the alarm sounds anew. This has gone on for two hours now. I've heard alarms for nine hours while suburbanites park in front of my building and ride mass transit to work. I've listened into the wee hours, when late night revelers are ensconced in some jazz club or restaurant, to some boor's car alarm screaming at every vibration of traffic.

I've considered demolishing the vehicle with a baseball bat, calling the police, paying thieves to remove it to a chop shop, or leaving a note on the windshield. I am at my wit's end! What do you suggest?

GENTLE READER,

Suggestion number one: It is indeed a good idea to reject responding to irritation with violence. This does not help to promote the quiet for which you yearn, although a great many people seem to think otherwise.

Suggestion number two: Take a look at the irrationality by which you have managed to turn a noise problem into an etiquette problem. "Revelers," "boors," even—heaven help us—"suburbanites" are malevolently wrecking your sleep while they callously indulge themselves in round-the-clock sensuality. Such wantonness must surely be punished.

Miss Manners hates to interrupt this exciting fantasy, but she asks you to consider that people might have alarms on their cars because they are afraid of their cars' being stolen. Suppose, further, that the alarms are set off because, in fact, there are thieves trying to steal those cars. While you're at it, you might even suppose that those people have come to your neighborhood in the middle of the night to attend to their elderly parents (who are succumbing to hysteria brought on by the noise, but we'll get back to that).

SEAT PLEASANT, MD.—An eighteen-year-old woman was shot and killed during a traffic dispute. The incident was sparked when a Jeep cut off her car and the occupants of the two vehicles began to argue, Prince Georges County police told the *Washington Post*.

Suggestion number three: In the light of these possibilities, examine the problem again. Is it that the car alarms are badly constructed so that they are set off by normal and legal street activity? Are there indeed multiple attempted robberies that are being thwarted by the alarms? Are the police ignoring either the thieves or the alarms (which probably violate noise ordinances)?

You have a civic problem here of no mean proportions. Miss Manners is sorry she cannot solve it for you, but can only recommend that you take the methods legally available to injured citizens. She can also save you from the additional problems that result from the line of thought you had been pursuing. The noises from which you suffer are unquestionably infuriating. What is worse is the number of people now wired to go off without warning.

The Idealist's Reaction

DEAR MISS MANNERS,

I was participating in a peace demonstration when a filthily attired older man and his three friends began harassing me. After several minutes, the man told me to begin supporting the war movement, "or I will stop treating you like a lady." He proffered his fists and then stuck his index finger in front of my nose.

After a moment's reflection, I arched my eyebrows, looked him directly in the eye and said, in my most menacing tone, "How dare you threaten me? Who do you think you are?" Apparently stunned, he backed off, and the four of them left, shouting comments again—only when they were far enough away that I could easily ignore them. While this approach succeeded in avoiding a physically violent conflict, it did leave me itching to point out that:

1. Not beating someone up is hardly considered a luxury in polite society.
2. If his original behavior indicated some type of special treatment for "ladies," he certainly did not have a very humane view of women.

Considering the context of such verbal conflicts, is it best to ignore discussion of these factors, or are they adequately conveyed by taking offense at the instigator's words? I have been trained in the martial arts and anticipate that I could easily physically subdue such a man if the need arose.

GENTLE READER,

Congratulations, but (aside from the fact that there were four of them) Miss Manners thought you were against settling conflicts violently. Isn't that why you were out marching?

That your attackers declared themselves authorities on judging proper ladylike behavior ought to have raised some doubts in your mind about the usefulness of engaging them in a discussion of manners. Miss Manners should hardly have to point out to you that they were no gentlemen. Why do you now wonder whether you should have debated them—or fought them? It seems to Miss Manners that you behaved like a perfect lady—a perfectly justifiably outraged lady. What is more, it worked. You sent them packing. Had you been less confident of your physical superiority, it would also have been ladylike to walk away without a word.

The shouts-from-a-safe-distance were a pathetic attempt to cover their shame-facedness at the very proper dressing-down you gave them. Miss Manners congratu-lates you on using ladylike behavior in place of violence, and urges you not to have regrets about your success.

The Driver's Reaction

DEAR MISS MANNERS,

While I was driving to work the other day, I glanced at my clock and realized that I had to get across town in under five minutes. The woman in front of me was driving incredibly slow, so I passed her up. As I did, I noticed she raised her middle finger at me. I somehow guessed that this was not a polite gesture. Was I wrong to pass this person? I had to get to work! I got there 30 seconds early, but if I hadn't passed her, I surely would have been late.

GENTLE READER,

Oh, you were in a hurry, were you? It's so annoying that all those other people clutter things up just at rush hour. A lady in labor may assume that her need to get through is more acute than the average motorist's, but it is not clear to Miss Manners how you arrived at the conclusion that your need to get to work took precedence over everyone else's.

That is not to say that one car cannot courteously pass another. It is part of road etiquette that motorists should make it convenient for one another to travel at a rea-sonable range of speeds. Whether you passed the other car courteously or not, Miss Manners is unable to judge from this distance. But the reaction of the other driver is not difficult for her to judge. As you correctly assume, the gesture she performed is not a polite one under any circumstances.

The Driver's Reaction (Boston)

DEAR MISS MANNERS,

Is it ever appropriate to give someone the finger, particularly when driving? I live in Boston.

GENTLE READER,

Certainly not, what are you thinking, goodness gracious— Oh. You live in Boston, do you? Miss Manners remembers glimpsing you and your fellow sportsmen out her carriage window. It was not a pretty sight. Insulting people in the streets is neither a proper nor a sensible sport, even in Boston.

VALLEJO, CALIF.—A driver was shot and paralyzed after he accidentally cut off another driver. The wounded man told police that the shooter was visibly angered by being cut off, pulled alongside him on Interstate 80 and opened fire, the *San Francisco Chronicle* reported.

WHO (BESIDES MISS MANNERS) DESERVES RESPECT?

DEAR MISS MANNERS,

Everyone wants "respect." The panhandler on the street wants it. The young person alienated from parents wants "respect." The minority populations want "respect." How do we interpret this intangible demand? My dictionary says "a gesture of esteem." Should it be freely given? Does it become commonplace, like "Have a nice day?"

GENTLE READER,

Would that it were commonplace. Contrary to what you who disdain "Have a nice day" seem to believe, there are worse things loose in the world than the habit of issuing conventional pleasantries. You might try listening to some of the unpleasantries people are in the habit of issuing right and left.

PRINCE WILLIAM COUNTY, VA.—A man was shot in the neck by a passing motorist during a tailgating altercation on Interstate 95, the *Washington Post* reported.

Respect is due to all human beings just for being human beings. On top of that, there are certain categories for which extra respect is required—the elderly, one's parents, that whole slew of relatives including the crotchety ones, members of the clergy, holders of high public office, and one's teachers, bosses and superior officers. Did Miss Manners overlook anyone? Rock stars? People who are bigger than we are?

Anyway, you see the point about categories. You, who have the acumen to notice that conventionalities lack originality, have also doubtless spotted a flaw here. There may be people in any of these categories who do not exhibit admirable behavior. Miss Manners has heard all about your aunt who makes such awful remarks about everyone, your congressman who distinguished himself in such an unusual way, and all those other unsavories whom you have had the misfortune to encounter.

NORTHERN VIRGINIA—State police received 46 reports of shootings by motorists in less than a year, most the result of rude driving such as going too slowly or tailgating. Police said one woman, who was trying to exit off Interstate 95, was shot at after she failed to move over to allow an impatient driver to pass her.

How to resolve this contradiction? Well, Miss Manners does excuse you for withdrawing respect from those who have committed heinous crimes. Otherwise, we separate basic respect from respect for a particular individual, the admiration that your dictionary means by esteem. Although you can respect an individual for his or her achievements, you may also withhold the admiring kind of respect while delivering the kind due to the person's age or position. That is what is meant when people say (as they do, alas, only too often, when given the occasion), "I respect the office, but not the man."

Panhandlers, young people and members of minorities (or majorities) are indeed due respect as human beings. This includes treating them with courtesy and dignity, whether or not you like them personally or wish to accede to their requests. If they get old or appointed to the Supreme Court or you go to work for them or they adopt you, they qualify for another dose of etiquette, mainly concerned with forms of address and precedence. Whether they win your respectful admiration on top of that is a matter entirely within your giving.

WHO (BESIDES MISS MANNERS) PRACTICES ETIQUETTE?

A funny thing happened to Miss Manners just as she was about to declare that this society has gotten to the point where any infraction of courtesy, no matter how slight, is presumed to be viciously intended provocation, requiring belligerent retaliation. There seem to be no more presumed accidents, accorded the benefit of the doubt. A small misstep is always interpreted as a purposeful attempt to take advantage of others. When one person in a crowd bumped into another, the traditional remark used to be "Excuse me," and the response a forgiving smile. Now the obligatory exchange seems to be "Watch where you're going!" which is as likely to come from the bumper, so to speak, as from the bumpee, and the response a snarled "*You* watch where *you're* going."

The funny thing that happened to Miss Manners, perhaps not a scream at the time, was what we still call an accident because it happened on the highway. It was a minor accident, one car bumping into another with no serious damage, but it nevertheless heralded all sorts of inconvenience and delays while the police were fetched, information exchanged, and damage assessed. This is not the sort of situation designed to foster tolerance and patience.

NEW YORK, N.Y.—A driver was shot five times and killed after he chased down a car that had cut him off while changing lanes. The angry driver had followed the offending car, pulled in front of it and forced it to stop in the left lane of the Harlem River Drive, police told the *New York Times*. Drivers and passengers then got out of both cars, argued and shots were fired, killing the man.

The driver of the automobile Miss Manners occupied immediately, and correctly, assumed full blame. When he emerged from the car to meet the innocent driver, who turned out to be a young man apparently just out of college, Miss Manners would have predicted one of the following greetings:

"You ought to be locked up, not let loose on the road."
"Believe me, you're going to pay for this."
"Okay, let's have your license—if they were dumb enough to give you one.
And did you find an insurance company dumb enough to insure you?"

Actually, those are cleaned-up versions of what Miss Manners expected. Intervehicular communication is not conspicuously polite these days, under the best of circumstances. Instead, when the two drivers emerged from their cars, the innocent one, as well as the guilty one, opened with an urgent inquiry about the other driver's welfare and that of the passenger (who has the honor of telling you this story). Reassured on that point, the young gentleman seemed to look as sympathetically at the state of the offending automobile as at his own. During the exchange of information and the division of chores, he remained calm and helpful. Not once did he allow himself to express blame or irritation. Miss Manners wished she had had an etiquette medal to award on the spot.

In addition to the sheer gladdening of her heart, not a common result of an automobile accident, Miss Manners was gratified by the practical results of this unusual behavior. A difficult hour was passed as pleasantly as possible under the circumstances. Had the gentleman who caused the accident not already assumed full responsibility (Miss Manners only travels with perfect gentlemen), the desire to offer generous compensation would have been inspired by the obvious generosity of the victim. It would have been a literal example of politeness paying off.

Recriminations left unspoken are stronger than those expressed. While it is understandable (but not forgivable) that those who have suffered wish to inflict suffering in return, they might note that kindness is equally contagious. Snapping at people, whether or not it is justified, does not inspire courtesy.

The incident left Miss Manners with little heart for complaining about how strangers treat one another, although she has countless counter-examples of trivial daily accidents. In some regions, people even pride themselves on their rudeness level, taking it as evidence of sophistication and explaining it as a natural reaction to crowding. Well, then, Miss Manners reflects, the height of sophistication must be toddlers in a small sandbox, banging one another with their little shovels. True sophistication is understanding that crowded conditions require the restraint of etiquette as a buffer—more, not less, than comfortable ones.

TORT REFORM THROUGH ETIQUETTE

In accounts of lawsuits, those involving ghastly crimes as well as those that may seem (to uninjured parties) petty, Miss Manners keeps seeing the same curious word— *Apology.*

> *If only they had apologized.*
> *And I never even got an apology.*
> *Of course, I had to sue them—they refused to apologize.*
> *I don't care how many years he did; I still feel he owes me an apology.*

Apologies consist only of words. One can never be sure that they are sincere. When an offending action is also a violation of the law, the victim and society have much more tangible retributions available. In some of these cases, large sums of money are involved; in others, substantial jail sentences are available. The apology is a mere form of etiquette. Why are angry citizens and their tenacious lawyers so eager to get them?

Trust Miss Manners to understand this apparently strange phenomenon. The function of the apology—an acknowledgment by the transgressor that the victim is justified in being outraged—is to reassure both the injured individual and society itself that the moral world exists. A society sizzling with evil is bad enough, but one in which criminals suffer only social consequences (and not even Miss Manners claims that an apology should take the place of fines or jail), but not moral consequences, is intolerable. In such a world, getting caught by the state would be the only deterrent to crime. The victim's own sense of right and wrong, wildly present because of the injustice suffered, would count for nothing.

Because there is some talk in legal circles about the possibility of mandating (presumably apologetic) confrontations between the transgressor and the victim if the latter wishes it, Miss Manners had better issue instructions for serious apologies, in contrast to the ordinary Whoops, sorry variety.

What is required is a statement of moral agony proportionate to the crime, and an absence of excuses. That the criminal has come to realize the enormity of the crime, suffers from torturing remorse and will live with guilt forever is about right. No hedging along the lines of "I'm sorry I caused you pain," with its strong implication of "but when I weighed this against my own desires, you lost," is allowed.

WINSTON-SALEM, N.C.—Supreme Court Justice Sandra Day O'Connor condemned lawyers who resort to "Rambo-style tactics" to win cases and called for more civility: "Unfortunately civility is hard to codify or legislate, but you know it when you see it. It's possible to disagree without being disagreeable."

Apologies for purposeful violations may be acknowledged without actually being accepted, although politeness requires that apologies for accidents be accepted. "I'm so terribly sorry I stepped on your toe," for example, demands the nearest thing the victim can manage in the way of a smile and the patently false declaration of "That's quite all right." Nevertheless, apologies even for unforgivable offenses should be offered in whatever way seems acceptable—if not face to face, then in writing.

The person who flares up at the apology spluttering, "What? She did that, and she thinks an apology will make everything all right?" may nevertheless be eventually comforted by seeing what seems to be remorse. If not mollified, the victim is given help in believing that the offender, having to exist on the same moral plane as himself, also wishes the crime undone, not only because he was caught but also because it has brought him eternal moral suffering.

The Hedged Apology

DEAR MISS MANNERS,

I've observed, in the media, numerous occasions when famous people (politicians mostly) make derogatory jokes or statements about minority groups, which create unmistakable public indignation. Making fun of Judge Lance Ito of O.J. Simpson Trial fame, for instance, has backfired on more than one embarrassed celebrity.

Later, the offending parties reluctantly offer to "apologize IF I insulted anybody." Maybe I'm wrong, but I thought that one can only truly apologize when one unequivocally acknowledges either the inappropriateness of one's action or, at least, the offense it has caused to others. If anything, this kind of defensive posturing is an additional affront, because it basically demonstrates that the offenders still don't think they did anything upsetting at all.

NEWPORT, ORE.—An "apology ad" program in this community requires some criminals to place advertisements, complete with their photographs, detailing their crimes and apologizing for them.

GENTLE READER,

Funny how long it takes the word to travel on some matters of etiquette, and how short on others. Miss Manners is always amazed to hear of people who have not yet heard that expressing bigotry is rude. It is true that while this rule has been around forever, it was so often flouted that many did not realize it was on the books. But in the last decade, it has been so thoroughly enforced in the public arena that one has to wonder about those who missed hearing about it.

Meanwhile, everybody has been quick to pick up on the unauthorized, legalistic, keeping-the-fingers-crossed non-apology. In the version you report, clear offenders of the rule against bigotry are hoping to establish that their motives were pure.

This is not "I'm sorry I said something offensive," but "I'm sorry I said something that lent itself to being misinterpreted as offensive."

Miss Manners can't quite decide whether this ought to be counted against them (as seeming to pass the blame to the targets) or allowed to pass (as blaming themselves for poor choice of language rather than admitting to harboring unpresentable feelings). Anyone who tries to follow up with a comment on how surprisingly sensitive anybody is who is offended loses all benefit of the doubt.

The Value of Mere Form

Knowing that the value of etiquette is beyond measure, Miss Manners was interested to hear of a family that is setting a not unreasonable price on it: $141.6 billion. This would not be unreasonable if suggested flatly as what good manners are worth, in the sense that a cash figure is put on something priceless and irreplaceable, as for insurance purposes. (There are times when Miss Manners wishes she had insured poor old etiquette, because it seems certifiably dead.) The amount was actually calculated as interest on a loan, for a legal case against the United States of America, on the merits of which Miss Manners does not venture an opinion. She is interested in the etiquette angle, which leaped out at her, although it was unaccountably omitted from the news account from which she extracted the facts.

Here is the story, along with Miss Manners' solemn promise that it will eventually bring her to her point: It seems that a Pennsylvania merchant and landowner named Jacob De Haven lent $450,000 in gold and supplies to the Continental Congress in 1777. His farm adjoined Valley Forge, and George Washington, as Commander in Chief of the Continental Army, had declared, "Unless aid comes, our affairs must soon become desperate beyond the possibility of recovery. The Army must disband or starve." Mr. De Haven responded, the Army did not disband, and the rest, as they say, is American History 101.

Only the Nation's benefactor neither made it into history nor got his money back. He attempted to collect, his descendants claim, but did not achieve satisfaction. They tried to do it for him. A bit of research proved that the Continental Congress offered 6 percent interest on loans in those days, and thus the United States owes Mr. De Haven's estate $141.6 billion in today's dollars with interest compounded daily. Compounding it yearly brings the debt down to $98.3 billion.

A United States Claims Court judge ruled that the time allowed under the statute of limitations has passed, but the case was then brought before the United States Court of Appeals for the District of Columbia. Neither the Treasury Department nor the 800 De Haven collateral descendants (Jacob De Haven died childless) seemed to think that the amount would actually be paid. But—thank you for your patience; here comes the point—the descendants indicated that they might accept a thank you instead. Or perhaps a statue of Jacob De Haven from a (belatedly) grateful nation. "They understand about the deficit," said their lawyer. "But they want some acknowledgment of what Jacob De Haven did."

FLORIDA—A teenager whose date failed to show up to take her to the prom sued the young man for damages.

Do you hear that, you who don't write thank you letters? You who grumble that people ought to give you presents for the pleasure of giving and not expect you to have the burden of thanking them? You who postponed thanking and now claim it's too late? Thanks and apologies are properly tendered immediately, but in their absence, the desire for them does not simply fade away. It is better to make a late acknowledgment than to allow an unpaid etiquette debt to be compounded daily. A nice thank you, even 219 years late, or $141.6 billion: That is the choice.

Chapter Five

THE LAW TAKES OVER
FROM ETIQUETTE

ETIQUETTE-FREE SMOKING

In full-page newspaper advertisements, a tobacco company started reaching for—of all things—courtesy. Reacting against laws banning smoking from many public places, and perhaps anticipating its being outlawed entirely, this cigarette manufacturer declared that "we believe that common courtesy and mutual respect are still the best ways for people to solve their differences. By respecting each other's rights and preferences, both groups can easily work things out. Smokers can ask before they light up. And nonsmokers can recognize that smokers have a right to enjoy a cigarette—especially in separate, designated smoking areas."

Miss Manners can't argue with that. It would be arguing against her own innocent past. For years and years, long before there were laws restricting smoking, she pleaded with smokers, whose rights nobody then disputed, to show courtesy to those who found smoke bothersome. Ask before you light up, she said. Otherwise, do your smoking in separate smoking areas. Wait till the others leave the table. Put on that nice smoking jacket you got for Christmas, so that you can change into something less pungent when you join the nonsmokers. Please.

Miss Manners can no more claim to have invented this masterly diplomatic solution than can its current promoters. Approximately from the introduction of tobacco until the early part of this century, these were the etiquette rules that prevailed.

The system worked then because ladies enforced it. "Don't you bring that filthy habit in here," they told the gentlemen they knew best, with what would probably now pass for restrained courtesy. "If you want to smell like a cesspool that's your business, but I won't have it in my parlor, and that's that." To those with whom they were on less intimate terms, they replied, when their permission to smoke was sought, "Oh, dear, I'm so sorry to inconvenience you, but I'm afraid it does bother me. I wonder if you would mind awfully smoking elsewhere?" The question was rhetorical.

Miss Manners would not go so far as to say that no ladies smoked. When the gentlemen were left to their port, cigars and racy stories, fondly believing that the ladies had retreated to do nothing but powder their noses and discuss their children, she went with the ladies. Never mind what they discussed or did; she'll never tell. Miss Manners is much too discreet to let anyone know about the tiny cigars she enjoyed with the wife of a public official who soon after became famous for putting his title on cigarette packages.

Whatever sins were committed, the principle was upheld that smoking, being an intrusive habit like playing portable radios or blowing bubble gum, required the sincere consent of those present. That principle was tossed aside when ladies began to smoke openly. From being a question of gentlemen against ladies, a contest gentlemen of sense knew they would lose, it became the majority (which, after ladies began to smoke openly, meant smokers) against the minority.

The etiquette of the situation having been abandoned by its former enforcers, the majority started following that popular alternative to etiquette known as majority wins, minority loses. The concept of separate areas, such as smoking rooms, was abandoned, and smokers started lighting up everywhere, without caring who might be bothered. This ugly disregard was expressed, in the vernacular of the time, as "Tough!" Anyone who was such a wimp as to suffer from the presence of smoke was supposed to learn to live with that tough luck so that more robust people (or so they thought of themselves) could smoke wherever they chose.

Surprisingly, annoying habits annoy people. When people have been annoyed long enough, they strike back, often in annoying ways. When etiquette fails, the next recourses, as we know, are law and that ever-popular standby, violence. Such are the alternatives, Miss Manners feels obliged to remind those who laughingly dismiss the claim of etiquette because of the weakness in its appeal to voluntary restraint.

So now, dear children, you know why we have laws restricting and banning smoking. When smokers were in the majority, they refused to recognize the claim of mere etiquette to practice consideration for others and the new majority, remembering this, is not going to trust them to behave. Nonsmokers escalated the battle with the argument that vicariously received smoke was injurious to their health, brought in the law and won.

Aside from the ignominious defeat of etiquette, that should have been the end of it. But as nonsmokers began to feel cocky, they, too, started feeling that they needn't bother following etiquette. Not content to institute nonsmoking laws, which Miss Manners sadly agrees is the sensible recourse when etiquette rules are flouted, they have also taken up jeering at smokers. So now smokers, with a history of institutionalized rudeness behind them, are more likely to be the victims of rudeness. They are the ones calling for courtesy.

Both sides will have to forgive Miss Manners for not being jubilant about this appeal to the very solution she has been advocating, not only in this dispute but in all matters of social behavior. The reason that she is not jumping with glee, but sobbing quietly with her head on her desk, is that the basic situation has remained the same: those who have the power exercise it without regard to the feelings of others, who plead in vain for courtesy.

The idea that you should not annoy people, even if you have a right to do so and the numbers on your side—even if the feeling of the society is such that you are allowed to get away with it—has been lost. Both sides now behave equally badly. Those who do not smoke, along with those who do, have reduced the claim of courtesy to ashes. Great clouds of bitterness hang in the air. Bringing in the law and administering it without a supplement of etiquette has not solved the problem.

Appealing the Decision (Denied)

DEAR MISS MANNERS,

If you are invited to a nonsmoker's house for a party or just for an evening, and they know that you are a smoker, are you expected to excuse yourself from the conversation and go outside to smoke a cigarette by yourself, or should the host/hostess allow you to smoke in their home and stay with the conversation?

I am a smoker, and the majority of my friends have put me in this extremely uncomfortable and ostracizing position. I feel if they have invited you, knowing of your habit, they should not only allow you to smoke, but expect it and prepare for it. Not all smokers are inconsiderate. We don't all dump ashes on the floor or blow smoke into your face. We just unfortunately have this habit. By providing an ashtray, opening a window or using a fan, you can at least make your guests feel comfortable and wanted.

GENTLE READER,

No, not all of those guests. Some of them are bothered by any proximity to smoke. Miss Manners believes you when you say that many smokers do not mean to be inconsiderate, but in that case, they must pay attention when the etiquette rules are changed. It is no longer the case that smokers' comfort prevails over that of people who are made uncomfortable by smoke. Smoking in anyone's house must be presumed to be off-limits unless the hosts specifically invite their guests to do so.

Appealing to Reverse an Appeal (Denied)

DEAR MISS MANNERS,

My husband and I, who do not smoke and do not enjoy being in a smoke-filled room, invited three other couples, none of whom we knew very well, for cocktails at our vacation condominium. Shortly after arriving, one of the women asked me if I minded if she smoked. Now, of course, there is where I made the mistake—I said, "No, it's all right." She AND her husband promptly lighted cigarettes and continued to smoke one after another the entire time they were here, which was about two hours.

None of the others were smoking. It was a chilly day, so we couldn't suggest moving to the balcony, and as our living room area is not immense, the air was soon heavy with smoke. This couple are perfectly charming people otherwise, but needless to say, we will not invite them back in a hurry. I would like to know if there is anything I might have said in a light way that would have discouraged the smoking without alienating these people.

GENTLE READER,

Now just a minute here. Let Miss Manners see if she has this straight.

These people asked if they could smoke.

You told them it was perfectly all right to smoke in your house.

Now you want to banish them for doing so.

It is all very well to toss off the remark that giving permission was a mistake, and Miss Manners will get to the point of answering your question about how to refuse such permission politely. First she must object to the tone you take, in citing your guests' enthusiastic compliance and your resulting suffering, as if they somehow should have known that smoke would bother you, in spite of your very direct statement to the contrary.

The answer you should have made was "Oh, dear, I'm afraid it does bother us." The whole scene would then have been avoided. As it has now taken place, it would be a shame to lose the friendship of this couple who are, by your testimony, charming, and by Miss Manners' decree, considerate. (Rude smokers don't bother to ask; some go so far as to argue with objections.) Invite them again, but this time say in advance, "You know, I was too timid to say last time that I prefer that you don't smoke. But we so enjoyed your visit, and I hope it won't annoy you not to smoke while you're here."

The War Continues

Dear Miss Manners,

I witnessed a six-foot-tall man in his 40's strolling over to the smoking section of a restaurant where a man in his 80's was celebrating his birthday by smoking a cigar. The other man calmly crushed out the cigar, announcing, "I find your smoke offensive—I am allergic" and unconcernedly walked back to his table.

I also saw, at a private party where ashtrays were provided, a woman with her leg in a cast who was smoking, when a much younger woman joined the group and blithely announced, "Would you mind putting out that cigarette? I just can't stand the smoke." I am pleased to report that one of the men suggested that the allergy sufferer might find it desirable to move elsewhere. When was the last time you heard anyone say, "I'll go outside so you can enjoy your cigarette in peace"?

Are these anti-smokers free from the restraints of ordinary politeness? Was the world created solely for their "health" and convenience?

Gentle Reader,

Miss Manners, who starts coughing when rudeness brandishes the lofty banner of health, nevertheless finds that you err in suggesting that non-smokers should do more of the retreating. Non-smoking is a nuisance to no one. The situation is only parallel in that the same principle that bans smoke also bans the intrusive and offensive practice of rudeness by non-smokers. Requests to restrain intrusive habits are not discourteous if they are made politely and reasonably, although this excludes making them inside clearly designated smoking zones.

And Continues . . .

DEAR MISS MANNERS,

Last Sunday, outside the airport, standing in the taxi line, I lit up one of my dreaded cigarettes. As you know, domestic flights are non-smoking and I hadn't been able to smoke for a nail-biting, turbulent three hours. I am a 20-year old female college student, very aware of the risks involved in smoking. I am also aware that my smoking bothers others. I try to be very careful so as not to let my smoke be inhaled by others.

Suddenly, from behind me, I heard and felt someone blowing into my hair. When I turned, I discovered a distinguished looking man staring menacingly at me. In answer to my puzzled expression, he said, "I was just blowing the smoke back at you." I mumbled an embarrassed apology and put out my cigarette. I understood the man's frustration and disgust at my smoking, but he could have just as easily asked me to put out my cigarette, instead of creating a drama. Am I right to feel offended by this man's action?

GENTLE READER,

Miss Manners is not a smoker herself, but she has noted that foul emissions from some non-smokers are hazardous to the public welfare. What impresses her is your behavior. Not only were you prepared to respond to a polite objection, but you responded politely to someone who was being offensive in public.

And Continues . . .

DEAR MISS MANNERS,

My husband and I are in disagreement as to whether or not it is prudent and socially acceptable to discuss nicotine patches in the company of smokers. We are both non-smokers and feel that these patches are a wonderful development, but Tom believes that any smoker who is confronted with this subject will feel criticized or personally attacked.

I believe that smokers are not that overly sensitive to the subject, and will accept the discussion as simply another intellectual review of the latest advances in medical technology. I feel that a brief inquiry as to their impressions concerning this product will only be viewed as polite interest in their opinion. If the smoker pursues the discussion, I would follow his lead. If he makes a brief, aversive response, I would immediately change the subject to eliminate any discomfort on his part.

GENTLE READER,

Do you have these little intellectual discussions about nutrition with people whose weight you believe to be unhealthy, or about cosmetic surgery with people whose looks you don't like? Miss Manners doesn't trust your disinterestedness, any more than your husband does, and he knows you better. Bringing up the subject of problems you identify in people you meet socially is the height of tactless nosiness. Polite people take care to avoid discussing any weaknesses they believe their listeners might take personally.

And Continues

DEAR MISS MANNERS,

I am a fifth grade student, so if you do not answer me, I'll understand. My friends' mothers often smoke. I hate the smell of it. When they are driving, to "relax" themselves in the car, they smoke. How do I ask them to please not smoke? P.S. Thank you.

GENTLE READER,

As the daughter of a lady who spent her career dealing with the questions of fifth graders, Miss Manners is not likely to overlook your polite and reasonable request.

You cannot lecture or reform the mothers of your friends, so don't even think of any approach that includes suggesting that they refrain from smoking for their own good. But you can apologetically confess to them your own problem: "I appreciate the ride, Mrs. Antropus, but I have trouble when I smell smoke." Given the choice between smoking and the probable consequences to her own sense of smell that this statement would politely suggest, a reasonable person would put out the cigarette.

The War Escalates

DEAR MISS MANNERS,

I have a problem at work. Most of my co-workers smoke, and I don't. Since I work for the government, they aren't allowed to smoke in the building; they have to go outside. They do this frequently during the day, and I'm beginning to feel really angry and resentful. When they go out, I'm left to pick up the slack. (We are secretaries, and are expected to answer the phones.)

I would like to solve this problem in a constructive way, without being so resentful. I know that getting sarcastic is not the solution, and neither is resuming my smoking habit. But if I just let the resentment build up, sooner or later I'll blow my stack and say something I shouldn't.

Gentle Reader,

Miss Manners would like to draw to your attention that you are not talking about the pros and cons of smoking, but about the terms of working. The issue is the regulation of what is known as a "coffee break," whether it is for coffee, cigarettes, candy bars, gossip, romance or any combination. In some work places, the time and length of coffee breaks are spelled out; in others, they are left to the discretion of workers. If the smoking rule has inspired your co-workers to abuse the privilege at your expense, this should be drawn to the attention of supervisors.

You need not complain about specific workers, or report their practices with rancor. The simple request for breaks of equal time and duration ought to suggest the need to curb abuses. (Miss Manners says this with some trepidation. Suppose your supervisor merely agrees that you, too, ought to be able to abandon work frequently, and yours is a government office that Miss Manners has been trying for years to reach on the telephone?)

A Truce

Dear Miss Manners,

My husband and I don't smoke, but some of our smoking friends have been coming to our home for over twenty years, and it seems inhospitable to require them to step outside, possibly into inclement weather, as my husband now wants to do. Inviting someone to my home and then not allowing them access beyond the front stoop has a very rude feel to it. In deference to our nonsmoking friends, I've offered the compromise of a "smoking room." My husband declined this proposal.

I realize that to align oneself with anything other than the non-smoking camp these days sets one up to be burned at the stake, side by side with anyone lighting a cigarette. But when considering the comfort of all our guests, do we allow the majority to rule and withdraw our hospitality to the 25% who enjoy smoking? Isn't that like telling them, "We love you and want you with us—but not if you behave the way you normally do"?

Gentle Reader,

Normally? Miss Manners normally puts on a tea gown at the close of day and lies back languidly with one of dear Mr. James' new novels, but she wouldn't do it if she were a dinner guest at your house.

Come to think of it, the tea gown disappeared from the scene about the same time as the smoking room. (Unfortunately, so did Mr. James.) Coincidentally, that was about the time that people started talking about social life in terms of rights rather than comforts. None of this improved the quality of social life.

However, reviving the smoking room, as a graceful alternative to porches or battles (and perhaps the tea gown, a graceful alternative to the sweatsuit), would improve things. If you have any spare space that could be ventilated and made comfortable, Miss Manners considers that it would be an enormously hospitable addition to your house.

ETIQUETTE-FREE SEX

The popular belief that one cannot practice both etiquette and sex has always puzzled Miss Manners. While it is recognized that both inspire strong feelings, the prevailing thought seems to be that one cancels out the other.

The Victorians' enthusiasm for etiquette is generally excused because they were born before sex was invented and what else was there to do? They probably wouldn't have cared for sex, anyway. It is hard for people in our enlightened age to imagine that it would have been worth doing something in private when one couldn't talk about it afterward on television.

Miss Manners can't help noticing that the parents of people alive today are not likely to be Victorians, as that dear lady passed away in 1901. As it happens, many of the parents of today's grown-ups were born in the present reign. However, good children still honor them with the name of dear Queen Victoria or, showing more patriotism and knowledge of history, of our own Puritans, for the privilege of taxing parents with the sin of having taught that sin was sinful.

There never has been a better excuse for the wild life than that it is an understandable, if not justified, reaction against being repressed by parents. Never mind that this was the same excuse used by those parents and their parents before them—it's so good an explanation that it has been passed down in some families for generations. Miss Manners regrets that the openness of today's parents could spoil the tradition.

It is difficult to maintain that a parent has taught that sex is wrong when strange but chummy grown-ups appear at the breakfast table.

Miss Manners is pleased to discover that there are children who manage to keep up the tradition in spite of these handicaps. The apparent contradiction is explained by each young generation with the presumption that no matter what appearances suggest, their parents could not have had a greater interest in the activity than the supreme happiness of begetting them. The lack of further interest is even more obvious if those parents have energy left over with which to nag their children about manners—speaking of having nothing better to do. If that isn't proof of a devotion to repression, what is?

How odd, then, that it turns out that there are no exceptions to the rule that no social activity—not even extremely sociable activity, the kind that takes place between two people, of whom at least one has some predilection for the other—functions well without etiquette. In both work and social settings, the same people who discarded all those pesky etiquette rules are busily devising one regulation after another to regulate behavior between the sexes.

Fine, Miss Manners supposes—but do they have to go and misrepresent what proper etiquette is? The idea that the present climate is a bewildering change, because pouncing on ladies used to be an officially approved sport, is a nasty one—and not even, like some nasty ideas, true. Etiquette has always hissed villains who tie ladies to the railroad tracks, foreclose on their mortgages, or give them poor job ratings if they do not surrender their virtue, and it has always snubbed suitors who press their suits, so to speak, with force. Miss Manners is only too happy to hand these people over to the law, which should have been after them long ago. Etiquette's weapon of disapproval is not strong enough to discourage outright scoundrels. She is only saddened because the need for such legalism was created by an etiquette vacuum.

By the time people are old enough to seek romance, they are supposed to have had enough practice in reading the social signaling system to understand whether they are being encouraged or rejected. A society without such training, Miss Manners regretfully acknowledges, cannot be trusted with subtleties. Hence the formalization of courtship rules.

Etiquette has also long known how to deal with the troublesome matter of disapproval of people's romantic partners, whether as individuals or by general classification. The apparent tolerance expressed by silence was not originally mandated for the benefit of unmarried couples, whatever their gender. It was directed at wedding guests who, no matter how socially suitable the match, would be thinking one of two thoughts: "What does she see in him?" or "What does he see in her?"

Etiquette Reaches Its Limit

Dear Miss Manners,

I have waist length hair, which I usually wear in a single braid. What should I say to total strangers who always want to fondle my hair? I totally abhor this and feel this is very ill-mannered.

Gentle Reader,

One does not properly address total strangers who attempt to fondle one. One requests the police to address them on one's behalf.

I. Sexual Harassment

Sexual harassment is the modern name for ungentlemanly behavior that is also unprofessional behavior—two grievous violations of etiquette that everyone is trying to pretend are brand new. Well, Miss Manners supposes they are, in that although both the problem and the rules that would have solved it have been around forever, the latter are fresh from not having been used.

Before the era of business hugs and sensitivity sessions, gentlemen maintained the convenient fiction that they were at work to get something accomplished rather than to make friends. They treated one another with formal respect and kept their hands to themselves.

At least, that was the expected practice—Miss Manners does not make the sentimental mistake of believing that disobeying the rules of etiquette is too interesting an idea to have occurred to our forebears—when there were no ladies around. Obviously, when ladies entered the working world, they should have been accorded the same formal respect. That was obvious to Miss Manners, anyway, but she was a mere slip of a girl in the 19th century, and didn't speak up loud enough.

The gentlemen didn't, as we say in contemporary parlance, get it. Even those who did not believe that the only excuse for having ladies around was to please them, aesthetically and otherwise, could not make the simple leap of applying their standard business manners to their new colleagues. Instead, they reached for the social manners they were accustomed to applying to ladies, and offered little attentions that they believed ladies always appreciated. Meaning to be polite, the gentlemen of business deferred to the ladies of business in everything other than those trifles—power and money—that the gentlemen preferred to keep to themselves. In return, they looked to the ladies to be gracious hostesses, serving whatever refreshments were taken and fussing over their personal comfort.

Mind, we are so far only talking about gentlemen of good will. They were only guilty of unprofessional, not ungentlemanly, behavior. Incapable of distinguishing their relation to these new colleagues from their association with the ladies they knew socially, they were using gallantry when they should have been using good business manners, in the belief that this was the only proper way to treat ladies. As proof, they had the happy reactions of their wives and daughters to such chivalry. That there is a difference between what a lady appreciates from her husband, father or friend, of whom she is presumably fond—or from a

---

SACRAMENTO, CALIF.—A male student in the Psychology 100 class at California State University filed a sexual harassment claim after he had to sit through a lecture on female masturbation, according to the *Wall Street Journal.* The lecture—which included how-to tips, close-up slides of women's and adolescent girls' genitals and denigrated male genitalia and childbirth—left the plaintiff feeling "raped and trapped" and as if "I wanted to vomit," the *Journal* reported. "In these periods of political correctness we tend to be compassionate to women but there may well be a kind of insensitivity to males. The effect is unfortunate," a psychology professor (who questioned the propriety of the masturbation lecture in a general psychology course) told the *Journal.*

---

suitor, whom she may dismiss at will, and who incidentally visits her at her convenience, not when she is trying to get some work done—was overlooked.

This brings us to those who practice ungentlemanly behavior, not even using proper, if inappropriately transplanted, social manners. The etiquette of friendship with ladies, and of welcome romance, required a gentleman to put himself under the lady's command, and strictly forbade him to probe a lady's attractiveness without her encouragement. The shabby combination of approaching a lady in a personal way while making clear one's power over her was always known to be rude. Cads did it because they knew they could get away with it, as the ladies were too afraid of losing their jobs to complain.

Proper workplace manners require that the workers be accorded tasks, salaries and deference by job, rank and performance. This requires the amazing feat of ignoring their gender. Miss Manners never promised that etiquette was easy, but the problem of sexual harassment would not exist if that unnatural rule about ignoring gender were observed. No recognition of gender at all means not even that couched in gallantry, which is why ladies-first, ladies-get-the-coffee, and even don't-the-ladies-look-great-today are banned. Miss Manners finds it high time that gentlemen of business realize that things have changed and learn to compliment female workers on their work rather than on their looks.

Admittedly, it is hard to hang on to proper office demeanor when it's Cookie Exchange Day, or when a facilitator has come in to make everybody confess something deeply personal and damaging. Office-mandated pseudo-friendship has, by weakening the habit of professionalism, helped disguise harassment. For that matter, Miss Manners is nonplussed at what happens to professional etiquette when the definition of sexual harassment is "unwelcome sexual attention on the job." What, pray, is welcome sexual attention on the job? It may be all very well for the two people concerned, but how welcome is it to those paying for their time, expecting service or having to cover for them? Even if office romance can be considered just another time-waster, no worse than talking about it at the water cooler, how welcome is it to those who find that the office network is dramatically different from the organizational chart?

To those who tax Miss Manners with having no heart—who argue that without workplace romance, the world would soon cease to exist, as no one has a chance to meet romantic partners except on the job—she admits one exception. An invitation to socialize after work is allowed, provided it is unaccompanied by coercion or the insinuation that it is part of the job, and that no is taken for a final answer.

Taking No for an Answer

DEAR MISS MANNERS,

I'm currently single, attractive and available. However, I've been trying for one year to catch this perfect man. We work in the same place of business, so I see him often, but he's a hard catch.

I've given him many signs that I'm interested, and he also has shown some interest, yet nothing has happened. His schedule is very busy, and mine can be.

I'm now wondering if this man is just playing games, really interested, or gay. I've heard he was married. But my concern is how to catch him. I want him! Do I give up? Or go for it? Do I openly confront him?

GENTLE READER,

And demand to know why he has behaved pleasantly to a co-worker, if he doesn't mean her to catch him? Or explain that while being gay might be an acceptable excuse for not having a romance with you, being married isn't?

Miss Manners wouldn't put it past you. She is afraid, however, that the most you can properly do is to propose to the gentleman that you get together outside of work. If he says he is too busy, you are required to accept this answer as final—gracefully and cheerfully so as not to disturb the working relationship.

There are two warnings Miss Manners should give you:

1. Being busy is etiquette's euphemism to allow people to show lack of romantic interest without resorting to such unpleasantries as "Not if you were the last person left on earth." It is a safe assumption that anyone truly eager to begin a romance finds time for it, in spite of all other demands.
2. Romantically pursuing colleagues who do not respond to restrained hints is not only rude now, it's illegal.

A Proposal to Replace Harassment with Neo-Discrimination

DEAR MISS MANNERS,

Manners are serious business. What used to be bad manners is now a federal crime. After being victimized on a spurious sexual harassment charge, I sought out the advice of experienced businessmen and lawyers. Prudent men everywhere should adopt the following rules for dealing with women at work:

1. Never be alone with any woman. You never know when you might need a witness.
2. Given the choice of dealing with a man or a woman, deal with a man. Even then be careful what you say, because overheard remarks not directed at a woman can lead to sexual-harassment charges.

3. Whenever possible, deal with women indirectly. Instead of face-to-face communications, prefer memos, electronic mail or intercom. If you do not look at women, you cannot be charged with inappropriate looks.

4. Confine all face-to-face interactions to strictly business. No chatting. No compliments on appearance. No discussion of personal problems, yours or hers. Do not give them rides home after work.

5. Never get closer to any woman than arm's length. That way, you can never be charged with inappropriate touching. Never, ever touch any woman.

6. Whatever your opinions about women, keep them to yourself. Free speech no longer applies in the work place. Matters of opinion—including graffiti on men's room walls—that upset women have been judged to be sexual harassment.

7. Never have a dating or sexual relationship with any woman with whom you work. If she gets promoted or receives any special treatment, you can be charged with discrimination by those, male and female, with whom you were not having sex and who did not get promoted or special treatment.

These rules may seem severe or extreme, but believe me, they are not. They are in line with current federal and state laws, and certain union work rules are even more draconian. We are in an era of new Victorianism, a new formalism in male-female relations.

Gentle Reader,

Miss Manners promises you that she is even more distressed than you are that rules of etiquette should have to be turned into law because people are not willing to obey them out of simple decency, but must be forced by fear of punishment. What an embarrassing failure it is for etiquette that it cannot mandate respect in the work place, without having to get its big brother, The Law, to threaten to beat everyone up.

Also, Miss Manners always sympathizes with people whom the justice system fails. The law is supposed to clear innocent people and offer them recourse against those who bring spurious charges. It is not her job to try your case, of which she knows nothing. It is your proposed etiquette that interests her. So she went fastidiously past your wounded tone and examined the rules you so bitterly offered.

You know what? Some of them constitute discrimination against women, which could land you right back in that legal tangle you did not seem to relish. You cannot refuse to conduct ordinary business with the otherwise appropriate people because of their gender.

Other rules that you offer as draconian are very sensible rules, indeed. Of course, you don't want to be overheard around the work place making tasteless remarks. Of course, you should keep your personal problems to yourself during work hours. Of course, you should keep your *hands* to yourself. Of course, you shouldn't air opinions at the office that anyone at the office might find personally offensive. And, right again, you should not, repeat not, be writing on the men's room walls.

These restrictions are known as professionalism. Even in work places that were all-male, anyone who went about spouting unpopular opinions, blabbing about his personal life, grabbing people and defacing the walls was in trouble. Gentlemen were expected to observe professional etiquette. Miss Manners lives in hope that they will someday learn to extend this courtesy to their female colleagues.

A Stricter Rule

DEAR MISS MANNERS,

For any man in the work place, those rules the man wrote in must be resolutely followed. Failure to do so will result in loss of career and most likely a jail sentence. At the last place I worked, the employee manual clearly stated that even to look at a woman was grounds for a sexual harassment charge. That, among other reasons, is why I now work in a private contracting capacity. I am not in contact with any one place or person long enough to be accused.

Thankfully, I have never been accused, but I have seen several coworkers lose jobs, home and bank accounts because of an innocent remark or misconstrued glance. Hopefully, I will never be accused; for even in private, I no longer touch or make any sexual advances to any woman, not even my wife.

Displeasing Compliments

DEAR MISS MANNERS,

Every time I wear something new at the office, or something I haven't worn in a long time, my boss has an annoying habit of saying, "Is that new?" or "Have I ever seen that before?" It irritates me no end, because it's really none of his business. Then he'll say, "Turn around," like I'm supposed to model it for him (which I don't).

What is a good comeback line? Last time he asked, "Have I seen that before?" I replied, "Probably not." He gets offended easily, but I'm about to blow up. Also, when I dress up a little more than usual, he says, "Going dancing after work?" To me, this is sarcastic and makes me mad. What can I say that will shut him up?

GENTLE READER,

Miss Manners wishes she shared the popular faith in the snappy comeback. Alas, not every misunderstanding has an instant cure, or Miss Manners would merrily spend her days giving off cracks like sparks wherever she went, and leaving everyone the wiser and better behaved (except Miss Manners, who would be in danger of developing a self-satisfied smirk).

What you characterize as a mere annoying habit has a complicated history, which both genders need to understand more fully. Miss Manners guarantees that if your boss were challenged on his habit, he would be truly flabbergasted. Whatever non-professional pleasure he may also have in this routine, he would be able to declare honestly that he thought women liked to get compliments on their clothes, and that he cannot possibly imagine why you take offense when he was saying only nice things. He thought ladies got annoyed when they wore something new, or made special efforts to look nice, and nobody noticed.

What is more, he would be able to produce many people who share his puzzlement, and conclude that ladies are impossible to understand any more, and that you, in particular, are a sourpuss. Miss Manners hastens to add that these people would be dangerously wrong. You are quite right to object to this behavior, and the etiquette error that your boss is committing is more grave than even you suggest. Nor is it excusable on the grounds of ignorance.

Perhaps you do not fully understand it, either. If you had to acknowledge that you are pleased when your friends compliment you on your appearance, and that you don't really believe that your boss has a prurient interest in you (Miss Manners doesn't have enough information to be sure, but feels that you would have mentioned it),

Within the space of one week, the chief executive officers of two publicly held companies were forced to resign because of alleged sexual harassment of female employees, the *Wall Street Journal* reported. "The unprecedented pair of CEO ousters seems likely to send a strong message to top corporate executives and could further strengthen efforts to banish sexual harassment from the workplace," the *Journal* said.

would you think that you had undercut the reasonableness of your objections? (You would not actually have done so. Miss Manners is just trying to establish the extent of the confusion on both sides so that she can begin clearing it up.)

The premise of your boss's behavior, which was never correct but was once widely held by both genders, is that ladies are always flattered to have their personal attractions noticed, no matter where or by whom—even by strange men making remarks to them in the street. You can read modern versions of this idea in fashion magazine articles that urge working women to break out of the dress-for-success rules and dare to look sexy at work. This is an odd campaign at a time when people are only beginning to recognize how widespread are sexual harassment and other professional handicaps that women have long endured, but then, Miss Manners supposes she should not be looking to the fashion industry for philosophical guidance.

Gestures that call attention to the gender of some workers—if the gentlemen rise when the ladies arrive at a meeting, or show an interest in their clothes—undermine their professional identity. Manners and attentions that would be welcome in private or social life, where gender is indeed a factor, are thus damaging in the workplace.

Now—about that factor of rank. Your boss outranks you. Employees do not properly correct the manners of their bosses, even though they do not have to put up with being treated improperly themselves. Miss Manners suggests that you tell him pleasantly that you find discussions of your clothing to be non-professional, quickly adding, "It's not that I don't love being complimented. If you can compliment me on my work, I'd be very pleased."

Embarrassing Comments

DEAR MISS MANNERS,

A friend and colleague has confided that she has been repeatedly shocked and embarrassed by comments made to her by a professor at the university where we teach. It is apparent that the professor believes that by commenting suggestively about my friend's physical attributes, he is paying her compliments. It is even evident that he imagines that he is treating her as an "equal" by sharing his locker-room thoughts in what he thinks is a lighthearted manner.

Needless to say, she finds his behavior less than amusing. Gentlemen colleagues have been sympathetic and they, too, have been embarrassed by this man's treatment of my friend, but no one has hit upon an effective way to correct this situation. The lady has not dignified this man's remarks with a reply, more because of her shock than because of her reserve. None of us wishes to hurt the offender, who, incredible as it may seem in light of highly publicized recent events and of the steady advance of women in the business world, appears to be acting out of real ignorance and insensitivity rather than with malice or even conscious disrespect.

All of us would like to foster and preserve a pleasant working environment. Is there a way for the ladies and gentlemen in our department to put a stop to this offensive behavior without being unkind, offensive and uncivilized themselves?

Gentle Reader,

Miss Manners has been trying for decades to expose the flaw in the argument that a lady armed only with the gentle example of etiquette can exercise control over someone who is determined to be impervious to the feelings of others. Long before what you call "recent events," she warned that someone who presses unwelcome attentions cannot be controlled by etiquette because he is choosing to operate outside the domain of etiquette.

Nowadays, this behavior, which has always been rude, is also illegal. If there is a university left in America that has not made a massive effort to educate its employees about sexual harassment—then you should get yourself over to the administration this very minute to find out why it has not.

It is true that etiquette kindly makes allowances for ignorance, and tries to find delicate ways to discourage people from offensive behavior that they actually intend and believe to be charming. This should never be interpreted to mean that offenders have no responsibility for observing the reactions they evoke and for changing their behavior accordingly. Still less does it mean that their targets have the responsibility of delicately re-training them.

The only thing that should stop your friend from filing charges against this professor is a genuine belief that he fails to understand that his attentions are unpleasant, romantic attentions of any kind are unprofessional behavior and she does not like what he is doing. It is hard to imagine anyone so insensible and still capable of teaching a class, but if that is the case, your friend—or perhaps those gentlemen eager to be helpful—should do him the favor of kindly alerting him to the fact that what he is doing is now called sexual harassment. Never mind the fact that he will protest that he never intended it as such. If you believe that this is a case that may be settled by etiquette, then you may graciously assure him that you are sure that he didn't mean it. The test of that will be whether he stops doing it.

II. PRIVACY

Didn't Miss Manners admonish you not to go around broadcasting the details of your private life? And by the way, isn't "private life" a quaint term for the first thing everybody tells everybody else about these days?

Nobody listens to Miss Manners' plea for personal reticence, based on remembrance of the bad old days, when job descriptions contained the information that servants were not allowed to have suitors, and spouses had to pass muster with recruiters. Drunk with the concept of openness, people can no longer imagine a reason, other than false shame or silly squeamishness, to stop the national flood of intimate information. Those few who wish to be conventionally circumspect are prodded and exposed, and finally blackmailed with the argument that not talking is tantamount to admitting that one has something dreadful to hide.

Amidst all that torrent of confession, the pouring of one's private emotions all over strangers is put forward as evidence of fine feeling, as if being emotional were not the human condition, but a special virtue. Apparently only good people cry, although it is a long time since Miss Manners has heard a poor, thwarted villain chuckle malevolently. Credit is claimed for the most basic and common emotions. Surely Miss Manners is not the only person who considers that, for example, love of one's own child is a minimum requirement for humanness, not cause for bragging. Yet she doesn't remember anyone else's thinking it odd when a politician was introduced at a national convention as demonstrating character worthy of election to high office because he visited his hospitalized child. It's not discretion that makes Miss Manners wonder what someone might be hiding, but rather the blabby bathos of expecting to be admired either for harboring normal human emotions or for confessing to human weakness.

Now look what those silly ideas have engendered. We have been having a variety of unseemly public debates in which fitness for one's professional life—the very opposite of private life, requiring quite different abilities and attractions—is measured in terms of one's most personal conduct. What does the personality of one spouse say about the character of the other spouse? Are adulterers fit for public office? Should gays serve in the military? No wonder no one gets around to the dull questions: Does he know how to do the job? Did she have any relevant professional experience? Is she bright, never mind emotional? Does he know how to make tough decisions without letting his personal feelings get in his way?

Miss Manners cannot help suspecting that the rationale of private life's being the key to professional life was revived to satisfy our natural, but nevertheless improper, urge to gossip. It has ended in turning over tender matters to the harsh scrutiny of the law. The collective opening up of private life is being institutionalized, with unpleasant results.

During the height of the debate over whether gays should serve in the military, someone suggested that there might be a difference between being on duty and being off duty. People who work when they are on the job have always thought so, but it would be nice if this concept spread to the majority. It is a triumph of professionalism, as well as of respect for the worker's personal sovereignty—the right to a personal life not being something free people should have to surrender in return for their paychecks.

Putting private life on the public agenda legitimizes what is only gossip, if muttered informally, but becomes discrimination when it is turned into public policy. Surely the zeal with which people speculate on the unfathomable relationship between private life and its possible public consequences could be well applied to punishing actual cases where private behavior—from innocent mutual flirtation to criminal sexual harassment or rape—is practiced on the job.

Miss Manners considered "Don't ask; don't tell" a good first draft. She would suggest that a policy of "Please spare me the details of what you do in private" and "Please don't give me your opinion of my choice" apply to everyone, and be known as, "Don't brag; don't pry." As her Victorian friends used to say, "You can do whatever you want to do in private, just as long as you don't scare the horses in the streets."

A Reply

DEAR MISS MANNERS,

You have suggested that in places of employment, the specific nature of one's sexual orientation is not an appropriate topic of conversation. To the extent that this refers to descriptions, graphic and otherwise, of behavior, I concur completely. It is nobody's business what one does sexually. That has been at the very center of the message of the gay and lesbian civil rights struggle for at least a generation.

However, you could unfortunately be interpreted to be implying that any mention of one's sexual orientation, for example using the correct gender pronoun in a conversation with coworkers about spouses, or replying to an inquiry as to how one spent one's weekend by describing the rally one may have attended (in an attempt to secure the end of discrimination in the work place, for instance) is, in and of itself, bad manners.

I am confident that you could not possibly have meant to suggest that who one is, as opposed to what one does sexually, is a matter to be kept in strictest privacy. The logical consequence of such a ban would mean never seeing pictures of my employees' children or meeting their husbands or wives for fear of being confronted with the admittedly somewhat personally distasteful evidence of their sometimes virulent heterosexuality.

I would hope you would elaborate on the difference between privacy and oppression, the first of which I join you whole-heartedly in supporting, and the second I hope you will join me in condemning. Please forgive my presumption in writing to correct what I see as an error in expression and not, I sincerely hope, in opinion. I can only say that when you suggest that one who would discriminate against an individual because of that person's sexual orientation is acting in defense of the noble principle of privacy, you would seem to have hold of the wrong end of the stick.

Gentle Reader,

Miss Manners thanks you for putting this so kindly. Not everyone does.

Miss Manners has an obvious bias toward conventional ways of living. By that, she means that she approves of trying to get along with one's neighbors, children and relatives, even if it involves following a few conventions, such as blowing the nose into a handkerchief instead of a sleeve. Who lives with whom, and who marries whom, is something that she considers to be outside her or the neighbors' jurisdiction. A strait-laced horror of snooping is an important part of what she means by being conventional.

Indeed, Miss Manners has come to believe that the basic political division in the society is not between liberals and conservatives, but between those who believe that they should have a say in the love lives of strangers and those who do not. Privacy is thus not an incidental part of her philosophy.

It is not identical with secrecy. One's family and whom one sees socially are, as you say, part of one's identity. Miss Manners has never objected to the photograph on the desk, the introduction of spouse, spouse-equivalent or friend, casual or otherwise, in ordinary conversation or social gatherings involving co-workers. Society has a legitimate claim to know whether an individual lives as part of a couple, because social

life is based on these units. Rather, Miss Manners would argue that there is an obligation not to drive people mad by making them guess who officially goes with whom.

It is when false friendship and pseudo-intimacy lead colleagues to feel they
should evaluate one another's private lives that trouble occurs. That, among other reasons, is why Miss Manners so opposes the colleagues-as-buddies model that is so prevalent in the modern work place.

The offenders, she agrees, are those who feel they have the right of approval,
not those who may be disapproved. Her objection to the unprofessional set-up is that
it fosters the assumption that everyone is entitled to express an opinion about everybody else's business.

The Political Display of Affection

Dear Miss Manners,

Putting moral and political considerations aside, it seems to me the controversy
surrounding the issue of homosexual rights has to do mostly with the question of public behavior. During a major march, I was struck by the flagrant and affected displays
of public affection which dominated the gathering. Is this the right for which homo-
sexuals march?

I admit to being raised in an environment which encouraged public modesty.
My parochial high school and college had relatively strict codes governing public displays of affection (what we called PDAs, or the six-inches rule). I also admit to having
a homosexual orientation myself. After a dozen years of defining my own lifestyle,
which included a five-year monogamous relationship, I still have little sympathy for
the type of public behavior which typifies the stereotyped gay lifestyle.

Does Miss Manners feel that PDA standards apply to everyone, regardless of
their orientation? It seems to me that a good dose of modesty would go a long way toward curing our national homophobia.

Gentle Reader,

The etiquette point is easy. Yes, Miss Manners agrees with you that the rule
against public displays of affection apply to everyone. (She presumes you are talking
about affection in an advanced state; a society that approves public hand-holding, for
example, has no business deciding who should hold hands with whom.) All the world
does not love watching lovers in action.

The assumptions that got swept in along with this point do not so easily obtain Miss Manners' agreement. One of them is the marchers' idea that forcing people to watch acts of which they disapprove is an effective tactic for promoting tolerance. The other, yours, is that shielding people from such observations promotes tolerance.

Such displays, whether intended to shock inadvertent onlookers or simply to ignore their sensibilities, are bound to inspire additional antagonism. Many who would not dream of interfering in private arrangements do so when those arrangements affect them—when they become involuntary onlookers because the acts are performed in public. Unfortunately, Miss Manners cannot share your optimism that the battle over this public arena is all there is to homophobia. In that case, homophobia would be quite a new phenomenon in the society.

She does emphatically share your conclusion that it is a mistake to obscure an issue (that one's private orientation is not society's concern) in which progress is finally, although slowly, being made by taking on an issue (whether one should be able to make love in public) that is practically its opposite, and which you and Miss Manners are hardly alone in finding offensive.

Resisting Intrusiveness

Dear Miss Manners,

I am extremely progressive politically, and honestly, I don't harbor one pet conservative notion. But I feel that sexuality is a spiritual, private experience, and though I feel passionately and have the same physical responses as any other woman, I feel intensely private about this in the presence of anyone but my partner. But except for my parents' generation (I am 28), no one else seems to feel this way. And even some older people surprise me.

My sister and brother both take me aside to interrogate me and make sure there is nothing "wrong" with him. To my embarrassment and anger, they have both asked whether I am orgasmic. Friends have used vulgarity to "desensitize" me by graphic and soul-less displays of obscenity. Co-workers do the same thing. These are intelligent people—teachers, professors, psychologists, activists, social workers, officials, lawyers, etc.

I do not behave in an uptight way. I'm not particularly shy. I have a good sense of humor. If no one dissects other things of profound grace and beauty (and, in doing so, would malign them), why do people feel compelled to talk about sex? I don't see people pinning their gardener friends to the wall, saying, "WHY do you grow orchids?" Nor would they say to Brahms, "Why are you writing this tender music? Wouldn't you rather write ugly music?" Nor, at a ballet, "I'll bet that dancer's about ready to drop that ballerina—I'll bet it would make some chaotic noise and just ruin it for everybody and be outrageous!"

I simply don't get it, and frankly, don't want to. I feel like Nureyev at a mud wrestling contest. I don't want to be a shrew or a rude prude, as it were. I can't say I'm old-fashioned: I'm not.

Gentle Reader,

Gracious. Miss Manners congratulates you on making a stirring speech, complete with politics, spirituality, psychology, the arts and romance, with due attention given to the elements of age, intelligence and professional status—all just to point out that people are nosy and vulgar and should mind their own business.

They often don't, as you have pointed out. Miss Manners is pleased to hear that you refuse to cooperate with them.

Pastoral Intrusiveness

Dear Miss Manners,

My pastor believes in a rigidly legalistic code of sexual morality that means no sex outside the bonds of heterosexual matrimony.

I don't care that he believes that, but he also thinks God wants him to routinely question members of his flock as to their sex lives. I have seen Hollywood gossip columnists who cared less about who was sleeping with whom than this man. He asks the married folks if they are committing adultery—although he has the good sense not to do so while their spouses are within earshot. He asks the single people if they are committing fornication or if they are gay. If someone aspires to being a Sunday school teacher or board member, the grilling is worse.

This Gentle Reader hopes Miss Manners will agree with her that such questions are rude, boorish and offensive, and do not cease being so just because the asker is a man of the cloth and asserts that God put him up to it. My question is what to do about it. When it has been my turn to be asked, I have thus far managed to keep my tongue and temper under control and refrain from telling him off, but the temptation to say what I think is becoming stronger. I am also tempted to tell him that his nosiness fosters lying and hypocrisy for the simple reason that nobody in their right mind is going to tell him the truth.

I was raised in this church and have many dear friends here, and the pastor is otherwise a deeply devoted shepherd who loves his flock and sincerely has their best interests at heart, so I really don't want to leave, although I've considered that, too. Is there a polite way to tell this boor to stay out of my private life, or am I stuck with it until he or I move on elsewhere?

Gentle Reader,

Miss Manners shares your surprise that God would be so relentlessly interested in hearing prurient details, considering the other sins in which a modern flock might be indulging. It also seems to her that your congregation has a problem more complicated than if such questions were being asked by mere acquaintances.

The technique of personal confrontation to solicit confessions is not an unusual one nowadays, however distasteful you and Miss Manners find it. If members of the church feel that this is not the way to go about tending to their spiritual welfare—if, as you suggest, it inspires them to lie as well—your pastor should be told. Far from accomplishing what he wishes, he is merely leading people into subterfuge.

However, if the real problem concerns the morality of the issue—a conviction on the part of the pastor or of the congregation that one of you is in disagreement with the other about whether such activity is actually sinful—you had better get that out in the open. Giving him a chance to persuade you of what he considers right would be more dignified to both sides than the method he is presently using, which smacks more of snoopiness than of morality.

Practicing Intrusive Tolerance

Dear Miss Manners,

When I encountered a man I knew from a few years ago, he was in the company of another man. Various inferences indicate that they are a "couple." This is perfectly all right with me, although I do not know if they are aware of my attitude.

If this had been a man-woman couple, I would have been at ease in asking, tactfully, about their relationship—"Oh, is this your wife?" or "Are you married now?"—without causing an affront, if perhaps risking some mild *faux pas*—"Oh, my goodness, no, this is my cousin"—and a polite laugh by all of us. Is there a way of making my openness known without risking a serious affront? Does current convention require that I abide by the etiquette restrictions of a homophobic society?

GENTLE READER,

It seems to Miss Manners that your anxiety to prove how tolerant you are has blinded you to the basic requirement of tolerance, which is allowing people some privacy. If, indeed, you would demand to know whether a heterosexual couple were married or planning to be so, you would be guilty of a rudeness only too likely to cause them embarrassment. One of these days you will offer your merry questions to an unmarried couple in the midst of emotional turmoil over the fact that one of them is eager to marry and the other isn't. At that time, Miss Manners would only be able to advise you to run for cover.

Such information is for others to announce about themselves, not to yield under questioning. If you feel that the two gentlemen you met have made it clear to you that they are a couple and you wish to show your pleasure in their happiness, why don't you just invite them over for dinner?

III. COURTSHIP

Even allowing for the way nostalgia softens and glamorizes the past, Miss Manners is sure she recalls a time when two people having a romance were assumed to be fond of each other. "Great and good friends," we used to call them when the association took a particularly enthusiastic and active turn. How did such dear friends come to think of themselves as enemies in need of legalistic protection from each other? She means *before* one of them got tired of the other.

Miss Manners is not speaking of people with lecherous and/or criminal intent. She is referring to couples with foolish expressions on their faces and the belief that they are participating in an unprecedented miracle. Far from considering themselves opponents, they are reveling in the discovery that they are truly and uncannily one. They both like the outdoors, for example. Or the indoors. Whatever. It is perfectly amazing.

True, society was always cynical about this. All sorts of devices—chaperones, curfews, shotguns, girdles, rules that college roommates had to be of the same sex—were invented to keep such friends from having too good a time together. None worked, of course, except for the useful (possibly, as it turns out, essential) function of complicating a relatively simple act so as to make it a challenge. Nevertheless, these customs—and society itself—acquired the nasty reputation of being barriers to perfect bliss and, by extension, to world peace.

It took a tremendous effort for lovers to get rid of all those impediments. There were so many different little and big restraints woven into the pattern of proper courtship. Finally, the entire structure was destroyed—the rituals by which the society brought eligible people together, right along with the ones that tried to keep them from getting too comfortable together. After the barriers fell, Miss Manners remembers a few frenzied years, when lots of people kept themselves busy trying out the new freedom. Then, suddenly, they got up and started agitating for legalistic codes to regulate courtship.

What's the matter? Weren't they having a good time? Never mind. This brings us to the great prototype of such efforts: the Antioch College Sexual Offense Policy. There was a time when nearly every conversation landed there, even if it started with farm prices. The entire society was rollicking with merriment at the very idea of a college's promulgating rules of courtship, in which one party was required continually to ask explicit consent of the other to each of a series of specific acts: May I do this? Is it all right if I do that?

Miss Manners was not amused. It struck her as proper and natural that people indulging in such a consequential activity as romance should want it to be governed by etiquette. That they came up with something awkward and adversarial unfortunately does not surprise her.

There was no going back to the old system. The matron-police who scowled at lovers were unavailable for a return to duty. Left unemployed for so long, they all went off to law school. So today's lovers, who have forgotten about demanding to be left alone, follow the spirit of their time and demand that the law act as their chaperones. Similarly, the very people who scorned marriage because it inhibited freedom and spontaneity are in the habit of marching off to court to demand protection and responsibility in connection with their extralegal unions.

All this racing around the board to get to square one strikes Miss Manners as unnecessarily tiring. But if this is what it takes to make everyone realize that love is incompatible with perfect freedom because it involves more than one person, she supposes it is worth it. Couldn't we just improve the explicit consent code? Miss Manners agrees that ongoing feedback is needed to make sure that everyone continues to be happy as things go along, but using the Q&A format has its drawbacks for the worthy but inarticulate. Cads are notoriously eloquent. Those who have exhausted their persuasive powers by setting up the occasion will be out of luck, and George Gordon, Lord Byron, will get all the ladies. But then, he always did.

Miss Manners is aware that explicit permission is built into the code because there is a presumption that no one would bother paying attention to the old vocabulary of gestures and expressions. The old-fashioned young gentleman who froze and retreated when the young lady on whose chairback his arm had come to rest squirmed away, instead of leaning back into his embrace, has been replaced. The new, meaner model is supposed to be chortling with the realization that it is safe to go ahead and grab her, because her signal would never stand up in court. That is what bothers Miss Manners the most. Everyone seems to concede that it's such a selfish world now that it would be preposterous to assume that two people pursuing love have any interest at all in each other's happiness.

Anticipatory Rejection

DEAR MISS MANNERS,

I want to share with you a printed message that I use to dissuade homosexual men from becoming preoccupied with me. I ask all heterosexual male readers to use this message whenever it appears necessary.

"Dear Sir, I want you to know that I am heterosexual, and currently preoccupied with maintaining heterosexuality. I hope you find someone soon. I apologize if my suspicions that you are (1) gay and (2) interested in me are incorrect. Please know that you are lovable like the women I want. I observed your nervousness when near me, and suspected that a romantic attraction to me had developed in you. Note: I have not described my theory to anyone, and I will not do so."

GENTLE READER,

A gentleman who summarily hands out rejection letters to people who have made no advances to him is going to have trouble maintaining any kind of sexuality, Miss Manners is afraid.

RETROACTIVE MISUNDERSTANDINGS

Although she doesn't know what aroused everybody else's interest in the succession of legal charges of date rape since that term came into use, Miss Manners was riveted by how they illuminated differing perceptions of the courtship rituals of our time.

The defense in these cases seems to be saying that it was clearly understood that an invitation had been issued and accepted to a single mating, with the vaguest romantic preliminaries and no subsequent expectations. Its explanation for ensuing hostilities is that the other side had agreed wholeheartedly to the lack of courtship, but secretly expected this attention after the fact, and brought the lawsuit in retroactive anger that it was clearly not going to develop.

PRINCETON, N.J.—Writing about so-called "date rape hysteria" among campus feminists, a Princeton University graduate student wrote in the *New York Times*: "feminists are responding, in this time of sexual suspicion, to the need for a more rigid courtship structure. The message represents, in part, a nostalgia for 1950's style dating. For Johnny picking Susie up for a movie and a Coke."

The prosecution takes the position that the encounter contained no promise of consummating a relationship that may not have existed previously, but was a limited social contact of which the terms were to be negotiated as it developed.

In other words, one person understood the occasion in question to be a one-night stand, which by definition has no future, and the other, a date, which lives in expectation of a rosy future. Each side is scornful that the other was not able to understand the nature of the event from the sending and receiving of such social signals as costume and venue.

Social signals? The subtle reading of etiquette's symbolism? In the unlikely event that Miss Manners could trust anyone in this literal-minded society to make such judgments, she would not consider dress or location to constitute serious consent. However little she may approve of bad taste, she realizes that fashion is too driven by its need for novelty to enable anyone to use it as a guide to the thinking of the body inside. Even before the invention of carjacking drove courting couples indoors, she lost interest in maintaining the assumption that no lady would visit a gentleman in his quarters for respectable reasons.

The ability to observe nuances and clues is, Miss Manners agrees, indispensable to the atmosphere of romance. When it comes to major decisions, however, it is considered polite to offer a formal proposal.

In a well known dirty trick of an earlier era, a gentleman who impulsively kissed a lady might well be informed how happy she was that they were now engaged, and her family would quickly appear—amazingly quickly, in fact—to congratulate him and negotiate the terms. The technicality that he had not mentioned marriage was not considered important. His behavior had clearly shown that that was what he wanted. What else could he have meant?

Now we have to remember that similar behavior on the lady's part does not entitle the gentleman to consider that she has dispensed with the formality of consenting to what was once considered an act of marriage.

In both cases, couples need to be allowed to state what they do and do not mean, to be believed and, if there is any doubt, to be questioned. Miss Manners does not deny that it is possible that someone will be so overcome by your charms as to want to surrender to you immediately, just as it is possible that someone will be similarly prompted to make over a fortune to you. She is only warning that in both cases one has to be certain before taking possession.

Retrogressive Suggestions

DEAR MISS MANNERS,

Everyone seems to be utterly unaware these days that if a young lady (of any age) consents to being alone with a man, she has surrendered her right to say "no" to sex. If you go to a man's car, hotel room, apartment, home, whatever, alone with him, sexual consent is implicit. To scream rape later should subject the accuser to ridicule.

To avoid rape (not including abduction by a total stranger or forcible entry into one's home, etc.), all one needs to do is have a chaperone, friend, or stay in safe public areas. The responsibility for a woman's virtue lies with her. Her conduct alone is responsible for the phenomenon so wrongly designated "date rape" or "acquaintance rape." If her judgment should prove unwise, she should learn from the mistake and get on with life. The courts should not be cluttered with such nonsense.

GENTLE READER,

How's that again? Chaperones? Off limits areas? You rather caught Miss Manners by surprise, but now that you mention it, etiquette books of the past always did contain instructions about ladies' needing chaperones to ensure that the gentlemen behaved themselves, and about ladies' losing their right to be treated decently if they crossed any one of a number of thresholds and borders.

Miss Manners does not write etiquette for the past, as she cherishes the fond notion that we have learned something during this century. So with your kind permission, she would like to adapt the tradition you mention for future use.

What we have learned is that society was after the wrong people. Attempting to control philandering young gentlemen by restricting the freedom of innocent young ladies did not make a lot of sense. Even now, although it is not totally unheard of, ladies are almost never responsible for committing rapes. Your suggestion is similar to the advice piled on potential victims of muggers to lock their houses, keep off the streets and stay out of parks, various neighborhoods and other areas designated as dangerous—until they have virtually interred themselves and given over free use of public areas to the criminal element.

It doesn't seem quite fair, does it? So if we are therefore to anticipate rapes, it seems fairer to set a watch on those who might commit this crime, and to keep them out of places where they do it. Perhaps we need chaperones and off-limits areas for gentlemen.

Miss Manners does not claim to be happy with this solution. It is not right to punish innocent people of either gender because of the statistical likelihood of their doing something wrong. It would be fairer, and safer, if all people took care not to place themselves under the protection of near-strangers who, for all they know, may harbor criminal tendencies.

Another Suggestion

DEAR MISS MANNERS,

Although I do not agree that any female who consents to being alone with a man is consenting to sex, I have wondered about women putting themselves in harm's way, especially in light of the Mike Tyson case. What did the rape victim think this guy wanted? After all, he didn't ask her out to dinner and a movie. On the other hand, when she had second thoughts and said no, I believe Mr. Tyson should have backed off.

Perhaps when a woman, especially a young woman, wins her rape case in court, the judge should also "sentence" her to a program designed to teach people how to avoid becoming a victim and to some hours of community work, talking to high school and college students about her experience and what she learned in the program.

MATING RITUALS

The Improper Introduction

Miss Manners is not volunteering to go around policing eager couples, but she has always rejected the modern demand to recognize the one night stand as a social form, complete with well-understood rules by which compliance could be easily deduced at the first sign of interest. It is not a proper event, and she wants no part of it.

She may not be naive enough to believe that love prompts all human couplings, but she does maintain that civilized people do not normally participate in mating that is totally unadorned by social ritual. Conventional social ritual requires people to learn each other's names before consummating their devotion and perhaps, for those who want to be not just intimate but sociable, to learn something about each other's background, history, activities and interests.

Anyway, the one night stand could not be the unmitigated source of pleasure that its advocates claim. Surely something not worth repeating couldn't have been all that much worth doing in the first place.

There's a reason Miss Manners is so grumpy about this. She is sick of hearing the one question that people still expect etiquette, rather than law, to solve: They want to know how politely to ask a stranger with whom they want to be intimate if that person can be trusted.

WASHINGTON,—D.C. A 15-year-old girl stabbed a boy who had been teasing her with an 8-inch knife in the school lunchroom of their junior high school. Classmates told the *Washington Post* that the two students disliked each other and that the boy shoved the girl's chair and was "messing" with her.

Having done away with the tedium of waiting to meet eligible people gradually, through activities of mutual interest, and the discomfort of enduring candidates put forward by their own friends and relations, unattached people have now taken to hawking themselves through commercial advertisements. Naturally they want the same sort of guarantees about what they are getting, as with other advertised goods.

Miss Manners is afraid that there is no getting around the fact that a stranger is someone you don't know anything about. She can no more produce a clever and polite question that would determine whether a stranger could be trusted not to transmit a fatal disease than she could determine if a stranger in the airport is trustworthy enough to watch your luggage for you. Is it reasonable to expect etiquette to fix a problem that was created by the abandonment of etiquette?

She is, however, willing to supply another solution: etiquette's old standby, the Proper Introduction. Those hoping to find romance should intensify their usual sociability, accepting and issuing lots of invitations to see people they know who could make proper introductions to those they don't know, and participating in activities where the roof, as they used to say, constitutes a proper introduction.

Wait! Don't go away!

It isn't just the old killjoy spirit that makes etiquette insist on a proper introduction followed by some degree of acquaintanceship to precede intimacy. Such poky old forms are there to help ensure that people are not at the mercy of strangers, whose character is unknown to them and who thus have no reputation or responsibilities to maintain. Sensible people wouldn't hire someone to work for them without any references, and the proper introduction serves a similar purpose.

It is by no means a foolproof protection, Miss Manners is sorry to say, but people do tend to behave better when not doing so might come to the attention of those to whom they have ties of family or long-standing friendship. The chance that they could be axe murderers without their friends having guessed is not eliminated, but it is lessened. It seems to Miss Manners that romance, under the best of circumstances, is reckless enough without adding to its perils.

The Proper Introduction

It is so unjust to charge that anyone so conventional as to go in for proper introductions must be trying to discourage romance. From the beginning of time, conventional society knocked itself out trying to throw eligible people together—goodness gracious (Miss Manners wails), that has been society's main impetus. Why else would those with comfortable mates and armchairs at home go and plan and attend so many functions, from hoedowns to debutante balls, where they have to stand up and even dance?

It was considered a social obligation to introduce your friends to others among your friends whom you thought they might like, in the way of friendship as well as romance. Parties were arranged to include a mix of people who might not have met; introductions were performed all around; and seating was arranged so that new friendships might be sparked.

This required the cooperation of those who were to be introduced. They had to have the faith to believe that their friends' friends were worth knowing, and to be willing to show up in an open frame of mind. Single people arrived singly, and couples fanned out separately after they arrived, doubling their chances of meeting people they and their partners might like. In return, they kept meeting people who were known, liked and recommended by people who knew, liked and recommended them.

Then the prime objects of this attention renamed themselves singles and ungratefully let it be known that they would waste no more time with doubles. They took things into their own hands, and all sorts of people into their arms.

Miss Manners, who loves happy endings, even if they haven't taken the path of etiquette, was sad, although not surprised, that there weren't many. The spurning of these social forms created an epidemic of loneliness. She can't understand why, in a society where everyone is whining about not being able to meet anyone, from prospective mates to anyone at all who doesn't work in the same place, the traditional methods of enlarging social acquaintanceship are still being scorned.

Single people who are invited to social occasions—notably weddings, but also ordinary gatherings—where they are likely to find other single people among the guests, scramble around to find someone they can take along for companionship, rather than take the chance of relying on whatever new companionship they might find there.

Working people who claim to have no time to socialize with friends nevertheless find time to celebrate their colleagues' birthdays and give showers for people whom they barely recognize.

The blind date is labeled a sign of desperation, even by those who resort to advertising for strangers to love them.

People who are willing in theory to go out will nevertheless ask a prospective host warily, "Who's going to be there?" to avoid taking a chance on just anyone the host might also happen to like.

There is only one aspect of the situation on which all those people with their dismal social lives agree: that they are glad to be free of stuffy old etiquette, which was slowing them down.

The Retroactive Introduction

In examining the rituals of modern courtship, Miss Manners is appalled to find the occasional reference to an apparently new custom: in the early stages of romance, just as the flames of love are beginning to catch, one member of the couple hires a professional detective to check out the other. And here Miss Manners thought that was a ritual associated with a much later stage in the courtship—the divorce. It's so annoying when people mix up their rituals like that.

She is, however, far from disputing the necessity of knowing someone's background before allowing one's affections to become irrevocably attached. Stories of love at first sight notwithstanding, there is usually a stage at which one realizes that one could well become—but is not yet—so passionately involved that one's entire happiness would be in a certain person's hands. This is an extremely good time to consider coolly how good a gamble one would be making.

Past performance is hardly a perfect measure of this, but it is all there is to go on. Many people are quick to toss this evidence aside, under the gratifying argument that one is so special oneself that one is bound to be treated better than one's predecessors—that her deceiving a number of previous husbands only shows that she has never before found the true love for which she has been yearning; or that his beating up all his girlfriends shows that they never understood how sensitive he is. As a lady of Miss Manners' acquaintance put it when explaining, decades after the fact, how she became the third (but by no means last) wife of an alcoholic playboy, "I thought all he needed was the love of a good woman. And you know what? Turns out that wasn't all he needed."

Still, ignoring evidence so staggering that it should warn against sitting next to that person on the bus only indicates that the window in which one can make a cool judgment has already been closed. At that point, there is no prying it open, as many a well-meaning friend and relation can attest. Nobody listens to advice from friends and relations, of course. But why not hire a detective, while there is still time? Who else can do so thorough a job?

BOSTON, MASS.—In a story on the death of slow dancing, one middle-aged woman told the *Boston Globe:* "When the slow songs started, they would come and ask you if you would like to dance. They had more manners then."

One reason why not is that checking up on people—a.k.a. snooping—is itself such an offense that it seems justifiable only when it produces proof of criminality. When innocence is uncovered by such means, innocence gets furious.

"You don't trust me!" it declares indignantly and, as it happens, irrefutably. But why should one trust someone one knows nothing about? This is also an irrefutable point.

To Miss Manners, the underlying problem is that society is not performing its natural functions, and it therefore makes people who need these functions rely on paid substitutes. Like the rest of matchmaking, the task of supplying information is being put into the hands of professional specialists.

Amateurs are actually better at society than professionals. Background material is going to come from the subject's acquaintanceship anyway, whether it is collected by a detective or given firsthand after a proper introduction. While detectives may reasonably argue that they are more discreet and thorough than friends, they have the overpowering disadvantage of not being easy to disavow. Even the client who gets a magnificent report is bound, one day, to refer, in the intimacy of confidences, to knowledge not yet confided. Those whose tricks detectives bring to light may turn out to be the people who hired them.

Proper Impropriety

DEAR MISS MANNERS,

You have often underlined the difference between manners and morals, which is the only reason I dare ask you to address the issue of etiquette for the principals in an affair. I suspect that etiquette must ultimately be guided by moral objectives—of which there are very few in an adulterous relationship.

GENTLE READER,

Miss Manners presumes that you do not intend to shock her delicate sensibilities by suggesting that people who have broken one rule, whether of morals or manners, might as well break them all. Sinners are not excused from being polite. One of the underlying directives of manners, as well as of morals, is a requirement to spare the feelings of others. Although the fact of adultery itself (a moral rather than a manners issue) is almost certain to violate this, there are also etiquette rules derived from the same directive that should be observed. These also apply to non-adulterers, but here are some that may be especially relevant to an affair:

> Third parties should never be placed in a position where they feel they must assist in a cover-up of behavior they do not approve.
> One should not violate the privacy of one's spouse, even on the classic excuse that the spouse doesn't understand one.
> Family loyalty requires protecting and defending relatives from criticism and ridicule, even that which has been prompted by one's own behavior.
> Third parties should not be made to witness any physical displays of affection.
> The possessions of a spouse should not be lent for use without that person's knowledge and consent.

That last rule does not refer to the body of the adulterer, which is, as Miss Manners noted, subject to the jurisdiction of morals rather than manners. The etiquette rule means that the lover should not be allowed to use the spouse's bathrobe.

When It's Over

DEAR MISS MANNERS,

A friend at work is having some difficulty breaking off a disastrous love affair. I call it disastrous because her former boyfriend has stalked her, invaded her privacy, and even made threats of physical violence, among other outrages I won't describe. Several of her friends have advised her to break off all contact with him, but so far she refuses to take this step. Last night, she accepted several long phone calls from him late at night—in which he pleaded with her to give him "another chance"—and she ended up losing so much sleep that she came to work today five hours late. She explains that she is "not very good at being mean."

She says they haven't been "intimate" for over a year, whatever that means, but during that time, she bought him a leather jacket for his birthday, and did him many small favors, such as balancing his check book for him every month. She explains that she is just trying to be "friends" with him, and she would do as much for any friend. I think she is telling the truth.

While I don't condone his behavior, I suspect she is contributing to the problem by performing acts of "friendship" which he is apt to misinterpret as meaning more. Can you suggest any rules to govern how one should behave toward a former lover with whom one wants to be "just friends," so as to leave no room for misinterpretation? This seems to be a common problem.

GENTLE READER,

Miss Manners is not going to attempt making rules for people who are hanging around with those they know are bad for them because they are still in love. As you have discovered, people in this state do not pay the slightest attention to friends or reason.

She does think it useful to say something about the demands of politeness in such a situation—the factor of not being mean, as your friend calls it. Perhaps removing the etiquette excuse will help to alert your friend to the danger in which she is placing herself.

Under ordinary circumstances, etiquette requires former lovers to be civil to each other and to speak civilly about each other. Even if they have been married. It neither precludes nor requires friendship; it just stands wistfully by, because it knows how rare such friendship really is.

The circumstances you describe are not ordinary. Physical violence and stalking are crimes, and heaven knows what those unspeakable outrages may be. Beyond sadly condoning recourse to the law to prosecute crime and protect the innocent, etiquette also uses the social weapon of refusing to have anything whatever to do with those who have put themselves outside of the bounds of decency. So it would be perfectly polite, not to mention wise, for your friend to cut off all contact with this person. Persuading her to do so is, Miss Manners is afraid to say, another matter.

Date? What's That?

Long, long ago, when boys and girls had separate dormitories, hairdressers and attitudes, there was a social form known as the Date. Those who are tickled by quaint customs from the past may be interested to know how this worked. Gather 'round Miss Manners, children. And pay attention, because there is going to be a lesson about modern romance.

To arrange a date, a boy called a girl several days or even weeks in advance of the time he hoped to see her, and invited her for an occasion he had planned, such as dinner and a dance or, less momentously, the movies and a snack. He assumed the part of host, with such obligations as picking the girl up at her home, making all arrangements, paying all bills and returning her home.

The girl could accept or refuse the offer, but once the date was made, it could not be broken short of an emergency that passed muster not only with the boy but with the girl's mother. This was a matter of considering not only the boy's possible hurt feelings, which the girl may have been willing to endure, but also what word of such perfidy might do to the girl's reputation with other potential suitors.

During the course of the date, the couple were considered paired. Flirtations with others were supposed to be discreet. For example, each could dance with others, provided the boy never left the girl stranded and saved the first and last dances and suppertime to spend with her. Even if neither had any intention of seeing the other again—and there was no obligation to do so—they both spoke of having had a wonderful time. No matter how many dates a couple shared, no exclusivity was assumed; this had to be the subject of a specific agreement.

This sort of thing had been going on for some decades before astute people noticed that it meant that the girl had to wait to be asked out, and that the boy always had to pay. It was also pointed out that boys and girls got to know each other only under these artificial circumstances, as opposed to a natural social life, where friends could get together in groups, and pairings could occur as nature dictated.

"Dating is extinct. It's a really weird way of getting to know someone," a 24-year-old girl told the _Washington Post_. Instead, the _Post_ reported, young people "group date" with friends, avoiding the risks, rejections and demands of a formal date. "The problem is, we haven't created a new dating ritual. We've deconstructed the old rituals but we haven't found a new one. . . . We're not even addressing the issue," a young lawyer told the _Post_.

As it happens, Miss Manners is sympathetic to these objections. Once when she was staying in the guest suite of what had been an exclusively male college when she had first visited— thus living out one of those fantasies come true too late—she was discussing the state of male-female relations with a contemporary. They were having breakfast in the crowded student dining hall.

"Were you ever here years ago?" the friend inquired.

Miss Manners blushed and acknowledged that she had been, more than once, even in the company of more than one gentleman.

"Didn't all the boys stop dead when a girl entered, stare at her, and then turn back, obviously to rate her attractions?"

Miss Manners blushed again and murmured that she had noticed something of the sort. Her friend then waved at the scene around them, with boys and girls jumbled together at various tables in comradely conversation, and asked, "Don't you think this is an improvement?"

Miss Manners does think it an improvement. She is not describing the date to young people who follow the newer custom in order to persuade them to bring the form back as a regular (as opposed to occasional grand occasion) practice. Nor is she only trying to amuse them with the follies of the past. Rather, she wishes to point out what it was about the date that was valuable and could be salvaged to smooth current awkwardnesses.

Exactly because the date was artificial, it gave everyone a set pattern, and a polite one, of how to act. This is not such a terrible inhibition as may be imagined; rather, it frees people from the inhibiting fear that often accompanies enforced improvisation. There are fewer hurt feelings when everyone must pretend to have a good time.

More than that, the date required the participants to give each other a trial for the period of an evening, with both on their best behavior, endeavoring to contribute to the success of the date. In the unstructured social comings and goings of today, it is far too common for ladies and gentlemen to dismiss each other after a quick look or remark. An attitude of "What are you going to do to impress me?" accompanies one of trying too hard to make an instant impression, or, in reaction, not trying at all to be agreeable. Knowing that one will be exclusively paired, at least for a while, after such a quick choice has been made, also has a discouraging effect on romance.

It strikes Miss Manners that the cause of gender equality would not be damaged if both boys and girls considered themselves obligated to make sustained, polite and charming efforts to get to know one another; and that the cause of romance might be advanced.

Serious Dating

DEAR MISS MANNERS,

As awkward as it sounds, I am not skillful in romancing. So there are basic things that confuse me:

In modern life, what are the definitions of "going out as friends on a one-to-one basis," "dating," "seeing a person," and "going steady"? Are there any generally presumed duties, obligations, rules, with which people comply in these stages? What is the proper way to handle the situation if my boyfriend or regular date is "shopping around" for partners and therefore multiple parties may be involved?

Here is the scenario that bugs me. After my boyfriend and I have agreed to "go steady" (he selected this term, though I don't thoroughly understand its meaning), he immediately said we should still "go out" with others as friends.

This seems to me a wide-open, no-strings-attached arrangement. Each party has all the opportunities to check out other people. However, I don't know if this means we can both "date" other people. He said that people tend to behave more loyally and faithfully to their partners under such arrangements. I simply don't understand the logic or the psychology behind this.

He thinks it is fair because we are both seriously choosing a partner for life, so we should do as much looking around as possible. If in the end we still find each other the best, we will know in our hearts that we have freely chosen each other as our best choices. I am confident that my boyfriend is interested in me but he is still window shopping.

I find myself flush with jealousy when he is approached by other ladies, so I don't know if I suit this wide-open arrangement. But I don't think I have a choice because it seems to be the way people do it now.

Gentle Reader,

What constitutes a "date" nowadays is practically a metaphysical question. With all the possibilities you mention, and Miss Manners has heard of a great many cute variations besides, it remains oddly true that the only real distinction between romantic relationships is between the married and the not-married.

We all know permanently faithful couples who have not married, for one reason or another. And heaven knows there are married individuals who never for an instant, maybe not even at the wedding reception, considered the possibility that they might not be available to whoever else happens to wander by. Nevertheless, nearly all people who truly want to commit themselves forever (along with some triflers who want just to be at the center of extravaganzas) want the legal, social and often the religious sanctions of marriage.

The old-fashioned social system recognized this by having only three possible terms for couples: married, engaged or just friends. That last term always covered a lot of territory and nowadays, that territory has become riddled with land mines. You can hardly condemn anyone for having lots of friends, and yet it is often not possible to tell until it is too late which ones might develop romantically.

We still haven't developed a satisfactory word for the unmarried couple who act as a social unit (a problem Miss Manners has been trying to solve for years, but doesn't have the energy to get into here). But that arrangement is one of many that people improvise for themselves. They may have different spoken or unspoken understandings about behavior for their duration (the rules are not, as you seem to suppose, decipherable from the term used) but they are all characterized by the non-marital freedom to terminate the bond at will.

A commitment between unmarried people, no matter what it is called or what the terms set in advance, is always going to be subject to unilateral alteration at any time. This is always going to infuriate the other person, whose indignation will be understandable, but nevertheless that is the basic nature of the arrangement. Unmarried people are, after all, not married.

But the whole matter has become complicated by the more, ah, rigorous forms that courtship often takes now—courtship which may lead to marriage, but might take years to get there. Even before the attendant dangers turned lethal (are you following all these euphemisms?), this took away the respectability of an unmarried person's exercising the freedom to have more than one sweetheart at a time. Those exciting but still socially condoned characters the belle and the man-about-town have come to be called by less glamorous names.

Hence the return to the language of quasi-commitment that your boyfriend is using when he quaintly says you are going steady. Meant to confer some sort of respectability on a non-marital love affair, this nevertheless really means what the intermediary stage has always meant: We're together until one of us would rather not be.

In that sense, Miss Manners is afraid you must recognize what you already know—that your boyfriend considers himself free to shop around and to drop you if he finds someone he prefers. Even if you are convinced that he will not actually do so, you will have to decide if you can bear this stage, whether you want to alter the terms of the arrangement to suit an uncommitted relationship and finally, if you even want to continue.

You might, however, keep in mind the fact that you are equally free. And that there is no reason that you need to give the gentleman the peace of mind that comes with smugly believing that while he vacillates, he can be sure that you will be there if he decides he wants to marry you.

This brings etiquette to one more complication—an age-old one this time, but one that is highly relevant. That is that the capacity to be unfaithful has never yet been tempered by the calm and fair acceptance of a partner's merest hint of harboring the same possibility.

Chapter Six

ETIQUETTE'S DEFENSE SYSTEM

REPUTATION

As if etiquette isn't unpopular enough, Miss Manners occasionally has to argue against compassion and forgiveness. It's so unfair. She feels like the high school debating champion who has been assigned "Resolved: The school year should be extended, homework should be increased and instead of a senior prom there should be a review session the night before graduation to check that seniors haven't forgotten what they crammed for examinations."

Miss Manners against compassion? Isn't she always nagging people to do nice things for others and refrain from hurting their feelings? Isn't that what etiquette is all about?

What hurts Miss Manners' own feelings is the claim that given a conflict between the letter and the spirit of the etiquette rule, she would merrily throw over the manners principle to stick by the etiquette rule—especially if this offered an opportunity to stick it to someone else. "I'd like to thank you now," a dignitary of Miss Manners' acquaintance told her guest of honor publicly during an official meal, "but I suppose Miss Manners would disapprove." Oh, right. As if it were Miss Manners' purpose in life to stamp out gratitude on technical grounds.

As for forgiveness, etiquette is the inventor of the apology, a device expressly designed to cancel misdeeds. Unlike its successor, the punitive damages award, the apology is available free (although flowers are always welcome). Etiquette also supplies the polite response to an apology: a gracefully murmured, "I'm sure it wasn't your fault," and "Of course, I knew there must be some explanation."

Yet—wait while Miss Manners takes a deep breath—there is such a thing as fostering bad behavior by misplaced compassion and forgiveness. When all transgressions are automatically explained away and immediately wiped from the record, there soon is no standard of good behavior. The more tolerant and understanding the society becomes, the worse the situation seems to get. People of widely varying political views have noticed that the criminal justice system suffers from the same horrifying and unintended consequence. Miss Manners is not the only person to be puzzled that modern juries are increasingly sympathetic to criminals—and that the society at large is reluctant to hold criminals' records against them—while the citizenry from which those juries are drawn is increasingly terrorized by crime.

Her habit of suspecting the best of people has her worrying that this arises from a kind but mistaken sense of manners. Decent people now feel obliged to consider everyone innocent after being proved guilty. Faced with the individual instance, they generously make allowances—just the sort of allowances for which Miss Manners is always pleading. That the person who did wrong perhaps didn't realize it. Or probably had a good reason. The catch is that when this decent compassion is used as a general rule, rather than remaining an exception, crime is defined out of existence. Either there was a good sociological or psychological reason for committing any crime or it was an irrational act. It seems as wrong to condemn someone who was merely the instrument in an inevitable chain of cause and effect as it does to convict a crazy person. There isn't anyone else in the dock.

Miss Manners does not want to pursue this point in respect to crime. She tends to be an old softy herself. Only when the argument is used to deprive etiquette of its one protection—the option of showing disapproval of people who behave rudely, mostly by avoiding them—does she tear after it. When people maintain that you can't expect this person to be polite because he's had a difficult life, or that one not to be rude because she is too busy to be bothered with etiquette, they give notice that everyone has license to be rude.

When people treat transgressors as members of society in good standing, they destroy the usefulness of reputation as a guide to character. It sounds polite to whitewash blemished records, on the grounds that someone who did wrong "has suffered enough" (been caught) and "paid his debt to society" (done time). But if personal history never counts, society only ends up assessing people less fairly, by using that easily manipulated ersatz substitute—image.

Miss Manners objects, and not only because society needs protection. She objects philosophically, too. So there.

The manners system, no less than that of morals, is based on the presumption that human beings have souls and free will and all that good stuff. Of course they are influenced and handicapped by the circumstances of their lives, and giving them compassion and assistance is the proper response to that. However, it is ultimately their ability to determine their behavior, rather than merely to be acted upon by events, that gives human beings their dignity. Puppets with no autonomous power of decision, and therefore no responsibility, would not merit respect—the one offering of etiquette that everyone on the street admits craving. Their lives would be merely records of the way they were buffeted about by the past. No credit would be due to the virtuous. If there are no bad reputations, there can be no good ones; if there are no villains, there are no heroes. There are merely the lucky and the unlucky.

Miss Manners isn't really arguing against compassion, which is one of the foundations of her calling. She is only warning against overusing it at the expense of another such value—respect.

Precedence among Heroes, Criminals and Victims

The polite way to talk about crime has changed dramatically in recent years. There is a general perception that manners are always declining, but in this respect there has been a leap forward into politeness—beyond it, Miss Manners would say.

Some years ago it became customary to react to news of a violent crime by saying, "The poor thing, he's obviously sick." Miss Manners had to point out that, as polite as this sounded, it contained a serious omission. In the precedence system for those due sympathy on such an occasion, the victim is supposed to go before the perpetrator. So the correct order would be "The poor thing, he was shot [pause] by some poor person who is obviously sick."

That said, Miss Manners considered the problem solved (although she always forgets to allow for the time lag between her making a pronouncement and people falling all over themselves in their eagerness to obey). Sure enough, the victim soon started to be put in first place and awarded the highest honor. Victims started being called heroes. The term is applied only to victims of spectacular crimes—international terrorism and such—but it seemed a proper start.

Then picky Miss Manners noticed another precedence problem. It wasn't just that hero was an odd term for someone who had been drawn inadvertently into a horrible situation and had suffered terribly before, God willing, being rescued. Heroism, by her definition, is a risky action someone bravely undertakes voluntarily. But never mind. She had been complaining about victims' being slighted, and it seemed churlish to quibble when they were upgraded.

The trouble was that the rescuers were now being slighted. Miss Manners had said that victims deserved first place in line for sympathy, but this wasn't about sympathy. When it comes to heroics, the rescuer has first place, although victims who bravely or cleverly manage to rescue themselves especially qualify.

The young American pilot who was shot down in Bosnia and rescued by Marines was as troubled as Miss Manners by this error in awarding precedence. Throughout his hero's welcome home—the full treatment, complete with White House honors—he kept trying to tell people that he was "a scared bunny trying to survive," not a hero, and to point out that his rescuers, having risked their lives to save him, were the heroes of the situation. Nobody except Miss Manners (and, she hopes, those heroes whom he was vainly endeavoring to make the nation treat as such) was listening. Others kept calling the pilot a hero and all but ignoring the rescuers.

Another term that has puzzled Miss Manners in connection with crime is "a cry for help." Her first impression that this describes what the victim utters during the crime turned out to be a mistake. The only statement that now seems to be required of a victim, aside from whatever the police hope to get, is a fastidiously polite disavowal of any desire for revenge or punishment, with the explanation, "My only concern is that what happened to me not happen to anyone else."

"A cry for help" has turned out to be popular as the polite term for the crime itself—as in "It was a real cry for help; he shot eleven people in the mall." Miss Manners doesn't mind this usage; etiquette adores euphemisms, and this one has another manners element—compassion—thrown in. She only objects when the criminal element starts turning the phrase around, and using it to cast blame on the innocent.

You just can't trust those criminals. They rudely complain that the victim, or society, should have noticed the problem before they cried for help, and solved it. Criminals' polite families still say that they suffer for the families of the victim—but now they spoil it by going on to say that they are suffering too, and why doesn't everybody just call it even?

The polite criminal, not to mention the prudent one, is supposed to express remorse. Miss Manners can't help thinking that the frequent omission of this

NEW YORK, N.Y.—A public homecoming celebration in Harlem planned for former heavyweight boxing champion and convicted rapist Mike Tyson after he served three years in jail "set off a storm of controversy among Harlem residents," according to the *New York Times*. "Our objections to celebrating Tyson are based on a long history of his abuse and degradation of black women, a history that culminated with his conviction," one resident told the *Times*. Others maintained that a heroic welcome would be a way of saying that Mr. Tyson deserved a second chance.

nowadays, which shocks judges and produces longer sentences, is the result of dealing with a criminal class that never learned the most basic principle of manners—that other people actually have feelings—and the related etiquette rule—that one must at least pretend to acknowledge this. If a criminal's family is to be polite, it can say that it wished it could have helped the criminal in such a way that he would not have committed the crime. Still, the criminal's family is supposed to depict its suffering, however terrible, as secondary to that of the victim and the victim's family. Miss Manners wishes that criminals would put more thought into these questions of precedence. Perhaps the exercise would help them stay out of trouble.

Prejudice against Crime

Dear Miss Manners,

I am a sex offender who will be released from prison next year, after serving nearly nine years' time. While incarcerated, I've had some therapy, and I know that I will continue with support groups and counseling as needed, post-release. However, I've seen ever-increasing social prejudice scapegoating ex-offenders, and I wonder if I will ever be given a fair chance by society to re-start my life. For instance, I do not wish to lie on job applications or to a friend about my past; on the other hand, I do not wish to give out information that others would use against me.

Gentle Reader,

Miss Manners wishes you well and hopes that you are able to make your honest way in society. But she has trouble with the common assumption, which you make, about what it means to start afresh.

Ordinary society is not as obliged as the law is to ignore people's undisputed past records when assessing them, Miss Manners maintains. The law has harsh sanctions and the force to impose them, after which it must consider itself satisfied. Society must attend to people's histories to assess them—and in ways that the law doesn't need to use, because the law can assess blame through examining evidence and witnesses. A good reputation is therefore essential, except, of course, on talk shows.

Using reputation as a guide to character may easily become unfair. Malicious people are sometimes successful in damaging the reputations of blameless people. Damage can be so serious that legal redress is available against slander and libel. But you are talking about acquiring a reputation for what you *did* do. This is also hard, especially on someone who has reformed. However, it is not quite as unfair, is it?

Miss Manners would caution you to focus less on blaming society, as suggested in your loaded terms of "prejudice" and "scapegoating," and concentrate on building a good reputation. This is done by responding to any revelation from the past with expressions of remorse, but, most of all, by accumulating a record of good behavior.

Although people are understandably afraid of those with criminal records, you will find that there is a tremendous fund of good will nowadays for the reformed. Just don't push it by condemning people as prejudiced when they don't automatically consider that anyone's personal history is totally irrelevant if it happens to include being caught and doing time.

Two Replies

DEAR MISS MANNERS,

I wonder about the significance of your good wishes! The people of this great nation, by paying little or no attention to the notion of paying a debt to society, have done two wrong things. One is to tell an offender that hypocrisy is quite AOK—I can tell you that you have paid, as long as you don't really expect me to believe it. The second is that by the way we treat ex-convicts, we have created, in addition to their victims, a whole new class of victims. They are the victims of a vengeful and unforgiving society.

DEAR MISS MANNERS,

Will the victim of the sex criminal who whined about social prejudice ever be able to restart her, his or their lives? He chose to do what he did, and it doesn't seem too outrageous that he must live—forever—with the consequences, including social ostracism. I'm not sure why he directed his question to an etiquette writer, but I hope he understands that social scorn directed against those who have injured the innocent is not rude.

Choosing Etiquette's Punishment over the Law's

DEAR MISS MANNERS,

Several years ago, my lovely adult daughter confided that she had been molested during her adolescence. She was baby-sitting for a couple with whom we were friendly, and the children's father behaved criminally toward her as he took her home. When she finally told me, she insisted I take no action. Both we and her attacker's family had moved to other states.

A few years ago, we moved back, and one day I answered a knock at the door and found myself face to face with my child's molester. I was speechless with shock, and reverted to the formula manners I learned as a child, which encapsulates to "never give offense." I actually found myself chatting with the man. When he and his wife and teenage daughter unexpectedly came again and expressed a desire to return to the neighborhood, I was extremely cold. But still I felt that I behaved in a cowardly manner to allow them in at all.

My daughter, who lives with us, insists that no "scene" be made. I realize that I should have dealt decisively with this when he first arrived. What should I have done? What can I do now? Further contact with this man is unimaginable, although I bear his poor wife no ill will. I am sure that she has no idea about the event that occurred ten years ago. This is beyond the normal bounds of etiquette, and although I can manage a fish fork, I have no solution.

GENTLE READER,

"Never give offense" is not a correct rule of etiquette. Almost never, yes. But there are times when one must choose to offend, in preference to condoning, or even cooperating with, those who are not bound by standards of decent behavior.

Miss Manners would like to point out that it is just that incorrect desire never to give offense that prevents children from fighting or exposing the advances of adults. Prosecuting criminals is, indeed, a matter for law, rather than etiquette. Miss Manners will not therefore discuss your daughter's decision. But etiquette does have a supplementary form for registering social condemnation, which is what you are in a position to do.

Marie Antoinette pays the price for personifying an etiquette taken beyond all sensible and tasteful limits into snobbery and arrogance. As she discovered, people who rightly find this rude tend to go beyond the limits of civility themselves when expressing their disapproval.

You must cut the man dead. The way to do this while meeting your daughter's requirement that you not make a scene, and your own that you not involve his wife, is to send him a letter saying, "My family wants nothing to do with you. I'm sure I needn't tell you the reason."

Etiquette's Consolation

DEAR MISS MANNERS,

One of our co-workers has been sent off to the county lockup for a few months, and several of us who worked with him would like to send a note to let him know we're thinking of him.

A get well card just isn't quite the right message. Best wishes could be misconstrued, and Good Luck is out completely. See what a quandary we're in? We all realize that life's lessons are a little harder for some and that this particular lesson was probably appropriate under the circumstances, but we'd also like it not to be a completely negative experience. Can you help us do the right thing?

GENTLE READER,

What exactly is it that you hope will not be a negative experience? Jail? Or your card?

There's not much you can do that will render the former agreeable. Nor is there anything you do to assist in the teaching of the lesson you mention that would not also be disagreeable. The message for which you are searching is a simple "We miss you." You might add that you look forward to his return, a sentiment which he probably does not take for granted.

SHAME

Shame is the target emotion of the season, Miss Manners has observed. Pop psychologists have discovered it and issued instructions to the endangered population on how to identify shame within themselves and root it out.

Miss Manners can't help thinking that this is a great shame. It seems to be part of a long-term, ongoing campaign to rid us of pesky emotional discomfort. Guilt was long ago diagnosed as an unpleasant and destructive feeling, the potential consequences of which justified its victims in devoting major portions of their lives and incomes to exorcising it.

One might very well point out that Miss Manners is herself engaged in what must appear to be a related endeavor—averting social discomfort. Why should she be suspicious of the kindly idea of obliterating shame?

She can tell you without blushing. Shame is the proper reaction when one has purposefully violated the accepted behavior of society. Inflicting it is etiquette's response when its rules are disobeyed. The law has all kinds of nasty ways of retaliating when it is disregarded, but etiquette has only a sense of social shame to deter people from treating others in ways they know are wrong. So naturally Miss Manners wants to maintain the sense of shame. Some forms of discomfort are fully justified, and the person who feels shame ought to be dealing with removing its causes rather than seeking to relieve the symptoms.

Does this sound mean? Miss Manners doubts that people really want to relieve those who act shamefully of being ashamed, any more than they really want to relieve those who are guilty of crimes from feeling any sense of guilt. What has created the confusion, she believes, is that they want, as does Miss Manners, to absolve people who may be feeling undeserved discomfort, and they keep shoving perfectly justified internal punishments into that category. Just as the word "guilt" came to refer chiefly to a false sense of guilt, in association with matters for which the harborer of guilt bore no responsibility, shame is now coming to refer to a false sense of shame over matters that are in no way shameful.

False shame, in etiquette terms, would mean feeling shame because one is poor, ill or unfamiliar with the etiquette rules of a new situation. If one follows the principles of manners about being gracious and makes an honest effort to learn and follow the rules as best one can, the only legitimate shame will attach to anyone who did not respond graciously.

When people seek to eradicate all forms of shame, Miss Manners gets worried. How are they supposed to feel when they are rude? Proud? A great many do, and Miss Manners thinks they should be ashamed of themselves.

The explanation that people who behave badly will improve if you replace their shame with a positive self-image does not go over with her. Nor does she accept the brash argument that people who have obviously behaved badly should not have to feel shame because it might make them do something worse, such as striking out violently against society, or injuring themselves. By this theory, it seems to Miss Manners, it is people with no conscience who will behave the best. She believes that those who propagate such a dangerous idea ought to be ashamed of themselves.

Equal Opportunity Shame

DEAR MISS MANNERS,

You have mentioned that if individuals do not act in a manner generally approved of by "society," they have to suffer society's sanctions. Social control is an absolute necessity in any and every society, but especially in so large and individualistic a society as ours.

But how is this to be accomplished? We now have such a fragmented culture that peer pressure is diminished and rudeness and crime (extreme rudeness) abound. To complicate matters even further, it appears to be "politically correct" to advocate a pluralistic, multicultural society (I personally don't agree), so perhaps one person's bad manners were correct in his culture. If so, doesn't that negate the whole concept of manners in America and manners especially as a form of social control, at least in principle?

GENTLE READER,

No.

American manners draw on both a variety of traditions and on the original ideas of the country's founders, who had a specific interest in developing an egalitarian etiquette that would be different from the aristocratic traditions they knew. Nevertheless—and additionally allowing for the unawareness of newcomers and for regional differences—we can all distinguish good American manners from bad. When a character in a national television drama behaves rudely, no one mistakes this for politeness, not even those who cheer him on or laugh. Etiquette errors are often inserted deliberately into television commercials, because transgressions arrest the audience's attention. This ploy wouldn't work if everyone did not recognize these shared standards.

As to how we punish the bad, that is a more difficult problem. Society's consequences for violating etiquette are not—nor should they be—what society's consequences are for mass murder or grand larceny. For this reason, etiquette zealots are often frustrated enough to take matters into their own hands, delivering rude punishments for rudeness, much as outlaw vigilantes punish violations of the law by illegal means.

Obviously, Miss Manners condemns vigilantism. She also believes it to be based on an underestimation of what she has been pleased to call society's sanctions.

Shameless Bragging

Ever gratified to hear of sinners' awakening to the desire to help others, Miss Manners has been noticing an amazing phenomenon. Everybody who publicly confesses to behavior that the society used to consider disgraceful now admits to doing so solely out of the desire to be of public service.

"I'm speaking out so that my experience will serve as a warning to others," they will say.

"I want to reach out to other people who might have the same problems, so they know they're not alone."

"I wouldn't want anyone else to have to go through what I did."

"I want people to know that you can live through this and come out all right."

"If I've helped even one person, it will have been worth it."

This high-minded admission, along with the lurid confessions that go with it, has been common for some time now. It strikes Miss Manners and everybody else as being so laudably philanthropic that she is embarrassed to be harboring troublesome little questions: Does it, in fact, help others? Has all this open confession served as a deterrent to errant behavior? Are things improving?

Miss Manners doesn't know the answer, and certainly cannot presume to deny that the modest goal that these altruists set—of saving one soul—is achieved. She also realizes that the comfort of those who thus discover that they are not the worst people in the world must be considerable. But before she joins in the admiration for the courage exhibited by public confessors, she would like to explore whether perhaps some incidental damage is also being done. Could all this confessing be contributing to destroying the concepts—minor perhaps, but dear to her—of privacy and reputation?

That the privacy of the confessors vanishes is probably not something Miss Manners needs to worry about. Many people seem eager to abandon their privacy voluntarily, especially when there is a chance to do so on television. Others may have originally been prompted to go public involuntarily, by such institutions as our open criminal court system or our less formal blackmail system, but have subsequently chosen to expand public knowledge of their cases.

This is their privilege. Miss Manners is only puzzled as to why it is characterized as courageous to sacrifice a reputation one has already lost or that one is eager to exchange for attention. What does trouble Miss Manners is establishing the idea that there is no point in building a fine lifetime reputation, because a checkered past can never fairly be counted against one. Public confession has become an eraser of misdeeds, and the slate of a person who has committed serious transgressions can be quickly made as clean as that of someone who has managed to stay out of trouble.

Goodness knows that Miss Manners believes in the redemption of souls, or she would hardly be in the business she is in. The etiquette trade is big on forgiveness. She just can't warm to the idea that a newly cleaned record is considered no worse than one that was never tarnished. Or maybe better.

Understanding and forgiveness, two noble attitudes toward the morally weak, have quietly slipped into becoming admiration. It is beginning to sound as if those who have always managed to stay out of major trouble are not just dull (ever the downside of being known to be good), but lacking in imagination and spirit. Not being fully developed, they would have nothing useful to teach anyone else. A wicked past becomes a qualification to teach virtue.

Leaving aside the peculiar idea that anyone who hasn't erred doesn't know much about life (staying out of trouble cannot be as easy as all that, or more people might do it), aren't those who succumbed to weakness more likely to lapse again? Are they really safe examples to hold up? It's not that Miss Manners doesn't commend the spirit that has led these people, with all their other difficulties, to offer themselves as role models to others. It's just that she wonders how come we don't seem to have better candidates for the job.

Shameful Bragging

DEAR MISS MANNERS,

A well known local artist who was speaking at school was quoted in the paper as saying, "I am very, very wealthy." She told the students about her houses and cars, and about her ability to travel anywhere she wants.

The reporter said she wasn't bragging, she was trying to get across to the students that they can accomplish anything they want when they do something they like. "You have to do what you want to do in this life," she explained. "My daughter is gay and repairs cars. She is kind and beautiful." I was shocked—should I have been?

GENTLE READER,

What shocks Miss Manners nowadays is how many people are selflessly willing to sacrifice their privacy in order to serve as examples to others. We used to call this exhibitionism, and some of us still do.

However, Miss Manners finds the moral of this particular school lesson—you can become rich by doing whatever it is you feel like doing anyway—dubious at best. If the children are not already rich enough to own cars, the only valuable nugget of information here—that there is a kind-hearted car mechanic in town—will be lost on them.

LONDON, ENGLAND—In an editorial, *Country Life* magazine bemoaned the lack of proper sanctions to punish the young man who publicly discussed his intimate relationship with HRH the Princess of Wales. "These days it is difficult to imagine what horror a person would have to commit to achieve social ostracism," said the magazine.

SHOCK

Miss Manners considers it her duty to be shocked whenever possible. She has, for example, made it a point to act shocked for the purpose of encouraging young artists. It is naturally their ambition to shock the bourgeoisie, but the poor dears are unable to find anyone willing to own up to being bourgeois, much less to being shockable. *"Il faut épater le bourgeois"* has become the rallying cry of the middle class.

So she tries to make it up to them by saying "My stars!" when they show her yet another painted or sculpted version of what used to be known as ladies' or gentlemen's private parts. Etiquetteers are known to be a fastidious lot—the merest hint that the human body is capable of functions other than writing thank you letters is supposed to make their hair curl, which is why you don't find them hanging out at the hairdressers'—and Miss Manners believes that those of her noble profession have the duty to foster this belief. The ones who succumb and start issuing pseudo-etiquette rules about how to offer intense overnight hospitality to strangers, or about the correct way to serve illegal refreshments are not only betraying the cause but, Miss Manners believes, taking the fun out of life.

We have here a society crammed with people who have a desire to shock others, and nearly devoid of those who are willing to register shock. As a result, shocking people are running out of audiences and—since there are, in fact, limitations to the number of things the human body can do—of ideas. That is one reason why she would like to restore profanity to its real function, which is to shock people.

It was Miss Manners' dear Mamma who pointed out to her (once she was safely grown up) that parents who take calmly all of their children's attempts to shock them are setting themselves up for trouble. "The children will just have to keep going until they succeed," she warned. "If necessary, they will figure out that parents who can't be shocked by licentiousness can be shocked by prudery. Wild children can shock rigid parents, of course, but the reverse works just as well. People who oblige their children by going to pieces at the first naughty word will save themselves a lot of heart-break."

Sooner or later, then, we really are all shockable. Yet it is considered desirable nowadays to pretend that one is totally unflappable, with a reckless disregard of how difficult this makes life for apprentice rebels and for others eager to get a rise out of someone. Miss Manners is just being efficient when she presses a limp hand to her fevered brow at the first sign, and she recommends it as the proper reaction when someone violates good taste. For those with a smaller dramatic range, there is the raised eyebrow and the terse little comment, "I don't care for that," or "We don't talk that way in this house."

The tedious people on both sides of the question will break in at this point, Miss Manners is well aware, to demand to know either why something "everybody knows about" can be considered obscene in any situation, or how obscenity can be precisely defined so that it may be outlawed everywhere. Miss Manners herself tends to oppose turning such matters into law. As one who has long been in the business of telling people things they may not want to hear, she is extremely wary of official limitations. The law does not work as well in regulating taste for everyday life, because taste is too elusive and context-dependent to be defined in legal terms.

Manners are gentler, knowing that people nevertheless recognize what is good and bad taste, and asking them to close the bathroom door when nobody wants to watch. Dutiful parents teach this sense by example: "Yes, dear, that is the correct name for it, but it's not the term we use in polite society" and "I don't doubt that all your friends think it's smart, but I find it offensive." Eventually everybody develops enough of a feel for it to recognize what is offensive—most of all those who wish to offend. Otherwise, they wouldn't know how to attempt it. It seems to Miss Manners that the subtler and more flexible discipline of etiquette is better equipped than law to handle matters of taste, setting limits through social disapproval. But it requires the citizens to do their part by admitting to being shockable.

Defunct Shock

DEAR MISS MANNERS,

In the world in which my husband and I grew up, he would not have been able to throw me away (and our grown daughter along with me) after twenty-five years, without suffering the disapproval of society, which would have affected his career and reputation and income. Since by the time of the divorce he was a circuit court judge, that would have meant a sizable risk and he might have decided that it wasn't worth it to have lunch and eventually an affair with the new, younger, buxom court clerk recently assigned to him.

Surely no matter how kindly we try to view our fellow human beings, we know that many of us—most? almost all?—don't have the basic character and integrity to do the right thing for its own sake, or for our self-respect. Most of us need some fear to help us find the discipline to remain civilized. Increasingly, that has not involved what might be called religious fears. But until recently, there was still some concern for the disapproval of other human beings—that is, "society."

> **In a story on the "new" Marine Corps the *Wall Street Journal* reported that "Once notoriously foul-mouthed, Parris Island's drill instructors today are forbidden to use obscenities. At the same time, their recruits arrive steeped in casual vulgarity from pop music, cable TV, and every day conversation. So it is all the more unnerving to face a D.I. who appears to be insanely angry—but who never swears."**

Do you really prefer a world in which my ex-husband (and most other men) could do what he did and lose nothing? Do you think that is good for women? For their children? For society as a whole? Will you be willing to have your taxes go up to help support women like me as we age and are forced to go on the dole for thirty or forty years?

GENTLE READER,

Now, now. However bitter you understandably feel, you really do not want to put this to Miss Manners on financial grounds. That shifts the argument not just from morality to manners, but from manners to money. Surely, you do not want to find yourself arguing with other taxpayers about why people in their forties would be presumed permanently helpless to support themselves.

Besides, this approach is not necessary. Miss Manners is already full of compassion for you and deeply interested in the issue you raise about society's using the power of shocked disapproval in the interests of morality.

As you say, the expression of social opinion, as a way of punishing bad behavior, has largely been abandoned—unless, of course, someone lights up a cigarette. Lesser crimes, from abandoning one's family right up to murder, no longer inspire indignation. This attitude started some years ago, when exercising judgment (good) turned into being judgmental (bad). Later, confession was seen as compensation for sin, as in "Sure, he rapes and pillages, but at least he has the courage to be honest about it." Most recently, it has come to be considered bad taste to reach into the past and condemn anyone for anything that isn't actually happening at the moment: "All right, so she committed armed robbery, but that was last month, and she's been a model citizen ever since."

Whew. Now that you have concluded that Miss Manners is about to take up her trusty cudgel to defend you, if she can only stop trembling, let us discuss the advantages and disadvantages of these changes.

Increased empathy, forgiveness and the public's desire to mind its own business are all tremendous gains. Society's indifference to good and bad is, however, a loss, not only because it fails to encourage good, but because it suggests that there really is no such thing. Miss Manners would dearly love to keep the gains without suffering the losses, greedy as that may sound. Thus she believes that the weapon of disapproval should be used—but judiciously. We all know how common it is for public opinion to condemn someone in erroneous anticipation of the justice system.

The retreat from a blanket condemnation of divorce is, at least in part, an overdue acknowledgment that it is difficult for outsiders to judge what is going on in a marriage. In the past, people who had compelling reasons to leave a marriage, such as their own physical safety, were inhibited from doing so by that indiscriminate social disapproval. Even in clear-cut cases, the old way did not work as fairly as you seem to think. While a husband who behaved like a cad would initially come in for his share of disapproval, suspicion also commonly attached itself to the innocent wife, with such mean notions as "She probably drove him to it." A divorced husband was soon known as a "bachelor," which white-washed the marital record, while the wife forever bore the label of "divorcée," a term that managed to be simultaneously racy and pathetic.

In all sympathy, Miss Manners does not think you would be better off to be socially characterized as having been abandoned by a villain, than as simply a dignified lady, formerly married, but now living independently.

QUESTIONABLE SANCTIONS

Two new forms of rudeness have been identified, as if Miss Manners were not busy enough trying to stamp out the time-honored forms. They are "demonizing" and "stigmatizing," and they are masquerading as social sanctions.

It seems that everyone is running around demonizing and stigmatizing everyone else, or running around accusing one another of such, or accusing the people who make the accusations of demonizing and stigmatizing the people about whom they make them. It's all very unpleasant and confusing, and Miss Manners will have to do something about it. Please cut it out.

Cut what out? That's where the problem arises. Exactly what is meant by these two crimes is not totally clear, even though everyone seems to agree that they are heinous.

At first examination, the new rudenesses sound remarkably like some not-so-nice old fashioned ones: insult, and its wholesale application, bigotry. It is all very well to rename the practice of saying nasty things about people, either individually or in groups, but then no credit can be claimed for the discovery of new sins.

On closer inspection, Miss Manners noticed something slightly different in the use of the old and new terms. Classic insults and bigotry generally claim to identify what individuals or categories of people supposedly are, by accident of birth or nature. Condemning people as stupid, ugly, lazy, devious or shifty purports to target inborn characteristics.

In contrast, demonizing and stigmatizing seem to have more to do with matters determined after birth—the targets' views, profession, actions or plight. Examples would be those strongly for or against such hotly contested issues as abortion or the death penalty; politicians, lawyers or police; smokers or surfers; those who are homeless, ill or on welfare. In other words, your basic mix of citizens.

Miss Manners is not about to say that, oh, well, in that case, go right ahead. Vilifying people for their ideals, their legitimate professions or activities or, even worse, their misfortunes, is only marginally more edifying than insulting them for supposed circumstances of birth. Surely we can learn to debate issues, actions and situations without being hateful. (Surely not, the evidence suggests, but Miss Manners lives in hope.) It is one of the basic tenets of manners, long predating these new terms, that polite people can argue vigorously without calling their opponents or, more likely, their opponents' mothers, mean names.

Notice that such politeness does not preclude holding and airing opinions. Miss

Manners is prepared to argue (vigorously) that the only way to register opposing views is to do so politely. Introducing personal attacks always shelves the real subject of debate while personal taunts and counter-taunts are substituted for issues. Thus, the identification and condemnation of demonizing and stigmatizing ought to be right up her line. Yet—ever the fuss-budget—there is something about them that worries her.

A clear distinction has not been made between stigmatizing and demonizing people for matters that are, after all, respectable, even if hotly disputed, and for those that are not respectable. Sometimes, Miss Manners has noticed, what is claimed to be demonized is villainy or viciousness and what is claimed to be stigmatized is illegality, immorality or rudeness. The danger, then, becomes that of condemning people for condemning the corrupt. The new terms have been gratefully taken up by convicted criminals, who complain that they are being stigmatized, and by hatemongers, who complain that they are being demonized. By this usage, stigmatizing and demonizing are only new names for "passing judgment"—the phrase in use when the habit of distinguishing between good and evil came to be judged harshly.

Miss Manners has always advocated minding one's own business, which normally precludes gathering enough information to be able to render moral judgments on others' private matters. She has always been opposed to—no, horrified by—those who give themselves license to be rude to people who do not meet their moral stance on legitimately debatable issues.

Abandoning the exercise of moral judgment altogether, and refraining from punishing clear wrongdoing by social condemnation, is further than she is prepared to go. To maintain its standards, polite society has only its approval to give or withhold. It should strive to be fair, it should encourage reform, and it should recognize when a record of good deeds has become long enough to justify dislodging an older bad record. It really does not need to associate with people it doesn't trust. It should not be demonized, or even stigmatized, for noticing who has behaved well.

Suspending Judgment

Dear Miss Manners,

I certainly hope this is not a controlling move on my part: I work at a large senior high school, where there is a teachers' parking lot with a Do Not Enter drive located on the southwest side. Because some teachers have to drive around the lot to enter properly, they choose to enter by way of the Do Not Enter route. This really upset me and I spoke to the principal, who put a "That's naughty" memo in the weekly bulletin. I feel these people are breaking the law, setting a poor example of citizenship, and certainly not teaching our kids respect for rules. Is there anything I can possibly do to correct this without offending or seeming morally judgmental?

Gentle Reader,

Miss Manners is bewildered about what sort of example you want to set. You seem to feel strongly about the matter, and yet you keep apologizing, even going so far as to endorse the sort of moral neutrality to which you obviously object, by characterizing your own action as possibly "controlling" and "judgmental." She is afraid that this sort of talk convinces the young that it is wrong to care about the difference between right and wrong.

The difficulty, in Miss Manners' opinion, is that there are two problems here, a deep problem and a surface problem. It is one thing to identify a wrong and quite another to find the proper way to correct it when you are not yourself authorized to do so. The deep question is whether teachers who scoff at inconvenient laws are double offenders, in that they also set bad examples. The surface question is not so much whether one person has the right to condemn the illegalities of others, so much as how one can properly do this.

Miss Manners clearly agrees with your judgment that violating the law, regularly and in front of children, is outrageous. She also condones your first move at correction, which quite properly consisted of reporting violations to the obvious authority. It is too bad that the principal seems to have treated the matter lightly. There are other possible moves. You should bring the subject up at a teacher conference. Do so in a polite way, not only to minimize the inevitable annoyance, but because that creates a more receptive atmosphere for change. You could also report the violations to the police. Adding that "there are children involved" might arouse some interest in correcting the situation.

Chapter Seven

APPLICATIONS FOR
ETIQUETTE EXEMPTIONS

xcuses, excuses, excuses. Etiquette is all very well for those who can manage it, Miss Manners has been told by those who don't intend to try. People who have no emotions worth talking about, nor anything particular to do with their time probably ought to be behaving politely, they will concede.

Miss Manners nods graciously to acknowledge the description of herself. As for themselves, they continue, they can't, you see, because:

They had desperately unhappy childhoods.

Their children are driving them crazy.

They live in crowded cities.

They live in towns where etiquette doesn't matter because everybody knows everybody else.

Their jobs (saving lives, running businesses, whatever) are so essential that they cannot be bothered with trivial impediments.

They're artists and can't get people's attention by being polite.

They're politicians and can't get people's attention by being polite.

They're lawyers and can't adequately represent their clients by being polite.

They have an important moral message to deliver and can't get people's attention or adequately represent their cause by being polite.

They're in service professions and people aren't polite to them.

It's too hot out.

They are under stress.

It's too cold out.

They're in a hurry.

They're too concerned with looking after their own responsibilities.

Holidays always depress them.

They've been victimized in their love affairs.

It's raining.

They don't feel comfortable with rules.

The weather's too nice out to be bothered.

They're busy.

All right, all right. That's enough.

Suppose, for the sake of argument, that Miss Manners did grant indulgences to all the people in those categories. Who would be left to be polite?

As everyone gratefully leaves the premises, Miss Manners can see them waving pleasantly at her, wishing her a good time all by herself. She and whoever else cares about etiquette are more than welcome to go around practicing it, if only all those others are absolved from the obligation.

As a matter of sad fact, Miss Manners can't even count on the company of those who profess to care about etiquette. They too have applied to be relieved of the necessity for practicing good manners on the impeccable grounds that they are teaching good manners. The etiquette avengers—Smash, bam, that'll learn 'em some manners. And you wonder why Miss Manners carries a fan even in cool weather.

Never mind that for-the-sake-of-argument question. Miss Manners does not grant manners exemptions to anyone.

No, not even to doctors who explain that they are saving lives. If they would look around their own emergency rooms, they would find that some of those lives that need to be saved were endangered because a dispute over etiquette—typically, that someone felt treated disrespectfully—ended in violence. If they would talk to their insurers, they would find that rudeness is often what provokes patients to sue for malpractice.

Not to people who live in crowded conditions, because obedience to rules is especially needed then to prevent people from getting on one another's nerves.

Not to people who have been treated badly by their families, lovers, friends, because they, of all people, should know how it feels to be treated badly and make a special effort not to subject others to bad treatment.

Not to business people, whether they are CEOs or clerks, because there is a direct relationship between polite service and doing right by employees, employers and customers.

Not to people who have a political, moral or artistic message to get across, because people whose feelings have been outraged by contempt are not receptive to ideas and while the novelty of shock does get their attention, shocking behavior is no longer novel.

Not to people who claim that they live among people who don't care about such things, because there are no people who don't care whether they are treated rudely.

Not to people pleading weather conditions, because that argument is too silly for Miss Manners to consider.

Not to people who claim that they must attend instead to their family or other responsibilities, because keeping the world peaceful is everyone's responsibility, and besides, rudeness breaks up families.

Not to people who just don't feel comfortable being polite, because they need to consider the comfort of others as well, for selfish as well as altruistic reasons—those who have been made uncomfortable are not accepting it meekly.

Not to people under stress, because a lot of the stress in the modern world is caused by having to endure other people's rudeness.

Not to people in a hurry, because, for goodness' sake, did you ever meet anyone who didn't claim to be in a hurry?

Finally, not to people who are just too busy, because that would include everyone in the world. Except, of course, Miss Manners, who has nothing to do all day long except to persuade people that it is essential to be civil.

Creative Excuses

"Why, of course. Don't give it another thought. It doesn't matter in the least." That is the sound of etiquette being characteristically gracious and generous about accepting the excuses of those who break its rules. Why people should assume that good manners are practiced only by the heartless (presumably leaving consideration and compassion to be maintained by the rude), Miss Manners cannot imagine. The very system has built into it a requirement to ensure that sparing people's feelings takes precedence over mindlessly applying ordinary surface rules.

Good manners require the polite to defuse unnecessary embarrassment on the part of others. Some of the great etiquette heroines have even been known deliberately to repeat the etiquette mistakes of their guests so as to assuage inadvertent transgressors. Then what is this sound (not exactly coming from Miss Manners, because that would be unladylike, but reeling about inside her)? "Aaaaaaargh!"

That is the reaction of a forgiving, understanding, generous, lean-over-backward, noblesse oblige–crazed polite person when she has heard this kindness abused. Because everybody who violates etiquette rules (like everyone who commits a crime) has an explanation, the argument goes, there shouldn't be any etiquette rules.

Wrong. The rules are needed, and explanations for breaking them are judged on a case-by-case basis. Here are some judgments from the Supreme Authority.

A Gentle Reader attempted to defend "the man who licks his plate at the table and then eats from the pot with the cooking utensil" (thus revolting his wife) on the grounds that he "has an eating disorder. While discussing his manners may change his behavior—of which he is clearly unaware—I suspect it will also shame him deeply, probably into avoiding the dinner table and eating alone elsewhere. I know these symptoms because they were once mine. I got help from Overeaters Anonymous."

Miss Manners notices a small flaw in the argument. Had this behavior been politely allowed, the eating problem, if indeed that is what it is, would have gone undiagnosed. Let us hope that the plate-licker seeks a cure and does not come back to the table until his manners problem is cured.

The Gentle Reader who breaks the rule against gentlemen wearing hats indoors "because I am having chemotherapy, and I'll wear my hat in the house and at the table no matter what you say—it would be most rude of me to remove it" is of course exempted from it. His attempt to take this further by declaring that there should be no rule against hats in case anyone else requires an exemption is thrown out.

The claim that it is "extremely callous" to expect people to return wedding presents when they break off an engagement is made by a Gentle Reader who wants to use her distress to cancel her etiquette obligations to generous friends. "If a wedding is canceled a week before the ceremony, chances are the bride and groom are going through very emotional times. When mine was canceled, due to his sleeping with someone else, I was deeply depressed for weeks. I couldn't concentrate on work, cried nightly, lost all interest or willpower to do anything but sit at home. Even suicide seemed like an option. Thank goodness my friends were more understanding . . . I eventually got everything together, and most people were kind enough to allow me to keep the gifts they had bought. Perhaps charity and compassion are no longer considered polite and appropriate behavior? If so, I choose to be socially incorrect and instead support the people I care about."

Yes, charity and compassion are polite behavior. That is why we allow people a reasonable period in which to get their feelings together. We then require them to refrain from claiming that their suffering entitles them to abuse the feelings of others.

The Only-Joking Excuse

DEAR MISS MANNERS,

As a young African-American woman with a large number of intellectual interests and activities, I often find myself in culturally diverse and racially mixed social situations. One of my interests happens to be ballroom dancing. One evening I was finishing a particularly energetic polka when I was beckoned by Wanda and Rick, a white couple of my acquaintance.

She and I have been friends since college, and it had been understood that I would be her maid of honor. Imagine my dismay when Rick, whom I also consider a friend, begins to talk about how he wants to plan his wedding so that it will totally shock and/or annoy his conservative Catholic parents.

"Well, for one thing," Wanda chimed in, "the maid of honor will be black." This she said as if it were some type of diseased state which she had never previously noticed in me. Rick continued, within earshot of many

NEW YORK, N.Y.—Manhattan high school students sent an anonymous anti-Semitic note to a Jewish teacher and in Greenwich, Conn., five high school boys inserted a coded message of racial hatred—"Kill All Niggers"—into their school yearbook. But the *New York Times* **reported that, instead of recognizing this as blatant bigotry, many involved in the incidents analyzed them in terms of social class tensions, economic differences and the problems of adolescence. "Such cruelty among young people is hardly ever motivated by bigotry alone, and can often mask larger insecurities, frustrations, petty rivalries, hostilities and other emotions that are a part of coming of age," the** *Times* **wrote.**

others, to tell in detail how he was going to choose purposefully as his best man a "friend" from school who physically is my exact opposite (short, quite heavyset and with Anglo-American features) so that we can provide comic figures during the first dance at the reception.

I admit that I did not send this letter to ask Miss Manners whether or not I should feel insulted. I do. I write to question the propriety of mentioning such a thing, the absolute disregard shown for my feelings and the feelings of Rick's "friend," and the maturity of a couple who would consider such a thing amusing.

They consider themselves "liberal minded" individuals. I am convinced that among people of my generation, the belief is held that as long as one spouts politically correct dogma, one may say anything one likes and hide behind "just kidding" or "only joking." Furthermore, they are less likely to demonstrate racist behavior, despite personal tenets. While I feel Rick and Wanda are not ignorant people, I do think that they, like so many people in the age range between 16 and 30, have decided that good manners are synonymous with the evils of hypocrisy and voting for the Republican Party. Much has been said about the negative effects of blatant racial prejudice in America, but little has been done about teaching young people to deal with a racially tolerant and culturally diverse atmosphere.

Since college, I have been a bridesmaid for four friends, all of whom were white, but none of whom seemed to consider my race a decorative novelty. All were asking me to participate in their lives in a specially dignified way. Maybe Rick and Wanda thought they were "only joking," but I found their remarks neither witty nor friendly. Since when were the physical attributes of a maid of honor meant to supersede her friendship with the bride? How does Miss Manners feel that I may politely broach this subject with Rick and Wanda in order to let them know that I don't dislike them, but that I did dislike their actions?

Gentle Reader,

You did happen to mention, in rather peculiar terms, that your friends don't care for etiquette. Miss Manners might point out that people who do not practice etiquette are constantly prone to insulting other people whether they intend to or not. As you recognize, they have insulted one of their best friends.

It is not only the racial reference. You have been told that what you naturally assumed was an honor and an act of friendship is intended as a farce. Miss Manners does not want to hear about how liberal they may otherwise be. She is waiting to hear you report that you have informed these awful people that you do not wish to make a public spectacle of yourself at their instigation.

The Ignorance Excuse

When people stopped slapping one another across the face with their gloves, Miss Manners permitted herself to rejoice at what she took for progress. If she didn't dare hope that this was an improvement in human nature, she did imagine it an improvement in the great cause of repressing that nature before bringing out the pistols.

As it turned out, people were merely forgetting to wear their gloves, which is hardly progress. How to insult their fellow creatures is something they remembered perfectly well. Exchanges of contempt go on as always, only more bluntly and directly than of old.

Why should Miss Manners care if the old symbolic vocabulary of insult is disappearing? It is surely not her responsibility to preserve gestures by which people can give and take offense. If there are fewer ways of indicating that one person finds another despicable, so much the better. Or so she would have thought. Wrong.

The problem is that this symbolism has apparently been forgotten only by the people who are still running around performing such gestures. Those on whom they are performed understand them as insults and react accordingly, sometimes to the bewilderment of the insulter. The result is that etiquette warfare is being declared by people who later claim that they had no intention of doing so. They had no idea that certain behavior, which seems natural to them, is taken badly.

The classic gestures of contempt include:

Pretending not to recognize someone one knows, which is called the Cut Direct (to distinguish it from the indirect method, a curt nod or frozen smile, which, although not exactly brimming with warmth, at least acknowledges the other as a fellow human being while warning him not to approach).

Refusing to shake hands with someone under circumstances where it is clearly expected— i.e., the other person has a hand hanging out waiting.

Refusing to break bread with someone, which can take the form of ignoring offers of hospitality, or of refusing refreshment in an unapologetic and pointed way, as if to say that one cannot avoid being in that person's presence, but wants to make it understood that no pleasure is taken.

Returning a letter to the person who wrote it.

Returning a present to the person who gave it with the explanation that it isn't satisfactory.

Criticizing people's looks, families or manner of living to their faces (as opposed to the perhaps more damaging but less embarrassing method of doing it behind their backs).

This sounds like normal modern life, doesn't it? Miss Manners should not be surprised. We do live in a state of etiquette warfare, as a jittery society always on the verge of feeling wronged by one another's behavior. But wait. Couldn't there be some mistake?

Etiquette always recognizes that possibility. Built right into its system is the obligation to explain away any of these gestures one might have made, and to examine the ones directed toward oneself for extenuating circumstances. The person who seemed to be performing the Cut Direct could be nearsighted. The one who didn't shake hands might have arthritis. The person who seemed to disdain an invitation might not have received it. The one who won't break bread may have an allergy.

And so on. These are honorable excuses, and, if offered or anticipated, serve to defuse the sting:

"My answering machine wiped out all my messages, so I had no idea about your party— I'm just sick about having missed it."

"Was that you who passed me the other day? I was so preoccupied it didn't really register with me until later that I must have walked right by you."

"Not only did I have no idea that she was your sister-in-law, but I realized afterward that I had given totally the wrong impression—what I was trying to say is how much I admire her."

The devastated tone goes a long way toward showing that the insulting gesture was not meant in an insulting way. When those who commit these gestures do not realize that what they are doing is potentially insulting, they tend to offer explanations instead—and these tend to be stunningly insulting.

They return presents with the explanation that they can't really use what was chosen, they ignore invitations because they confess they can't make up their minds in advance

NEW YORK, N.Y.—A senior Time Warner executive, meeting with opponents of obscene rock and gangsta rap music produced by the company, refused three times to read aloud the violent and sexually explicit lyrics of one song, according to an account of the meeting in *The New Yorker* magazine. Asked if he considered the words "vulgar and potentially damaging to children," the magazine said the executive answered: "Art is hard to interpret."

whether or not they want to go, they ignore acquaintances because they were in a hurry and, best of all, they criticize people because they want to help them out by opening their eyes to their own inadequacies. In other words, they take pains to explain that they do not value the other person's company, offerings or feelings. That is not what Miss Manners would call a proper excuse.

The Sanitation Excuse

DEAR MISS MANNERS,

At a gathering I hosted, my friend Susan reached out her hand to another guest and said, "Hello, my name is Susan." The other guest replied, "Hi, I'm Mary," but pulled back her hand and bluntly said that she did not shake hands because she did not want to pick up any germs.

My friend was embarrassed, and I was aghast. To make matters worse, at this same gathering, Mary hugged many people she knew. Although she is a friend of many years, I am now reluctant to invite Mary to any future gatherings that may introduce her to new people. Do I have a duty to my guests to invite polite people? What should I say if Mary asks why she was excluded?

GENTLE READER,

To refuse to shake someone's hand is etiquette's second highest symbolic insult, right up there next to slapping someone across the face with one's gloves. But then, if Mary had been wearing her gloves, as Miss Manners keeps telling all ladies to do (to no avail whatsoever on any occasion short of a snowball fight), this problem wouldn't have arisen.

Leery as Miss Manners is of self-declared phobias, she would have let Mary's action pass had she exclaimed apologetically, "Oh, dear, I'm afraid I can't shake your hand; please forgive me." No explanation need have been provided, but an apology was necessary, lest poor Susan conclude from the bald action that she had been publicly snubbed. To add the explanation about germs would be insulting, not to mention unconvincing, in someone who then went around the room distributing hugs.

The way it happened, Susan was snubbed, and you do have an obligation to protect your guests from any such affront. Should Mary inquire why she has been dropped, you might just murmur, "It's a question of germs," leaving it unclear as to whether you are protecting her or quarantining her.

The Multicultural Excuse

DEAR MISS MANNERS,

I am in my middle thirties, female and white. In the course of daily business, I am often addressed in public places by young black men who make eye contact and offer a friendly greeting that invites conversation, usually, "How you doing?" While I applaud friendliness and greetings in general, I do not know these individuals, and find it difficult to strike a balance between rudely cutting them and making an over-friendly response that could be (honestly or deliberately) misinterpreted.

I am not greeted in this way by people of any other age, sex or ethnic group. Given that these young men have a cultivated "cool dude" appearance and appear to be about the age when young men are notoriously bent on proving their machismo, I am driven toward the unattractive conclusion that this is a form of baiting, and that the object adds an extra level of complication to the common experience of keeping an over-familiar masher at arm's length ("Take it easy, lady, I was only saying hi"), since the greeting is always a little cozier than I care to hear from a stranger of any race or sex, at least in the kind of urban environment where you practically have to breathe defensively.

Do you know of other women, white or black, who can throw some light on what I experience as provocative over-familiarity? Do I treat it as gallantry, a tentative come-on, or an attempt at petty social blackmail? How do I handle this? If these young men are, in effect, daring me to knock a chip off their shoulders, I need a response that will politely neutralize them without rebuffing the occasional person who is, in fact, merely being friendly.

GENTLE READER,

Miss Manners insists on removing from this situation two elements that are irrelevant: race and friendship. If there is any race or ethnic group in which the young men do not consider it fun to bother strange young women on the streets, Miss Manners would like to know about it so she can offer her congratulations.

This is not to be interpreted, however, as acceptance or even resignation on Miss Manners' part. "Custom" it may be, but neither among African-Americans, nor among any other demographic group known to Miss Manners, do the elders—that is to say, the mothers and fathers of the young ladies being harassed—consider this a legitimate custom.

Nor can it be construed as friendliness, as if you were talking about offhand pleasantries in a village where everyone knows everyone else at least by sight. It should never be treated as such. The young men's intentions may range from merely showing off to one another to dangerous designs, but no lady should engage in any dialogue with them, even to the extent of delivering a "rebuff," which will be considered a challenge. Rest assured you are not rudely cutting these people—a "cut" is the refusal to recognize someone one actually knows. What you are doing is refusing to get to know anyone under such circumstances.

The Tragic Excuse

DEAR MISS MANNERS,

People who are grieving should not be expected to follow the established etiquette of society. They are on a different planet mentally.

My twenty-six-year-old son is close to death with a brain tumor he has been battling for 18 months. I have received a vast array of condolences, such as cards and flowers. I cannot bring myself to write thank you notes. Some day, later on, I'm sure I will. Privileged, tragedy-free people should try to understand that when a person is grieving, it is a very different and sacred world he lives in. All semblance of normality ceases. We grieving people need a large measure of quiet and compassion from society. It is a time, frankly, that the expectations should fall entirely on friends to make allowances, give freely and unconditionally from the heart, and be able to say, "Oh, forget it. You have enough troubles."

GENTLE READER,

Miss Manners does not suspect your friends of thinking, "She owes us a letter of thanks, and it would be rude of her to keep us waiting." That is the kind of meanness of which people suspect manners, but which manners, as well as you, would classify as rude.

It is much more likely that your friends are thinking, "I wonder how she is, but I don't want to intrude by calling. I wonder if there is anything I can do—whether she'd like some practical help, or emotional support—but I suppose if she did, she would let me know." So they do nothing and, when grief is compounded with loneliness, the grieving person begins to think that no one cares. The cards and flowers eventually stop, and there is a vacuum.

This is why even under such tragic circumstances as yours, Miss Manners does not give anyone a permanent excuse (allowance for delay, of course, being made under such circumstances as yours) from acknowledging kindness. Silence, however understandable, seems to rebuff friendship—on which those who are grieving, of all people, will need to draw.

The Success Excuse

"Do you know what it's like," the usually sunny lady inquired plaintively, "to be written off as a success?"

Miss Manners is not sure that there is such a thing as a usual complaint in the etiquette field; she has long ceased to be astounded at the ingenuity that can be expended in inventing forms of offensiveness. This complaint was so unusual that it took a while to establish that it wasn't about something else—for example, its opposite.

No, the lady was not talking about how people treat failures. Those whose misfortune is perceived as chronic may be rudely put down by the more fortunate, and those who have reversals of fortune are sometimes callously deserted by their former supporters. Neither situation was the topic under discussion. Nor did this appear to be a complaint about impolite (even if understandable) reactions to success-inspired arrogance or ostentation. As far as Miss Manners could ascertain, the transgressions under discussion were unprovoked by gloating.

Its victim even denied that they could be the result of envy. "I'm talking about the same people who were always my friends—even about my relatives," she said. "I really do think they're pleased that after all these years my efforts are being recognized and rewarded. These are the people who encouraged me all along. I couldn't have done it without them. They don't mean to be unkind—on the contrary. But it's as though I've forfeited my standing among them by being lucky. The kind of consideration they used to show me—the kind they expect from me—no longer seems to apply."

Miss Manners asked for specifics. "Everybody always talks to me about money. When I didn't have much, the same people would never have dreamed of speculating about how much—how little, rather—I had. But now it comes into everything. Let's say a friend complains to me about being tired or overworked. I sympathize and admit that I'm tired, too. 'You?' he'll say, 'Why, you must be laughing all the way to the bank.' So I've learned never to mention my work, even when everyone else is talking about theirs. But it doesn't help. Sooner or later someone will turn to me and ask, 'Still raking it in?'

"Notice the 'still.' This not only emphasizes the fact that my success is precarious, but makes me sound selfish, as if I've been hogging it for too long. Needless to say, I try not to report my little ups and downs. If something nice happens, the same people who used to jump up and down with glee for me are now bored and ask, 'What did you expect?' If I have a set-back, instead of commiserating, they say, 'So what—it's not important.' "

Miss Manners inquired whether things were all right when the subject of work didn't come up. The lady looked embarrassed. "No, you see . . . well," she confessed, "my personal life is under control, too. In fact, it's kind of nice. It's another thing to be careful not to mention. If your children turn out well, nobody wants to hear about it. But this is beginning to sound as if I just want to talk about myself. That's not my point at all. What I miss is just being considered to share a common humanity. I seem to have been disqualified from showing the interest I always had in other people's triumphs and troubles. If I'm happy for someone else, that person will say, 'Of course, I know it's nothing in comparison to what you do,' as if I were trivializing the accomplishment. And if I'm upset for someone else, I'll be told, 'You wouldn't understand,' as if I'd never had any worries and wouldn't know how to cope with them if I had. I'm not asking for credit because I have my life more or less in order—I just want to be treated like everyone else again."

Miss Manners wished her success. She disallows treating people rudely on the grounds that life has treated them well.

The No-Fault Excuse

Dear Miss Manners,

I would like to share with you an example of what I suppose could be called the Etiquette of New Age Psychology, and to ask your opinion as to what actual message was meant to be communicated to me. My sister and I had a bit of a misunderstanding over a proposed visit. Later, my sister, who has been in counseling and support groups, wrote me and said, "I am sorry if you felt badly about what happened, but I am not responsible for your feelings." The incident itself is not of great significance, but I am left perplexed over the letter. I don't know if I've received an apology or have been soundly told off. What would you say?

GENTLE READER,

Miss Manners has been trying very hard to translate this statement into "Sister, dear, I hope I didn't hurt your feelings," but it doesn't work. It keeps coming out sounding more like "Well, tough."

Let us nevertheless take the kind view, which is that your sister is merely repeating a formula designed to keep one from blaming others for one's disappointments, and that she does not realize how mean a substitute this is for graciously making up after a tiff. Taking responsibility for oneself does not mean indulging in hit and run rudeness. It is, in fact, an evasion of responsibility to pretend that one can act without acknowledging the effect one can have, for better or worse, on the feelings of others.

Chapter Eight

MOVING TOWARD AN ETIQUETTE-FREE SOCIETY

The sergeant at arms, that patient old soul who enjoys the official privilege of thinking of himself as being intimidating (courtesy of legislators whom he prides himself on greeting respectfully by name), is in danger of being thrown off the floor. Those who are working to rule him out of order are the very members of legislatures and other civic and educational institutions who most flagrantly disobey the rules against swearing and shouting insults. They protest that the etiquette traditionally maintained to keep their working discourse civil violates their civil liberty to be rude.

Curiously enough, Miss Manners, too, believes in retaining the civil liberty to be rude, although she wishes that so many people wouldn't exercise it so often. She hates to be the only person who acknowledges that we've never had totally unrestrained speech (everybody else allows the one famous exception, of not being permitted to shout "Fire!" in a crowded theater, and barely notices such other necessary restrictions as laws against slander and perjury), but she is in no way suggesting further limiting speech under the law. That would indeed be an intolerable inroad on freedom.

The more practical and benign way to manage institutions in an orderly fashion that permits them to serve their legitimate functions is, and always has been, etiquette. That is why Miss Manners is offering her protection to that stalwart etiquette-enforcer, the sergeant at arms. He may be armed with something more threatening-looking than her raised eyebrow (formidable a weapon as that is), but neither he nor she gets really rough on offenders. They only insist that those who do not care to behave properly at a given time, place and activity must either stop being disruptive or go away, so that those who wish can conduct in peace the activity for which everybody else has gathered.

Is that so unreasonable? An awful lot of supposedly bright people, notably educators and public servants, don't seem to be able to resolve the free speech–etiquette paradox. Even proponents of speech codes are given to claiming that they are not trying to restrain speech, but only dangerous conduct; they are redefining the speech restrictions they suggest as conduct-provoking "fighting words." For good reason, nobody believes this, not even those who claim it, which is why they are so easily intimidated when their own speech codes—which of course are intended to bar offensive speech—are challenged.

An institution has to be able to require adherence to etiquette in order to further its particular mission without these admitted restrictions on speech at certain times and places necessarily constituting an abridgment of rights guaranteed by law. An atmosphere in which people refuse to respect authority, do not observe a recognized schedule for speaking, trade personal insults and air personal prejudices, or engage in distracting and irrelevant activities (that means you with the bubble gum) is incompatible with thrashing out disputes rationally and successfully. The more controversial the ideas people want to express, and the more serious the arenas in which they want to put them in opposition to the ideas of others, the more everybody needs etiquette. It takes a great deal of strong form to bear the weight of conflict.

The regulative function of etiquette, upon which all society's institutions depend, requires participants in adversary proceedings to present their opposing views in a restrained manner, to provide a disciplined and respectful ambience in which to settle conflicts peacefully. Under those now-challenged rules of decorum, debate is more productive, not less, than if there were no restrictions on insult and invective. Far from stifling ideas, the rules allow them to be effectively and forcefully discussed. Etiquette restrictions permit people to attack ideas without allowing them to attack one another, and protect the discussion of offensive topics without permitting the use of offensive speech. Everybody gets a fair chance to talk. Some people may actually find themselves listening to others, although etiquette merely requires them to assume the posture of doing so. The focus of the debate is kept on the business at hand, rather than on ruining and defending reputations.

Miss Manners has always had a hard time associating herself with the other great defenders of free speech. To which side should she rally: the left, which defends obscenity, or the right, which defends bigotry? Etiquette is firmly opposed to both obscene talk and hate talk. That is why it marks off limits, the times and places at which certain types of speech will spoil things, without conceding that this undermines liberty. As Mother would say, "You can perfectly well say what you mean and still keep a civil tongue in your head, but if you can't, you may leave the table. Now!"

Institutional etiquette is slightly different from the everyday variety, and more akin to law, in that it carries practical consequences for violators. In most activities, including legislative sessions and other meetings, people who disobey the rules are merely asked to leave the meeting place, so that the activity can resume; at worst, they are shown formal disapproval by being censured. However, it is true that people who pick the wrong organizations in which to be rude—the military, for instance—are in big trouble.

Typically, the body of rules that a particular organization has determined is necessary for it to accomplish its business includes the requirement to be polite and orderly, forms for acknowledging authority and respecting peers, instructions about when to rise, limitations about who speaks when, and perhaps a dress code. The work of a dear colleague of Miss Manners', *Robert's Rules of Order,* is an etiquette book of such rules. Its section "Decorum in Debate" includes the admonishment that "it is not allowable to arraign the motives of a member, but the nature or consequences of a measure may be condemned in strong terms. It is not the man, but the measure, that is the subject of debate."

Now, just when the citizens are no longer sure that personal rudeness is as romantic as they once thought because they have lived with the unintended results, new anti-etiquette forces have arisen to challenge institutional etiquette. These idealists have had a high success rate.

Disdaining etiquette has become a matter of principle with some members of the academic community, who believe that by upholding rudeness, they are upholding freedom of speech, even at the sacrifice of education. University speech codes proscribing hate speech have had to be rescinded in spite of complaints from the targets of such rudeness that they can't study or benefit from classroom instruction or enjoy the sort of scholarly atmosphere and benefits for which they went to the university in the first place. It is not possible to conduct a class without any restrictions on behavior among the participants other than those provided by law.

But having been told that they have the special mission of fostering free speech, members of the academic community have increasingly abdicated the responsibility to enforce and obey the standards of speech required for their incidental mission of educating or being educated. As a matter of fact, the university's mission is not to foster free speech but to foster free inquiry. And free inquiry—the pursuit of truth—is not possible when there are no etiquette restrictions on speech. Miss Manners does not want to hear any more lip on the subject.

Less loftily, politicians are attacking etiquette on principle. In the Pasadena, California, City Council, a member was censured for cursing and screaming invective during the session. The American Civil Liberties Union defended him by attacking the council's "courtesy code" ordinance as "silly," "goofy," "embarrassing" and "a laughingstock by First Amendment standards." In its triumphant press release, the ACLU characterized the council's retreat from its own code as "a victory for all of Pasadena." In other legislative bodies, such as the United States Congress, discourtesy is now commonly practiced and rarely challenged or punished.

Is this, indeed, a victory for the citizens? Is it, as its proponents claim, a victory for the First Amendment? Miss Manners thinks not.

It is true that candidates who use rude attack methods on their opponents are often elected to office. Voters seem to feel that politicians who wax emotional about what they claim they cannot phrase politely, or who refuse to show tolerance to those who disagree with them—who are, in other words, what we used to call "unstatesmanlike"—are more sincere than less aggressive politicians. So the people are getting whom they want.

What we all want, which is good

WASHINGTON, D.C.—A debate on the floor of the U.S. House of Representatives became decidedly unpleasant when one member referred to "homos" and then shouted, "Sit down, you socialist!" at another member who objected. Name-calling is against House rules. One congresswoman asked: "Do we have to call the gentleman a gentleman if he is not one?"

government, may be something else. Confrontation is riveting to observe, but Miss Manners would like to suggest that running a government, and changing it in response to the needs and desires of the people, is better accomplished by boring old cooperation, persuasiveness and consensus building.

The victory of the anti-institutional etiquette forces is not yet complete. Those who wish to participate in university classrooms or legislative bodies are still expected to restrain their own speech to the extent of ensuring that everybody doesn't talk at the same time. That, too, is an etiquette rule designed to permit the activity to achieve its stated goal. Any day now, Miss Manners expects to hear of its being struck down as goofy, silly (what could be more embarrassing?) etiquette.

Free Speech at Christmas

DEAR MISS MANNERS,

Last Christmas, there was a story in the paper about a five-year-old who upset her kindergarten classmates by telling them there is no Santa Claus. When the teacher asked the little girl to kindly keep that information to herself, the child's mother became indignant. Claiming abridgment of her daughter's freedom of speech, she removed the child from the school.

This incident has nothing to do with First Amendment rights and everything to do with manners. The essence of good manners is being loath to offend another person when there is no constructive reason to do so. A young woman with good manners is reluctant to inform her great-aunt Alice that she (the young woman) has moved in with her boyfriend or has taken a lesbian lover, if that information is bound to pain Aunt Alice.

Parents who do not want their young children to believe in Santa Claus, the Easter Bunny, or the Tooth Fairy may so instruct their children. If, however, they want them to have good manners, they will tell the children that it is wrong to use that special information to hurt other children who have different beliefs. The parents will explain that just because something may be "true" is not sufficient reason to talk about it. People with good manners do not initiate conversations about other people's weight problems, physical or intellectual handicaps, or possibly outmoded beliefs if those beliefs aren't harming anyone.

GENTLE READER,

Miss Manners deeply appreciates your support, but she wishes you hadn't mixed up the little girl's declaration with that of the hypothetical big girl, Aunt Alice's niece. There is quite a difference between the question about the existence of Santa Claus and the existence of someone who is sharing one's apartment. Anybody who has ever made a request of both types knows the difference.

Couldn't you have made an analogy to a young atheist's refraining from debating theology with her religious aunt (or a religious young person with her atheistic aunt)? Then it would have been a clear cut case of not challenging others' beliefs, rather than concealing one's own living arrangements.

The rule is not to denigrate others' faith by declaring that what they believe is not true. Miss Manners thinks that rather too much was made on both sides of a small child's artless challenge, but agrees that the difference between what is open to class debate and what is personal should have been taught. How right you are that this is a question of manners, not of rights.

Miss Manners agrees wholeheartedly that truth is not a defense against bringing up hurtful subjects. How much we must conceal about ourselves from our dear aunts is a another issue.

CHICAGO, ILL.—"The Chicago City Council went on record . . . against slurs and name-calling. It was, of course, a painfully close vote that came only after a vicious round of finger-pointing, shouting and racial posturing. The lack of civility surprised no one. The Chicago City Council is not one of the world's great deliberative bodies," the *Washington Post* reported.

ETIQUETTE-ENHANCED DISSENT

Someone who can take it but not dish it out: That is a widely held definition of the polite individual.

It is not Miss Manners' definition. She has enough trouble trying to persuade people to behave like human beings without scaring them into thinking that they will thus put themselves at the mercy of other human beings who can't be counted on to act like human beings.

When the going gets rough between people of opposing views, with both sides wanting to make their positions, and their opposition, clear and public, you will not find Miss Manners cowering in the background, nor fluttering about, pleading with everyone to stop fighting and make nice. She refuses to concede that it is impossible to fight and be nice—well, anyway, courteous—at the same time. Indeed, she argues that manners are more important when strong viewpoints clash than when everyone is just ambling along thinking pretty thoughts. If there are no orderly forms of registering dissent, then there are no alternatives to either involuntary compliance or violence.

It is therefore with interest and appreciation that Miss Manners takes note of those nice people at the Harvard Law School who are helping her out by issuing guidelines on proper and improper forms of protest against public speakers. A committee of professors, administrators and students, seeking "to balance the rights of speakers with the rights of people to protest and dissent," issued a report on the etiquette involved. They don't call it etiquette, but that is what it is. Their rules include:

Confining picketing outside meetings to orderly forms that do not prevent people from entering the meeting room.
Limiting the distribution of written protests inside to before or after the formal meeting.
Restricting to the back of the meeting room those who are engaged in prolonged protesting that is likely to block anyone else's view.
Permitting short spontaneous responses from the audience, but banning sustained noise that would prevent the speaker from being heard.

Miss Manners applauds these guidelines, but at the appropriate time and not in such a way as to interfere with anyone else's hearing them. Although she has never actually been able to bring herself to boo, not even on a dreadful night at the opera (thinking it punishment enough when she refrains from applauding or remains seated during a standing ovation, wearing an icy expression), she recognizes that there must be ways for audiences to register negative, as well as positive, responses in a restrained fashion.

Speeches, by their nature, suggest more give-and-take with audiences than do artistic performances. Miss Manners does not approve of preventing speakers from speaking, nor of any actions that would intimidate other members of an audience from hearing, seeing and, if they like, showing approval. There is plenty of opportunity for a skilled dissenter to frame a rebuttal as a question after the lecture, although it is a violation of etiquette (and of audience patience) to use that time for counterstatements or prolonged commentary. The American tradition of heckling should properly be limited to short (and, if possible, witty) replies to a speaker's propositions.

By way of compensation for those whose indignation is unbearably stifled by these rules, Miss Manners will whisper (so as not to disturb anyone else) the most effective way of registering contempt. That is to get up when an offensive point is made and walk out. When this is done early on (so as not to suggest that the motivation is to get home at the hour promised to the baby-sitter), in apparent reaction to what is being said, it is devastating. A dignified expression of disgust may be worn while this is done. The gait is rapid to suggest the inability to endure any more. Stepping on anyone's toes on the way out would, however, be a violation of the proper etiquette of protest.

Responding Politely to Protests

DEAR MISS MANNERS,

What are the proper responses for graduation audiences and dignitaries when the "surprise" of a disruption occurs? At my graduation, many years ago, two or three "political radicals" tried to express their anti-establishment (or whatever) beliefs by snubbing the dignitary who was presenting us with our diplomas.

Those student actions were not flamboyant or even noticeable to most of the audience—to this day, most of us have no idea what they did. Nevertheless, the dignitary halted the ceremony to deliver a five-minute harangue against "immature" behavior which the audience applauded in a standing ovation that remains the most humiliating moment in my memory. My fellow graduates and I had been shamed and degraded as a group. Even though I graduated with top honors, I can never look back with pride at that day. I have always felt that a true gentleman would have ignored their offensive behavior to ensure that the occasion be properly—and happily—observed.

GENTLE READER,

Miss Manners assures you that you need not remember your graduation with shame. It is high time you began to recall it as a period piece, typical of a certain era.

This is not to say that she sympathizes with those who attempt to refashion the graduation program on the spot, whether they are demonstrators or speakers who seize the opportunity to lecture demonstrators. A small disturbance can, as you say, be ignored. If there is a large one, the presiding official should politely ask those who refuse to participate in the planned program to leave and, if necessary, should pause while they are escorted out. A sermon on manners is not appropriate for any graduation ceremony at which Miss Manners does not happen to be getting an honorary degree.

ETIQUETTE ON TRIAL

Etiquette went on trial in 1970, and a case in which it was pitted against the United States Constitution ended up at the United States Supreme Court. Etiquette won, you may be surprised to hear.

Like many another defendant wailing, "But I thought we were so happy together," Miss Manners was shocked to find herself in court. Etiquette and law have had their differences, and Miss Manners has made no secret of the fact that she thinks the law has been encroaching on her territory. But on the whole she thought they worked well together. She has been known to threaten wrongdoers with, "All right, don't listen, just go ahead and keep it up, but you wait till the law hears about this, then you'll be sorry." In return, she has created order, if not coziness, in the courtroom.

Courtroom etiquette, transmitted through an unwritten tradition that has been preserved for centuries, has always been stricter than the etiquette generally prevailing in the society. In enforcing standards of dress, modes of address, rules about when to sit and when to stand, restricting offensive language and requiring people to speak only in proper turn and respectful terms, courtroom etiquette overrides many of the very rights it may be called on to protect. Even in litigation in which the very issue of freedom of speech is being upheld, total freedom of speech is not permitted.

Like the rest of the society, jurisprudence has its problems with deteriorating standards of etiquette, as the public noticed with distaste when watching such interesting trials as O. J. Simpson's became the national pastime. Dress has deteriorated, language has coarsened and snacks and chewing gum have entered the courtroom.

Lawyers used to follow otherwise obsolescent rules of etiquette—refraining from chasing clients or advertising their services and conducting cases with such expressions of respect for their adversaries as "my learned opponent" and (in Massachusetts) "my brother" or "my sister." Jurors—who could be counted upon to be solemnly dutiful back when they could concentrate on the cases instead of worrying about their media images and book offers—used not to feel free to complain about the conditions of the job, such as boredom and incompatibility with one another.

(Witnesses, in contrast, have always been treated rudely. As dear Anthony Trollope puts it in his novel *Orley Farm,* "To stand in a box, to be bawled after by the police, to be scowled at and scolded by the judge, to be browbeaten and accused falsely by the barristers, and then to be condemned as perjurers by the jury,—that is the fate of the one person who during the whole trial is perhaps entitled to the greatest respect, and is certainly entitled to the most public gratitude" for only "doing a painful duty to the public, for which they were to receive no pay and from which they were to obtain no benefit. Of whom else in that court could so much be said?")

Judicial procedure now looks more like ordinary society, which is to say it freely displays the messy clashing of egos in pursuit of gain rather than a solemn ritual. Miss Manners can't help thinking that this lowering of dignity has contributed to the public's lack of faith in the fairness of the system. That the adversarial method is the best way to achieve justice is one of the society's deep beliefs. When such conflict looks little better than the ordinary street fight, which bullies tend to win, it's hard to believe that the results will be any more just.

There is, however, still one model of decorum Miss Manners can count upon to be present at a trial. If there is one person whose clothes, speech and demeanor are designed to demonstrate respect, with regulative, symbolic and ritual etiquette all operating at top capacity, it is the person on trial. Any well-advised defendant goes on full etiquette alert to show respect for the judge, the jury, the judicial process and the community at large, in the hope of planting the feeling that someone who would not dream of violating the etiquette of the society would be even less likely to violate its laws.

Almost any defendant. Then there was the Great Court Etiquette Rebellion of 1970. Abbie Hoffman declared that decorum itself was an instrument of repression, and he and the other Chicago Seven defendants broke an impressive number of etiquette rules at their trial—addressing the judge by his first name, wearing judicial robes, putting their feet on tables and chairs, speaking out of turn, shouting, swearing and generally carrying on to the astonishment of all. This tactic was adopted at other trials of the era.

Left spluttering at this unaccustomed defiance, the judges sought to establish order by using the weapon of contempt of court. They ordered defendants manacled and gagged and had them removed from the courtroom altogether, even though these remedies, in turn, violated the judges' explicit Constitutional commitment to conduct a fair trial, at which the defendant has the right to be present and in a condition that is not prejudicial to the jury's findings.

That, dear children, is how we got to the point where the United States Supreme Court had to decide the momentous question: Which is more important, a defendant's rights, guaranteed by the 6th and 14th Amendments, or mere courtroom etiquette? The case about what judges can or cannot do to restore decorum was *Illinois v. Allen,* and on appeal, the Supreme Court found that a misbehaving defendant may be removed from the courtroom. Those Constitutional rights could be forfeited by failure to observe the etiquette of the courtroom.

LOS ANGELES, CALIF.—Judge Lance Ito was infuriated by spectators at the O. J. Simpson trial who ignored rules against chewing gum and eating food in the courtroom, according to news reports. The Judge barred offenders from future court sessions and even showed videotape in court of a gum chewing spectator, a local television reporter.

Miss Manners hopes everyone is properly horrified. Although she highly approves the ruling, even she does not claim that etiquette is more important than the Constitution. She only recognizes, as did that other Supreme Court, that it would be impossible to hold a trial without judicial etiquette; the pursuit of justice is not possible in a courtroom in which mayhem and invective are permitted.

Adherence to etiquette is a prerequisite for all the practices of a democratic state, including such governmental business as legislative sessions and judicial proceedings. Allowing etiquette to be abandoned would sabotage these institutions in their pursuit of justice and freedom. Just as Miss Manners has always said.

Rudeness in Pursuit of Justice

Dear Miss Manners,

I happen to work in one of the professions in which being rude often gets results when being polite does not. I am a lawyer. Of course many lawyers are polite and respond well to courtesy. But a significant number interpret courtesy as a sign of weakness and insist upon a level of intimacy that would make a talk show host blush. Ordinary formality (such as the use of "Mr." or "Ms.") is interpreted as an ominous threat, and treated accordingly.

Male colleagues lead co-ed luncheons with detailed discussions of the conception and delivery of their children. Superiors comment publicly on ordinary costume jewelry (pearls!) and hair color. An executive recruiter tells me that a prospective employer is on anti-psychotic medication. An interviewer informs me that an acquaintance has left his employ because she had a mental breakdown as a result of her job. Married peers (men) regularly ask me if I am now "dating" anyone. Receptionists snap "You weren't 'cut off'! You were disconnected!" Adversaries hang up instead of politely saying "See you in court!"

And it isn't just me. A friend who is also extremely proper recently received an unbelievably personal and obscene letter from an adversary. I'm beginning to suspect that one must be willing to roll in the mud in order to practice law. But I just cannot stoop to this level. I don't expect miracles and I don't expect to substitute courtesy for competence. But it seems to me that unless we maintain some standards, the profession will become unbearable.

Gentle Reader,

A great many people believe that the profession is already unbearable, Miss Manners regrets to say. These people do not need to hire lawyers to defend them from the results of making such a charge. They are lawyers.

In bar associations all over America, little Miss Mannerses (not that you'd immediately recognize them as such) are busy drawing up etiquette guides (not that they necessarily call them that) for the legal profession. It is not only the occasional incident where lawyers have resorted to fisticuffs that has upset them; it is a general deterioration of the standards of what should be a gentlemanly and ladylike, albeit vigorous, profession.

CHICAGO, ILL.—A report for the Committee on Civility of the Seventh Federal Judicial District recommended that new lawyers read and abide by a 38-step code of conduct and that already practicing lawyers be given civility training. "It's not reality," San Francisco lawyer Melvin Belli told the Associated Press. "To come in and say now they're going to get a post-graduate course in civility is like going out in the jungle and teaching orangutans to use a knife and fork." And a prominent New York lawyer told the AP: "Generally speaking, it's not Mr. Good Guy who always wins the litigation. Hopefully, nobody ever called me Mr. Good Guy."

Miss Manners must gently point out that you, too, suffer from the idea that rudeness is a professional asset, although you don't want to indulge in it. "It often gets results," you claim. Allow Miss Manners respectfully to disagree. Judges, juries and clients respond to politeness and are antagonized by rudeness. Nor could lawyers use rudeness to intimidate other lawyers without their cooperation. You should stop cooperating. It is as much your privilege to insist, "I prefer to be addressed as Ms. Hand," as it is another lawyer's to request, "Call me Joe." What strikes Miss Manners as professional weakness is yielding and letting him remake the rules. Nor are you required to testify about your personal life. "I don't care to discuss it" or "I'll let you continue your gossip, but I have to get back to work" may be said politely. When someone indulges in violations of professional confidence to you, the least you can do is to respond, "Oh, really? Is that public knowledge?"

Indeed, like most professions, the law is, as you say, tough. Miss Manners would think that anyone practicing it successfully would have the strength to set her own standards and not give in to bullies.

ETIQUETTE-FREE RECREATION

ATHLETICS

For a while there, Miss Manners thought a new sport was sweeping the country. Every time she glanced at the sports news, she saw groups of people, some in uniform and some not, pummeling one another. What were the rules? What was the object? What was the proper cheer? How could you tell who had won?

Athletics, she is well aware, is heavily dependent on etiquette. In addition to the rules defining the game, each sport has rules about dress, behavior and respect for authority. Underlying these is the mannerly expectation of fairness and self-control known as sportsmanship. So much for the perception that etiquette is only for sissies who prefer tea time to honest sport, or weaklings looking for an excuse to avoid contests they would lose. Physical contests without etiquette—attacks with no holds barred—are never classified as sport. Assault and battery are more like it. Or at least, "You kids cut that out."

It turned out that the fights Miss Manners had been seeing telecast from sports arenas had no rules. The object was to overthrow rules in favor of—whammo! (of either the spoken or the physical variety). Preliminaries varied, and could be recognized as hockey, basketball, tennis, baseball or soccer, but the free-for-all that developed from each was pretty much the same. Sometimes it involved the players' leaving off the game to attack one another or a referee; sometimes it was the fans bashing one another; and sometimes it was between the crowd and the players. Fists, sports equipment, bottles and seafood were being thrown wildly. No skill and little prowess were involved—just unrestrained anger.

Miss Manners, who is probably suspected of confusing the etiquette of the sports arena with that of the quilting bee, nevertheless understands that proper behavior for sports spectators is almost always highly informal and often pleasantly rambunctious. The etiquette varies depending on the sport and the occasion—the Super Bowl is not Ascot—but cheering, booing and shouting encouragement or the witty criticism known as heckling are acceptable.

Unfortunately, the traditional cry of "Kill the umpire" sounds quaint, now that there has been at least one instance of an athlete being murdered by a disgruntled fan. Sports behavior has deteriorated to where it no longer meets the expectations— not just of Miss Manners, but of the participants. Disillusioned with athletes because they no longer are good role models (which is to say that they do not exhibit the mannerly values of good sportsmanship), the fans have turned vicious and vulgar. They often say it is because they feel the players have been unmasked as greedy, lawless businessmen.

Still, fans are copying athletes' behavior. They frequently see athletes hitting and yelling at one another, which gives the fans license, if they need it, to do the same. Players are furious and bewildered at being subjected to this level of taunting from the stands, even when it mimics their own behavior, and some are retaliating in kind.

Large numbers of people in these crowds complain that they can't enjoy a game, or safely take their children to see one, because of shouted obscenities and racial epithets, and such obnoxious behavior on the part of other fans as spitting and deliberately smearing food around. Owners and sports commissioners complain that things are out of control and talk about bringing in the law.

"There has to be a line drawn in all sports, between what you are allowed to shout because you paid for a ticket and what is unacceptable no matter what you paid," *Sports Illustrated* quoted the NBA commissioner as saying. "We have to begin drawing that line now."

The law has already been invoked in amateur sports, where rancor has led players to consider their injuries the malicious fault of opponents rather than a risk

"He never even came over and said he was sorry," complained a man who sued his friend because of a torn ligament acquired when the two men collided in a Sunday afternoon softball game, according to the *Wall Street Journal.*

SIMI VALLEY, CALIF.—Formal handshakes at the end of high school sporting events were banned here because they often touch off violence, and some players spit on their hands before the handshake, some mutter insults and increasingly the situation degenerates into fist fights. The ban was eventually reversed, but not before much soul-searching occurred in the area's athletic community. "The old adage—it isn't whether you win or lose but how you play the game—may have become old-fashioned," one school sports director told the *New York Times.*

"Both athletes and coaches around Los Angeles say sporting contests have become more intense and rough at all levels in recent years. 'Trash talk' has been spreading, with players muttering running insults at opponents. Parents fight each other in the stands and on the playing field," the *Times* reported, adding that a Little League player near San Francisco fatally struck a teenager in the head with a bat he was swinging at a rival who taunted him.

of the game. It is clear that health clubs and gymnasiums, where anger about other people's behavior is the cause of threats and fistfights, will also be turning to the law for help.

The person most in despair over all this is Miss Manners, because using the law to regulate sports arenas would be a double defeat for etiquette. The first defeat would be yet another instance, and probably a highly unsuccessful one, of trying to force people to behave themselves when they refuse to do so voluntarily, with heavy policing and serious punishment. The second would be the overthrow of sports as one of the best exemplars of manners. With its high sense of ritual, its symbolism in dress and gesture, and, most of all, its requirement of showing respect to the game, to its judges and—against all natural promptings—to opponents, athletics served as a model of etiquette in action. When this is thrown aside in favor of displaying the nastier side of ambition and greed, everybody loses.

Sportsmanship

DEAR MISS MANNERS,

The parents who helped organize my 11-year-old daughter's baseball team have a daughter the same age, who swears and becomes very argumentative if children don't do what she says. I have stepped in with a little advice on how to compromise, and how swearing is unproductive, and I have brought the problem to the attention of her parents. Now my daughter and she are getting along better—and the swearing has been directed at other children on the team. But I also notice a coldness towards my daughter by the parents. She sits on the bench more and is less active as a team player.

WIMBLEDON, ENGLAND—A tennis player was fined a record $15,500 by Wimbledon officials for verbal abuse, failing to complete a match and unsportsmanlike conduct after he called the umpire "the most corrupt official in the game" before walking off the court and told the crowd to "shut up" when they jeered him while he was arguing a ruling by the umpire.

Gentle Reader,

Somebody needs to be teaching sportsmanship here, and Miss Manners regrets to say that the parents who organized the team have disqualified themselves. The only lessons they seem to have succeeded in teaching their daughter are:

> *If you get caught and penalized, direct your foul play elsewhere.*
> *If anyone complains, get your agents to punish them in an apparently unrelated move.*

These may not be lessons you want your daughter to learn. If you expect baseball to provide her with more than simple exercise of limb and lip, you must find her coaches who insist upon good sportsmanship. Miss Manners would not be surprised to hear that the parents of the children serving as replacement targets would prefer that as well.

CONCERTS AND THEATERS

Can you get tickets to hear a famous musician lecture on manners? Probably, although these events are unscheduled. Jean-Pierre Rampal stopped playing the flute one day and started lecturing parents in the audience about the etiquette violations of their children. Sir Georg Solti stopped conducting to do an etiquette critique of the entire audience. Jessye Norman begged an audience which had been applauding her after each song to stop, because they were ruining the cumulative effect of the song cycle. A number of performers have greeted latecomers with sudden silence, followed by such inquiries as "Have trouble parking?" or "Why don't I just wait until you get comfortable?"

Why, the music world has gotten so etiquette-conscious that a star was fired from the Metropolitan Opera for arriving late for rehearsals, leaving early and being unpleasant and inconsiderate of others who were trying to pay attention to the music. Miss Manners was astounded. She thought that kind of rudeness, under the name of temperament, was a job requirement for a diva.

Nevertheless, even she didn't think that performers were prepared to tolerate late arrivals, early departures and outbursts from their audiences. She is also aware that members of audiences are even less willing to tolerate offenders in their ranks.

We have been through all this before. In the good old days for which concert-goers mistakenly yearn, musical performances and socializing were not considered mutually exclusive pastimes. Miss Manners' dear friend Stendhal, one of the great music appreciators of all times, described in *The Charterhouse of Parma* the unexceptionable behavior of his music-loving heroine in the early 19th century: "She would go and shut herself up alone for hours on end, at the Scala. . . . Going home, she would improvise on her piano until three o'clock in the morning. . . . One evening, in the box of one of her friends . . . she made the acquaintance of Conte Mosca, a Minister from Parma. . . . She returned to the same box the following evening; this intelligent man reappeared and through the whole performance she talked to him with enjoyment."

Nobody called out, "Hey, lady!" to Contessa Pietranera (later to become Duchessa Sanseverina-Taxis and still later Contessa Mosca), "some of us are trying to hear something besides your yapping." Only in the mid-19th century, when silence during the music was demanded by performers, did the expectations of audiences begin to change. It was through the written etiquette instructions passed out in concert halls and the furious admonitions of annoyed performers that the concept of respect for music, not to mention allowing others to hear, was finally established.

In recent decades there has been serious backsliding. Miss Manners attributes this not only to a generation of anti-etiquette activity but also to confusion with the laxer audience etiquette for television and other home entertainment. Without denying the pleasures of talking during and back to performances, she notes that these habits require the consent of the rest of the audience, which is possible to obtain only among friends, and not always then.

Whole audiences have to be retrained to attend public performances. Yet Miss Manners really does not want to revive the habit of having musicians lecturing their audiences, not only because they might reserve some of their indignation for the manners of their own profession, but because inflicting public humiliation is itself rude.

Some concert halls have instituted pre-concert etiquette lessons through program notes, signs forbidding people to take candy inside, and announcements from the stage. (Miss Manners has not yet seen surtitles reading, "Cut that out. Can't you see people are trying to sing?" Nor, in spite of complaints about electronic devices and clunky jewelry, has she heard of concert hall guards being brought in to pat down the audience members and confiscate their potential noisemakers.) Audiences are filled with vigilantes who correct one another by means of shushes, icy stares and the occasional whack with a rolled-up program, but the melees that ensue are also distracting.

Everybody admits that these combined forces have not met with notable success in teaching etiquette. People of all ages continue to wander in and out at will, chew food and rattle candy, talk, snuggle, squirm, cough and snore. Those who are rebuked either go on doing what they are doing or step it up to retaliate.

Miss Manners will now take over and give master classes in audience manners. Please sit up, keep still, pay attention and don't throw long-stemmed roses until she is finished.

The first semester covers everyday manners that everyone is expected to know:

- Because audiences gather for the purpose of hearing and seeing a performance, not one another, making noise and other distractions is rude.

    Questions? Yes, your beeper, watch alarm, and cellular telephones are such distractions, and Miss Manners doesn't care how important you are. Get a paging system that vibrates without making noise. No, your low cut dress on opening night does not qualify as a distraction. Miss Manners hopes you are not offended to hear that.
- If seized with illness at a public event, you are supposed to remove yourself or, if incapacitated, allow yourself to be removed if not cured on the spot with a cough drop or a nudge for snoring.

    Questions? No, it's not a one-cough-and-you're-out policy, but three will do it. Yes, Miss Manners knows that sleeping is not an illness, but noisy sleeping might as well be.

The second semester takes up specialized manners for a particular event, which anyone planning to attend is required to learn for the occasion, such as:

- While audience enthusiasm is accepted on almost any terms at most types of performances, this does not apply to classical music, where there are often pauses, separating movements of a symphony or songs in a cycle, where silence is required. When in doubt, wait, no matter how overcome with emotion. Even at the end, applause should not begin until the last strains of music have died away.

- Displays of appreciation other than clapping vary with the type of event. It is rude to throw flowers at some, your underwear at others; it is disastrous to confuse the two. Purrs as well as catcalls are specific, the one for classical music being "Bravo," with the ending adjusted according to the gender and number of people being addressed.

- Hot dogs and beer may be consumed during baseball games, and edibles it may be just as well not to be able to see during dinner theater, but concert and opera audiences, as well as other theatergoers, are supposed to wait for the intermissions. Miss Manners, who is not without pity, recommends that Wagnerites have picnic hampers available for the first sign of a break.

- Most events, although not necessarily the most unbearable ones, have intermissions and other authorized times in which members of the audience may make a break for it.

Miss Manners will now take questions.

What should have been done about the elderly lady who was breathing irregularly and noisily, but was apparently unaware of causing disturbance because of what observers diagnosed as senility? How could the gentleman who crossed his leg over his knee be informed that the bottom of his foot was poised threateningly only inches away from a lady's pastel pink skirt? Why don't people leave their children at home?

Wait—you who asked that last question. Didn't Miss Manners hear you at the opera board meeting, lamenting that audiences were aging and plotting ways to attract younger people? Are we reaching the point here where concertgoers, like the audiences of some less lofty forms of entertainment, come expecting a good fight in the stands? Does everybody believe that people deliberately spend substantial sums on tickets for the thrill of coughing and sleeping in public? Are children automatically considered to be present at classical musical events against their will to serve the pretentious and tyrannical wishes of their parents, and to be plotting a terrorist's revenge against the entire audience? If little Mozart squirmed at some performer's efforts, it would be taken as evidence that children are by nature incapable of appreciating good music.

Come on, people—music is supposed to have a calming effect. Concertgoers are supposed to assume good will among their numbers. Miss Manners is by no means minimizing, much less defending, the flouting of etiquette that is now common in music and other audiences. But breathing? And crossing the knee?

Well, all right. The polite way to deal with repeated accidental annoyances is with an apologetically regretful look (following a discreet tap, if necessary) that seems to say, "Oh, dear, you're probably so carried away with the music that you didn't notice you were humming." Or snorting. Or pointing your foot at my skirt. Miss Manners admits this doesn't always work, but neither does saying, "Shut up," and at least the polite way is silent.

Playbill, **the national theater program-magazine, reports that during one recent performance a member of the audience asked a woman to stop talking. "I can talk if I want to!" the woman retorted.**

The second line of defense is the intermission plea to management to change one's seat, with the reasons stated. Since changing people's seats is a nuisance at best, this encourages the management to do the dirty work. The polite method for ushers is to report apologetically to the offender that another unspecified person claimed to have been troubled—perhaps unreasonably, but if anything could be done to help, it would be appreciated.

In sum, challenges are not issued because they invariably lead to more disturbance, not less. If all you people are going to teach one another audience etiquette by force, Miss Manners won't be able to hear the music.

Parental Guidance

DEAR MISS MANNERS,

At band and choral concerts and other school activities where parents come to enjoy their offspring's performance—How loud should babies cry during performances, and should slightly older children be allowed to just talk in loud whispers, or is banging the seat in front of them with their foot mandatory? How fashionably late should entire families (including grandparents, cousins and the like) arrive? When they do, is it important that they disturb an entire row of people when they sit down, or is it only necessary to alert a few people that they made the event?

Should adults be restricted only to noises such as loud coughing, or are other noises, such as gum popping and/or snickering considered part of "having a good time" for peers who know the performers? In the case of coughing, is it O.K. to come if you are getting over a cold, or should you only force yourself if you have pneumonia? Does a person with a camera need to push in front of everyone possible, or can they simply arrive on time and obtain an unobtrusive seat that allows them to get the pictures they want?

I know it would be impolite for principals or teachers who have worked with the students for many weeks or months prior to the performance to clarify these behaviors ahead of time on invitations or prior to a performance. However, is there anything I can do as a parent who would like to enjoy a performance without certain interruptions? I know you recommend a cool stare, but I have found in the past that those who are ignorant of the appropriate behaviors also seem oblivious to the reactions of those around them.

GENTLE READER,

Much as Miss Manners admires your ability to tell your complaint backwards, she advises you to come out with it, straight—at a parent-teacher meeting in your school. If you state your case in a good-natured tone, implying that everyone understands the problems that led to these transgressions, you will enlist sympathizers even among those who committed some of the etiquette violations but suffered from others.

Indeed, any parent ought to be sympathetic about the difficulties caused by crying babies and bored toddlers; parental pride prompting the desire to attend an event one isn't really well enough for or to record the occasion; the logistics of getting a multigenerational family anywhere on time; and silliness associated with the age group of one's own child.

Putting rules of behavior on an invitation would damage the dignity of the occasion, in Miss Manners' opinion, although she feels less strongly against polite admonitions on programs. Instructing the students ahead of time, perhaps in an assembly, and asking them to explain the rules to their families, would be best. It can all be classified as education, rather than as an announcement that the school expects its guests to be rude.

As for on-the-spot corrections, one step up from that glance is a whispered "I'm sorry, but I can't hear [or see]." If you say this self-righteously, the offender will turn defensive; if you say it sympathetically, as if truly sorry to have to add to the difficulty, you will awaken the desire to make amends.

Lawn Audiences

Dear Miss Manners,

Four of us went to an outdoor program of concert and comedy. Everyone brought chairs or blankets for the lawn, but other people brought the short beach chairs and ours were higher, regular folding lawn chairs. (This was our first experience at bringing our own chairs, and since I have arthritis of the hips and spine, the higher chairs are more bearable.) We arrived early and took a good place in the center. Later, a group of eight took a position behind us. As the program started, they began making rude remarks about our blocking their view. Since we were there when they chose their location, we ignored them. They brought their own libations in those quart sized insulated bottles with a straw in the top, and as they became more inebriated, their comments were louder and more profane.

Should I have explained the reason for the higher chairs, moved to the very back of the lawn behind everyone, or left early? How much should you let bullies intimidate you? It spoiled what should have been a wonderful, balmy evening with a full moon. What would you have done?

Gentle Reader,

Wait. Miss Manners is having enough trouble struggling to do the proper thing now. Your position is loaded with appeals to which she is sympathetic—your illness, the fairness of letting the people who arrive first choose the best spots, the unreasonableness of people first settling behind you and then complaining, their drunkenness and the rude and obnoxious method of complaint they sought. Yet what she would have done then was to offer to exchange places with them.

Why? Because politeness requires being taken advantage of? No. It doesn't, and Miss Manners can more than hold her own without resorting to retaliatory rudeness. The fact is that lawn audiences can reasonably expect a height level common to all, and you exceeded it. View-blocking chairs should be placed to the side or back of the lawn. If someone had a legitimate reason to stand up during a performance in a regular auditorium, you would expect that person to stand at one side, rather than in the middle of a seated audience.

Boo!

DEAR MISS MANNERS,

Attacking the disgusting habit of people feeding their faces in crowded public places requires more than a delicate, ironic touch. It is not in the same category as using the right fork. The only appropriate approach to the subject is with a bludgeon or a sledgehammer.

Incidentally, it is not clear to me who is paying you off, but I note that you have steadfastly refused to discuss in your column the gross habit of people eating and drinking in crowded movie theaters. The distinction you make between smoke being blown in one's face and having to take in the nauseous odor of popcorn is ridiculous. Nausea is a manifestation of one's health being affected. Self-restraint is not going to correct the situation. Arbitrary NO FOOD AND DRINK IN THE THEATER regulations will.

GENTLE READER,

Thank you so much for your demonstration of bludgeon-sledgehammer tactics. Miss Manners doesn't care for noisy eating in movie theaters, but much prefers the crunch of popcorn to that of character assassination.

Chapter Nine

JETTISONING PROFESSIONAL BEHAVIOR

*I*t has now been proven possible to bring down the reputation of a once esteemed, even venerated, profession—even without requiring a large percentage of its members to do time. Politicians, athletes, physicians and lawyers are among those managing this feat with some success.

Miss Manners recognizes that casting aside professional ethics is the simplest way to alert people outside of a traditionally respectable profession that their respect is no longer fitting, and it's time to bring out the joke books and catcalls. This method has been used frequently to enlighten the public about public service. There is, however, a less hazardous way for practitioners of a profession to make it clear that dignity and public service have been replaced by arrogance and greed. All they have to do is to cast aside professional etiquette.

The process is started by new members of the profession who declare that the "gentlemanly" behavior that had been professed (and sometimes even practiced) by the older members is hopelessly old-fashioned, as evidenced by the fact that the name excludes ladies. This criticism is readily accepted, because the term "gentlemanly behavior" is so patently old-fashioned that the old gentlemen themselves are ashamed of it.

Rather than make that crucial improvement of extending the etiquette of the profession to ladies and then requiring ladies and gentlemen alike to follow the improved standard, the critics continue with their complaints. The old manners are also, they charge, hypocritical. They often require behavior suggesting that making the most money possible, as fast as possible, is not the sole objective of the profession. They suggest—get this—that in the rush for financial gain, some holds really are barred.

Taking down those barriers will, they declare, both decrease hypocrisy and increase profit. Among the customs thus trashed are: treating rivals, colleagues, subordinates and those who preside over the profession with courtesy and respect; counseling clients against spending their money wastefully; treating courteously even clients who are desperate for the service; negotiating compromises rather than using only attack methods; and conducting all professional proceedings, no matter how adversarial, within the bounds of polite restraint.

Miss Manners is pleased to report that not everybody who listens to this stirring argument in favor of rudeness immediately exclaims, "Wow! Just shove everyone out of the way and go for it! Why didn't we think of that?" Habit and perhaps an ingrained touch of decency make most people hang back. Only a few advocates of the new frank rudeness start putting it into practice. They rush crudely after business, denigrate their competitors, thumb their noses at the regulators of the profession—and succeed.

What do you know—it works. Their audacity not only makes them look tough and confident, but makes the polite members of the profession look weak and deceitful. The public begins figuring that everyone in the profession is really like that, and therefore it is wiser to trust the person who at least baldly admits it than the sneak who pretends otherwise.

That's where the reformers figure the story ends. For those who nevertheless cling to the profession's etiquette, they have early retirement—and, for Miss Manners, a pat on the head. "Sure your way is nicer," they tell her. "And it was fine when there wasn't so much competition and people didn't care about making that much money. But," they add, while Miss Manners is busy puzzling about what era they could have in mind—certainly nothing she has ever known or heard tell about—"it won't work now."

As it turns out, that is not the end of the story. Having been taught, and then shown, that a profession once thought to be noble and selfless is actually brutal and ruthless, the public ceases to trust anyone in it at all—not even those who have kindly admitted that they are only in it to win and to enjoy its perks and spoils. Although the services of the profession may still be necessary, its reputation is destroyed. Physicians are seen as not caring about patients, lawyers about justice, politicians about the public good, athletes about a fairly won game—they all just want to pummel one another and gouge the paying public.

Or so that public comes to believe. Accepting the (false) premise that there is something inherently compromising in being paid for one's work, they discount the hardships of a worthy profession, and the possibility that anyone could have chosen it with a nobler motive than personal enrichment. Once that word is out, the temporary advantage that the advocates of rudeness had over their colleagues is gone and the entire profession finds itself in trouble. To be held under suspicion and in contempt for belonging to a profession that performs services for the society is neither pleasant nor easy.

Therefore, various professional societies are groping for a remedy—trying to reinstitute the very concept of professional etiquette. Their begging for voluntary submission to any standards of civility now has to contend with the refusal of individuals to sacrifice what they still see as the edge that they might get from flouting existing standards.

Miss Manners urges the professional societies to persevere. Even

DALLAS, TEX.—**Texas courts approved a Lawyer's Creed in an attempt to stamp out rudeness in the legal profession, according to the Associated Press. "No more obnoxiousness. No more tit-for-tat unprofessional behavior. No more stalling tactics. And no 'allusions to personal peculiarities or idiosyncrasies of opposing counsel' will be allowed," the AP reported, quoting a Texas Supreme Court Justice as saying: "It's kind of like dieting. It's a battle that we can win, but it's not going to be done overnight."**

the sharpies among their ranks will find it more difficult to gain the trust of those who can plainly see that they are neither ladies nor gentlemen.

Publishing the Rules

Dear Miss Manners,

I belong to an employee involvement team at a large manufacturing firm, where we have been plagued by many situations in which our co-workers did not show what we consider to be proper office etiquette. We are all "professionals" and should know the proper way to behave in this environment, but for those who don't, should we try to tell them?

We have been considering publishing a list of these improprieties, but doing so in a manner that will promote awareness, not reproach. We cannot decide if publishing such a list is proper office etiquette. It would be embarrassing to commit a breach of etiquette in an attempt to promote office etiquette.

GENTLE READER,

Etiquette is not, in itself, offensive. Miss Manners feels obliged to point that out. Nor is writing etiquette books rude.

What you fear—and Miss Manners admires you for understanding this—is breaching a rule of etiquette that forbids pointing out other people's unintended transgressions of etiquette, especially if doing so causes them public embarrassment. That is why you should not single out individuals, or publish examples that are obviously traceable to a particular person. Establishing a general code of etiquette is not offensive, because everyone believes it to be directed toward everyone else.

This calls for—yet another team, Miss Manners is afraid, because obtaining general consent on desirable office standards will make them easier to enforce. Put out a call for those willing to undertake such an august task, and circulate their decisions before proclaiming the code. Most of what it contains will be the ordinary rules of the society—the ones you point out that people should already know—but some may be peculiar to your place of employment. Never mind the funny remarks that the office wits will scribble on the margins. One of the notations should be that humor—provided it does not violate rules against meanness and obscenity—is an office asset. And a solace to those in the etiquette business.

Counterproductive Rudeness

You have perhaps heard of the influence that the possession of political power is supposed to have on social behavior among the inhabitants of Washington, D.C. Miss Manners, whose birthplace Washington is, knows it to be a sweet village where affability and modesty are the qualities most respected. The very idea of rank is repugnant, because the egalitarian ideals shared by all citizens are especially revered by those who have the privilege of serving them.

For those who have heard contrary rumors, Miss Manners presents the following real life story. To be sure, it illustrates horrendous rudeness in your capital. She is using it to demonstrate that rudeness is not always practiced because it is expedient. Even bad behavior seems to be uninfluenced by—well, influence.

Imagine the scene, in an important federal office: Someone wishes to present views to a high ranking official and is fortunate enough to have secured an appointment with that personage. The petitioner states his case as forcefully as possible. Only instead of addressing it to the official himself, the visitor rudely ignores him and directs his efforts at agreeableness toward one or another of the official's subordinates.

How could this happen? How can a lobbyist, or the representative of another government agency, or any taxpayer who wants something done commit such an error? Perhaps there will be less surprise when Miss Manners mentions that the official involved uses a wheelchair. The incident is one that happened more than once to Evan J. Kemp, junior, when he was Chairman of the Equal Employment Opportunity Commission.

Mr. Kemp's position did not exempt him from the rudenesses almost inevitably experienced by people with disabilities, the most common of which is to be ignored. Mr. Kemp's fiancée is asked in restaurants what he wants to eat. Like everyone else who uses a wheelchair, he has often been talked about in his own presence as if he were not competent and treated as a nuisance when he travels.

However, he does cheerfully report some progress in public attitudes. Formerly, when he was going down the street minding his own business, he would occasionally be offered money. Now, at least, he is asked for it.

Miss Manners has long known of the peculiar and illogical breach of etiquette by which people treat anyone accompanying a person in a wheelchair (or with another visible disability) as that person's custodian. But even Miss Manners is astonished to hear, in this cynical age, that such a rude impulse will be expressed in defiance of the immediate practical interests of its possessor. Not only disabilities but gender and race often seem to obscure what ought to be obvious clues to importance. Miss Manners used to be on a board of directors where others routinely ignored the CEO when they had financial questions and addressed her assistant, on the assumption that a gentleman would know more about money than a lady.

In ordinary human relations, basic politeness dictates that everyone

Doctors who are sued frequently for malpractice are seen by their patients as disrespectful, rushed, inaccessible and poor communicators, according to a study published in the *Journal of the American Medical Association*. "Many [patients] indicated that they had been yelled at and that they believed that their physicians had no concern for them," said the report. The report studied one group of doctors who are sued frequently but relatively unsuccessfully and suggested that the source of the lawsuits was rudeness rather than actual malpractice.

be accorded the simple dignity due a human being, without assumptions being made as to his or her capabilities or lack of them. In the professional realm, one would think that self-interest would reinforce the respect due, in addition, to position. Miss Manners will confine herself to labeling anyone who fails to do this as rude. She leaves it to others to characterize the judgment of those who allow themselves to insult the very people they wish to impress.

BASIC WORK ETIQUETTE

What is it going to take to make people realize that formal manners must be reinstituted in the workplace? That the chummy atmosphere of first names, friendly retreats, on-the-job celebrations, work-related parties, friendliness merging into flirting, background music and leisure clothing isn't working?

It is Miss Manners' contention that professional behavior should be strictly professional—if that does not sound unreasonable. This concept does not cover any remarks or behavior that call attention to gender, however charming such overtures might be in the social arena, but goes further than that. It also means ending the inappropriate use of the forms of friendship and leisure in the workplace, and no longer requiring pseudo-socializing after hours as part of any job.

Comparisons of co-workers to family and friends are sweet but unfortunate, especially when you think of how some people treat their families. Relatives can't be fired when they fail to perform, and should be able to draw on quantities of sympathy and tolerance that are not available in the corporate world, no matter how syrupy the language in which employers attempt to disguise harsh reality. As for friends, one of their greatest advantages is that you get to choose your own, and you can avoid them when you're annoyed or bored with them.

The proper work demeanor is cordial, cheerful and obliging, but somewhat distant and impersonal. The only people who seem to get this right nowadays are colleagues who are having a secret affair. They actually take the trouble to maintain a formal and professional demeanor, while those who don't much care for one another are being prodded to pretend that they are pals.

Of the people who have failed to notice that proper manners for employees and their bosses have changed in recent years, a disproportionate number appear to be bosses. Miss Manners cannot pretend to find this odd, but she does find it disturbing. It is one of the fundamental principles of manners that responsibility for treating people well increases with the degree of one's authority over them. That everyone is supposed to be polite to everyone else all the time anyway makes this difficult to explain.

Here is a brief review for those who have failed to catch on to the manners changes that have occurred since they first went to work—or who grudgingly go along with the new practices, but believe, deep in their hearts, that they grew out of a lot of ridiculous fuss about nothing. Miss Manners will group these by issue, because that is the way they are identified by employers who scratch their heads and claim they just can't understand why the employees feel so strongly about this or that. However, she will point out that two simple principles—that businesses should be businesslike, and that dignity goes with every honest job—would serve to explain them all.

The Name Issue. Most workplaces have abandoned the custom of secretaries' being addressed by their first names while they were expected to address their bosses by title and surname. Miss Manners approves, but the usual solution, of using first names all around, is not acceptable to her. It is as if the ever-horrid custom of a male boss referring to his female secretary as "my girl" had been equalized by introducing the practice of her calling him "my boy."

The nonreciprocal use of first names to denote inferiority has not been totally forgotten; there are many people still around who fought long and hard for the right to be addressed with formal respect by those who outrank them. In a work setting, what the higher-ranking person calls friendly may be indistinguishable from what the lower-ranking person considers patronizing. Anyway, paying someone does not, under respectable conditions, buy friendship.

Having said that, Miss Manners will discreetly look the other way when first names are used in highly informal businesses, especially those where today's lower-ranking staff is the source of tomorrow's bosses. Bosses should still be extra careful to use full names when referring to their subordinates among outsiders who might assume that first names indicate a lack of respect for the jobs these people hold.

The Coffee Issue. It's not the coffeepot that sent the ladies in the workplace into revolt, but the symbolism. The idea of any female present being a sort of wife-on-the-job is especially cherished by those who think of a wife as hostess and caretaker, with no such loving services provided in return, although they may have noticed that their wives have revolted against this, too. Personal errands should not be slipped unofficially into any job, to be performed in addition to a full day of work. Unless they are specified in the job description, recognized as a needed part of facilitating the boss's work, they should be reciprocal or treated as an occasional great favor.

The Dress Issue. Because there is a wider range of fashions for ladies than for gentlemen, Appropriateness vs. Freedom of Expression battles often involve women. Both male and female secretaries can be asked to maintain whatever the workplace standard is in the way of formality—it's the one that applies to the bosses themselves—but should not be subjected to critiques of individual outfits or styles.

The Compliment Issue. If personal criticism is objectionable, then why aren't personal compliments charming? Because no employee should be subject to personal appraisal from a boss, even if the judgment is favorable. Proper compliments have to do with job performance, and the best of all are the ones that go into the paycheck or the record.

Girls and Boys at Work

Dear Miss Manners,

While working for a large corporation, I was secretary to the manager of personnel development and education. He is an elderly gentleman. Quite a few times he referred to another's secretary as their "girl." I corrected him on many occasions, saying it was very rude and demeaning. He insisted it was proper, had always been proper, and I was just being extremely picky. I cringed every time I heard it, and I'm sure he's still doing it. I still work for this corporation. Please, help me set this guy straight.

Gentle Reader,

For his sake, and the sake of the company, you might start by gently breaking the news that times have changed. It was never correct to refer to an adult employee as a girl, but it was usual. To do so now that it no longer is common is to suggest to prospective female employees that they will be unfairly treated in the company—not the message a personnel department generally wishes to send. It is too bad that he has interpreted your explanation to be an idiosyncratic complaint. The next step is to send a tactfully worded memorandum from the company's female staff that they would all like to have the practice discontinued.

Equal Etiquette

But they mean so well, the gentlemen of the old school protest when complaints are made about how they are treating their female colleagues. Haven't they welcomed ladies into their midst with open arms? Oops. Haven't most of them learned, by working at it for about twenty years now, that they are not supposed to call them "ladies"; they are supposed to remember that ladies like to be called "women."

But it's so difficult. Perhaps "open arms" was an unfortunate choice of words, but really, it was just an expression not intended to offend anyone, they explain. Ladies—women—are so sensitive nowadays. Oops. They didn't mean to suggest that they are more sensitive than regular people—that is, themselves. Of course, the ladies are regular people, too. And they are trying to be sensitive. But see how confusing it is?

Miss Manners doesn't happen to believe it is all that confusing. Treating professional colleagues in a dignified and professional manner should not be something new or difficult for gentlemen. Because it is so simple, suspicion is cast upon the inability to master the forms.

Oh, all right. For those who insist that they mean well, but can't quite get the hang of what they are expected to do, here is a special gentlemen's (so as not to say old duffer's) guide to behaving with traditional propriety toward ladies who are colleagues.

There is a lesson right at the start: Miss Manners, being a sweet little old-fashioned feminist, is allowed to use terms that gentlemen should not. Note that she has done so in strict accordance with an important rule they must learn, which is that word usage must always be parallel. "Ladies" is fine, provided those who are not ladies are referred to as "gentlemen." The term of respect, "Sir," becomes "Ma'am"; "Mr." in front of a title, as in "Mr. President," becomes "Madam President." Miss Manners would have thought that checking what the male term would be and then using its equivalent to be a rather simple way of getting it right. A gentleman of her acquaintance assured her that it was, just as he supervised signs going up on matching bathrooms, neatly labeled Ladies and Men.

The central lesson requires only two skills, both of which even admittedly unenlightened gentlemen proudly claim to know. They are supposed to understand professional behavior, having practiced it on one another for generations. They also profess to understand how to treat a lady.

To begin with the second part, crudity is never allowed in the presence of ladies, much less directed toward them. Pestering a lady is also ungentlemanly. Assuming liberties is a dreadful transgression of gentlemanly behavior. Only a cad would fail to take the slightest hint that he has offended a lady, for which he accepts her word and offers the deepest apologies.

In the old rules about the way gentlemen do business, they are required to maintain a respectful distance from one another, so as not to confuse personal likes and dislikes with professional relationships. Rank is the key to the only precedence system they use. If there happens to be a personal interest, it is put severely aside. Fathers who take their sons into their businesses have been lecturing them on this point for centuries.

The professional behavior ought to be enough of a modern guideline, because it requires a gentleman never even to seem to notice that the colleague he treats in a professional manner is a lady. He treats her according to her place in the work scheme, and strictly avoids any show of personal interest. If he fails, the gentlemanly code toward ladies should kick in. This strictly enjoins him from making personal remarks or overtures, as it has traditionally been the lady who got to choose whether or not she wished to enter a personal acquaintanceship with someone whom chance had sent her way.

See how easy it is? Miss Manners knows better than to suggest that the confused need only behave the way they have been behaving all along. Rather, she suggests that they behave the way they know they should have been behaving all along.

SYMBOLISM AT WORK: CLOTHING

The Dress Code Issue

A number of professional establishments not hitherto known for their insouciance (would you consider that a fair description of the Central Intelligence Agency?) have instituted Casual Day, or Dress-Down Friday, rescinding, for at least one working day, the expectation that business clothing might be worn for business. Employees report for work on such days dressed for leisure.

It is not hard to see where this one is going. Or that nobody but stuffy old Miss Manners sees anything wrong with merrily tossing aside those sober garments and following. Why, the adherents invariably ask, should people go around dressed as if they were attending a funeral?

This is a careless question, indicating an ignorance of how people dress for funerals nowadays. Leisure clothes are worn then, too, by people who don't see why they should have to go around dressed as if for work. So the question becomes why anyone should have to wear formal clothes at any time, for any occasion. The central figure at a funeral may not be in a position to dictate, but even if a bride is able to persuade a few of her closest friends to play dress-up with her, is that any reason why the wedding guests should surrender their comfort and individuality?

Comfort and individuality are the two big rallying cries of the No Dress Standards movement, and even Miss Manners is susceptible to their attractions. The goal of etiquette itself is often cited as "making other people feel comfortable." That is an interest of etiquette (which can also, under extreme provocation, provide freezingly polite methods of making other people feel decidedly uncomfortable), but not its only goal. It also provides a symbolic code by which one can read other people's attitudes and intentions quickly, before it's too late. Clothing is an important part of that symbolic vocabulary.

Miss Manners recognizes that not all places of employment want to symbolize seriousness. Those that want to symbolize imagination, creativity and daring encourage eccentric dress; those that want to symbolize responsibility and reliability do not. Clients want to see different qualities in their advertising agencies and caterers than they do in their financial advisers and heart surgeons. This part is at least understood by the employers. A standard caveat of Casual Day at serious institutions is that it is not the day to schedule meetings with clients. Dressing down is only for the privacy of the workplace.

Studies have been produced to show that both morale and productivity rise on Casual Day. Miss Manners has a simple way of dealing with such figures provided by sociology or its gullible younger sibling, the polls. She just dozes off the minute she hears the phrase "Studies show . . ." and wakes up in time for the study that shows the opposite.

That is what she is expecting when the novelty of play day wears off. Having conceded that the dress code is not an essential requirement, employees will have little trouble dropping it every day. Employers, who had relatively little trouble making people understand what formal work clothes were, will find themselves haggling ever more pettily over the differences among open shirts, T-shirts and tank shirts; sneakers, mules and sandals; sundresses, sweat clothes and house clothes.

Then the employees will start complaining about one another. Misbehaving male workers will charge that the females are dressing provocatively, while female workers will charge that males are dressing offensively. What that will do to the workplace atmosphere is nothing in comparison to the contribution of those who jog or bicycle to work and no longer need change clothes when they get there.

Still, the worst loss will be in symbolic statements. When there is a dress code, an employer who invites employees to forgo it because of weather emergencies is saying, symbolically, "We know it's a hardship to be here now, and we appreciate it." Employees who show up in leisure dress for weekend work are saying, symbolically, "Please note that this is not my regular shift—I'm giving up my free time to be here." These are two important messages Miss Manners feels sure they will be sorry to lose.

Deciding What to Symbolize

DEAR MISS MANNERS,

I am a writer, and I've begun attending science fiction conventions as a guest, speaking on panels, reading my work, giving autographs, etc. Since the people who attend the conventions pay to do so, I feel I should respect that and wear clothes that are dressier and suitable for a professional appearance.

My husband disagrees. He argues that since the people attending usually dress in jeans, as do many of the professional guests, I'm being needlessly formal. The conventions are exhausting, and I would prefer more comfortable clothes, but as you've pointed out, sometimes it's better to be uncomfortable and feel appropriate. What do you suggest?

ARMONK, N.Y.—IBM, renowned in corporate America for its rigid dress code of white shirts and dark suits, has adopted a policy of allowing headquarters employees to wear casual dress. The *Wall Street Journal* reported that IBM employees at other, already casual, locations seemed to have adopted a chinos-and-loafers dress code just as rigid as the old one.

GENTLE READER,

Miss Manners suggests that there is a big difference between being a performer and being a member of the audience—between those who pay to see someone, and those who are paid. Movie audiences dress for comfort, too, but they expect to see performers who are properly costumed for whatever they are there to represent.

From your description, you wish to appear as a professional author and lecturer who considers the occasion and the audience to be significant. Others who appear at a science fiction convention may wish to appear as something more, shall we say, unusual; Miss Manners is grateful they are not asking her for suggestions on how to do so.

Uniforms

The modern record of etiquette in exercising control over fashion is not glorious, Miss Manners has to admit. The campaign to persuade ladies not to show their ankles (on the grounds that there is no use in unduly exciting the gentlemen when we're all too busy doing interesting things to pay them the attention they would like) is not going well.

Even if she were not afraid of bringing down the house, Miss Manners would not want to suggest that anyone follow her personal preferences. She was schooled in a time when Worth was the name of the tailor, not of the first thing everyone was supposed to notice about the clothes, and a true lady packed away the new clothes she had received from Paris for at least a year so that they wouldn't be startlingly stylish when she first appeared in them. (Come to think of it, that is not a bad routine for the young to take up again. By the time the year ended, they could be the first to use the clothes to herald the nostalgic revival of that year's fashions.) She would, however, like timidly to suggest that there ought to be more and better working uniforms available for ladies.

Horrors! she hears the female population saying. Or would, if ladies still limited themselves to such delicate expressions of outrage. (There will be a short pause while Miss Manners realizes that her eccentric use of the terms "ladies" and "gentlemen" under all circumstances, intended to encourage civilized behavior, will not do in this discussion.) How dare anyone think of curtailing women's freedom, limiting their options, suppressing their creativity and squelching their individuality? They will wear what they please, and no longer be shoved into anyone else's restrictive ideas about what they should look like. (Of course, every one of these stirring voices comes from someone dressed in black, but never mind. Freedom to choose includes being able to choose to look alike.)

Progress has been made since the decades it took to wrench both employers and workers away from the idea that women should always look as if they were appearing for social purposes. Either silly supervisors were demanding that they wear skirts for manual labor, and were puzzled about why they were encumbered in doing the job, or they themselves were showing up in frills for office jobs and were puzzled about why they weren't treated seriously.

In some occupations, such as those of judge, chef or doctor, the problem is solved by a simple symbolic covering—the judge's robe, the chef's apron and hat, the doctor's white coat—over the individual's own clothes. In others, for example in the costumes of such athletes as swimmers or tennis players, a women's equivalent exists that is both practical and appropriate to women. There is now a reasonable standard for manual labor, with nearly identical costumes for male and female and for dressy office jobs, where a woman's suit or dress is obviously equivalent to a man's suit.

Miss Manners is still concerned now about women who already are in uniform, or who are dissatisfied at not having a uniform-equivalent at all.

The first category includes not only the military and the police but also occupations such as waitressing and bus driving, where a standard look is acknowledged to serve an important utilitarian purpose. Being in jobs formerly open only to men, many of these women are being dressed as honorary men. The silliest example must be the staffs of expensive restaurants. To its disgrace, etiquette used to have the idea that formal service could be provided only by males, as a result of which waiters served delicate tidbits in high-tipping places while waitresses lugged trays in places where tips were scarce. Now, fortunately, one sees both genders working in formal restaurants, but the waitresses generally wear masculine evening clothes, as if they had to be made honorary males in order to qualify for the job. What this says, symbolically, is that the job is still a man's job, but women are nevertheless being allowed to perform it.

Some airlines have devised smart and suitable uniforms for women, but the military services tend to give women dowdy uniforms, while the men's equivalents have a dashing glamour, or to make women wear men's ties rather than a female version, such as a scarf. (Both skirts and trousers being standard female apparel, especially when physical labor is involved, the distinction need be made only on ceremonial occasions.)

The second category consists of those, such as diplomats and other dignitaries, who are expected to supply formal wardrobes for public social-like appearances. These jobs, too, were formerly occupied only by men, who, like the waiters and orchestra players, need only have one set of formal clothes to look well dressed and smart. Obviously, women's evening clothes, with their individuality and fragility, are inappropriate, not to mention ludicrously expensive, to wear to such jobs. What is more, they are distracting. A woman who is a diplomat will, of course, wear a dressy outfit when the men wear morning clothes, but she is apt to find herself evaluated for fashion in a way the men are not.

The old-fashioned solution was not to allow women to hold official positions. It solved the problem all right, but Miss Manners never cared for that way of doing business. When women were present, they were there in their social capacity as wives. So even in the most august pseudo-social situations, such as state-sponsored ceremonies and entertainment, women in an official capacity still run the risk of being classified as accompanying relatives.

Miss Manners doesn't approve of dressing working women either as men or as their wives. Yet she doesn't much care for the helter-skelter solution by which, for example, male musicians wear evening dress while the female members of the orchestra tend to go in for black sports clothes. What is still needed is a female equivalent of formal clothing to be worn professionally (as opposed to socially, when taste has more or less free rein). It should be practical and durable, so that one can wear the same thing over and over again, but not masculine.

Considering that her own taste runs to leg-of-mutton sleeves, Miss Manners does not presume to make particular suggestions. If she did, she might point out that the simple black coatdress, in short or long versions (which could be worn plain for jobs requiring manual labor, or with jewelry and other accessories to provide individuality and variety for official appearances) is being freely and nearly universally worn now, anyway. Someone who took the initiative to design and institute this as standard formal dress for working women might earn the gratitude of those who would then have a lot of discretionary money available with which to dress themselves imaginatively in their private lives.

SYMBOLISM AT WORK: HONORIFICS

Generic Names

Some time ago, in relation to a discussion about what to call waiters or waitresses when one wants to summon them for another round of the same, a Gentle Reader was prompted to admit to Miss Manners "the solution we used to have" in his day: "All waitresses are called Mabel. All Pullman car porters are called George. All soldiers are called Joe."

Miss Manners promptly filed this information under *T* for Trouble. She did not care to inspire outraged replies from Mabels, Georges and Joes who did not happen to be, respectively, waitresses, Pullman car porters or soldiers. Especially Miss Manners did not care to inspire outrage in non-Mabel waitresses, non-George Pullman car porters and non-Joe soldiers over the indignity of summarily being assigned generic first names. This is similar to another offensive relic of the past recommended by an impatient nobleman: He used to call all his servants by the first names of those who had originally held their jobs, feeling that, having once troubled to learn a set of names, one needn't bother to do it again just because the bodies had changed.

The reason that Miss Manners brings this up (and out of the Trouble file) is that a similar practice is arising now, for different reasons. Let us say you telephone the Whiffle Company and explain your business at great length to the proper agent. Because there might be some sequels—perhaps you haven't made up your mind yet about your transaction, or perhaps another one will follow it and you don't want to have to repeat the entire story—you ask the person's name.

"Denise" is the reply. If you ask "Denise Who?" (a precaution Miss Manners takes in the hope of not having to be so cheeky as to address a stranger by her first name), the reply is "Just ask for Denise." In some cases, you call back and ask for Denise and are asked "Which one? We have several." In others, the name may turn out to be a code name for anyone covering that telephone, and the new Denise will know nothing of what was told to the old Denise.

Miss Manners understands the modern problem of identifying employees of a large establishment to their customers without providing personal information that cranks could use. First names do provide quasi-anonymity. However, she is not satisfied with that solution to the problem. The free usage of first names in business is thoroughly associated with two offensive practices:

1. The faked assumption of personal ties. Don't you feel like an idiot when the caller whose intimate greeting you respond to warmly turns out to be a salesperson who got your name from a list?

2. The outmoded assumption that only certain jobs are entitled to dignity, and that those holding them may treat their employees or others familiarly without any mutuality. This is what your doctor is assuming by addressing you by your first name while expecting you to say "Doctor."

Miss Manners proposes a twofold solution: Where there are regular contacts, people should trouble to learn one another's full names. Anonymity is not possible under those circumstances, but the dignity of addressing everyone by title and surname is. When it is not necessary to know the individual, a job title alone can be used. There is no disrespect in addressing someone on the job as "Waiter" or "Clerk" or "Mr. President," for that matter. In telephone encounters, a frank code—"When you call back, tell them that Operator 43 handled this call"—is preferable because it is more businesslike. That gentle "Just call and ask for Denise" only encourages the cranks.

First Names

DEAR MISS MANNERS,

Preceded by my résumé and cover letter (with salutation to Sir or Madam), and attired in my navy blue suit (from which all dog hairs have been painstakingly removed), I—a middle-aged woman seeking employment—cannot help but proceed with a feeling of formality. I greet my interviewer and express my thanks. Almost immediately, I hear my given name being tossed into the sentences which flow from the mouth of my potential employer: "Nancy, we are a team spirited company. What, Nancy, do you think you might contribute to our game plan?"

I find the use of my given name to be jarring and unnecessary. I am the only person being addressed, and I am paying attention. I feel like a fifth grader who is suspected of daydreaming. Worse yet, I am baffled as to how I should respond. May I, as I have been doing, speak without calling the interviewer anything? Does he expect me to call him Mr. Jones? Does she expect me to address her as Peggy? I fear that either of the latter two might be interpreted as my disapproval of their using my given name. I do not wish to insult them. What is the game, and how should I play? I want very much to work.

Gentle Reader,

Wanting to work is a very good reason not to indicate, during a job interview, that one is suffering under the silliness of a prospective employer's misuse of manners. It is also a good reason to attempt to accommodate oneself to puzzling expectations. So Miss Manners will allow herself only a brief shudder at this patently phony attempt to suggest that you are being interviewed for the position of work place buddy in a place where everyone is equal (except of course, when it comes to such trifles as duties and salaries) before answering your question.

Address your interviewer formally to show your own professionalism and respect. When you are then told, "I'm Brad" or "Call me Peggy," as you undoubtedly will be, you must look flattered and may do so or just stop addressing the person by name at all. At the moment, it is their work place, and their standards prevail. Miss Manners wishes you luck in getting the job. Perhaps then, you will eventually be able to help these people establish a more professional tone in the work place.

VANISHING PROFESSIONAL DEMEANOR

The Brush-off

Dear Miss Manners,

I have been conducting a job search for over a year now, applying for positions at many different universities, and have received numerous rejection letters. I have noticed a pattern developing. With very few exceptions (Vanderbilt was a class act from start to finish), the most prestigious universities in the nation have been responsible for some of the least gracious correspondence I have ever experienced. Some of the letters have been downright insulting!

Meanwhile, I have received letters that left me feeling favorably impressed, from institutions that are anything but elitist. I was raised to believe that sensitivity to the feelings of others is, in itself, a mark of personal distinction. How can so many highly regarded academic institutions employ so many ill bred people and not have their reputations suffer?

GENTLE READER,

Because those are their recent graduates who can't get jobs elsewhere. Also because, although any institution that is more sought after than seeking may know that its reputation will suffer, many also believe that behaving insufferably is a sign of distinction.

Miss Manners wishes to point out two serious mistakes in this rude way of thinking. The first is that arrogant people are much more likely to be perceived as uneducated louts than as important people who can't be bothered being polite. Thus, the victims of this rudeness, far from believing themselves to have been scorned by their betters, are bound to have (and to spread) doubts about the quality of an institution that has such low grade employees. The second is that every institution makes personnel mistakes, but to insult, as well as merely to reject, people who will turn out to be raging successes later can be devastating. The more powerful these people turn out to be, the more they will enjoy telling how they were misjudged and mistreated. No institution should risk setting itself up as the butt of such a story.

Nosy Questions

DEAR MISS MANNERS,

In two job interviews, I have been asked, "Now, tell us about your parents." I was completely taken aback, particularly when I was told that someone "not open enough" to talk about her personal life was not suitable for employment with the company, and that I should take my résumé and leave at once.

My family circumstances are best left undisclosed. It is sad but true that the offspring of two troubled, alcoholic and abusive parents are often regarded as irredeemably troubled themselves, despite strenuous efforts to raise oneself into a decent and worthwhile individual. I do not wish to carry this handicap into the workplace, nor do I feel obligated to do so. Can Miss Manners suggest a gracious refusal that will communicate to potential employers that one is a worthy and dedicated employee, regardless of a dislike for wanton personal "sharing"?

Gentle Reader,

Miss Manners has long been puzzled about the prevalence of the *Chorus Line* job interview you describe. (You may recall the long-popular musical show by that name, in which applicants for dancers' jobs in the show-within-the-show were selected less on how high they could kick than on how freely they would kick around their families.) Do employers need to go to that much trouble to find employees who associate work with the opportunity to sit around and talk about themselves?

Never mind that you have special reasons for not wanting to discuss your parents. Unless you are applying to be a guest on a confessional talk show, your personal life should be off limits to prospective employers. A lot of effort has been put into barring them from prying into personal matters, such as whether an applicant has children and how she plans to manage home responsibilities while working.

So try this: "I am discreet and loyal. For that reason, I'm afraid I can't discuss my dear family with you. But this also means that I would never disclose company business to competitors, or stir up trouble on the job by grousing about my employers or gossiping about my colleagues. You would be able to depend on my discretion absolutely."

A company that did not appreciate these qualities more than a predilection for personal confession is probably not a good place to work, anyway. It is going to go under, while its customers or clients cool their heels and its carefully selected employees are busy being open about themselves.

Relaxing

Just how happy-go-lucky do you want your surgeon to feel? While you are lying there, all fetching and oblivious, he is apt to be happily relaxing to his favorite music while doing his little job on you. The custom of using music to cut by is now widespread, according to the *Journal of the American Medical Association,* which ought to be looking around for a critic to review CDs.

Background music in the operating room is merely an extension of the widely accepted idea that people work better to music. Offices, factories and stores have been broadcasting music for almost as long as elevators. There are strong claims that it reduces tension and increases productivity. Of course, productivity, not to mention creativity, is often the result of tension. Still, we wouldn't want people to get all worried and bothered about their work, certainly not our own surgeons. Surely nothing matters so much that it is worth getting tense about.

WASHINGTON, D.C.—The District of Columbia Bar's Task Force on Civility in the Profession and its three subcommittees, The Subcommittee on Civility in Litigation, The Subcommittee on Civility in Negotiations and The Subcommittee on Legal Education and Lawyer Training Concerning Civility, are hard at work, according to an article in *The Washington Lawyer*. However, "There will be no quick fix! It will take time to change the legal culture, if that is what it is," the article said.

Only grumpy Miss Manners can be expected to be against workplace music, because it violates professional manners, or it would if there were any left. The generation that grew up with its homework spread out on the floor in front of the television set assures Miss Manners that it has no trouble at all doing two things at once. No problem, as it is fond of saying.

Not so fast. Miss Manners has another problem, and this is one that is perhaps too advanced for them, rather than too old-fashioned. It is that we are finally beginning to recognize that there may be a difference between having the right to indulge one's own tastes and having the right to inflict them upon others. Retreating from this realization will cause more trouble than it can ignore. The long and bitter struggle over smoke has finally established the idea that intrusiveness is a public problem. The problem with background music is that some people's easy listening is other people's strenuous listening. Enjoyment of music is a question of taste, and no form of it can please everyone. Especially if there is anyone else in the crowd who, like Miss Manners, gives music her undivided attention (and part of her disposable income) when she can, but cannot concentrate on anything else while it is playing.

This means that when music is played at work, someone's taste is intrusively foisted on someone else. In the case of the operating room, it is the surgeon whose taste prevails, and certainly everybody wants him to be happy. The patient, being anesthetized, needn't be consulted, although some doctors say they play music as the patient is going under on the grounds that it is reassuring. Provided, of course, the patient's last thought isn't "I'm trusting myself to some kid who thinks my operation is some kind of entertainment." But there are other people working in that room. Is having a relaxed surgeon worth risking, for example, a jumpy and distracted anesthesiologist?

The Etiquette-free Ritual

Except for a few details, the ritual of the retirement ceremony hasn't changed much over the last few decades, Miss Manners has observed. Some sort of party is still usually given, with a representative of management presiding. The difference nowadays is that newer workplace-social customs may be honored by the company's allowing, or encouraging, the other employees to arrange and pay for the party, preferably on their own time.

A boss still customarily expresses praise for the retiree's years of service, but in keeping with modern ideas of humor and candor, these remarks are now sprinkled with mild personal insults. Gratitude is no longer expressed, it being frankly recognized that however many years the arrangement may have endured, it was, after all, only a commercial bargain, in which loyalty and affection would not have prevented either employer or employee from abandoning the other at any time along the line.

A commemorative present is still commonly given, but it is not likely to be a gold watch with an inscription from the employer, for the very good reason that the employer didn't provide it. Other employees are now asked to chip in, and one of them is assigned to go out and buy something.

All participants in this ritual still promise to keep in close touch. This means that a month or two later, the retiree will drop by at lunchtime and, if everyone is not busy giving a shower for a new temporary worker, rejoin the old gang. Their conversation will consist of this week's workplace problems, interlaced with the overly hearty demand, "So what are you doing with yourself?" Everyone will privately vow not to repeat the occasion. At that point, true retirement will begin.

Miss Manners would not presume to interfere in such a well established ritual. Ultimately, she recognizes, whatever satisfaction anyone finds in retirement will have to do with that person's interests, circumstances, attitudes and activities, rather than with the send-off. What concerns her is the practice of speeding the retiree along with a massive dose of rudeness preceding the retirement party.

This professional innovation may be related to new laws proscribing age-mandated retirement. Kindly intended social policies may actually encourage unkind manners, Miss Manners has been sorry to observe. Rudeness is the main tool in the now-common technique by which supervisors encourage voluntary retirement. The idea is to bully and taunt the employee into feeling so worthless that retirement will be seen as an escape from embarrassing oneself further.

Some of the workers to whom this is applied may actually be slowing down; others may have never been swift. Still others may be meeting the highest standards, but are nevertheless considered undesirable because their salaries have risen with seniority and their places may be wanted for younger people.

Miss Manners is not seeking a futile quarrel with the harsh realities of the workplace. But she deplores the practice of sending off longtime workers—whatever their past or present merits or limitations—in a state of humiliation. Surely there must be a better way to handle the necessary progression of the workplace than to make people who have had honorable careers feel as though they have ultimately failed. Until there is a change, however, Miss Manners can only make the victims of this technique— and their colleagues, who could be helpful in bolstering their confidence—aware that it is a rude subterfuge, applied on the basis of age rather than competence.

Not Giving Up

DEAR MISS MANNERS,

As a middle-aged adult, I have observed the gradual erosion of behavior in much of everyday life. The amenities, when practiced at all, are now often reserved only for selfish ends, such as cajoling friends for favors, impressing superiors, or consummating deals.

I have witnessed so-called professionals in business and industry freely ply their talents for misinformation, obfuscation and plagiarism in the pursuit of salary increases, promotions and currying favor with the influential. Management, generally aware of the situation, ignores or even encourages it, since they are frequently engaged in the same activities themselves.

People have either deliberately or, I suspect for the most part, inadvertently distanced themselves from manners because good manners are simply no longer expected of them. When courtesies go unrecognized and therefore unacknowledged, they are unappreciated and fall into disuse. Despite material abundance, a stable government, a secure middle class and expansive freedoms, the populace invariably reveals a mass appeal for the ill-mannered, vulgar, sensational and transient diversions of the lowest common denominator.

GENTLE READER,

You must understand how Miss Manners feels when people tell her that they are eager to learn about etiquette, in which they strongly believe—and then reveal that what they mean is the command of tricks to show off at a restaurant in front of an employer or client.

All is not lost, however. Miss Manners has come to understand that even this unlikely introduction to manners can be used to plant the idea that behaving politely is an advantage in society. Also, greedy, ambitious people are slightly more palatable with a gloss of manners than they are without.

ETIQUETTE-FREE SERVICE AND PUBLIC SERVICE

MINDLESS POLITENESS

You encounter a place of business where agreeable behavior is so widespread among the employees that it seems to be a company policy. What is the first adjective that comes to mind to describe this?

For some people, the word is "mindless." What are they thinking?

What brought this to Miss Manners' mind was an irate letter to the *Washington Post.* (The letter-to-the-editor is one of Miss Manners' favorite literary genres. Her hobby is searching for the rare ones that don't use the word "ironic.") This one was spluttering over a story about the McDonald's fast-food restaurant in Moscow, which the letter writer believed erroneously elevated the company into being a " 'perfect' icon of American culture. The McDonald's empire represents more than just a food service," he continued. "It constitutes a mass encroachment on the individuality that we Americans have cherished for more than 200 years. The company not only makes robots of its employees, it also demeans its patrons with assembly line service by people who are told to smile and be nice."

Doesn't everyone know that surliness is not only an inevitable result of living in freedom but The American Way? Miss Manners, for one, does not. From its inception, America was distinguished by its citizens' openness and helpfulness to strangers. The hauteur of aristocracies in class-divided societies was thought to be as offensive here as the obsequiousness of their lower classes. The classic American demeanor is neither, but straightforward, easygoing and pleasant. Not that we've seen a lot of that lately.

Miss Manners fears that the gentleman who wrote the letter has a lot of company among those who believe that it is demeaning to act or be treated nicely. If you are nasty, the argument goes, you are truly being yourself. This would tend to suggest that people who claim the right to be themselves have perhaps a justifiably low opinion of themselves. Have you ever heard anyone declare "I just want to be me!" in asserting the right to go around being nice?

WASHINGTON, D.C.—"The U.S. Postal Service is hoping to erase the image of postal workers as sullen and slow with charm classes that teach window clerks to be courteous to customers who become surly waiting in line," the *Washington Post* **reported.**

Even if the intent were to project all one's moods, up and down, onto hapless business acquaintances, the cause of freedom would be badly served. When we extol individuality, we do so still willing to try to get along with others. In business, being pleasant and efficient, without exposing one's private emotions, is called a professional demeanor. This is not to be confused with the inappropriate use of social manners on the job: Miss Manners is as opposed to chumminess in business as she is to crossness. It is equally for the protection of the employee and the customer that they should not expose their private feelings to each other.

We expect a standard of service in all professional endeavors, in which fairness precludes inflicting unpleasantness on the innocent. Or even the guilty. Would any American want the police officer stopping people on the highway to be entitled to act out a personal bad mood, or the defending lawyer to expose personal dissatisfactions to the judge or jury?

Thought-out Rudeness

DEAR MISS MANNERS,

I have noticed—as I'm sure others do but overlook—that more and more, when an employee in a service, public-oriented position (whether it is the Department of Motor Vehicles, county clerks, utility reps or your local five and dime) makes a booboo, that person spends not one calorie to apologize for their mishandling of the matter. For example, the warm body behind window two at the DMV forgot to return my license that I gave her with the extension card and a $5 bill, to request my driving record. I had to go back to get it. She made no attempt whatever to acknowledge or say anything remotely like an "oops" or apology. There seems to be an underlying mannerism of disassociating a boo-boo from oneself. If I missed the class in 1990s attitudes, could you please send me same so I can fit into the quagmire?

GENTLE READER,

Miss Manners is not giving lessons in the callous behavior currently known as attitude. It seems to her that people are managing to develop this well enough on their own.

As you have noticed, encountering these attitudes is not pleasant. An "Oops, sorry" and a regretful smile would not have cost this warm body anything, and would probably even have produced a sympathetic "Oh, that's all right," perhaps accompanied by a smile from you in return. Thus a mean exchange would have been transformed into a kind moment.

Miss Manners' theory about the cause of such routine rudeness is

NEW YORK, N. Y.—In one of its recurrent "politeness" campaigns, New York City civic leaders distributed 10,000 apple-scented air fresheners to cabdrivers, launched a "sensitivity program" to teach police, subway workers and other city employees the importance of being polite and started a subway ad campaign exhorting New Yorkers with slogans such as "Instead of Making a Wise Crack, Crack a Smile." The newspaper report added that surveys in urban areas such as New York and Miami have shown that rudeness ranks among the top deterrents to return visits by tourists.

that people want to distance themselves not only from their own mistakes, but from the professional role itself. A ridiculous over-emphasis on professional status—as if it were a key to individual worthiness—has resulted in many people actively seeking to show their contempt for their own jobs. The result is as sad as it is annoying. Miss Manners seems to recall that a widespread American belief in the equal dignity of all honest labor used to demand that one give respect as well as expect to receive it.

Thought-out Ridicule

DEAR MISS MANNERS,

At my dentist's, I had a more involved procedure done than usual and was nervous. The assistant took my blood pressure as the doctor stood there with his back towards me, and upon discovering that I was nervous, they both laughed. Then I was not only apprehensive, but angry and frustrated. I wanted to belt both of them. But I truly didn't want to do them bodily harm and I did need their services, so I restrained myself and sat in silence.

If they had wanted to know if I was nervous, all they had to do was ask. After all, we patients trust them. It seems to me a blatant display of power abuse, only for them to satisfy their nosy curiosity. Nothing was done to alleviate my anxiety.

A friend of mine was insulted by the same assistant who exclaimed, "Isn't that the same dress you wore last time?" (My friend, who dresses impeccably, was hurt but said nothing.) Should we have said something immediately and walked out, or was sitting in silence the best thing?

GENTLE READER,

Do you pay these people to insult you? Miss Manners understands that the best of dentists may cause some pain, but generally not by sneering at the patients. She would certainly recommend walking out, if this is at all feasible. If not, it might be prudent to wait until the procedure is over before voicing your dissatisfaction, which you might be moved to repeat in writing to the nearest professional association affecting these people.

New Service Techniques

Puzzling Explanations

Is there a modern business manners program that Miss Manners doesn't know about, where special training in politeness avoidance is given to those who deal with the public?

Miss Manners trusts that she will not be suspected of anything so low as sarcasm in posing this question. She puts it in a tiny voice, with her most sincerely more-in-sorrow-than-anger facial expression (this resembles that upside-down look that inevitably accompanies a murmured "Awwwwww"), because she is genuinely puzzled. Business people assure her that mannerlessness is the one area in which all job-seekers show up already well trained.

Perhaps so. There is certainly a lot of talent along those lines on the market, and Miss Manners, who is not totally unaware that there seem to be some problems with etiquette in the society, would be inclined to accept this explanation. Indeed, she would naturally be the first to sympathize with employers who cannot successfully pro-hibit bad manners on the part of the people they pay to please their clients. What got her thinking that something more complicated was going on was hearing the same phrases being used by people in different businesses in different cities.

At first she suspected they were coming from company legal departments—not to pick on poor old lawyers again, but because the phrases seemed to be so carefully crafted to be devoid of promises and admissions. Instead of "I'll see to that" or "Sure, we'll take care of it" or "Thank you" or "I'm sorry," service people now say, "I hear what you're saying," "It's not my fault," "I wasn't there when it happened," "There you go," and "I can understand that you feel that way." The new statements may be less satis-fying, but they are presumably safer in case the transaction gets to court.

Even more neutral and standard is the simple "Okay."

CUSTOMER: "I waited three months for that piece of junk I ordered from you, like an idiot, and when it finally came, you sent me the wrong size, a color that makes me sick, and the one flimsy material I told you specifically I didn't want. Plus it didn't work. When I took it back, you refused to take off the delivery fee, in spite of the fact that I was in the store when I ordered it and you couldn't give it to me be-cause you didn't have them in stock, even though you'd advertised them that very day—which should have told me something right there. You refused to pick it up again but made me make a second trip to bring it back, while you're still charging me for 'delivery.' "

BUSINESS REPRESENTATIVE: "Okay."

CUSTOMER: "Wait! Now I get another bill, dunning me for something I don't even have anymore, and you had the nerve to add a penalty charge, claiming I refused to pay for it, when I hadn't even gotten it for weeks after you promised it. There's been nothing but incompetence on this whole matter, from beginning to end, and you still haven't got it right."

COMPLAINT DEPARTMENT PERSON: "Okay."

Out of delicacy, Miss Manners will not report the continuation of this proto-typical exchange. The customer was already inadvertently (and unattractively) spraying the telephone with moisture while talking. The simple response of "Okay"—suggesting that the course of events as narrated was perfectly all right with the repre-sentative of the institution responsible—so added to the rage level that any pretense at civility was abandoned altogether.

Then Miss Manners began to suspect the airlines of originating these responses.

If they didn't invent "We are sorry *if* this has caused you any inconvenience," with its odd element of doubt, they are the ones sending it around. Surely it is safe to assume that no one is gratefully surprised to be allowed to spend more time on an airplane or in an airport.

That curious apology is at least an approach to politeness. Things turn ugly when an airline employee announces that the delayed flight will be ready for departure at 9:57 and shrugs and turns away when the passengers point out that it's now 10:02 and the aircraft has not yet arrived. Miss Manners discovered how far this technique had spread when, nine weeks after ordering an item promised for delivery in "six to eight weeks," she was assured that "It will be delivered exactly when we said it would."

An approach that no sensible person would think up without corporate assistance is to counter evidence that something didn't work by saying, "But that's our normal procedure." Think about it. Who would want to brag that an error was company policy? Miss Manners' favorite example is the official in an airline baggage department who crisply told that to a passenger whose bag didn't arrive on the same airplane. "It will be here tomorrow," he declared, obviously without doing any checking on the bag's whereabouts. "It's normal procedure to have the bag arrive the next day." (Naive Miss Manners would have thought it was normal procedure to have the bag arrive with the passenger. In any case, it arrived two weeks later, and a month after that, a letter arrived from the company saying that the bag could not be found.)

Explaining that nothing can be done because a particular error, although unfortunate, cannot be rectified, could reasonably be used as a final admission. It is now often used as the first. When Miss Manners called back her former answering service to inquire about a wrong number she had been given, she was assured, "That's what we have—there's no way of checking what it ought to be." The ingenious sleuthing technique Miss Manners successfully used—calling Directory Assistance, giving the name, and then just asking for the number—was apparently unimaginable.

Miss Manners has enough faith in humanity to believe that most people, when given a problem, attempt to solve it, which in most cases is the simplest recourse and leaves everyone happy. Surely employees have to be retrained into making these weird declarations. Miss Manners suspects the motive of this may be to goad the customer to madness, at which time the company begins to look like the reasonable party.

Missing Explanations

DEAR MISS MANNERS,

A recent flight I was on which was supposed to depart at 9 a.m. did not depart until 4:30 p.m. After we had been on the aircraft for three hours, with captain and stewardesses assuring us all the while that we would be leaving in "just a few minutes," I began to grow increasingly impatient. After four hours, I felt I had to take some action. I asked a stewardess if I might leave the aircraft to attempt to secure a flight on another airline.

The flight attendant apologized and said that we would be under way "shortly" and that the delay was not her fault. I said that regardless of whose fault it was, the passengers should be realistically told when the plane was going to leave. I asked why the plane was not leaving and she said she did not know. She informed me that I could not leave the aircraft, but that if I returned to my seat, she would show a movie to help kill time.

I became quite angry and told her that as an employee of the airline, she should be embarrassed by such outrageous behavior. I said that the passengers deserved an explanation and that showing a film to placate us was not an acceptable solution. I then returned to my seat before I completely lost my temper. When we finally arrived, more than eight hours later than scheduled, I immediately wrote a letter to the president of the airline expressing my outrage.

Is what I did in the immediate situation proper? I realize that the flight attendant had no control over the aircraft, but she was the only one there at the time, representing the airline. While I tried to control myself, I'm afraid that after four hours of outrageous treatment, the tone of my voice may have been somewhat angry. Is there special dispensation in this case?

GENTLE READER,

Miss Manners has been on enough such non-flights to understand how you felt and worry about how you acted. A planeful of trapped people going nowhere and not believing the encouragement they are offered is an etiquette time bomb, which is why Miss Manners does not give special dispensations. An outbreak of rudeness among passengers and crew—and Miss Manners has unfortunately witnessed them—does not relieve cabin fever.

Leaving aside matters that rest with God (the weather) and aviation law (mandating when passengers may or may not disembark), the etiquette question is how the airline might soften the inconvenience to their clients. Of course, the crew should provide frequent bulletins. Even negative information, that no official word has come, helps convince the passengers that the crew is on their side instead of meanly plotting to hold them there punitively. Distractions—drinks, movies—are useful provided that they are not offered as a substitute for news and assistance.

Most of all, the crew should apologize—often and profusely. Never mind that they are not at fault; people like to have their suffering recognized. The passengers are not looking for someone to blame so much as they are looking for relief from their sense of the injustice of the situation. Individual defenses by the flight attendant or anyone else do not interest them. They only want to hear that an airplane they have paid to get them somewhere fast is sorry it cannot.

Defusing Anger

In the standard exchange involving a person making a complaint and the person receiving the complaint, usually on behalf of a commercial establishment, there are, Miss Manners has observed, two obligatory roles. One person must say something along the lines of, "This is the most outrageous thing that ever happened. I can't imagine how anyone could be so stupid. I'm going to find out exactly how this came about, and believe me, I'm going to do something about it right away." The other must say, "Look, mistakes happen. This is just not all that important. There's no use getting upset, because these things happen all the time. It's not really anybody's fault."

Now here comes the peculiar part: The person at whom the complaint is directed gets to choose which role he or she wants to play, and the complainer has to take the other. That's right. Although the complainer always starts out making speech #1, the complainee may also make speech #1, in which case the complainer is forced to respond with speech #2.

TORONTO, CANADA—Canada's largest pizza chain, threatened by competition, established a policy of giving customers their pizza free if the delivery driver fails to smile, and then firing the driver, according to the *Globe and Mail.* "That's corporate policy. It's not cutthroat. It's getting back to basics. It's service," the chain's executive director told the newspaper.

Miss Manners realizes that this is a difficult concept. It must be, because those who are obliged to receive complaints, either occasionally or as a wearisome way to earn a living, don't seem to have caught on to the possibilities of the switcheroo. It can't be pleasant to have someone screaming at you, but nevertheless, here is the way the standard exchange goes:

COMPLAINER (in more or less normal voice, with just a small edge to it): "This is an outrage."

COMPLAINEE (in bored tone): "Oh, calm down. It's nobody's fault, it just happens occasionally. It's really too late to do anything about it."

COMPLAINER (shrieking): "You mean it's happened before? Is everyone here an idiot? I've never seen such bungling in all my life. Well, it just so happens that my cousin is a lawyer, and you haven't heard the last of this. There is no excuse for this, none whatsoever."

And so on and on and on.

Here is the same situation, except that the complainee has decided not to take abuse, and so has preempted that function.

COMPLAINER (same voice): "This is an outrage."

COMPLAINEE (with note of abject desperation): "It certainly is. I can't imagine how this could have happened, but you may be sure I'm going to do something about it. I feel terrible because it must be my [our] fault. I can't apologize to you enough. We pride ourselves on getting things right, and this is intolerable. Please give us another chance. Let me see what I can do to make it up to you."

COMPLAINER (grudgingly at first, but warming up to subject to counter threat of Complainee continuing in the same vein): "Oh, that's okay. We all make mistakes. It's not all that important."

What makes the switch work is the impossibility of two people keeping up an argument in which both are carrying on from the same point of view. Miss Manners is astonished that so few people avail themselves of this simple technique to neutralize what is otherwise a nasty exchange, sometimes even with later consequences. Perhaps they are aware that they will never hear from the lawyer-cousin, who is used to hearing highly unreliable accounts of so-called outrages, and doubtless fed up with being asked to do petty tasks for free.

Sustaining Anger

DEAR MISS MANNERS,

I was insulted by a person acting in an official capacity (she is an assistant attorney general) with whom I was negotiating on behalf of my client (I too am a lawyer).

WASHINGTON, D. C.—A onetime supporter of Mayor Marion Barry and member of a local Advisory Neighborhood Commission told the *Washington Post,* **in a story examining the breakdown of the city: "The response of the city back in the late 1980s was not courteous to those of us who paid taxes. . . . There was insolence on the telephone. Employees did not give their names and did not follow through."**

She had indicated that she required the approval of her supervisor on certain points. Consequently, when we later reached an impasse, I stated that if she was unable to grant our request (or did not have the authority to do so), I would like to discuss the matter directly with her supervisor.

She said that was not how they did things in her state, and, after some audible fuming, told me I was behaving "like an ass" and demanded the name of my "supervisor." I gave her the name of the partner at the large law firm where I am an associate, and repeated my request. After she stated she would only tell her supervisor to call me, I asked her to do me the courtesy of telling me his or her name, so I might know who was calling. Finally, she did so.

Frankly, I found her conduct unprofessional, outrageous, unwarranted and offensive. Shortly thereafter, she called me back and apologized for "flying off the handle," but explained that she was very frustrated, had a heavy workload, etc. I did not feel the apology was sincerely offered, but did not know how to react without seeming churlish. I made noncommittal remarks like "Hmmm, I see," in response to her catalogue of complaints.

Would it have been proper to say, "I'm afraid your remarks were terribly offensive—I cannot accept your apology"? I did not mention her behavior to her supervisor because I did not want to get her in trouble—however, I don't believe she appreciated how shocking I found her conduct (or want of conduct). Perhaps I expected too much and should be content with what I received?

GENTLE READER,

Well, you could sue her. You already thought of that, didn't you? Miss Manners commends you for rejecting the idea. In the milder realm of etiquette, an apology is considered sufficient restitution for a slight. However, the tone of the apology is supposed to be commensurate with the extent of the slight—the greater the offense, the more slobbering the apology—and Miss Manners takes it that you did not find this one satisfactory.

Rejection of an apology can only be considered a request for a better apology. That is why one does not issue a blanket refusal. It would sound as if you expected the debt to be paid in blood or money. Rather, the offensive apology is met with the sort of noncommittal words you issued, followed by prolonged coldness. Eventually, the offender notices that the offense has not been erased by the apology, and is supposed to be moved to offer one that will work.

Breaking Bad News

Breaking tragic news to someone who will be deeply affected by it is as tough a problem as etiquette is called upon to handle. Knowing that one will cause pain by what one says is dreadful. Miss Manners has no pity for people who enjoy heralding tragedy (and there seem to be a lot of those around), but she has a great deal for those who must do so, and, from distaste for the task, bungle it.

Callousness is rarely the problem, although the instances in which it occurs are memorable. People who receive a curt announcement, without preliminaries or condolences, find themselves adding to their grief an anger that never subsides, even after the shock itself has eased. Relatives of victims of the Lockerbie air crash reported that they first found their calls for information to a government "24-hour hot line" unanswered, and then finally "they'd call us and say, 'We found your child's remains,' and sign off, 'Have a nice day.'"

Surely most people know the basic formula for breaking tragic news: First one announces that bad news is to come, to get the person's attention, to establish that it

> NEW YORK, N.Y.—"I have always considered courtesy a sign of weakness," a former cab-driver was quoted in the *New York Times* as saying.

is not some sort of perverse joke and to avoid baldly blurting out the worst. Before the person has time to race over all the catastrophic possibilities, the victim is named. Here there is a pause only if the news is of a death. Otherwise, it must immediately be said that this is not a death but an accident or whatever, with as optimistic an interpretation as can be honestly stated. Both unwarranted optimism and undue pessimism can cause lasting extra bitterness.

Then the circumstances of the tragedy are explained, fully but without grisly details. If something must be done immediately—if the person is being summoned to the hospital, for example—that is said next, preferably along with a plan for assistance in getting there. The person who is being told of the tragedy will not, of course, take it all in. Denials must be answered calmly, and incomprehension met with patient repeating.

Most people can manage all this. It is what they add to it that gets them into trouble. In the vain hope that there is some way to tell of a tragedy that will remove its effect of pain, some people try to add reassurance that everything will be all right. To someone whose world is suddenly clearly not all right, this is infuriating.

Equally misguided is any effort to make a moral lesson of the tragedy. The bereaved may find great solace in doing this later themselves—in organizing or supporting an organization that seeks to prevent such tragedies as they have suffered. But to tell people that "This needn't have happened if . . ." followed by a denunciation of the carelessness of the victim (whether it is for exercising too little or too much, for being on a street occupied by drunk drivers, or for living at a time before some disease is cured) is galling.

Finally, the bearers of tragic news should beware of describing to its recipients what they must be feeling, or predicting the course of their "process of healing." Miss Manners received a heartrending letter from a lady widowed in an accident in which she was also injured. "The hospital sent a widow to speak to me, and she informed me that she had lost her husband a year earlier, that she had recently gotten engaged, and, when I expressed doubt that I would want to marry again, scoffed at my grief and love for my husband by saying that I wouldn't feel like that for long. Were I not under the influence of narcotics, I would have thrown her out."

The popularity of "support groups" should not obscure their limits. Knowing that others have gone through similar tragedies may be a help, but it should be remembered that every tragedy is not only commonplace but also unique.

Too Good to Be Polite

There is no such thing as being important or powerful enough to be entitled to be rude, as many a toppled monarch and defeated statesman has found out. There is not even such a thing as being too noble and self-sacrificing and dedicated to serving the public to have to be bothered with mere etiquette.

When the high pressure, stressful, crucial, overworked and noble profession of medicine complained that its inestimable service to the public should not be hampered by mere etiquette, Miss Manners suggested it take a seat in her waiting room. There were a lot of professions represented there already—government officials both powerful and petty, police, artists, athletes and cabdrivers—all listlessly leafing through back issues of the *New England Journal of Medicine* and complaining of stress. They're working too hard, they've got deadlines, they have to make quick deci-

A former cabdriver wrote in a letter to the editor of the *Washington Post* that hacking a cab is hard work but quite profitable if the cabby is deferential, polite and helpful. "A cabdriver is, after all, a freelance servant. Lousy servants make lousy tips," he wrote. As an example, he told of a man who got into his cab, slammed the door and was quite rude. "I said, 'Yes sir, right away,'" the former cabby wrote, adding that he ended up with an apology, a $10 tip and $250 the next day for driving the man and his son on an all-day tour.

sions about crucial matters, they're exhausted, pressed for time, and they know that what they do takes skill and dedication and is important to society. So they want it understood that they cannot tarry for mere etiquette. It was going to be a long wait, because Miss Manners doesn't give exemptions for public service. Stressed people need more etiquette, not less.

Suddenly Miss Manners went bursting into her waiting room and, in defiance of etiquette's rules of precedence, told Medicine, "Please come in; you're next." (This rule does not apply in hospital emergency rooms, but the failure to explain that the urgency of patients' complaints is factored into the order leaves people highly indignant. They see patients who arrived after them being taken before, and assume that normal etiquette is being violated out of arbitrary favoritism.)

Medicine's medical problems seemed to be critical. Doctors are skipping the niceties for lack of time when talking to patients' families, according to an article en-titled "Your Child Is Dead." A surgeon and an anesthesiologist had a disagreement and slugged it out on the floor of a Massachusetts hospital's operating room while the anes-thetized patient quietly waited for a gallbladder operation. Malpractice suits are often discovered to have an etiquette problem at the root: ignorant old Dr. Housecall, who hasn't read a medical journal since the Middle Ages, is forgiven for his mistakes, while Dr. Hotshot makes one trivial false move and gets sued.

Medical habits are also spreading. Lay people, having learned from the legal profession that rude behavior is interpreted as forceful and dedicated, have now picked up from medicine the idea that everyone else's time is less important than their own.

It used to be the exclusive privilege of doctors to set up an exact appointment on their own turf, and then not keep it, offering the patient no explanation, no apol-ogy about running late, and no estimate of how long the wait would be. (Note: Miss Manners knows that there are times when it's impossible to calculate how long it will take to do a good and careful job, and not even she wants slapdash medicine, but that explanation has been abused too much to be perpetually credible.) True, a related but even higher-ranking profession, plumbing, did something similar by instructing clients to wait at home all day for the practitioner to show up, but at least the clients were on their own turf. Now, virtually all business people invite their clients to come to their offices—at a time when they are too busy to see them.

When Miss Manners examined the medical manners problem, it turned out to be an intellectually rather snazzy one—the old mind-body problem. Health care work-ers deal every day with a problem that has baffled everybody who approached it since the dawn of philosophy: the paradox of body and personhood.

In their work, it is essential that they take the scientific view of the body, as an object with natural properties. Nevertheless, patients do not resign their personhood when they seek health care, and must also be treated with dignity, which is not easy to do with someone who is practically naked, clutching a sheet, looking alarmed and maybe not telling a full story. When the patient is not safely anesthetized, medical prac-titioners must recognize the nonmaterial properties of the person—nuisance-making ones, such as free will and emotions—even though this can interfere with dealing with patients as objects of benevolent medical intention.

This is where etiquette comes in. Requiring the forms of dignity and respect, even when the need for them is not obvious, is perhaps counterintuitive. Acting on one's intuitive feelings is not all it's cracked up to be, anyway. Miss Manners frequently hears from terminally sick people complaining that their friends and relatives shun them because their condition makes them unattractive. She also hears, regrettably, from those shunners who shamelessly admit to it and take the liberty of excusing themselves on the grounds that they find visiting the seriously ill and the dying upsetting, frightening and depressing. It would take manners for them to do so anyway, ignoring and concealing their distaste for someone else's sake.

The nobility of health care workers is that they never commit this unspeakable rudeness, and their problem of philosophical confusion is not a bad one, as excuses go. Too bad Miss Manners doesn't accept excuses. Respect is due to everyone, simply for being human. Here are some perfectly ordinary manners from which hospital staffs, in spite of the basic and valid asymmetry in the relationship between those with more authority and those with less, are not excused:

When doctors first approach a patient, even on hospital rounds, they must introduce themselves and anyone with them and explain who they are. They must not touch anyone, even for an examination, without asking permission, or do a medical procedure without saying what it is. All instructions should be put in the form of requests using the word "please." This doesn't make the instructions optional; it just makes them palatable. If they must inconvenience people, they must acknowledge that they have done so. They must not gossip about people where they can be caught—which includes discussing patients where they, or other patients or visitors, are likely to hear.

They are not excused from following the dress code of the profession. The symbolism of neatness and cleanliness is perhaps obvious, but the white coat and other professional clothing act just as powerfully. That's why there have been efforts to detrock the white coated people in advertisements who are selling over-the-counter remedies. The white coat symbolizes the kind of authority that tells you you really have no choice but to obey if you care about your health.

The other thing Miss Manners wishes to say to the overworked, overstressed medical profession and all the amateur healers they have inspired is "There, there." She hopes they feel better. A good dose of etiquette will help.

Making Patients Wait

DEAR MISS MANNERS,

As I understand it, when two people have an appointment, whether for business or social purposes, and one of them is unable to meet the other on time, it is that person's responsibility to notify the other of the delay. Is this indeed the rule, and, if so, are physicians exempt from it? I have spent many hours in physicians' waiting rooms and I have yet to have a physician's office phone me to warn that the doctor is running late.

In self defense, I have taken to phoning the doctor's office first, to make sure she is running on time before leaving for the appointment. When I recently tried this, I was told that while my gynecologist would not be able to see me on time, if I were to arrive late, I would be put in the queue behind the patients that had arrived earlier, regardless of when my appointment was. I brought this up with the doctor herself (after a 45 minute wait in the waiting room), and her defense was that the other patients would be irritated if I were to wait in my own office (and get some work done), arrive at a time when I could be seen, and then be shown in before them.

This seems to me a curious and self-serving view of etiquette. Rather than invest the time and effort to treat all patients properly by phoning them if there is to be a delay, instead insist on mistreating all patients equally. I understand that in a medical practice, there is an unavoidable variability in the time required to attend to each individual properly, and I would not complain about a ten or 15 minute wait. But if the doctor has fallen significantly behind the appointment schedule, I see no reason why she should not be held to the same standard of courteous behavior as the rest of the business and social world.

Gentle Reader,

Miss Manners doesn't want to hear the outrage from physicians and their staffs, along with their high-minded justifications about saving lives and the patients' money, that will be generated by your complaint and Miss Manners' agreement. The fact is that these people have presumed on the good nature of people such as yourself, who are ready to be accommodating about the occasional emergency and even the routine short delay. Everybody who wants good medical care will agree that some inconvenience might be necessary so that all receive whatever full attention is needed, which cannot be exactly gauged in advance.

This does not, however, explain why virtually all patients seeking routine care are kept waiting for long periods of time, virtually every time they go to the doctor's. It has just come to be one of those institutionalized rudenesses of the profession—the way opera singers are indulged for having tantrums.

Perhaps it is the patients themselves who need to alter this unfortunate practice. Heaven knows that Miss Manners has tried to appeal to doctors to do this voluntarily, but without noticeable results. Since your doctor has presumed to speak for the other patients—suggesting an unfair scenario in which the other patients would be led to believe that you merely walked in late and got served out of turn—perhaps you should ask them to speak for themselves. A waiting room caucus, in which people documented the inconvenience each had, and asked jointly for a change in the system, might make more of an impression.

Making Visitors Wait

Dear Miss Manners,

Ours is a professional management office, not some showroom for farm equipment or lingerie (not that it would make a difference) and it amazes me, in this day and age, how many men will say "honey," "baby" or "dear" when approaching the receptionist. When they are asked to wait, they invariably act as if it is the receptionist's duty to entertain them, laugh at their joke or carry on a continuous conversation.

We have tried, unsuccessfully in most cases, to ignore them by continuing with our work, but they don't take us seriously when we tell them that we are sorry but we must complete a project.

Many job applicants—male and female—also carry on continuous chatter while filling out the application. We don't wish to lose our jobs, so we are always polite and professional and greet the rudeness with a smile. We are all tired of biting our tongues and are thoroughly disgusted by the lack of professionalism we have to deal with.

BOSTON, MASS.—Boston University created a program in health care negotiation and conflict resolution at its medical school to teach medical students how to cooperate. " . . . the team also trains practicing doctors, nurses and other health professionals in techniques of negotiation and mediation and offers its services to help resolve conflicts before they escalate to violence or legal proceedings," said an account of the team in the *Washington Post*. A BU social scientist who helped set up the team told the *Post* that the solution to conflicts in the medical profession is often quite simple: "A revolutionary concept: The apology. If you say, 'I'm sorry,' it's over. If you don't, it's gonna cost you $22 million."

GENTLE READER,

Miss Manners doesn't countenance annoying people who are trying to work any more than you do. And she is thinking of restricting legal use of the term "honey" to people who have been married so long that they can't remember their spouses' names.

But she does have to ask herself why all those people are being kept waiting so long in your office. Do they have appointments? It has become an increasingly common business practice to set appointments on one's own turf and then keep people waiting. Reception rooms everywhere are filled with people who have showed up on time for appointments and are kept cooling their heels. Talk about unprofessional behavior . . .

What that amounts to is wasting the time of visitors who then become bored and waste the time of whoever is around. One rudeness begets another.

As you suffer the brunt of this, it would be in your interest and that of the other receptionists to ask that this practice be discontinued. The argument that you cannot both entertain other people's visitors and do your own work ought to be a strong one.

When the expected visitors whip right through the reception area to their appointments, you can be firm with anyone who does not have an appointment. Say politely that they are welcome to stay on the understanding that there is no one available just now—including, unfortunately, yourself—to talk with them.

Miss Manners only requests you to donate a fraction of all that time she has saved you to tolerance for the nervousness of job applicants.

Waiting on Home Turf

DEAR MISS MANNERS,

Our listing with the realtor specifies that agents should call me at my office before showing the house, so that I may leave work (without pay) to go home to get the dogs out of the house. Over the past ten months, all the agents who have made an appointment to show our house do not bother to call to cancel the appointment when they decide not to show the house. We don't care why they don't come; we just want to know that they will not be coming.

Are sellers so unimportant that our time is worth nothing? Do agents feel that we are at their mercy to sell our house? Would you not cancel an appointment with a doctor? Your hairdresser? Your garage mechanic? We had a call half an hour before I was to serve Easter dinner to my family and friends, but I agreed to let the house be shown two hours later. Instead of enjoying dinner, I had to scramble to clean up quickly so there wouldn't be stacks of dirty dishes.

No show, no call.

I lost three hours of pay last week. This week, my husband had to cancel an important appointment. I could go on and on, but since I am more thoughtful than the agents, I will spare you. This problem has been voiced by other home owners, as well.

GENTLE READER,

It is Miss Manners' theory that rude business techniques ought to be self-correcting, since their rudeness should naturally drive customers away. There should be only polite businesses, because the bad ones should have gone bankrupt. Miss Manners would not have to get involved.

Why doesn't this theory work? Is it that there are no businesses that are both polite and efficient, so that you are indeed at the mercy of the rude? Miss Manners sincerely hopes not. Her fear is that the system isn't working because people feel that protest is useless, possibly even rude.

Well, it's got to work eventually, if people really refuse to do business with those who treat them badly. Somebody has got to notice that there would be a market in doing business considerately. Surely there must be real estate companies that realize their customers still live in the houses they are trying to sell. Cooperation in showing those houses is disrupting enough

SAN ANTONIO, TEX.—A television reporter was fired for being rude to the President at a press conference. "From the time they enter journalism school through their burgeoning careers, many reporters are taught to be aggressive, questioning, thick-skinned, cynical and, if need be, downright pushy in their efforts to get a story. Rarely are they warned that they might be fired for this behavior," wrote the magazine *Editor & Publisher* of the incident. The magazine also noted sharply differing opinions among journalists about whether the reporter should have been fired.

to the residents, without adding to their burden by treating them as inconsiderately as you describe.

Refusing to be treated rudely is not rude. True, you could make it rude by using the first methods that come to mind, such as addressing your complaints to "Dear Idiots." But as long as it's crisply and politely done (as opposed to methods that spew bits of your lunch over everything), this is smack within the realm of etiquette, where disapproval is the means of control.

In business terms, such disapproval begins by drawing to the offender's attention that you are being poorly served; it continues, if you have the patience, by drawing this to the attention of supervisors, and it culminates, at any point in this process when the customer has had enough, in breaking off the business arrangement and explaining exactly why to the heads of the organization.

The Public's Right to Know

When Miss Manners reassures people who are besieged by busybodies that politeness does not require them to satisfy idle curiosity, she feels a twinge of disloyalty to her profession.

Not to the exalted profession of etiquette, of course. As protector of privacy, etiquette does not hold people hostage so that they can be interrogated. To free the innocent from the intimidation of bullies who falsely imply that it is rude not to respond to rude inquiries, etiquette provides a range of responses. (These start with absentminded evasion—"How much do you make?" "Yes, I really love my job"—and move on to frosty refusal—"Oh, that's just private business of my own, I can't imagine that it would interest you.")

But Miss Manners is also a journalist, a profession that not everybody immediately associates with politeness. She may escape its unpopularity on the charmingly mistaken grounds of being a sweet old thing who wouldn't know real news if it bit her, but her dear colleagues are not in high repute these days. Not that they ever were, but back when journalism had no pretensions to respectability, they didn't arouse such irritation.

This distresses Miss Manners, who knows journalism to be a highly etiquette-dependent, if not always etiquette-practicing, profession. No one is obliged to talk to a journalist, as one sometimes is to a police officer, judge or tax auditor. What would happen to journalism if everyone were to refuse to answer nosy questions? The insinuation that "No comment" is the desperate admission of the guilty would soon lose its punch.

What would happen to The Public's Right to Know?

It bewilders Miss Manners, as it does the rest of her profession, when that stirring phrase is classified by the public as a desperate excuse. As the public's representative on the spot, the journalist should not be condemned as any more curious than

Queen Victoria popularizes the white wedding dress. Although she was not heard to scream "We're the bride, so we can do whatever we want," she nevertheless must be held responsible for this extra financial burden on brides' parents and for the nasty custom of comparing the purity of the dress to that of the bride.

the public itself. To take the trouble to get the public the information it wants, the nosy old things, and then be chastised for it, doesn't seem fair. Nor is the old mirror trick fair—blaming the reporter for the state of society being reported.

Still another misunderstanding arises from failure to distinguish the professional manners of news gathering, in regard to ferreting out information, from social manners, which insist that this be done delicately, if at all. The journalistic community itself makes that mistake when it periodically jumps on one of its own for asking and pursuing rigorous questions at press conferences. Using press conferences to flatter officials, or to preen for the bosses back home, is a violation of professional manners. It is not a violation to ask difficult questions, the very purpose for which the conference is intended.

One more rationalization before Miss Manners, having established her bias, does her job of condemning rudeness in journalism: The publicity-madness of the public is a contributing factor. Today, almost any reporter (so as not to say media personality) is in the position of the handsome young prince in Thomas Mann's *Royal Highness*, who has never in his life arrived at a train station that was not covered in bunting, nor seen anyone approaching him who did not wear a foolish smile. This is not good for the journalistic soul.

With that odd phrase, Miss Manners' defense stops. What offends the public—journalists who barge into public events and private lives, creating a ruckus and embarrassing people with opinions or accusations disguised as questions—is rude by all standards, including the professional ones. No one is exempted from having to show respect for inadvertently conspicuous citizens, and even—would you believe—for their (deliberately conspicuous) political representatives.

The argument that journalistic rudeness ultimately serves the public is a false one, because these techniques rarely produce information. Those who disrupt events, disassociating themselves symbolically by flouting the standards of dress and decorum of others present, cannot expect to find out what they would in the fly-on-the-wall position.

If you ask a rude question, you're going to get a rude answer, and rude answers are not informative ones. Miss Manners has never learned anything from a reply to such crass inquiries as "How do you feel about your children being killed?" although she sometimes has from the polite inquiry, "Is there a lesson for society in all this?" No one seems moved to open up after being asked, "What are you trying to cover up?" but a polite invitation to "give your side of the story" yields amazing results.

Overexposure to thrillers and courtroom dramas has persuaded the society that truth and justice are only achieved through unpleasantness. Journalists, who have only to ask one polite question to have people pour out their hearts to them, should know better.

The Public's Right to a Response

DEAR MISS MANNERS,

As a legislative correspondent to a U.S. Senator, I am responsible for responding to the significant number of letters from constituents. Anyone who may believe that the art of letter-writing is dying need only come to our mailroom each day to see that the art is alive, though, in some cases, not well. Certainly, the letters are not filled with the pleasantries that personal mail may hold, but nevertheless, each letter deserves and receives a response.

Is there a proper response that etiquette dictates to letters sent to elected representatives? How many responses are appropriate to one individual constituent? I ask for somewhat selfish reasons. It is impossible for each person to get a personal response as the time involved is prohibitive. I was raised by an ardent letter-writer who has made me painfully aware that people prefer answers to their questions, not just acknowledgment of receipt.

Most members of Congress have a series of letters on the various issues that are active during the sessions. However, as I work on health care reform, I have found that constituents often write long, detailed letters about their personal cases, making the rote answers not only obvious, but also nonresponsive. Every letter is read, but specific responses to each are virtually impossible. I am aware that the White House sends one response: "Thank you for your input on the issues that concern you." Congressional offices are somewhat more specific, but do not offer a necessarily better answer.

WASHINGTON, D.C.—"I don't feel I am fearless but I find a way to ask questions so people wouldn't be offended," a television reporter told the *Washington Post* in explaining her success in getting both celebrities and ordinary people to talk to her, adding, "Very often I will say, 'I hope you don't mind my asking,' or 'You can answer that any way you like but I'd really like to know,' giving them the opportunity to not answer if they don't want to. When people know you have given them that opportunity, they will give you the answer you want."

Some individuals write back about the "canned" responses they have received, or write weekly on the numerous issues that concern them. While, in my personal correspondence, I feel that every letter deserves a response, I am less inclined to respond to a constituent who writes back in response to the response that I have written. Shouldn't the circle end at some point with neither party expecting a reply?

Gentle Reader,

Doesn't Miss Manners recall your employer's spending a good part of the campaign going around promising all the voters to keep in close touch? Correct her if her memory is wrong, but weren't there some ringing statements about "Let me know what you think—I'll be there for you"? And about the opponent's aloofness and indifference?

You are supposed to cope with the results of this impossible implied promise, and it is not surprising that in spite of your valiant struggles, you are finding the job impossible. Miss Manners is not advocating a campaign strategy that says, "Here's my general approach, and here's what I think on the current issues. I'll be tallying the opinions in any letters you care to send me, but basically, you're going to have to trust me. I won't have time to be your pen pal." It would be closer to reality, however.

Far from discouraging your sympathy with the constituents, she wishes to encourage it—although not to the point of encouraging Congress to vote itself funds to hire legions of letter-writers to enter into genuinely personal correspondence with everyone in America. Form letters are obviously form letters, no matter how clever the wording and sophisticated the technology. It is better to acknowledge them as such; the reassurance that the letters are nevertheless read and the opinions noted will be all the more credible with this admission. This should also discourage letters about having caught you giving canned responses, although you might have a second canned response ready just in case: Yes, you are right, we don't take the time to write individual letters, but we do spend the time necessary to read every letter we get, because knowing what constituents think is essential to the job of serving their interests.

You should be ready to hear from any one citizen on as many issues as concern that person. This is not a social correspondence where one dose of good wishes is supposed to last a long time. An expression of sympathy is certainly needed for personal hard luck stories, when it is not possible to say that the Senator can intervene in this particular case, or suggest other redress. It is possible to do this in a standard way, as well—by inserting a paragraph that the Senator was sorry to hear, etc. Just make sure you don't drop it into the letter of congratulation to the Animal Husbandry Youth Club.

Miss Manners urges you to give in to temptation when your heart is particularly touched, and to add a brief handwritten expression of sympathy and good wishes. It will only take a minute, and it will gladden not only the letter-writer, but Miss Manners and the person after her own heart who brought you up.

TOO GOOD TO BE TRUE

In the course of two weeks, three different people happened to mention to Miss Manners, in similarly awestruck tones, the name of the same chain department store. Each time she thought she must have faded gently out of the conversation for a moment because she had missed the standard shopping-talk opening, which is "You won't believe what they are charging for . . ."

The store in question did happen to be one of those where the goods are mostly priced for laughs, but the declaration Miss Manners heard instead, on these three separate occasions, was a wondrous "And everybody there is so nice!" There was a clear implication that the speakers—two gentlemen and a lady, all obviously not incapable of substantial shopping—were touched, even honored, to have been treated politely by people to whom they were handing over money.

Miss Manners' first thought was how sad it was that they seemed so impressed by what once was, after all, standard customer service. The reason the store had been mentioned at all (in what had been merely the kind of isn't-modern-life-dreadful? exchanges that are so cozy to share over a good meal when one has reached a certain age) was that the "niceness" represented a deliberate new commercial policy. Word had been getting around that this chain was successfully competing with similar stores by the radical policy of treating the customers civilly, and these shoppers were confirming that it was true.

Miss Manners' second thought, still tinged with pathos at such lowered expectations, was how smart it was of the store. Here was a dramatic advantage over its rivals that could be achieved for free. In commercial transactions, it is difficult to separate the question of efficiency from that of politeness. No matter how charming salespeople may be, the customer is not going to be satisfied with their behavior if they are unfamiliar with the stock, unable to settle reasonable complaints or too busy to give any one transaction proper attention. But in Miss Manners' experience, competence and civility often go hand in hand. The determination to satisfy customers' needs requires intelligent thought and empathy. The basic exercise needed to establish polite behavior—"How would I want to be treated under the circumstances?"—naturally leads to imaginative service techniques.

What were these miracles of niceness that so astonished Miss Manners' informants? Defective articles were accepted for return not only without suspicion but with apologies. A cup of coffee was offered to soften the fact that a customer had to wait. A spouse was paged in the store when the customer was lingering longer than anticipated. The purchase of one item was accompanied with an offer to go with the customer around the store to find articles needed to complete the outfit. The complaint that a garment's color had run in the wash was met with the offer to replace not only the item purchased, but all other clothing that had been ruined in that washing.

Except perhaps for the last example, none of these services should be considered extraordinary. But in an era when customers are used to being treated as wasters of the staff's valuable time, and as in the wrong until proven otherwise, they are all remarkable. Miss Manners hates to use the bribery of good-manners-is-good-business to convince people or institutions to behave as they ought to just because of common decency. But showing respect for the customer's time, and demonstrating that the customer's justified complaints require apologies and compensations, does seem to carry a tangible reward. Miss Manners doesn't need to buy anything at the moment, and lives far from the store in question. But she can hardly wait to go there and rediscover what it is like to be treated, on a shopping expedition, with ordinary civility.

A Reply

Dear Miss Manners,

Concerning one of your favorite themes, that of the rudeness of service people—I do not know if you, Miss Manners, have ever had the singular experience of working in a job which requires dealing directly, face-to-face, with The Public every day. I have spent the last 15 years in such jobs, usually working for large companies, and it is an experience that I would liken to being thrown to the lions every day.

A person employed in customer service is daily bombarded with a veritable smorgasbord of personalities, each with different attitudes, demands, questions and emotions. Among these will be a certain percentage who are irate, or at least dissatisfied, and although it is very rarely a direct result of some action or inaction of the service person, this is the person who must deal directly with the snarling customer. Politely. Happily. With understanding and compassion. And produce a satisfactory result.

They usually do not own any part of the company, but are at the bottom of the ladder, the lowest paid, the least respected, and usually they have no say in what their options are in dealing with customers.

All the training is worthless if it is impossible to implement. A store that requires that each customer be personally greeted must ensure that the ratio of employees to customers makes this possible. An employee alone at a cash register in a sea of customers cannot even ring up sales in an efficient manner, let alone greet every customer, assist customers in locating specific items, iron out problems, and keep the stock neat and orderly. It was up to me to become familiar with the products, at the same time that I was learning to operate the necessary equipment, meeting co-workers, and figuring out where the closest rest room was.

If there is an epidemic of unsatisfactory customer service these days, please quit bashing the store clerk who gets paid minimum wage, and start bashing the money-grubbing companies for not providing adequate training and incentives to their hard-working, loyal employees.

GENTLE READER,

Miss Manners does not know what it is to deal with the irate public? If she empathized with you any more than she does, she'd be weeping in your lap.

That service people are over-worked, under-trained and unappreciated, Miss Manners willingly acknowledges. She is only too ready to point this out to an unfeeling management (who also complain of being over-worked and unappreciated, but sympathy starts at the bottom of that ladder).

In her experience, the harried service person who casts a regretful smile and says "I'm so sorry, I'll be with you as soon as I can" brings out the best in that public. Miss Manners has a higher opinion of the public than you do—not of the public's initial reactions, heaven knows, but of its essential fairness. Many who see that you are trying will be softened; some may be moved to report your kindness to your supervisors.

However, she wishes that you would stop using the argument that you are not responsible for doing a good job because you are ill paid. It does not give anyone the incentive to move you into a higher paying job. Those who advance are more likely to be people who do the best they can under the circumstances, and offer management suggestions as to how the circumstances can reasonably be improved.

Please do not despair. Calming down irascible people is a satisfying, if overwhelming, job, as Miss Manners can assure you from experience on the front.

THE DEMISE OF DISINTERESTED FRIENDSHIP

"This is a mean town. Everybody you meet is always sizing you up, trying to figure what they can get out of you."

It doesn't matter on what vicious turf these bitter words are spoken. What intrigues Miss Manners is who these people are who take such a sad view of society. They are not the wallflowers you might suppose. They are not the quiet souls who cherish hopes of a companionable existence, only to find themselves brutally used—or scorned when they are found useless—by the heartlessly ambitious. They are not the people who have turned away from sociability, having become disillusioned with what they feel is its smiling deceitfulness. They are some of the most socially coveted and active people in town.

While enjoying popularity beyond any ordinary person's dreams, being courted, flattered and pursued, they privately voice this sad assessment of the social game they feel doomed to play. Miss Manners is particularly familiar with how this works in her little village, Washington, D.C. Flushed with triumph, the newly powerful note, with cynicism, how socially desirable they have suddenly become. Invitations, accompanied by flattering remarks, abound, and some are accepted. It turns out to be a great deal of fun to be thrown together with other important people engaged in exciting work at a very visible level. Also, the trappings of such entertainment are luxurious, being paid for by governments, businesses, other institutions, or individuals who can afford to make such entertainment a hobby. Most rewarding, there gets to be an aura of virtue about going out. It's no longer after-hours indulgence: They do it for the job, for the contacts, for the position, even for the Nation.

True, there is too much of it. They begin to feel it an imposition to have to be constantly entertained, even when the normal social expectation of reciprocation miraculously doesn't apply. The sacrifices of evening time are resented. Old friendships have already been put on hold and complainers written off as ungracious, but the inroads on family life are harder to accept or justify. Attempts are made at cutting back, but the notion that duty compels them to be entertained has taken a strong hold. Reclaiming the time for themselves or their families feels both pompous and selfish. Whatever off-duty time there is goes toward repairing the ravages of exhaustion.

These complaints are considered a hoot by their neglected friends, but Miss Manners does not doubt that the dissatisfaction is genuine. Costly trappings are of only moderate help in alleviating social tedium. Boredom may have gotten its name from the skill with which it is able to bore through whatever luxury has been piled on top of it as a disguise. It seems obvious to her that what is now called networking—the pursuit of advantage while holding and dispensing drinks—will never be as heart-warming as relaxing among congenial souls for the pure pleasure of it.

When the world-weary respond that they must network, not so much for their own personal gain as for the good of the enterprises they represent (such as the nation, or the livelihood of their employees), Miss Manners is still prepared to sympathize. She doesn't really believe it—she believes that if everyone stopped business-partying all at once, the world would go around just as fast—but, soft touch that she is, she sympathizes. No one should have to work straight through dinner, late evenings and weekends, even on a full stomach.

Although she is a stalwart opponent of socializing-for-success, and she knows a few brave and powerful souls who declared and proved that they could manage impressive careers effectively without constant partying, Miss Manners is aware that the pattern is there, and difficult to defy. She also realizes that even social lions need petting, without always being required to fetch the ball to get it. She could reassure these people that at some point, the social whirl ceases. All jobs come to an end, if only in retirement, and super-jobs are prone to ending abruptly. The invitations trail off.

When this happens, she expects the former job-holders to be relieved. She keeps forgetting that that's when they really turn indignant, angry and cynical. A deeper cry goes out—this time about how fickle all those new friends have turned out to be.

Friends? What friends? To anyone who remembers the original sensation of being suddenly sought after upon accession to influence, it should seem perfectly reasonable that one should be dropped upon losing it. Why were the sponsors of this social life so eager to have guests who never entertained them in return, who hardly kept up the social niceties, let alone the small attentions that maintain friendship? What else were the guests offering these new friends except the advantages and glamour of their positions? Did they fall for the idea that temporary alliances based on professional considerations constituted friendships, no matter how many compliments and flowers accompanied them?

None of this is taken into account to soften their disillusionment. Nor do they seem to notice that they had been going by this standard themselves. They spurned the attentions of the professionally useless, reciprocated favors to those who offered mutually advantageous assistance, and went just as doggedly after the more powerful as the less powerful went after them. When cutting back socially, the invitations refused were not those from the least charming people, but from those with least status. People who lost their jobs shifted rapidly into the category of those whom they said they really ought to see—but didn't.

There comes a point at which Miss Manners can no longer offer comfort to the hors d'oeuvres victims. That is right after she tries to reassure them that they still have their real friends, those who knew them before they were successful, who love them for themselves, and who seek no benefit from their friendship other than return friendship.

Their response is a bit of hemming and puffing, followed by the revelation that they no longer see those people socially. "There was no time," the explanation goes, and "We have nothing in common anymore." By this definition, having memories in common counts as nothing. All right. Miss Manners doesn't want to be maudlin and insist on old friends. Didn't they find people with whom they shared private interests and values and make friends with them?

Well, no. They had no time for such rituals of friendship as exchanging visits and presents, sharing holidays and gossip, attending parties and ceremonies. Or rather, they did those things all the time, but only with people from whom they wanted something professionally at the moment.

Those people, they complain, do not have the goodness to behave as true friends to them. Miss Manners would not expect them to. Why should they not be equally clear-sighted about being valued for their connections and power, and not for themselves? Miss Manners' infallible reason tells her that people who are too busy to make real friends will not have real friends.

The Voter as Friend

DEAR MISS MANNERS,

My husband is an elected official who enjoys a reputation for accessibility and conviviality. As a politician, he has managed to combine his love of public service with a down-home touch that has made him a "friend" to thousands of people across our state. I applaud his success and try my best to support him in his career. However, people are always making unannounced visits to our home (usually at mealtime) and often bring such items as unsolicited religious tracts or unsuitable eatables for the children. How can I put an end to this?

We constantly receive invitations to weddings, graduations and anniversary celebrations from people we may have met in a receiving line. Will a simple congratulatory note, typed by the office staff, suffice to recognize the event? We are often the recipients of gifts of paintings, needlework, pottery and the like that do not complement the decor of our home. After thanking the donor, I store these items in a closet. How long must I wait before I donate them to a deserving charity?

It is nice to know that my husband is well liked by a number of voters in our state. But I would like to separate our private lives from his public life. Is it possible to do this without being rude?

Gentle Reader,

Miss Manners has a wonderful double whammy for you. She plans to solve a major part of your etiquette problem with a nice little political advantage for your husband. You are going to learn to say "No" when people offer you presents. Not just a simple no, which might hurt people's feelings. This is going to be a high ethical no:

"Oh, how beautiful. What a magnificent painting. I love it! How incredibly kind of you to think of us. But . . . this just breaks my heart. We have an absolute rule against accepting anything from anyone. No exceptions whatsoever. You know how my husband is—incredibly strict about personal ethics. Believe me, I am so tempted by this, but we just feel it would be wrong to take anything. Oh, and taffy for the children! Aren't you wonderful? But I think it's better if the children don't even see it. Their father would never allow them to take anything, either, so there's no use tantalizing them. But there's no reason I can't tell him how generous you are."

All right. Now how do we get these people off the doorstep? "Why, hello! Oh, dear, I wish I could ask you in, but family dinner is the only time my husband gets to talk with the children without being interrupted—you know, he works late every night, and we just set this time aside as sacred. I'm not going to tell him you're here now, because I know he would insist on dropping everything to see you, but give me your number. And I really appreciate your stopping by. I hope it wasn't too much trouble."

Whew. Miss Manners is getting in the mood to run for office herself. You might remind her that she hasn't finished her own job, which is solving your etiquette problems.

Tracts on religion, politics or anything else should be accepted with thanks. The presents in your closet should never be donated to a charity remotely near the hometown of the donor. Invitations should be gratefully declined on your and your husband's behalf with a congratulatory note. A handwritten line is better, and required in social matters, but as we are not really talking about your social life, Miss Manners is lenient on this point. She trusts that you or he personally answers such invitations from friends, not only in handwriting, but on your own time and at your own expense.

The Spouse as Superfluous

"Oh, I never go there with him. Nobody ever talks to the wives." As a member of the We Thought We Fixed That Generation, Miss Manners was shocked to hear a lady make such a statement at what she had thought was a modern gathering. (That is to say, the ladies were complaining about stress from their jobs, while the gentlemen were bragging about how much time they spend with their children.)

Miss Manners dates back to the time when ladies were not just ignored on formal occasions—they were required to leave the table (after dessert, admittedly) so that the real conversation could take place. At any rate, it was claimed that this was why the gentlemen were getting out that bottle of port. This curious practice of offering gentlemen port, while offering ladies the opportunity to powder their noses, went on for a long time before a few pioneering ladies got the idea of keeping on going until they were out the door. As some of them had the car keys, and some of them held keys to the gentlemen's professional or personal futures, the practice of separating after dinner was abandoned. (Miss Manners had no trouble neatly sidestepping the question of whether these ladies she admired—and trotted along after—were not simply violating etiquette. The rule itself was wrong, because it violated a higher rule against treating one's guests unequally.)

WASHINGTON, D.C.—The *Washington Post* reported that the former Speaker of the House of Representatives is no longer socially desirable. "The day he lost the election, he was moved from the A-list to the C-list. And within a period of months, he will probably be moved off altogether," one Capitol Hill veteran told the *Post*, which also noted that "the socialite seated next to [the former Speaker] at a recent dinner party . . . privately observed that the placement reflected poorly on *her* status."

She thought the idea behind this custom had disappeared as well. Over the years, legions of gentlemen ruined themselves by basing their obligatory conversation with dinner partners on the assumption that ladies could be present at important gatherings only because they were there accompanying their husbands. The lady on the right would turn out to have just bought out the company headed by her dinner partner, and to have been wondering who there understood the future well enough that she should keep him on. The lady on the left was there with her husband, but didn't care for the condescending attitude toward a perfectly normal way for married people to go to parties. She would say so, afterward, to that important husband, who would turn out not to care to have other gentlemen slighting his wife.

This is why Miss Manners was startled to hear that bitter report of the old problem's persistence. But was it the old problem? You can't be too careful these days about checking to see if something apparently offensive was, in fact, initiated by the people it apparently offends, in the sort of neo-neo movement that makes Miss Manners' head spin. She will never condone You Can't Come In Here—exclusionary policies and attitudes based on conditions of birth, no matter who declares them—although she recognizes what an old-fashioned position that has come to be.

Why was the lady bitter about staying home, or going somewhere more entertaining? Miss Manners champions the freedom that released couples from mandatory in-tandem socializing, as practiced back when any married person who attended a social event without a spouse in tow was the subject of mistaken gossip. (The ones to watch, if you go in for that sort of thing, are the couples who arrive holding hands, ask to sit together, and direct their conversation to each other: if they are not at the very beginning of a marriage, they are at the very end of one.) It should now be assumed that an absent spouse has better things to do—other pressing obligations, as the explanation to the hosts should state.

Perhaps these events weren't really social functions at all, but after-office meetings with drinks, where both husbands and wives feel that their presence is superfluous because it is. Miss Manners, who abhors such fake socializing, would consider not attending to be a sensible solution.

No, it turned out that the events that this lady avoided were merely those of ordinary social circles—or what now passes for them. That is to say, some of the people present had been taught that if they were to get ahead in life, they must view all gatherings as opportunities to network. Others were seeking out people whose work overlapped with theirs only because they had never learned to make conversation unrelated to their professions. Still others thought that the way to open a conversation with a stranger was to ask, "What do you do?" and then to come up with some comment or question related to the answer.

They are all wrong, of course, and lacking in elementary social skills. That should not be interpreted to mean that they were callously angling to talk only to major figures, and would have spurned the chance to talk to those who just happened to be interesting. One need not trouble with such difficult cases, Miss Manners supposes, but neither should one trouble to feel insulted by the merely awkward and untutored.

Any lady who is gracious enough to overlook the fact that most people's social openings sound like personnel department forms, and to begin a genuine conversation—one that offers topics of general interest in the hope of stimulating a give and take of ideas solely for amusement, not professional profit—would be doing society an excellent service. One who chooses to avoid gatherings of go-getters where she will be snubbed would be doing herself a favor. One who went but briefed her husband afterward on which people should be avoided as crass would be doing her husband a favor.

Muddled Workplace Rituals

Chatting with the Boss

Dear Miss Manners,

My new boss at work seems to assume that everyone who works for her is an instant friend. I'm used to picking my friends, and feel I cannot be friends with any boss—a certain amount of distance has to be maintained. After all, she has more power over me than I have over her. (I felt this way when I was an officer and supervisor in the military, too.)

Her main fault is that she likes to sit down and talk and talk about personal matters to me in my office. How do I discourage this? She's preventing me from getting my work done! When she does this in her office, I get up and move slowly away and she gets the message.

Gentle Reader,

You will recall that in the military there are rules against fraternizing, actually put there for a reason unconnected with sabotaging American egalitarianism. As you point out, true friendship is impossible when one person can command it of another.

Miss Manners doubts that your boss understands that she is paying you to listen to her confidences and that it is not work that you enjoy. We shall not be so cruel as to point this out to her, but you can certainly point out how eager you are to do your real work. A bright declaration, "I'd love to chat, but that's not what you're paying me for—I've got work to do," cannot offend your boss, no matter how much it disappoints her.

Showering the Boss

Dear Miss Manners,

Where I am employed, the company president and his wife are expecting a baby. A fellow employee recently hosted a shower in their honor, to which all employees, male and female, were invited. Two weeks before the event, the president's wife typed up a list of items that she wanted and it was routed to each employee. The list included the item name, the price, the store where you could buy it, and even the aisle number in the store where the item was located! Some of the items were quite expensive (a high chair and car seat, for example) and some were underlined—indicating that they "really needed" that item.

A few people did not shop from the list, but most felt they had to. Some people who had already purchased a gift, purchased a second from the list. Everyone knew immediately how much everyone else had spent. I thought the whole idea of a list was brash. In fact, I was offended. Am I old-fashioned or overly sensitive, or is this in bad taste? It was as if she had just won a shopping spree at her favorite store at our expense. Please don't use my name or I'll lose my job.

Gentle Reader,

It is going to take more than Miss Manners' cooperation to save this job. It is going to take the cooperation of all the employees in making this a dignified job, worth having. You all need to unite in refusing to submit to what Miss Manners calls social harassment—in this case bordering on blackmail.

These may seem to be harsh words for a mere baby shower. But baby showers are social occasions, held among friends who hope to please someone they hold dear by giving her little items she may find charming or amusing. The boss's wife is hardly a friend, the items in question do not seem to be little, and the object is to appease, rather than please, the guest of honor. The term for things that are given in response to a demand and out of fear of losing one's job is not "presents" but "kickbacks."

NEW YORK, N.Y.—In a story on the complexities of interracial socializing, the *New York Times* reported that some African-Americans find the idea of a work-oriented social event awkward. "The social event as an extension of business, politics or work is essentially a white phenomenon," one African-American social theorist told the *Times*.

Miss Manners understands that you do not want to act alone. She advises all of you to appeal to the host, saying this has gotten out of hand, and asking that the event be canceled on some such excuse as that people don't want to take the time away from their work. If all of you together issue a statement declaring that although you wish the boss and his wife joy on the birth of their child, your devotion to the company prevents you from socializing, your point will be made.

Requiring Guest Duty

Dear Miss Manners,

I work in private homes as a waiter, and I have found that more and more often, hosts find it necessary to introduce me to a guest as I am passing drinks or hors d'oeuvres. This I find inappropriate. I am suddenly on a first name basis with someone I am serving. I have taken it as a rather patronizing attitude. Is this some kind of PC issue? Do I ask the host not to introduce me?

Gentle Reader,

Miss Manners is reminded of the old story (no part of which is guaranteed to be factual, or even close) about the lady who engaged Enrico Caruso to sing at her party, for which he said his fee was $10,000. That was fine, she replied, but he was not to mingle afterward with the guests.

"In that case, Madam," he is supposed to have replied, "my fee is $5,000."

Perhaps you should be charging more.

Nevertheless, Miss Manners must remind you that discomfort with being served by others represents the best sort of American sensitivity, however awkward the results. Nor is it new. Mr. and Mrs. Ralph Waldo Emerson kept trying to make their servant sit at table with them, which that person hated. There is more dignity in professional distance than forced and unsuitable friendliness. Miss Manners suggests you tell hosts kindly, "If you don't mind, I can do a better job if I don't do any socializing."

Food Day

DEAR MISS MANNERS,

I work for a large company which frequently celebrates special occasions by having "food days." In addition to asking individuals to bring in a homemade or store-bought snack to share with their fellow employees, a monetary donation is sometimes requested to purchase a gift.

Although the snacks and money are voluntary, several employees are disturbed with those employees who choose not to contribute to food day, or to the gift, but help themselves to food once it is laid out and sign their names to the gift card. I am often the individual who initiates these "food days"; therefore, I find myself in a predicament. I would like everyone to participate, but unfortunately realize that not everyone can afford to do so.

GENTLE READER,

What do you want to do—offer scholarships?

It seems to Miss Manners that with the best intentions in the world, you have set up a no-win situation. By not "volunteering," employees make themselves either wallflowers or sponges in their own work places. The temptation for non-contributors to wander over and join the crowd—or to keep to themselves while the fun is going on, with the resentment that is bound to create—is as understandable as is the resentment of contributors at finding they are inadvertently sponsoring their colleagues.

Please just stop. This is a work place, not a social hall. If you want to treat others to lunch, homemade or otherwise, by all means do so. Do not make this a part of the job routine, so that people are forced either to participate or to miss out on a company-wide event.

The Retreat

You are on a retreat with your boss and colleagues. A professional facilitator, hired to conduct the session, asks everyone present to tell a revealing personal story—something from childhood, perhaps, or later family life, that will enable others to see a side of you not generally known.

No job seems too dignified nowadays to be exempt from these investigations. The President of the United States summoned his cabinet to one, at which there were two professional facilitators, and people who had been through the searches connected with Senate confirmations were amazingly asked to come up with something that had been overlooked.

All right, so you may have to do this. How about:

"I was always the class bully. It started in kindergarten, when I made the other kids give me their cookies at juice time. I think this influenced me a great deal; it was so successful that I never really gave it up, but merely developed more sophisticated techniques. I realized that there is something in most people that makes them want to be pushed around, even in situations where I don't know any better than they do."

Or: "One of the things that always used to annoy me was having to be prom queen year after year. It took time away from my prize-winning science projects and when I wanted to relax, I would have preferred just to go for a drive in the country— my parents had given me a convertible for my 16th birthday. But I suppose it was my mother insisting that I had an obligation to go and wear their silly crowns that made me understand that being the best at everything is an obligation, and not the unmitigated pleasure everyone else seems to think."

No? What if these confessions meet the criteria of being honest and revealing?

Is it an accident that all successful people who find themselves probed in this way turn out to have been shy, homely, long-struggling and unsure of themselves? Miss Manners thinks not. She apologizes for offering manners assistance that sabotages the declared purpose of these situations, but she suspects that people who value both politeness and their careers have long been tailoring their tales.

Quite right they are, too. For a number of reasons, sensible people simply cannot cooperate with these outrageous but ubiquitous demands to surrender their privacy. The most obvious danger is that an injudicious admission could hamper one's career. One would have to be extremely naive to believe that employers honestly consider faults to be lovable assets rather than potential liabilities. Or that damaging information handed over willingly to non-intimates is somehow protected, as it would be if confided to those bound to one through love and loyalty.

There are other reasons for being wary, and these have to do with good manners. As any successful raconteur knows, the narrator must be the butt of his or her own story. Anecdotes that show how much cleverer one is than anyone else are socially obnoxious, no matter how true.

Self-satisfaction is irritating, no matter how desirable everyone agrees self-esteem to be. It is for the sake of manners, as much as anything else, that the greatest beauties in the world say such things as "I've never felt pretty—I've always been self-conscious because I know my toes are too thin."

Anecdotes usually have more than one character, and even though one may willingly surrender one's own privacy, manners demand not putting other people in an embarrassing light. Miss Manners would think twice about the wisdom of trusting an employee who can't even respect the confidences of his family. Finally, a polite person is considerate of those to whom he is talking and will not tell them a story that is too long, boring, or (for those who attend multiple retreats) may have been told before.

This is why there is a convention to such stories. They are all about being too fat or too shy, overcoming adversity, triumphing over temptation, and so on. Miss Manners recommends adopting such guidelines until such time as employers begin to realize that the presumption that intimacy can be forced, rather than developing naturally through the slow growth of trust and affection, is a false one.

Resisting the Retreat

DEAR MISS MANNERS,

Having sensibly rejected the too-frequent pretense that business functions are social gatherings, would Miss Manners kindly comment on the farce of enforced "retreats"? Employees are required to spend a weekend—presumably their own free time—at some resort, where they must listen to pep talks from the boss, engage in childish "psychological games" that are supposed to reveal marvelous insights into their own characters, and endure what is in effect a 49-hour staff meeting.

This idiocy is supposed to promote solidarity and familial feelings—i.e., agreement with the boss who mandated the whole pretense. Hasn't this sort of play-acting gone out of fashion? Except, of course, with the sort of trendies who are always ten years behind the times—relentlessly

THURMONT, MD.—The President, his Cabinet and top aides gathered at Camp David for a weekend retreat. Using professional "facilitators," the government officials went through "team building exercises" during which "most of the Cabinet and other senior aides told stories of their childhoods, professional lives or marriages—some revealing, some not," the *Washington Post* reported. The President was reported to have talked about "how he was a fat kid when he was five and six and how the other kids taunted him."

replaying the fads of yesteryear as the hottest new thing. Old or new, the idea is simply another type of brainwashing.

GENTLE READER,

Miss Manners wonders why it never occurs to the organizers of retreats that it is exactly the fact of not knowing one another's innermost souls that allows people to work together in respect and harmony. The sweetly misguided notions that no problems exist among different people except communication problems, and that we would all love one another if only we knew one another better, should have been exposed by time.

Do your employers not know that people's main difficulty nowadays is trying to balance their personal and professional lives? What you need to draw to their attention is that weekends away from home greatly aggravate that problem. If the retreats you describe are considered to be indispensable for the job, surely they deserve to come with financial compensation—at overtime rates.

The Official Party

DEAR MISS MANNERS,

When I served on a government delegation to arms control talks in Geneva, the head of the delegation, a high-ranking civil servant, marked the end of our stay by "requesting" that we attend a social gathering at his government-provided quarters. He also requested that we each contribute about $15 to pay for the food and drink at this party. I paid and attended, but grudgingly, and only because I thought it was polite. What is the proper way to respond to such "requests" without being rude and without jeopardizing my job?

GENTLE READER,

Miss Manners doesn't want to be selfish about this, but she knows that the minute she voices her agreement with your position, the head of the delegation will ask her to pay for this event. In her official capacity as U.S. taxpayer.

The fact remains that an occasion at which attendance does not seem voluntary, and at which guests buy their own refreshments, can in no way be described as a party. At best, it is a meeting with refreshments available for sale. To flush this fact out politely, you might decline the invitation by saying, "Oh, I really don't want to take time for partying. I think I'll do some more work in my room." If your self-styled host then claims that the gathering is necessary to work, you should agree to attend. You can still decline to pay, adding, "Fine, but I still think I'll have supper in my room afterward while I go over things, and I don't plan to drink because I'd like to keep a clear head."

The Collection

DEAR MISS MANNERS,

I know it is a tradition in the workplace to collect money to buy gifts for employees who marry, give birth or move away. However, my co-workers seem to be searching for additional reasons. In the past year, there have been collections for three local job changes, one move, two weddings, two babies born to employees, two babies born to employees' spouses, and one on the way. It's not that I'm a selfish person, but in today's economy, my husband and I have decreased our spending on our own family's birthdays, weddings, baby gifts, Christmas, etc. On what occasions and for whom is the gift-giving proper and when is it not necessary? I do not socialize with my co-workers outside of company functions, even though I have worked with them a few years. I prefer it that way.

GENTLE READER,

The only employee milestone for which Miss Manners believes a present to be necessary at work is retirement, and then the symbol of the employer's gratitude should be provided by the employer alone. The rest of this nonsense is—well, nonsense. Expensive nonsense. Colleagues are colleagues, who should not feel obliged to pretend that they are friends who take pleasure and excitement in the events of one another's personal lives. Many friendships do begin with working acquaintanceships, and such friends may celebrate one another's happiness, but that seems to Miss Manners, as to you, a far cry from the office collection.

That said, how do you get away from the pressure to go along with the pseudo-socializing demanded of you by people with whom you want to stay on pleasant terms? Miss Manners knows how difficult this is to do unilaterally. One gets the reputation for being mean or stingy. She therefore suggests putting the matter to an employer.

"On our salaries," one might begin, "the custom of employees constantly giving presents to other employees really isn't affordable." Your boss, being no fool, will claim to have no concern in the matter, and vehemently deny that there is any work policy requiring this. You may then suggest that, actual practice being contrary to the employer's expectations, a memo be posted stating that there is no such policy.

Christmas Presents

DEAR MISS MANNERS,

This year, my company sent me a gift box containing, among other things, ham, bacon and sausage. Last year, I received a whole smoked turkey. I have been a vegetarian for over four years, and am offended even by the sight of such frivolous expense of life. But I don't want to offend my company superiors, and I know all employees receive the same gift, so it might not be fair to make exceptions for just me. But how can I prevent this from happening next year, and what do I do with the corpses in the freezer? Should I send a thank you note?

GENTLE READER,

Unless you work for a grocery wholesaler, it seems foolish of your employer to spend money on presents which could have been put into a Christmas bonus. This being a business relationship, not a friendship, the company can hardly be expected to know what would please each individual, as demonstrated by the fact that even a conventional Christmas food item was offensively unsuitable in your case.

It seems equally futile to try to explain your individual preferences in the minimal thank you note appropriate for an impersonal gesture. If you must, Miss Manners suggests you thank them for the food "which, as a vegetarian, I do not eat, but which I have donated to the homeless." Just don't count on this being remembered next year, when someone else may be assigned to send out silly presents.

PROTECTING CHILDREN
FROM ETIQUETTE

About a generation ago, while Miss Manners must have been busy trying to hitch up the horses to one of them newfangled computers, parents switched their basic directive to children. Instead of saying, "Behave yourself," they started saying, "Be yourself."

Earlier parents, with their complicated and detailed definitions of proper behavior, had gotten mixed results from their instruction. In contrast, modern parents, who didn't want to inhibit their children's inborn gifts with the draggy old restraints of etiquette, found that their one simple demand was obeyed. Whoever else the children were considering being, they dutifully refrained. In due course, they grew up to be their natural selves, unimproved by etiquette.

The result turned out to be not as attractive as fond parents had imagined. Even those who didn't care what hardships their unsocialized young created for the community were shocked. Allowing children to be free of child-rearing did not, after all, produce a generation of happy, carefree, uncomplicated, altruistic and creative people. The experiment seems to suggest that a great deal of what we think of as "human nature" in the best sense—compassion, fairness, conscience—is, in fact, taught. We had always assumed that guilt and remorse were a natural consequence of doing wrong, but judges are now encountering legions of young criminals who have no such feelings.

The only idea with which we are indisputably born is to look out for our own wants, without regard to how this affects others. Infants may not be able to do things for themselves, but they have the even better idea of screaming and carrying on until other people do their bidding. Miss Manners does not argue that it is hard to deny them this when they are lying there, all helpless and drooling. She is only suggesting that after a while, preferably before they are able to fend for themselves at the dinner table, that ploy should stop working. Whether the caretakers act out of a desire to teach empathy, or are just plain exhausted, they are supposed to start gently pushing the etiquette lesson that the feelings of others must be taken into consideration.

Others? There are other people? And they have feelings? This is a difficult lesson, best taught at the start of life, when learning without conviction is easiest. No one has yet come up with a satisfactory substitute for etiquette training within the family, where the manners that are needed (although not always in evidence) are those associated with responsibility and compassion rather than individuality and strict justice—care of the helpless, respect for elders and for authority, empathy for all, the allotment of resources on the basis of need, the accommodation of differences—and there is ample opportunity for demonstrating such etiquette techniques as settling disputes through face-saving compromise.

From the earliest weeks of life, when an infant is taught to control hunger to fit into a social pattern in which people do not eat during the night; through babyhood, where etiquette skills include learning conventional greetings such as morning kisses and waving bye-bye; to toddler training in such less amusing concepts as sharing toys with guests, refraining from hitting, and expressing gratitude for presents, manners are used to establish a basis for other virtues. When this is not taught, the results are monstrous, as we have tragically seen from the behavior of children who have never really had the benefit of parenting.

Why those who are able to help their children should care to mimic such neglect, Miss Manners cannot fathom. Curiously, well-off parents are frequently the worst offenders. What now passes for conscientious parenting is making the outraged public demand that the schools attend to this task, or the hefty financial sacrifice of turning them over to professional child-care experts.

Dedicated teachers, seeing the need even if they don't agree that the job should be theirs, have tried valiantly, only to find that their efforts are usually doomed, because it turns out that etiquette skills are a prerequisite for learning anything in a classroom setting. Clinical psychology and the law have also tried to compensate for the decline of etiquette training of children in the home, but they face an almost hopeless task, in that the language of mental health and legal rights obscures the discourse by presuming a world in which people's behavior is guided only by the rules of law and medicine.

Miss Manners is in passionate sympathy with the problems of time and money that all parents face in a society that considers child-rearing to be an elective hobby. She hopes she does not sound as if she is minimizing parents' difficulties when they attempt to rear their children in an unhelpful society and while attending to immediate matters, such as providing the children with food and shelter.

She is only trying to help, and she is convinced that their task will be made easier when they not only give up the romantic myth that ideal behavior is that of the natural child unfettered by etiquette, but rid the whole society of such an idea. Naturally, no one wants to do or support child-rearing if it is detrimental to children.

The notion that etiquette is bad for children is also detrimental to adults, and not only because their own and other people's children feel free to treat them rudely. If uninhibited

RICHMOND, VA.—A new law attempts to make Virginia parents more accountable for their children's misbehavior in school by subjecting them to stiff fines and allowing a judge to order parents to meet with school officials to discuss a child's disciplinary problems. Virginia joins Alabama, California, North Carolina, Tennessee and Washington, D.C., in taking legislative action in an effort to force parents to take charge of unruly children.

childhood is the ideal state of being, surely no one would willingly leave it for a generation charged with responsibility. It puzzles Miss Manners that it is no longer considered fun to grow up and assume adult manners and privileges and sophisticated clothes, an attitude she keeps encountering symbolically in the resistance to any manners that smack of adulthood, rather than casual teenagerhood. People who grow old ought to be thinking about lording it over the young, especially in the activity in which Miss Manners is spending an enjoyable life—that of teaching etiquette. If there is no other reason, it gives the young people something to look forward to.

Free Children

Dear Miss Manners,

We believe that people should act in a polite manner when in certain places. Football, baseball, basketball, boxing and hockey, to name a few, it is okay to be boisterous. Tennis and chess are games where quiet is mandatory.

When we are at a hospital waiting for emergency or pharmacy, children are running around uncontrolled. Some parents try to discipline, but most children run them. Trying a small slap on the hand or butt brings charges of brutality (but not from us). It would seem that the whole family has to come, and teenagers come in to have a get-together with the injured person.

Most important to us is a pizza place where they have a theater organ. We go to eat, but we do want to hear the music. Some parents let their kids wander around, dance, sing and just plain scream. This may be okay part of the time, but when three or four adults act like the rear end of a large farm animal, it is a real pain.

We'd be glad to chip in a few bucks to hire an off-duty cop to keep order. Using Mace or a hollow point doesn't bother me, but you are only allowed use of same for defense. They have to put you in danger before you can act. Any ideas?

GENTLE READER,

Miss Manners' foremost idea is that it would be nice if you stopped fantasizing about maiming children.

Aside from that one little thing, she is with you. You seem to understand three basic etiquette concepts that a lot of people find extremely difficult:

1. Notwithstanding the popularity of the I-gotta-be-me mentality, context is crucial for setting proper standards of behavior. What is suitable to some activities may be offensive and disruptive at others.

2. Public entertainment is impossible unless everyone obeys the etiquette of the place, even when this includes such fine points as distinguishing between permissible whooping and impermissible screaming. (But people who are unable to enjoy themselves at a public accommodation should not pick fights with offenders. It is the management's privilege to maintain the necessary standard.)

3. No matter how many people plead the excuse of stress—and few people go to the Emergency Room because they are feeling mellow, or to accompany patients because they are looking for recreation—parents are responsible for keeping their children from disturbing others. Admittedly, controlling children without hitting them takes some advance work, starting approximately from birth, and doesn't always work in public. That is why children's wrists fit so nicely into the circle of the thumb and forefinger of an adult who is speaking very, very sternly.

Creative Children

DEAR MISS MANNERS,

We invited another couple, whose company we enjoy immensely in adult surroundings, over for a family dinner. Since their only child is now almost five, I did not anticipate a nuclear holocaust disguised as a preschooler.

He destroyed my dining room as well as a friendship. He interrupted the conversation constantly, he criticized the food, he demanded his own wine glass, he got up from the table at least nine times, he smeared food all over the table, his chair and his face, and he delighted in graphic descriptions of his body functions.

Our children, ages six and nine, were at first aghast, but were soon swept into the spirit of rebellion. When I reminded them that such behavior was not tolerated, my guests hurriedly jumped to their rescue, stating that "Children can only be children for such a short time, they should be able to enjoy themselves and do what they feel."

The dinner came to a quick end when I said that if what children feel is destructive or rude, they are expected to feel these emotions in the privacy of their rooms. Both of our children were immediately excused from the table and sent to their rooms until further notice. Our guests left soon thereafter, but not until the wife had made one more remark about "stifling creativity" and "inducing resentment in the child." I couldn't help but remark that her child had not done one creative thing all night. Destructive, yes; creative, no. Would you kindly explain to me why parents of rude, disruptive children describe their behavior as creative?

GENTLE READER,

Miss Manners would like to believe that parents only resort to such doublespeak in order to apologize for their out-of-control children. That would be understandable, but not forgivable. The polite way to apologize on behalf of one's children is, "I'm so sorry, I just don't know what got into them," and to haul them off the premises.

These parents—and many others, Miss Manners regrets to say—are so far from apologizing for the rudeness of their children that they have actually gone to some trouble, and endured a great deal of personal discomfort, to foster that rudeness. If your dinner was unpleasant, you can imagine what their lives must be like. They do this, poor things, under the misguided belief that it gives their children happiness. Did this child strike you as happy?

The notion that freedom to act on all one's whims constitutes happiness is mistaken. The whims soon come to be meaningless, and the child ends up being bitterly unable to understand why other people don't want to be with him. Miss Manners is pleased that you curbed your children's attempt to join the rudeness. She only wishes you could have done so as a part of your own child-rearing policy, without committing the rudeness of informing your guests that you disapproved of theirs.

PARENTAL WISDOM

Miss Manners would like to bring back the concepts that Mother Is Always Right and Father Knows Best. Remember how they worked?

Interviews done by the National School Safety Center in Los Angeles of fourth-through-twelfth-grade students nationwide said the students pointed to name-calling, cursing and staring—called "mad-dogging"—as the most common triggers of violence. "Adolescent profanity is so pervasive that it isn't considered aberrant by mental health professionals," the *Wall Street Journal* reported. A psychology professor who has written a book for teachers on how to deal with foul language in the classroom was quoted in the *Journal* as suggesting "dirty word etiquette," or making it clear when cursing is prohibited.

Mother said you would get a cold if you didn't wear your sweater, and you did. Or at least you sneezed once in her presence, thereby losing face. Father said you had to invite the class outcast to your birthday party, and five years later, this person, who had mysteriously evolved into being the class knockout, remembered.

Mother said you had to write thank you letters for presents you hated, and years later, you found that you thanked everyone automatically, even people who stepped on your foot. Father said you would get over being jilted, and you did, even if it took until halfway through your twenty-fifth high school reunion.

It was not a bad system. Mother and Father imparted their wisdom by the system of repetition (and repetition and repetition and repetition). One day the adult child, who had valiantly tried not to listen, was horrified to hear those same words being spoken when a parent was nowhere around. They were coming out of the former child's very own mouth.

Somewhere along the line, the system failed. This was the fault not of the child, who never willingly supported the system anyway, but of the parents. They lost the courage of their convictions. During an era that believed in the sweet but stupid idea that the innocent nature of children should be unrestrained by the evils of civilization, Mother developed doubts and Father fell for the argument that things are different now.

Noticing that the world was imperfect, they lost faith in their own generation, which they oddly believed could have made the world perfect if only it had been trying harder. Remembering the simple tortures of childhood, they endeavored to spare their own child any pain, even the normal pains of growing up. Believing fervently in democracy, they applied the idea to the family, generously discounting experience and education to give everyone an equal say. Instead of putting her energy into pounding her ideas into her innocent children's heads, Mother took up a new occupation: feeling guilty. Father took up the midlife crisis. This occupied them satisfactorily, while the children were left to their own devices.

Far from blossoming with the supposed wisdom of innocence, those idealistically neglected children simply found substitute leaders—celebrities, television and one another. The little ones were not each going off into his or her original direction, as one might suppose of creative individuals unhampered by worldly knowledge; they were following whatever tedious trends happened to come their way.

You would think that the horrified parents would have resumed charge when they saw that peer pressure, commercial pressure and just plain trash were no longer only competing with their own values, but were now in sole charge of setting the standards for children. But no. Rather than return to their own wisdom, in which they had lost faith, they directed their energies into trying to get other people to do the job.

They requested better television. They asked the school systems to assume such parenting functions as teaching the children manners, ethics and bearing up under the difficulties of life. They complained that rock and sports stars were not good role models. They urged therapists and others to instill in children a sense of self-worth—the kind of thing that children used to get from hearing, "Father thinks you're the most wonderful creature that ever lived in the history of the world" and "Mother knows you can do whatever you set your mind to do."

None of these people or institutions had the access and influence of parents, and even those who tried to do the job were handicapped by a lack of reinforcement at home. Miss Manners maintains that Mother and Father were wrong to give up on Being Right and Knowing Best. Perhaps she wasn't and he didn't, always. Do therapists and rock stars have a better record? Parents can at least give their children a standard by which to measure their own burgeoning ideas and the determination to do something, if only to escape parental authority.

Hope for the Future

DEAR MISS MANNERS,

In the United States from England for a series of short visits with friends my age (late 60's and early 70's) and with some younger-generation Americanized relatives and their families, I have been shocked by the prevalence of what I consider to be bad manners in this younger group. I apologize first for my own bad manners in criticizing my hosts, but I cannot refrain from listing the seemingly commonplace and accepted actions which offended me. If you say they are the norm, then I am hopelessly behind the times.

Cursing teachers has become rampant in Washington, D.C., area schools, according to the *Washington Post.* **"I explained why I was late [to my teacher], and she started going off on me about what I needed to do to get to class on time. I just freaked out and called her the *B*-word. I said, 'Shut up, [expletive].' I got Saturday detention, but I don't regret it. She deserved to be called that," a 17-year-old Northern Virginia junior told the** *Post.* **In student-teacher confrontations, "The *B*-word is strongly used, and the *F*-word. It's the first thing you think of," said another 17-year-old girl. A Northern Virginia child psychologist and school consultant told the** *Post* **that children are not being taught respect at home because parents aren't spending much time with them.**

1. Parents and children all interrupt each other (and guests, too) frequently.
2. Children and young people contradict their parents over small, inconsequential things that don't merit argument.
3. Parent-to-parent, child-to-child and child-to-parent, all engage in whispering sessions in front of company with no apology beforehand.
4. In restaurants, tasting the variety of dishes that have been ordered is done, not with a serving spoon from dish to dish, but by shared utensils from mouth to mouth.

5. Children rush ahead of adults everywhere—ME FIRST!—to the door, the taxi, the table, the theater seats. No deference to others, no "excuse me, please."

6. Parents kiss their children and teenagers directly on the mouth. This even with infants! My generation reserves this kissing for lovers.

7. Closed gates and closed doors do not signal privacy. More than once, a child or adult has entered my room without knocking or asking permission.

My own grandchildren (I have six, ages nine to 24), all brought up on the family estate where generations have lived, wear dirty, ragged jeans, listen to loud tuneless music, and use strange slang with each other. They are bubbly, enthusiastic, sometimes overly noisy and rambunctious, and certainly not perfect. But their well-mannered parents taught them to behave courteously and considerately toward all people at all times. They respect others' privacy and possessions, show consideration to young and old, have pleasant manners at table, are careful that no one is embarrassed or humiliated in their presence, and they even rise to greet me when I walk into a room where they are seated!

They have their awkward moments and they make mistakes, but I am proud of them and confident of their behavior in any situation. American parents seem to have lost control and have reverted to childish behavior themselves. Good manners is basic consideration for another's feelings, and it doesn't require money or even education to teach it. I have found it almost universally in the people of China and of Portugal, where good manners seem to occur naturally. There is too much rudeness in my country, and in yours, too.

GENTLE READER,

Indeed, there is, and Miss Manners is happy to discuss it with you, as you put it so politely. Had you made this an excuse for claiming the superiority of British manners over American, or the rich over the poor, Miss Manners would have been bristling too violently to do so.

As you know, your countrymen, as well as Miss Manners', have been lax in insisting that children exhibit the minimal proper manners you list. (We could quibble over the details, but we are in basic agreement.) What may well be the "norm," is not good enough. Good manners do not come "naturally" in any country. Parents must teach them. It was once considered natural to do so.

What happened in America was that a well-meant but sadly mistaken notion took hold that it was bad for children to teach them manners. However, the children who were reared by that nonsystem are of parental age themselves now, and are resolving not to make the same mistake. So there is hope here, Miss Manners wants to assure you—provided the rest of the world doesn't pick up the discarded experiment.

PARENTAL PROTECTION

Parents actually work for Miss Manners, running franchises for the daily teaching and supervising of etiquette in their own households. Conceding that this is an even rougher job than lolling around issuing pronouncements on the subject, Miss Manners would like to do something in return for parents who are trying. (The ones who aren't, parents who don't teach manners because all that matters is that the children should be happy, are already getting what they deserve, which is surly children.) In keeping with the state of the economy, it will not actually be a monetary bonus, just a gesture.

It will consist of mandating rules for treating a parent properly, and it is intended for the edification of those who might be so fortunate as to have one. Or two or four, as the case may well be. This is the aspect of manners that parents tend to neglect teaching, busy as they are with the basics.

There isn't much occasion for announcing that one must push in Mother's chair at mealtime (preferably with Mother in it, taking care not to run over her ankles) and then wait for her to begin eating—when she is actually in the kitchen, pleading with everyone not to leave the refrigerator door open while standing there chomping on what passes for dinner.

A remarkable number of fathers have been intimidated into dropping the lesson of respect known as Don't You Dare Talk to Me That Way. Some were persuaded by the peculiar argument that equality, a noble concept to which we all subscribe, should be applied regardless of age and generational standing. Others were stymied by being asked why parents deserve respect from children. (The reasonable response to that, which all parents should be able to say without pausing between the words, is "Because I say so and I don't want to hear one more word about it and that's final if you know what's good for you.")

Other parents have the practice of cajoling—so as not to say bribing—children to learn manners with the promise that they will lead to monetary and romantic success. The child who observes that he or she is already getting the maximum of love and money that can be expected from a parent may conclude that no effort is needed in that direction. Finally, even those parents who are the most conscientious about requiring that their children exhibit good manners toward others may be embarrassed to make demands on their own behalf. This comes easily, because, with the expert assistance of their children, mothers, especially, tend to spend most of their lives being embarrassed.

This brings Miss Manners to her first rule: It is rude to let on that your parents embarrass you, let alone to inform them of this choice piece of information. Parents are, by definition, a generation older than their children, but that does not mean that their clothing, manner of speech or cultural references are less legitimate, or that they are best kept hidden. Cringing on behalf of an adult relative is a bad habit, which leads to the high-risk business of offering one's spouse warnings and critiques before and after social gatherings. If you want to be embarrassed on behalf of a relative—have a baby.

Causing embarrassment to one's parents would be against the rules if it weren't inevitable. At least doing so deliberately is condemned. Family loyalty requires keeping secrets and guarding inside information, such as how Mother looks without makeup or how Father sounds when he is asleep.

Admittedly, parents get in there first with funny stories that humiliate their very own relatives. That is only because parents misjudge the age at which children can understand what is being said about them. Most guess that it's about 25. Miss Manners would not actually want to suggest that a polite child bargain for what ought to be given freely, but having an amusing story to tell about a parent presents an excellent opportunity for encouraging the parent to drop a story about the child that the child has always hated.

Parents who ask their children why they can't be like certain other, perfect children are setting themselves up for the nasty and futile game of comparison shopping for relatives. Nevertheless, it is rude for children to point out how much more pliable another parent is. It's untrue, too. Any parent who actually changes rules upon being told that all the other parents are more lax is probably too gullible to parent anyone. The worst transgression of all is playing the game of Making Parents Feel Guilty— chiefly because it's too easy.

Parental Pressures

Finding Time

Here's what strikes Miss Manners as a fair division of labor: She will nag adults to teach manners to children, and everyone else will find them the time in which to do this. After all, she can't do everything herself. It takes more time to work out, not less, when your exercise equipment is a hammock rather than a StairMaster.

While Miss Manners has been doing her part, others have not. Everybody is happy to help by deploring the behavior of other people's children. (Their own are too young and adorable to have to be polite, a state that continues right up until they reach the age when they are deemed too old and out of control.) It is only when it comes to the need for a society-wide effort to make the rearing of children compatible with supporting children that taxpayers discover that they have more important things to do.

Only there is no more important thing to do. We have seen the emotional damage done to children, and the physical damage done to the world, when children do not learn the lessons of manners on which civilization is based. Yet even Miss Manners has noticed that in order to teach children decent table manners, it is necessary to be able to buy the food. A reasonable society would be arranged so that everybody is able to do both. She is full of sympathy for parents who recognize the need for doing it all but are having a hard time managing. Oddly, this dilemma appears among the rich as well as the poor. Two-lawyer families seem to have as much trouble finding time for child-rearing as one-waitress families.

(Time out, while Miss Manners disavows the cheering support of those who think she is trying to lead a parade back to those wonderful days when we didn't have this problem because people—read: mothers—weren't so selfish. Miss Manners was around during those days, and the wonder of them escaped her. Her taste in fashion notwithstanding, she is trying to go forward, in the hope of creating wonderful days that never were.)

The old system was to divide life into private and professional halves, a.k.a. love and work, and to assign people one or the other by gender, regardless of ability or inclination. The private half included not only housekeeping and child-rearing, but running the social, cultural, religious and philanthropic life of the family and the community. The professional half may or may not have made a gratifying use of other talents; its basic requirement was to bring home the money with which to support the private half.

Miss Manners was not the only person to notice that the assignments were often unsuitable, and that the system only worked as a permanent arrangement, with those not earning the money being able to count on being permanently compensated from it for their private labor. So we changed, and ladies as well as gentlemen were expected to enter the professional life. The only hitch is that the reformers forgot to re-slice those two halves of life so that everyone got a share of each.

The work world is still designed for someone with no personal responsibilities, on the assumption the worker is able to supply a spouse to meet those responsibilities. Furthermore, an ersatz private life has been grafted on to the better-paying jobs, so that partying and travel, which used to be strictly within the personal realm, add extra time to the work schedule.

So now everyone still has only half a life, but it's the same half. Among the activities that have been largely abandoned are community work, recreational social life and other forms of pure relaxation. Only those margins left in the work week—as originally designed, like the agriculturally based school year, for a previous era—are available for child-rearing.

WASHINGTON, D.C.—In a story on murders motivated by a show of disrespect among street children, the *Washington Post* quoted a Howard University social work professor as saying: "The respect the kids demand is compensation for the very little courtesy they really receive in their lives. So their rules are very, very strict."

Some parents misguidedly feel that it is more important to spend that little time harmoniously than to use it to civilize the children, which children don't always welcome. Others trust that it will be done by equally harried nannies, day care workers or teachers—or by television, which then gets denounced for not meeting the responsibility.

Miss Manners is offering a better deal. If parents and everybody else short of time will just restructure the society so that a reasonable person can manage both a job and a private life, she promises to nag parents about how to behave.

Resisting Criticism

DEAR MISS MANNERS,

Three years ago, I quit a marketing position with a national corporation and took a job with a small ad agency in a smaller city. I made this move because it is more important to me to be involved in raising my kids than to climb the corporate ladder. I also realized, after ten years of fast tracking, that I wanted to develop avocations that may serve me well in later years. Neither my wife—who also "traded down" in responsibility and pay—nor I regret it for a second.

When I negotiated my position, I made it clear that I would be staying in the same field by servicing just one specific, long time client and would bring to the agency years of experience on the corporate side of that business. I would take a significant cut in pay and benefits in exchange for a 35-hour work week, four weeks of vacation, flexible hours so that I can deliver and pick up children, and no "new business" responsibilities. The boss agreed, and his decision has been rewarded. The client is happy to have a real professional rather than an ad man dabbling in various accounts. The boss is happy because billing on the account has increased every year, as has profit. I've simply eliminated the frills and busywork that previously plagued the account, in favor of sound decisions and execution.

My problem is with staff employees, although I personally get along with all of them. The details of my agreement were not published generally in the office. This is proper and desirable. Yet it is true that I am working under different strictures than the rest, and the differences occasionally grate. When I started, I dropped some broad hints regarding the nature of my career compromises, but time and turnover have erased that message and I'm not inclined to repeat it constantly.

I feel the attitudinal wrath when, twice each week, I leave at 3:30 to pick up my kids or take two hours at lunch to be a "room father." I am also the parent who primarily stays at home with a sick child. There is the occasional Friday afternoon that I take off to get a running start at a weekend building project. All of this is within the bounds of my agreement, and the boss understands. Those who do not understand feel that sarcasm is an appropriate mode for greeting and farewell on these occasions. Two employees have made a series of specific comments that I was obviously meant to hear, about their own lack of initiative being justifiable because "that's how it's done around here."

How do I make my position understood without the complete revelation of a personal agreement? Indeed, it would be embarrassing to require the boss to publish or publicize a summary of my "special" status. This would open several new rooms of sarcastic opportunities.

GENTLE READER,

First you must allow Miss Manners to express the highest admiration for you. Not only have you chosen a civilized life—and it has not escaped her attention that you are putting in a 35-hour-week, which is considered full-time in many jobs—but you want to keep your choice private. So why are they picking on you?

Such is the burden of a pioneer. Miss Manners hopes that someday employers will make it possible for everyone to manage a satisfying personal life while pursuing an interesting career, but your situation is a rarity. Something will have to be said about it unless you want to go on enduring these barbs. You need not say it yourself; your boss can do so.

As a matter of fact, it is his problem, too, as it seems to be affecting morale. The minimum explanation he can offer, if that is what you both want, is a public expression of his great satisfaction with what you are accomplishing. The implication is that anyone else who can be so productive under such circumstances is welcome to negotiate flexible working conditions with him.

PARENTAL WORRIES

Exposure to Embarrassment

DEAR MISS MANNERS,

The coach of my son's baseball team (for seven and eight year olds) was awarding trophies at the end-of-the-season celebration in a restaurant. At another table, a group of racially mixed teenagers enthusiastically and good-naturedly joined the cheering. One of the children in our group shouted a racially offensive remark to one of the teenagers.

There was a moment of horrified silence, and then all continued as before— except that the teenagers no longer participated. The parents should have reacted. An apology should have been offered, the child whisked away from the premises and punished for a serious offense. As this did not occur, I thought that the coach should have apologized on behalf of the group and said, "Wilbur, that type of behavior will not be tolerated here." I understand he was probably too shocked to react.

In the absence of all reaction, I should have done or said something, certainly to apologize, but also to impress on the young children that such behavior is never permissible. However, this might have exacerbated the situation.

Gentle Reader,

To what? Miss Manners can hardly think of a worse situation than allowing good-hearted young people to be insulted, unless it is allowing a child to get away with such behavior.

People who are immobilized with shock at the unexpected should never be left in charge of children. Miss Manners has been trying to imagine what prevented the coach, the child's parents or anyone else from acting. Did they think only of their children's celebration, and not how the other young people's day had been ruined? Were they in doubts about their parental duty of correcting such misbehavior? Did they (this would horrify her most of all) think that etiquette required them to ignore the transgression rather than embarrass the offending child?

Miss Manners assures you that the etiquette catastrophe of letting this pass overcomes any other consideration. She is grateful that you understand what should have been done and, if any such thing happens in your presence again, wishes you the courage of your convictions.

Exposure to Responsibility

Dear Miss Manners,

I am enclosing a sample of a card—printed "Thank you for your thoughtfulness and your gift of money," with my son's name—that I produced to use as a thank you for those people who were kind enough to send my son money for his high school graduation. I know my son and was aware that if I relied upon him to handwrite his thank you notes, they would never get done. What would be better, this or no thank you at all?

I typed up labels for each of the kind people who sent presents, and he signed them and sent them off. I received back in the mail one of the cards with the label torn off and a message typed on it: "This is really shabby. Keep your thanks!" The envelope was also typed, so the sender is unknown to me, or I would call and apologize for their finding the form of the note offensive. Now I am concerned that others might have been offended and I wonder if I should send a message of apology to everyone.

My husband and I feel embarrassed and wish to rectify the situation if you think it would be the right thing to do.

Gentle Reader,

Miss Manners appreciates your desire to do the right thing, even in response to a rude reaction to your well meant blunder, but she is not sure that you are prepared to hear what the right thing really is.

The right thing is to make your son write the letters. He need not apologize directly, but can start each letter by saying, "I wanted to thank you personally . . ." Never mind that you know your son and he'll never do it. You are the parents and moralizing, nagging and supervising is your task. By taking his tasks upon yourself, as you did by relieving him of the letter-writing chore, you are depriving him of growing into responsible adulthood as surely as if you had taken his school examinations for him or eaten his vegetables. Miss Manners knows this will be hard for you at this stage, even harder than the considerable task of writing humble letters yourself. But you must do it.

Exposure to Television

Dear Miss Manners,

My granddaughter is 16 and wears her hair in a blunt cut, ending about chin length. She is constantly pushing her hair out of her eyes, tucking it behind her ears, etc.

I tell her we were taught not to handle our hair. She says that it is not so any more and pointed out a T.V. starlet on a talk show, who constantly moved her hair behind her ears, pushed it out of her eyes, took the hair from behind her ears, and then pushed it off her forehead. I didn't hear what she said, I was so busy watching what she was going to do next with her hair. I claim that if you are going to wear your hair in a style that hangs free, you have to get used to it hanging in your face.

Gentle Reader,

Your granddaughter is learning proper behavior from T.V. starlets she sees on television? Miss Manners is afraid that you have more than her hair to worry about.

It is time to teach her that no era deduces that which it considers proper from the lowest common denominator of what is practiced. So however much we admire our T.V. starlets, we should not be burdening them with the responsibility of being models of propriety. When etiquette rules change, as they sometimes do, it is in consequence of changed conditions, attitudes or other circumstances. The rule you cite is not likely to change simply because while those who twirl their hair have always fancied the gesture to be sexy, those who observe it generally find it unappetizing.

Exposure to Failure

Dear Miss Manners,

I have a five-year-old and a seven-year-old who are beginning to play card games and board games. When I play with them, I could usually win, but I make enough "mistakes" so that they win about half of the time and lose half of the time. I do this so that they will learn how to play, enjoy playing, and learn how to lose graciously.

Some of my friends have a different approach. They play to win and beat my children unmercifully (and not even close). Is there an etiquette rule about playing with someone who is at a disadvantage, or is it okay to win continually, by a landslide, as long as one is a good sport about winning?

Gentle Reader,

What you are searching for is the sportsmanlike concept of a handicap, which lies conveniently between the ugly spectacle of taking advantage of a child who is also a beginner and the fraud of throwing games, which children can soon see through. Miss Manners urges you to proceed with humility when explaining that you are temporarily willing to start at a disadvantage until the child has had some practice at the game. It is only too quickly that children, with their agile memories, are able to crush their parents at games. You will then be grateful, in your embarrassment, to have explained the concept of the handicap, while your friends are finding out how it feels to be trampled by an unmerciful opponent.

Exposure to Extortion

Dear Miss Manners,

The past two years, my eight-year-old son has been invited to the birthday party of a young school acquaintance. At the bottom of the invitation, the first year, were listed gifts that he wanted. This was the first time I had encountered this. This year, at the bottom of the invitation it was noted, "Johnny would prefer gift certificates from the following stores . . ."

We had previous plans which took us out of town on the scheduled date, and I did inform the mother that my son would not be able to attend the party. The mother suggested I drop the present by before we left. I did not get by to do this. The following week in school, Johnny told my son that his mother said he should bring his present by some afternoon. Two days later, Johnny related to my son that his mother said to bring the present to school and give it to him.

I wonder if I am being unfair to be completely turned off by such conduct. I had a present for the boy (not a gift certificate), but I just can't seem to bring myself to give it to him. Am I wrong in not responding to this birthday? I do want my son to grow up knowing what is correct. I have always contended that if you are invited to a party it is wrong not to go, but for some reason, in this case . . .

GENTLE READER,

Because another mother is bringing up her son to be an extortionist does not seem to Miss Manners to justify your bringing yours up to be a victim. Not only does correctness not require that a present be sent when a birthday party invitation is declined, but it does not require accepting any party invitation, no matter how unattractive—only declining graciously. To spare both children, Miss Manners suggests that you simply explain to the mother that as your son did not attend the party, he will not be offering a present.

Exposure to Property

DEAR MISS MANNERS,

After nine years of marriage, we are expecting our first baby. We moved into a brand new house almost three years ago, and have since spent thousands of dollars on decorating, from upgraded carpeting and ceramic tile to exquisite draperies, furnishings and wallpaper. I am a very neat housekeeper, and take pride in keeping my house clean and orderly.

Both my sisters have children, ages two and four. When their families visit, the kids wreak havoc. They spill milk and juice on the floors, mash bananas into the carpeting, draw on walls and countertops, pick up and play with breakable items—sometimes breaking them—and just make a mess. I get irritated with my sisters and ask them nicely to please control and supervise their children. They sometimes attempt to, or say they'll clean up the mess before leaving—which they usually don't do. Sometimes I reprimand the kids myself, but it doesn't work for long.

My mom and sisters now say I am "too high strung" and need to "calm down." So what if food gets spilled on the carpeting or there's writing on the walls? They say it's my problem and I need to change. I say it's only common courtesy that when visiting other people's homes, you respect their property.

GENTLE READER,

Consider yourself lucky that you came to Miss Manners with this problem. Just about anyone else in the world would be chuckling maniacally, saying, "Just you wait until your own baby arrives, Mrs. Finicky. We'll see what happens to your 'exquisite draperies' then."

Not Miss Manners, who is pretty finicky herself. Nevertheless, she has managed to have generations of babies in the house without serious damage to the furnishings, their psyches or the spirit of hospitality. Although she has been known to remove a crystal vase or two from the immediate grabbing area of toddlers, she did it without putting any rooms of the house off limits.

She trusts that as a mother, you will accept accidents good-naturedly, but firmly teach that property—yours, the child's or anyone else's—must not be treated wantonly. If your sisters do not teach this to their children, they will have serious problems— both the sisters and, as they grow up, the children.

You have a problem too, of course, but Miss Manners does not consider it a psychological one. It is the problem of protecting your property. As they are all relatives, you may be forced to establish a safe play area, with toys, where the children can enjoy themselves but not at your expense. Because you are their aunt, you could help them by at least showing them that another way of life exists. This is done by inviting them over individually, when they are just a bit older, and showing them how to have a good time while gently explaining why it is not nice to do so in a destructive way.

Exposure to Rude Relatives

DEAR MISS MANNERS,

I have a seven-year-old who is, for the most part, very well-behaved. Yet, he is seven and has occasional lapses in his manners. In the privacy of our home, I point out and correct his behavior when necessary, but in groups of friends and family, I overlook small infringements unless I can catch his eye and correct him without embarrassment.

The problem is an uncle of his who is not very patient with children and who has taken to loudly reprimanding my son, even when his father and I are in the room, in our house as well as others'. It is uncomfortable for all of us and my child has asked why his uncle yells at him. I have told my son that his uncle isn't around children much and speaks before he thinks, but I'd appreciate a better solution.

GENTLE READER,

One of the most enjoyable ways of teaching children manners is by pointing out examples of manners in others, under strict oaths of secrecy not to let on to anyone that you are critical. What you have here is a super example of bad manners. It is very hard for children to learn that having good manners oneself does not give one license to go around chastising other people for their violations—that, in fact, doing so makes one lose the status of being well mannered.

A confidential critical chat with your son about his uncle's failing, of course accompanied by an injunction against letting on that either of you has found him rude, will make this unpleasantness less unbearable. You might also try telling the uncle that your child is doing the best he can, that you and his father are supervising his conduct, and that it would be a shame if he grew up to associate this relative with outbursts, rather than valuing him for his presumably more lovable qualities.

Exposure to Rude Strangers

DEAR MISS MANNERS,

My eight-year-old has sensory integration dysfunction, a neurological disorder which does not allow the senses to interpret stimuli correctly, thus often his behavior seems odd. When he is taken to a family restaurant, he looks like he is being spoiled, because I do not force him to eat food undesirable to him, and his use of utensils is good for him, but leaves much to be desired. We leave when I can tell he has reached his limit.

I cannot count the number of times that well-meaning people have given me suggestions about his behavior. Waitresses have told him, "You're a big boy now, eat with a fork, not a spoon," or "I would never tolerate those table manners from a child of mine." I never answer because I am enraged. Please remind your readers that all handicaps are not visible. The heartache for his plight is often great, but the comments from people are unknowingly harmful and cause me much grief.

GENTLE READER,

While Miss Manners is happy to pass on that reminder, she refuses to attribute these people's error only to a lack of medical knowledge. If they were not also ignorant of manners, they would be aware of how rude it is to monitor and correct other people's children's behavior.

Exposure to Abandoned Children

DEAR MISS MANNERS,

I would like advice on how to deal with the children in our new neighborhood—although the problem lies with the parents. They like to play with our children, ages three and a half and two. I don't mind if they come over, but they usually stay for hours, sometimes bringing their three-year-old cousin.

Last Sunday, the eight-year-old was here two hours when I sent her home so my kids could eat lunch. One minute later, she knocked on the door, explaining that "No one was home"! I feel the parents should call or bring the kids over, so I know when they are here. They should not climb the fence to our yard, and their stays should be short. When my six-year-old niece stays with us, I suggest they go to the neighbors' for a change. I know that type of retaliation is not correct, but it seems only fair.

GENTLE READER,

Retaliation? Just a minute here. Miss Manners admires your understanding of the situation, and she wants to help get you out of the difficult position that you are in. But let us have no talk of retaliating by sending innocent children places where they may not be welcome or supervised.

As you rightly point out, the problem was not created by children, but by parents. Neglecting to teach their children visiting manners is only part of the problem—they seem to be neglecting their children altogether, perhaps expecting you to pick up the slack, or perhaps not troubling themselves to wonder.

You do not want to humiliate a child, even one sent to you under these outrageous conditions, and you do not want to leave a small child to wander the streets. It is high time you set some rules with the parents. Just don't let the indignation you justifiably feel—and that you may perceive from Miss Manners' use of the snippy term "high time"—tempt you to be rude.

The polite approach is to tell them that you are concerned over the children's apparent misunderstanding of where they are supposed to be and worried about the dangers of their simply appearing when you may not be able to take care of them. "They're lovely children and we're happy to see them," you should conclude, "but please call before letting them come over, and we will certainly do the same when they suggest that our children visit you."

Exposure to Illness

DEAR MISS MANNERS,

I would like your opinion of the growing trend of deliberately exposing the world to contagion. At a lively neighborhood party my family attended, the hosts' young daughter had been sent home from school that day with stomach flu. She was apparently well enough to enjoy the party, but sick enough to spread germs among the guests. Many neighbors, including members of my own family, spent the ensuing holiday in a state of gastric upheaval.

I realize that all of us at times appear in public a bit under the weather, with colds and the like. However, I question the party hosts' decision to place the rights of their daughter above the safety of their guests. This nine-year-old could have been relegated to a bedroom with nourishment and a television or video games. The parents could have periodically checked on her without missing much of the activity.

GENTLE READER,

Just a minute, while Miss Manners recovers from your use of the word "rights," used in connection with a child's peevish desire to run about when ill. It is that sort of thinking, implying that responsible parenting is un-Constitutional, that has produced the outrageous situation you encountered.

If these people were unable to arrange to have a sick child cared for during their party, they should have canceled the party. If the reckless refusal to do either is a "trend" in your neighborhood, surely it is time you put a stop to it. The polite way to draw this to their attention is to ask after the child's health, adding that others have now come down with her flu, but voicing your faith that the parents could not possibly have realized that she was ill at the time of the party, or they would not have allowed her to expose others to infection.

PARENTAL TECHNIQUES

Teaching Context

"But you said it—so why can't I?" Almost as many children have caught their parents with this simple trick as have bamboozled them into extra privileges because "Everybody else's parents lets them." (Miss Manners never ceases to wonder at the simplicity of grown-ups. There are no such people as Everybody Else's Parents. And even if there were, why should they have authority over other parents?)

That parents have license to talk differently from their children does not excuse rudeness toward children. Age does have other privileges, however, and one of them is announcing sternly, upon provocation, "I don't care what I said—that's no way to talk to your mother" or "Kindly remember that I'm your father and you don't tell me what to do."

In order to claim such a privilege the parent must first teach the child the concept of context. This valuable lesson is often skipped nowadays, in favor of the naive and unworkable ideal of being true to oneself, in the sense of behaving in the same manner without regard to the situation, occasion or company. The child who is brought up to believe that he or she should choose what outfit to wear only on the basis of comfort and personal preference—never mind that Granny expects people to dress up when she takes them to a dressy place—will be innocent of that subtle but crucial social expectation of appropriateness.

Speech is not something that people judge solely on its content. It is not only what is said, but who says it, where and to whom. For example, members of a particular racial, religious or ethnic group may, when strictly among themselves, make jokes or use terms about that group that they would vilify any outsider for doing. Miss Manners has observed welling fury at some outrageous utterance suddenly disappear when the supposed offender, observing the reaction, hastily explained an affiliation with the group that had been unknown to the others.

Business rank is another factor. The boss who off-handedly remarks to a subordinate about the tediousness of a task will welcome a sympathetic smile. If the employee replies in kind, with something like, "Yes, it is a bore, isn't it?" the reaction, even if it is not spoken, is likely to be along the lines of "Then why don't you go find a job you like better?"

Isn't it unfair for the boss to condemn the employee for expressing the same sentiment? Only if you omit the context. The boss is certain of his or her own basic commitment to the job, and therefore intends the complaint as momentary exasperation. Not being equally sure of the employee's true feelings, however, that same boss may take any complaint, even an echoed one, to reveal deeper dissatisfaction.

The degree of family relationship is another factor. It is not uncommon, or even unreasonable, for siblings to disagree about everything, yet share resentment of any outsider who dares to criticize any one of them. (Such loyalty, which also has to be taught by parents, provides the first lesson in the folly of saying things to an outsider that one is unwilling to allow that person to say in return.) Within the family, there are questions that a parent may ask that a more distant relation cannot, or remarks that may be considered harmless when coming from a blood relative but intolerable from an in-law. Personal intimacy also plays a part among relatives, as it does among friends. The same advice that may be taken as an insult from a stranger may be interpreted gratefully as a sign of love from a close friend.

While everyone is supposed to speak respectfully to everyone else, the age factor means that younger people use more restraint and formality toward elders than is necessary in the reverse direction. To the perpetual complaint of "Unfair!" Miss Manners would like to point out that of all hierarchies, that of age is the fairest, in that one only has to wait one's turn.

The Look

DEAR MISS MANNERS,

I am concerned about how adults correct and/or remind children, in front of other people, to say or do what is correct. For a shy and sensitive child, such correction could have a negative impact on self-esteem. They may be too upset to speak at all. Or they may associate their discomfort with all social encounters and avoid these in the future. Some children seek revenge by refusing to speak, or making an improper reply to embarrass the adult.

To delay correction may lessen the effectiveness of the effort. To withdraw with the child for a prompt, private conversation may be awkward or not possible. To whisper to the child may seem rude. What would you suggest?

GENTLE READER,

You almost had Miss Manners there when you talked about "negative impact on self-esteem," a phrase that usually has a highly negative impact on her. Used as an excuse for not civilizing children, it encourages them to feel great about behaving badly.

As it turns out that you weren't actually tearing off in that unfortunate direction, Miss Manners apologizes. She really does thoroughly agree with you that the rudeness of embarrassing a child in public is a poor (although in extreme cases, necessary) method of teaching manners, being itself a demonstration of bad manners. For this reason, she has always advocated the Look. This is a way of looking at the child (tight smile, raised eyebrows) that passes unnoticed by the uninitiated, but that the child has been taught to interpret correctly as "Boy, are you getting yourself into serious trouble."

Using the Look to Protect the Child

DEAR MISS MANNERS,

While we were enjoying a holiday meal with some of my husband's family, my maternal reflex caused me to gently remind my six-year-old son to take his elbows off the table. A guilty flutter went around, and I realized that I was the only one at table who was observing the custom. My genial host opined that this was a relaxed family affair, so formal rules did not apply. The hostess disagreed, and added that it was my right and duty to correct my child, and that I ought to have support, or at least no interference.

To defuse the situation, I hastily explained the "when in Rome . . ." loophole to my little troublemaker, who was simply delighted at the dispute that had arisen. I don't want to raise my boy to be "superior"; that is, inflexibly correct, but I'm not happy teaching him to do as others do, either. I said no more, but I did ask that those present instruct my boy in the rules of their table. Since my husband and I have a "mixed marriage," such things can be extremely delicate, rich with undercurrents of meaning.

GENTLE READER,

"When in Rome" will only get you in trouble later, when your child wants to behave as badly as other children, who will make his relatives look like models of decorum. Miss Manners does not need to belabor the other dangers of seeming to criticize their behavior. She doesn't want to get dragged into those undercurrents, and neither do you. She will therefore give you an etiquette hydrofoil, so to speak, to enable you to skim along the surface without disturbing the waters.

It requires you to refrain from correcting your child in words while others are present. Lest you protest that she is betraying your noble dedication to the task of teaching your child better manners than the general standard of what he is likely to see, notice that she said "in words." Use the classic maternal look that says, "Stop that, or I'll get you later." If you are sitting next to him, you can also jog his elbow until he finds it less painful to put it where it belongs.

House Rules

Luckily, Miss Manners doesn't make house calls. Lucky for her, that is. What a life that would be. Slap the sidesaddle on the horse or, on a rush day, rev up the motorcycle, and zip around for the privilege of watching everybody slop around the house.

Presuming she didn't get killed for messing in other people's domestic arrangements, which is already a big leap, she would lose her etiquette license. As long as everybody is happy with the behavioral standards prevailing in a closed community, she has no business interfering. If people want to switch breakfast and dinner, or decide not to make the beds on the weekends, or ever, she will discreetly look the other way.

Of course, it is easy for Miss Manners to be tolerant about something she can't control. Nevertheless, she is so far from wanting to mess in this area that she wishes people would learn home etiquette programming, so that her help would not be sought as often as it is. Miss Manners is called in when there is no household etiquette consensus. One or more members are steadily defying the standards of other members, which does not make for a peaceful life for any of them. The question she is asked to decide is which preference is right.

That needn't be asked. Correctness, according to the world at large, is not strictly necessary in private. Here's your chance to create a private world that may be more easygoing—or less so, if that is your taste. The level of formality maintained can be whatever is mutually agreeable. Dressing for dinner can mean black tie, or it can mean covered chests and underwear, or it can mean something Miss Manners would prefer not to hear. The beauty of home life is that adjustments can be made for preferences and quirks.

True, it is infinitely easier on everyone if the style approximates that of the outside. It seems unnecessarily troublesome to burden children with remembering that what goes at home is off-putting elsewhere, so that they need to learn a whole second set of basic manners, usually referred to as company (but more frequently, these days, meaning job-seeking) manners.

When there is disagreement within the house, the higher form, as approved for general use in the society, should prevail. This is because good standard manners are not offensive, and there is no use trying to be clever by arguing that they are. Miss Manners has learned to be suspicious of the word "relaxing," which in this context has come to mean not caring about the effect on others in the household.

The value of not alienating the people among whom you live is something Miss Manners would have thought obvious. Apparently not. She is always being asked to bolster the argument of a complaining spouse, as if the mere fact that the spouse is being made unhappy were not argument enough.

Couples and roommates need to establish house rules, because they are apt to come from different traditions. These may go beyond conventional questions of etiquette to include who can finish up which leftovers in the refrigerator, and how one may mark one's place in other people's books.

Clue that making a house rule is overdue: *"You know what drives me crazy?"*

Statement to avoid: *"Just because you were brought up in a barn doesn't mean I'm willing to live that way."*

Parents not only need to establish house rules, but must steadfastly resist being talked out of their obligation to maintain them.

Handy statement: *"I don't care what other kids get away with, you are not allowed to do that in this house."*

Divorced parents and their subsequent spouses are in special need of house rules, as they may not care for other conditions under which the children live. The difference is that they do not have equal freedom to criticize those particular outside standards.

Handy statement: *"Yes, I know your mother says it's okay, and that's fine when you're with her, but in our house we have different rules."*

Grandparents are under similar tact restraints, not only to avoid undermining other authority to which the children are properly subject, but out of humility as well. At least one of those parents who is permitting the child to get away with murder is the product of the grandparents' own child-rearing methods. Exposure to grandparents' house rules gives both their and the grandchildren's generation a second chance. A pleasant visit, with an explanation of rules that are presented merely as alternative ways of doing things, can give an otherwise etiquetteless child insight and practice into a better way of life.

Handy statement: *"Yes, darling, but this is how we do things at Grandma and Grandpa's house."*

Statement to avoid: *"I know your mother knows better, but what can you expect with that father of yours?"*

Granddaddy's House Rules

DEAR MISS MANNERS,

Here are my Mealtime Rules for Special and Formal Occasions at Granddaddy's House:

Rule 1. On their arrival, guests will greet the dog and Granddaddy and permit themselves to be kissed (at least by Granddaddy). They will then put their overcoats and overshoes in the places provided, and not on the dining room floor or furniture.

Rule 2. No one over 18 shall appear in blue jeans or basketball shoes; adult males will wear coats and ties; juvenile and adult females will be dressed appropriately for the occasion.

Rule 3. For one full hour prior to the serving of the meal, the kitchen and other serving areas will be kept clear of all persons who do not have Granddaddy's special permission.

Rule 4. When all are called to the table, all will come to the table.

Rule 5. Persons will be seated at the places assigned to them by Granddaddy in consultation with their mothers, and they will remain at those places until excused or summoned for duty.

Rule 6. Since high chairs and telephone books will be provided for those too small to reach the table, there will be no eating while standing.

Rule 7. No hats, caps or other headgear shall be worn at the table by persons of either sex, save they be grandmothers brought up in a proper Victorian household.

Rule 7a. No outerwear will be worn at the table unless the heating system fails.

Rule 8. No dogs, cats, turtles, iguanas or pets of any other description will be allowed within 25 feet of the dining room during the progress of the meal.

Rule 9. The meal will be served according to the guests' sex and seniority. Persons under the age of four will be allowed to bang their dishes with their silverware, provided this is done moderately and from the impatience of hunger, not for the mere delight in the noise.

Rule 10. Persons will drink from the glasses provided, infants under 24 months excepted. At the table there will be no soda or other soft drink bottles.

Rule 11. All guests will sit at their places, converse politely with their dinner companions and not leave the table until they have been excused or until they have been asked to perform some chore.

Rule 12. Persons between the ages of thirteen and nineteen will not reply, "Oh, nothing," when asked what they have been doing. They will come prepared to give some account of themselves. Persons below and above that age bracket will confine themselves to a brief and temperate enumeration of their accomplishments.

Rule 13. Nobody save Granddaddy may complain of the behavior of another, whether the reference be to the immediate present days or to the events of past years.

Rule 14. People shall not shout from one room to another; in fact, people shall not shout at all.

Rule 15. No firearms or firecrackers will be let off in the dining room, either during or after the meal, nor will permission be sought to fire them elsewhere while the meal is in progress.

Rule 16. Persons will remain at their places at the table. When one person is requested to perform some service, all others are to remain at their places.

Rule 17. Once a person has finally been excused, he or she is history and will not linger in the dining area, hanging on a parent's arm, complaining that there is nothing to do, or seeking permission to go to McDonald's.

Rule 18. At Christmas time, whatever presents there may be will lie unmolested until, by general agreement, the whole gathering is assembled before the tree. At that point, the distribution will be orderly, with suitable pauses between each giving, so that the giver, the recipient and all others may enjoy the event.

Rule 19. Those up to the age of 16 who receive a mere item of clothing as a gift will put their bravest face upon the disaster.

Rule 20. Parents will not pass the day fretting over the lapses of their offspring, threatening them with bread and water, or promising to "punch them out" when they get home. Rather, before each and any of these formal and special occasions, each guest and especially parents, will review with themselves and their children the rudiments of table manners and hope for the best.

Rule 21. Nothing in these regulations is to be construed as preventing Granddaddy from promulgating additional ones on the spot.

Gun Rules

DEAR MISS MANNERS,

If my little Johnny wishes to play at Jimmy's house, how do I ask Jimmy's parents if they keep firearms and, if so, do they store them in a locked cabinet?

If I am giving a large party with many guests who are casual acquaintances, is there a polite way to remind everyone of the concealed weapons law in my jurisdiction? Or do I just have to hope? I have no wish to use etiquette as an occasion for proselytizing and am most anxious to avoid acrimonious debate with those who may be heavily armed.

GENTLE READER,

The day is probably not far off when people will install metal detectors on their front porches. If you wish to lead the way, Miss Manners asks you to ask to offer to relieve your guests of whatever sets the thing off, in the same hospitable tone in which you would ask to take their coats.

When one child visits another, the visitor's parent uses an apologetic tone—as if to admit that her fastidiousness is slightly comic—when she explains rules that may conflict with the standards of the household visited: "I'm afraid we feel Johnny is too young [never mind the fact that he may be 40] to play in houses where there are firearms. If that is a problem, perhaps you would send Jimmy to play with him here, instead."

TEACHING MANNERS FOR SCHOOL

Once again someone tried to tell Miss Manners a well known horror story about preschool, The Tale of the Fetus Pupil.

"Someone I know knows this woman who had amniocentesis because she needed to know the sex of her baby so she could apply to a good private school before anyone else his age," she was told.

"Really?" asked Miss Manners, polite in tone if not in intention. "What was the name of the school?"

If anyone can name an actual school that accepts fetuses on its waiting list, Miss Manners has yet to hear it. She is also skeptical when she hears pathetic stories of overprivileged children who have been denied their childhoods by parents training them to get into a place called The Right School, apparently a nursery that feeds directly into Ivy League colleges.

In these accounts, the children have been taught to read by flash cards before they can talk, and to do mathematics before they can find their thumbs. Admissions directors who see them when these prodigies are three years old (presuming that the preschools are not already filled with smug children who had the foresight to apply at conception) are apparently thrilled.

"Wonderful!" they say. "This one already knows everything we had planned to teach through the sixth grade. Let's take him in so that he can hang around bored while we teach less advanced children. He can sulk or make trouble while we attend to them." It strikes Miss Manners as an unlikely scenario. Whenever she has talked with the educators of very small children, the ideal candidate they describe is ignorant but mannerly.

Mannerly! Miss Manners is aware that the very mention of etiquette in connection with children excites both comedians and snobs with the idea of tots swaggering around knowledgeably amidst commercial luxury. The very idea of teaching three- or four-year-olds manners is even more shocking to kindly adults than the idea of teaching academic subjects to people whose amusement of choice is to watch their mobiles go 'round. What the adults envision is innocent children being forced to learn how to spar with a sommelier about the relative merits of wines.

Miss Manners also finds abhorrent the idea of teaching inappropriate rituals to small children for the sake of snobbery. But toddlers can learn toddler manners. When educators identify the school system's fatal problem as a lack of discipline, they are talking about the impossibility of teaching a roomful of children who have not previously been taught to keep quiet and listen even for two minutes, let alone to show respect for authority and consideration for their peers; who do not agree that communal goals may sometimes outweigh individual desires; who have no experience of methods of settling disputes nonviolently; and who are genuinely ignorant of what is and is not acceptable behavior in a classroom. A few toddler etiquette rules are:

> *Hitting is not a form of greeting.*
> *Food is not properly used for decoration, either of oneself or of one's habitat.*
> *Hitting is not a form of negotiation.*
> *It is physically possible to sit still for moments at a time.*
> *It is mentally possible to take directions from an adult.*
> *If you listen, you might hear something interesting.*

Such manners are taught by small reminders and restraints, and by adults regularly and pleasantly talking and reading to children. They make all subsequent education possible. A child who can't pay attention, or who disrupts a classroom, is a discouraging prospect for teaching. Schools that can choose their pupils prefer those whom they can begin to teach, not those who have to have remedial parenting done first.

Aside from whatever ambitions children may harbor for formal education, these manners are also the foundation for any kind of learning or socializing. No one wants to play with a bully, and a zero attention span makes it impossible to take in the amusements the world has to offer. Colleges that allegedly draw their enrollments from these preschools will be grateful. They have had their share of students who come to them pretty much etiquette-free, and they yearn for campus civility.

After decades of nearly laissez-faire administration, colleges and universities are once again clamping down on student behavior. "An increasing lack of civility among students, which has ranged from overt acts of racism to an increase in age-old complaints like playing loud music when other students are trying to study," was a reason given by the *New York Times.*

Remedial Etiquette

"Why don't the schools teach children manners?" Nobody expects Miss Manners to argue with this suggestion, which she hears with increasing frequency as the acuteness of the national manners crisis is understood. Rather, she is expected to be grateful that the heavy burden will be lifted from her own frail shoulders.

Indeed, Miss Manners is pathetically anxious for assistance. Even if she were of a mind to become the national scold, which is not her idea of either a feasible or an amusing job, issuing instructions for beginners and reprimands for violators is only a small part of her calling. Miss Manners is more useful as a judge than as a policewoman. Interpreting the rules, applying them to specific cases where there may be conflicts and extenuating circumstances, and developing them to keep pace with society's needs are the tasks to which she directs most of her attention.

BOSTON—A 3-year-old boy allegedly kicked a 3-year-old girl in the sandbox, leading the girl's mother to appeal to the judicial system to bar the boy and his mother from the playground. Neither Jonathan, the alleged perpetrator, nor Stacey, the alleged victim, has a criminal record, the *Washington Post* reported. A temporary restraining order and then a preliminary civil injunction to keep the children and their parents apart were issued. "If she could have at least apologized, fine. But this woman refuses to take any responsibility for her child's action," said Stacey's mother in an interview.

All this depends on the citizens' agreeing that they must practice good manners if we are to have a livable society, and their knowing just what constitutes such manners in our society. Why not let the schools teach that? This has been the traditional American cry whenever a need for nonacademic instruction arises in the society. American schools have always been expected to teach good citizenship. Later they were expected to teach skills necessary for business, health and even marriage and family living. With the perceived breakdown in morality now, the schools are besieged with requests to teach ethics. Why not throw in etiquette as well?

Miss Manners' objection to all of this is that the schools become overburdened with tasks that are basically impossible to teach in the classroom, to the neglect of those that are. It seems unreasonable to her to require academics to make up for the abdication of parental responsibility. Are the parents going to take over teaching history, literature, science and mathematics so that the teachers will be free to show children how to behave?

Because teachers are teachers, and can't bear to observe ignorance that handicaps children without trying to alleviate it, many of them, bless their hearts, do attempt to teach children the basics of civilized living that they are apparently not getting at home. Predictably, it is not working too well. This is because manners for children are a matter not of theory but of practice, and a child who does not daily observe the practice of manners on the part of his or her family, and receive daily correction from them on the basics and nuances of acceptable behavior, is unlikely to learn anything from lectures or discussions.

Manners should be first taught as a matter of rote. Children who anticipate the philosophical branch of the study of manners by asking "Why should I?" should be first told, "Because you want other people to treat you nicely," and, if that doesn't work, "Because I say so, that's why."

No classroom can provide such practice. Even to maintain a school code of behavior, to establish an orderly atmosphere in which learning is possible, the schools need the reinforcement of the community. Support for indecent dress, obscene language and lack of respect for others as an expression of student rights is not helpful. Miss Manners appreciates what help the school system can give in teaching the principles of civility, and, yes, she would be grateful for more help in the teaching of manners. That is why, when parents complain that somebody should be teaching their children manners, she agrees that somebody should, and then stares hard at them through her lorgnette.

Teaching Etiquette Anyway: Elementary School

DEAR MISS MANNERS,

I teach as a science specialist in an elementary school, taking each class but kindergarten for one hour a week, and I often take time to try to teach manners— "Excuse me," "Thank you," "I'm sorry."

Imagine a class of second graders without manners. Students interrupt while the teacher gives instruction, students yell at others when someone or something bothers them, regardless of instruction being present.

In this atmosphere, many good lessons are shelved until manners can be in-stilled. Those exciting sciences lessons that I do, containing hands-on experiments, need attentive listening. I have wonderful, bright students, but I'm sorry to say I have sacrificed learning time toward lessons on manners and truth-telling.

GENTLE READER,

Not much imagination is required nowadays to conjure up the scene you de-scribe. Children who are unable to benefit from the advantages of civilization because they have not been taught its most basic skill, manners, are everywhere.

Miss Manners blesses you for trying to do something about this. She only wonders that the children's parents cannot seem to see that they have prevented you from doing your job by making you do theirs.

Teaching Etiquette Anyway: High School

DEAR MISS MANNERS,

I am a high school chemistry teacher at a fairly good inner-city public school, and I never realized how important manners were until coming to a place that had very little respect for the basic rules of etiquette. How can I, as an adult white male and teacher, instill proper manners in teenage black boys and girls without being thought of as racist or ignorant of their culture? How far can or should I go in the much needed instruction of etiquette and not be rude myself?

GENTLE READER,

They are not chemists, are they? And yet you teach them chemistry. Don't you?

Perhaps not, Miss Manners is afraid, unless you can first teach them to behave in a classroom. She strongly suggests that you squarely face and challenge them to defend any such outrageous charges as you imply they may harbor. Sorry as she is to add to your workload, she is afraid that you must teach the theory of manners before you can lay down the etiquette rules that will finally enable you to teach chemistry.

You can show that what would be most disrespectful and degrading to them would be the belief that requiring manners exhibits disrespect for their culture. As you might point out, there is hardly a more obnoxiously racist charge than that civilized behavior is inherently white, and that it is phony and inappropriate on the part of people of color to attempt it. The conclusion of that would be that modern civilization, with all its rewards, belongs to whites, while others should remain on the periphery, in an unsophisticated (and happy-go-lucky?) state of nature. It is hard to think of a more bigoted all-purpose concept.

The truth is that your students don't really believe this; they simply share the universal desire to be free of rules by any argument that works on timid adults. Astonishingly enough they also despise rudeness—but only when it is practiced on them, instead of by them. Should they claim otherwise, they cannot then claim to be offended by disrespect. Showing respect to others is an etiquette rule, mandated only by manners.

Miss Manners understands perfectly well that different standards of behavior prevail among different people (age being more of a factor nowadays than race) and in different situations. The rougher manners that the young may enjoy in their social lives with other youngsters are not acceptable to their grandmothers or during organized sports or at funerals. Nor should these be acceptable in the classroom, where you will need to set rules that demonstrate respect for education, yourself as teacher, and one another.

They will then be able to learn chemistry as well as the enormously important lesson that etiquette being inborn in no one, can be learned by anyone—and used to great advantage by those who can practice it skillfully.

Basic Classroom Rules

DEAR MISS MANNERS,

By the time an adolescent has reached high school age, he/she has already developed a personality, and if a student is exhibiting disrespectful behavior toward authority or subject matter, it will take a lot more than one or two lessons, even an entire semester of etiquette, to change the student's attitude. Is the teacher trained to be Miss Manners? Are those "basic rules" universally accepted? Not everybody would agree as to what common courtesy means.

I don't believe that the idea of respect for others can be put on like a piece of clothing, whenever the occasion may arise. Respect for others is developed over time, from the cradle on, and becomes part of the personality. In today's educational reform environment, there are many parents who believe that the public school has veered away from the traditional three R's and should not be in the business of teaching their kids morality.

GENTLE READER,

Now, now, Miss Manners does not expect teachers to do her job. She expects parents to do it.

It is when parents fail to instill the principles of manners that we all run into trouble. The subject cannot simply be abandoned, because wild children ruin classroom instruction, not to mention society, for themselves and for others. Teachers must then instill and enforce the etiquette of the classroom—setting out rules that they require to be observed while the children are under their jurisdiction. Consensus for such ordinary and reasonable rules as sitting quietly, not chewing gum, raising a hand to be called upon to speak, and so on should not be requested or required, from either the children or their parents.

Miss Manners is well aware that this may not ennoble the children's souls so that they actually feel respect for others. If they observe the form, that will be enough, although feelings do sometimes spring from good habits, rather than the other way around.

The Teacher's Authority

DEAR MISS MANNERS,

I am a high school teacher who does not allow my students to chew gum in class. They claim that they have never heard that it is rude to chew with their mouths open in public (not to mention having wrappers and chewed gum everywhere but in the waste basket).

I can understand that they may want to freshen their breaths with gum after lunch, but they should remove it, wrap it in paper and dispose of it in the wastepaper basket before participating in class. They have challenged me to prove to them that their behavior violates the rule of etiquette. Need I ask?

GENTLE READER,

Miss Manners is surprised that your students have not heard of the rule prohibiting gum chewing in public, but shocked that they have not heard of the rule requiring following their teachers' instructions. It is time you taught them both.

PARENTAL BREAKDOWNS

When It's Too Late for Etiquette

By the time the law enters a household, it's too late for family etiquette. It's time to study Etiquette in the Courtroom, and Etiquette for Dealing with the Other Parent of Your Child Under Abhorrent Circumstances.

The reason Miss Manners is found sobbing by the hearth when the police arrive is not that she has been hit or threatened. It is that she has been defeated. Etiquette, not law, is the system that is supposed to prevail in family life, where fairness is supposed to take second place to fondness.

Family etiquette is not, however, a standard household item. It has been brutally assaulted by:

- The concept of the individual as the only really important unit, so that sacrifice for others, even in trivial matters, may be considered more foolish than admirable.
- The related presumption that the family unit may well be temporary, so that its members must protect their separate interests.
- The idea that the ideal family is one in which total relaxation excuses everyone from the effort and artificiality of tact.

Then things turn nasty, and everyone is surprised that peace and harmony, much less happiness, do not prevail in this etiquette-free environment.

Miss Manners is far from claiming that a lack of etiquette is the only cause of family failure. There is no polite way to say, "Darling, I've finally met the love of my life." She has even heard, with horror, of cases where etiquette was perversely used to create family conflict. Some parents teach manners rudely, through humiliation or other forms of cruelty. The result is that the children feel about etiquette the way several generations of high school students used to feel about *Silas Marner*—a rather good book, Miss Manners wishes to point out on behalf of her dear friend George Eliot, but one that crude and force-fed teaching made tiresome.

Yet the absence of household etiquette has two serious consequences:

1. A lack of consideration for others, even if only in minor matters, is an irritant that can act cumulatively to drive people smack out of their minds.

2. Failure to have a civil method for conflict resolution means that hurtful methods will be used instead, and nobody can inflict hurt as effectively as a relative-in-residence.

Small concessions do a lot toward heading off household antagonism among
people who presumably got together out of love in the first place. When these occur
anyway, there must be a polite technique for solving them.

The law forbids doing this through violence, although it has great difficulty
with enforcement because of the complicated mix of emotions involved. Etiquette
concentrates on providing forms that air disputes without causing lateral damage.
Thus, it also bans such acts of warfare as name-calling, threats, door-slamming,
dish-smashing, shunning and the use of privileged information—confessions
uttered under trusting circumstances—as ammunition. Children must be taught that
these methods of fighting are as out of bounds as the direct physical attack.

Anybody who thinks it is impossible to have a family fight without such techniques is lacking in imagination. In a basically warm family, the cold observation of
formalities is startlingly effective in expressing unhappiness. It also enables people to
debate the problem rather than desperately defend a general onslaught on their character, freedom and territory. And it keeps the police from the door.

THE GOOD, THE BAD
AND THE VULGAR

POLITICAL CORRECTNESS

Political Correctness is like cholesterol, Miss Manners has decided. It used to mean nothing but trouble. Then it was discovered that there was a good kind as well as a bad kind.

Actually, the only person to have discovered Good P.C. is, in all modesty, Miss Manners. Bad P.C. is something everyone knows about. It has become a national resource, supplying huge amounts of both outrage and hilarity. Its detractors define P.C. as ridiculous, touchy, hostile, humorless responses to ordinary, previously acceptable, harmless, even pleasant, human discourse. This is illustrated with no end of stories about innocent people being vilified for saying or doing something unexceptionable:

> *"All I did was tell him, 'You did a great job,' and he snarled that I wouldn't have been so condescending if he'd been white."*
>
> *"When she came back from sick leave, her boss said she looked great, and she slapped him with a sexual harassment complaint."*
>
> *"They won't let us put on* Everyman *because they claim he's elitist." (History and literature provide frequent targets because Bad P.C. works retroactively: Having been born, written and died long before the standard was recognized is no excuse.)*

Miss Manners finds herself being drawn in because insulting people on the basis of what was clearly said or done out of nothing but good will is, obviously, rude. No question about it. In fact, this is so obvious that Miss Manners has become slightly suspicious of those stories. When (as a polite cover-up for her inability to double up in shock or merriment at yet another of these tales) she asks dainty questions, some of these incidents turn out to be not quite so clear-cut. Perhaps there was a previously omitted detail, such as that those pleasantries the lady was so touchy about had included a little friendly but unauthorized touching. Or that the gentleman who was so surly about his work was getting the dirty work not assigned to his peers.

Condemnation of P.C. has become so popular that the distinction between reacting to imaginary slights and reacting to real ones seems to have gotten lost. The anti-P.C. forces have succeeded in casting suspicion on anyone who won't accept the expression of bigotry with equanimity. So one day Miss Manners woke up from her afternoon nap and found that the bigots had managed to position themselves on the side of politeness and to define as rude the people who objected to bigotry.

Talk about outrage! P.C. at its most spluttering is nothing compared to Miss Manners' state when she found she was being yoked with the defenders of bigotry. Bigotry is rude. (Practicing it is immoral, but expressing it is rude.) Reacting against it rudely is also rude; that's the Bad P.C.

But reacting against it in a civilized fashion is not rude. That's the Good P.C. This is actually more in keeping with the basic principles of manners, dignity and respect than is ignoring bigotry, which may superficially—but deceptively—appear to be the polite response.

Here's how it works:

1. In identifying any rudeness, including bigotry, consideration must be given to motivation, so that people who are trying to be polite are not condemned on small or obscure technicalities. (This does not mean that ignorance of society-wide standards is a defense, as Miss Manners keeps pointing out to those who have not yet heard that "honey" is not the female form of address equivalent to "sir.")
2. Those who believe that they have identified a new form of bigotry or other immorality are obliged to make their proposed rules known and accepted before they start attacking people for disobeying them. (In simpler times, Miss Manners could have taken this for granted, but impatient moralists now like to open with the punishment.)
3. Moral superiority does not confer immunity from the very standards

one is trying to enforce. (Hurling epithets, invading privacy and inflicting humiliation are not legitimate weapons, even against people one wants to punish for hurling epithets, invading privacy and inflicting humiliation.)

4. Moral inferiority doesn't confer immunity, either. (It has become common now to preface offensive statements with, "I suppose I'm not being politically correct, but . . ." This does not work on Miss Manners, who has never let people off from the charge of being rude because they acknowledged that they are being rude—sort of the opposite of the temporary insanity plea.)

5. Objections to bigotry should match the severity of the transgression, ranging from "Surely I must have misunderstood you" to "I beg your pardon!" to "How dare you!" to "You will be hearing from my lawyer." Properly used, however, all of these are perfectly polite responses to highly impolite behavior.

6. Finally, preempting the term because it is catchy and declaring one's own political views to be the standard of political correctness, even if they are irrelevant or in opposition to what is commonly understood by this, is another form of Bad P.C. It is rude to add to the already sufficient amount of confusion in the world.

A Reply

DEAR MISS MANNERS,

I hope you aren't suggesting that persons opposed to the mindlessness of political correctness are bigots. Any decent person would be properly outraged at blatant racism or sexism, but decency would require that this also include racism or sexism against white persons and males.

Some minorities and women seem to consider it their right to make such remarks: An Hispanic magazine named a "Gringo of the Year," although "gringo" is a disparaging term for white. Black comedians sometimes refer to "honkies." If a white did the equivalent, he'd be lucky to escape without a severe beating.

Universities tend to be bastions of political correctness, with a common double standard that allows feminists to state their ideas while persons who offer any critical comments are accused of "attacking" females and "creating a hostile climate" for women. Government employees are threatened with sexual harassment charges for simply stating that women are being given special privileges in employment and promotion, which they are.

Political correctness is insidious in that it absolves a person of thinking for himself, aside from the obvious lack of logic involved. It's an attempt to prevent the free and open discussion of ideas, i.e., it's a threat to free speech and freedom in general. It's astounding that liberals have gone from advocating free speech in the '60s to promoting politically correct only speech.

GENTLE READER,

As Miss Manners understands it, you and she are in perfect agreement that there should not be a double standard that permits some people to practice racism and sexism while others may not.

Your solution is to allow everyone to do so. Miss Manners' is to discourage anyone from doing so. Fairness is certainly one of her concerns, but civility is another. She has observed that trading insults prevents and substitutes for—rather than constitutes—free and open discussions of ideas.

An Anti-Feminist Interpretation at Dinner

DEAR MISS MANNERS,

A former friend often accepted my invitation to a meal and then, after I had changed all arrangements so she could attend, called and canceled at the last minute. I understand her motivation, in that she is a very self-effacing person who does not think that she is important. My position is that she does not respect the work that I put into having guests, and is incredibly rude.

It is really an anti-woman act, which devalues the work of cooking, cleaning, hostessing, preparing, etc.—usually women's work. I have never heard this tack taken in regard to this kind of behavior. She considers herself a feminist and would be appalled at the idea that she is denigrating women. Do you think this view would change her behavior?

GENTLE READER,

No, Miss Manners doesn't think your friend is demonstrating disrespect for women's work. And no, she doesn't think she is motivated by feelings of unimportance.

Miss Manners thinks this person is rude, rude, rude, and that her motivation is to consider her own convenience without regard to how she inconveniences others, regardless of gender. Isn't that bad enough? Do you have to make it sound respectable?

Never mind. Miss Manners has now gotten a grip on herself. Sure: If you think you can improve your friend's manners by claiming that you understand her motivation but that she is practicing sexism, go right ahead. Just please show Miss Manners the courtesy of doing it out of her earshot.

A Racist Interpretation at Dinner

Dear Miss Manners,

I am an Asian professional woman married to an American. On a number of occasions when we entered suburban restaurants, the waitresses who approached to seat us pointedly ignored me, speaking to, and looking only at, my husband. Please explain what prompted such behavior and advise on how it should be handled. We don't have such problems in classier, cosmopolitan, downtown restaurants.

Gentle Reader,

Miss Manners suggests that you stop brooding about possible racial or gender discrimination, which is bound to spoil your digestion, and check out the etiquette.

NEW YORK, N.Y.—"Has hatred become hip?" asked a *New York Times* story on the increase in racial and sexual prejudice showing up in pop music and comedy. "Ethnic stereotyping runs deep in American popular culture. Blacks have been caricatured since the days of slavery; during World War II, the Japanese were portrayed as evil incarnate. Ethnic jokes have always been comedians' staples. But the triumphs of the civil rights movement of the 1960s, and the feminist and homosexual rights movements that followed, made prejudicial statements less tolerable in mainstream society, almost taboo. Now, that taboo is cracking," the *Times* reported.

Apparently, your suburban restaurants are more aware than the downtown ones of old-fashioned restaurant tradition. This required that all questions and directions be spoken between the service people and the host of the party, rather than the guest. A lady would give her order to the gentleman, who would then relay it to the waiter or waitress, a charming bit of stage business that has been all but lost now.

To Miss Manners' mind, this was the—as you say—classier method of service. The only erroneous part was the assumption that the gentleman was always the host (the advantage to the lady being that he also made that assumption and picked up the check). Restaurateurs had an unnaturally hard time understanding that a lady who was acting as hostess should be treated as one, with the orders of her guest or guests going through her. Miss Manners still gives her order to accompanying gentlemen, when they are her hosts, just to see the startled look on everyone's face, sometimes including the gentlemen's. If you feel it interferes with your dignity to allow your husband to seem to be in charge of your wishes, you can always speak up for yourself, and for him, too, if he doesn't charge you with sexism.

An Interpretation of Seafood

Dear Miss Manners,

At a dinner for a member of government, his wife (I don't want to name names as that is tacky, don't you think?) commented on how delicious my dinner of scallops looked. I asked if she would like to taste it and she said yes, so I put several scallops on a plate and passed them to her. When the evening was over, my husband said he was embarrassed and appalled by my behavior. He says one should never ask someone except family if they want to taste and that in public, it is poor manners. Was I politically incorrect?

Gentle Reader,

How would Miss Manners know? You forgot to tell her whom you voted for.

Extolling Vulgarity and Bigotry

"You know he's only saying what everyone is thinking but doesn't dare say."
"Oh, come on, she's not saying anything you haven't heard before."

Miss Manners has heard both of these statements so often lately that she may get to the point where she prefers the bigotry or vulgarity that invariably precedes them. Almost, but not quite. The idea that there should be no safety mechanism between the thought and the word has never appealed to her. You show her someone who incessantly condemns hypocrisy, euphemism and circumlocution, and she will show you someone who is up to no good.

Blatantly anti-etiquette, the quest for total expression has left behind an almost unbroken train of disasters. Remember "It's just a communication problem"? That was the byword for more than a decade. No relationship was exempt from the promise of improvement through total frankness. Wives and husbands who had thought they were viewed through the kindly light of marital approval found out otherwise. Opponents, who might have tolerated each other on the notion that disagreement did not necessarily indicate inferiority or bad faith, were treated to a full blast of enmity.

Yet these examples seem pleasantly naive to Miss Manners, compared with the malevolent frankness now coming into vogue. The redefinition of loathsome sentiments as admirable because they truly express what is being thought has truly shocked her. Admittedly, Miss Manners is easily shocked. She considers her ability to be so a public service. It is a performance that is, if she may modestly say so, greatly in demand. If more people practiced it, the level of shocking statements could be kept tolerable. But no, they have to brag that they welcome bluntness, no matter how unappetizing it may be.

Those on the search for a good shock have been trying to undo the greatest etiquette advance of our age, the condemnation of bigotry. When the nostalgic moan about the decline of etiquette, Miss Manners turns contrary and points out that it is only recently that frank expressions of prejudice have become socially unacceptable. That lascivious and bigoted statements no longer pass uncensured is enormous progress.

To be sure, there are many people who cannot spell and who therefore equate censureship with censorship. They do not understand that an etiquette rule is not the same as a law and that disapproval and the desire to keep rude people at a distance are not the same as throwing them in jail. Miss Manners defends the right of the rude to make horrid statements, although not in her presence.

What appalls her is the defense of such statements as truthfully representing what people think. Very likely they do. But so what? That it is only human nature to harbor ugly, harmful ideas, some of which may be the fleeting thoughts of otherwise reasonable people, and others of which may be deeply rooted prejudices, does not even surprise her. However, the belief that these thoughts might therefore just as well be let loose in the world to spread their damage, or that there is actually something courageous about expressing them, will drive her to ordering smelling salts by the case.

Is It Rude to Avoid Vulgarity?

DEAR MISS MANNERS,

I was dining in a local restaurant where I have been going with my family for years—fortunately not with children this time—when a male stripper appeared, during one of those now-omnipresent birthday celebrations at an adjoining table. He began to dance and move in an obscenely suggestive manner. I was informed by a delighted observer that the young man would soon strip down to his G-string.

Appalled by the whole business, I left, having first explained my reasons to my companions. On the way out, I told the headwaiter that I did not intend to pay my portion of the bill, since I had neither expected nor desired to participate in this show. A follow-up call to the management revealed that my companions had not only paid my share, but had "apologized for my behavior." My departure had been quiet and unnoticed.

Several people I have since spoken with tell me this—the appearance of a male stripper, that is—is becoming an increasingly common practice. Please advise on what the appropriate response should be for unwary customers.

GENTLE READER,

Unwary Customer did just fine, it seems to Miss Manners. It is Unwary Customer's friends and Restaurateur who transgressed—not by enjoying a stripper, but by falling all over themselves with embarrassment because you refused to do so.

When toleration is expected for practices that are likely to offend many people, it seems to Miss Manners only fair to extend toleration to those who don't want to witness such practices. Your friends who apologized for your behavior and the manager who ignored your complaint were not willing to do this.

Bullying everyone into accepting a low standard is not the answer. If the restaurant is not clearly one where strippers entertain, the party hiring one should have been required to take a private room.

Is It Polite to Stare at Vulgarity?

DEAR MISS MANNERS,

The man in a nearby apartment (I am an adult male living alone) has started to watch hard-core porn videos after hours. His viewing room window is clearly visible from a room I use heavily and his blinds remain open.

I am not so much looking for advice about what I should do as much as about what I should think. Which, if any, of the following apply?

What he does in his castle is his own business. If it's legal and he's not hurting anyone else, it's none of my business and if I don't like it, I should pull my shades.

His having his blinds open is ethically out of bounds, perhaps some form of exhibitionism, and I should tell him about it.

If he wants to put these movies (and implicitly, his behavior) on public display, he has, in effect, invited me to watch with binoculars or sell tickets if I so choose, and neither he nor I has any grounds for complaint.

Whether I like it or not has no bearing upon whether or not he should shut his blinds. It is not the identity, moral system or preferences of me, the observer, that have any bearing upon whether or not he should shut his blinds, but solely the nature of the activity itself.

GENTLE READER,

It seems to Miss Manners that you are showing far too much interest in the nature of your neighbor's habit. Getting out the binoculars or opening an acquaintanceship by going over to discuss his moral character or psychological state would involve you more, rather than less, with his tastes. The only alternative you consider is to dismiss your own objections and either cut off your entire outside view or continue to endure seeing pornographic movies.

It is true that there is a lot to think about here. Protecting the inadvertent viewer from offensive material involves a delicate balance between freedom and that protection. The definition of what can be considered a rightful affront to public sensibilities is notoriously elusive. Yet Miss Manners can't help noting that whether hard-core pornography should be visible on a residential street is not a question on which you are likely to encounter opposition. The neighbor himself may not have intended this. Surely your objective must be not to have

SAN FRANCISCO, CALIF.—**"Cyber solicitation" of teenagers who ran away from home to meet sexual partners they found by computer is an increasingly common crime being investigated by the Federal Bureau of Investigation, according to Reuters. Such cases have added to the debate about how to regulate pornography, obscenity and solicitation on the Internet.**

unacceptable pictures thrust into your view. But then, you did tell Miss Manners you want to think about the problem rather than inquire how to solve it.

TOPICS THAT USED TO BE BANNED

One way to get the young people's attention at dinner is to tell them about the old-fashioned etiquette rule against discussing sex, religion or politics at the table. "You're kidding," they always say. "Why not?" In the age of information, if not enlightenment, people can't imagine what could possibly be said on these tired old subjects that would bring on the sort of juices that fight digestion. Who cares how many angels dance on the head of a pin, or who else does what to whom?

Miss Manners, who sees a need to get that rule out and active again, suspects that those who laugh it off simply don't recognize the dangerous subjects under their plain old names. Try calling sex "alternate lifestyles" and see if you can get a pleasant and interesting discussion on it going among people of different orientations. Religion may not inspire heated theological controversy in general circles nowadays, but as a cultural factor it can get people pretty worked up. When was the last time you were part of a reasoned give-and-take about prayer in the schools? Or had a calm debate about religious positions on abortion?

Politics only sounds tame because there is not much incentive to argue about who is going to win an election when you can court tedium by quoting polls at one another. Calmly talking about what everyone present agrees upon isn't banned, no matter how inflammatory it may be elsewhere. Comforting as it may be to launch a unanimous attack on people who aren't represented, vigorous nodding and pronouncements of "Yeah, right" don't constitute a discussion, anyway. It's a bit different when any specific political issues come up—say, war and peace, crime and justice, education, the economy, the environment, health, welfare, animal rights. And that's just for starters.

Perhaps you begin to see the problem. Probably the only principles on which everybody agrees are the right of free speech and the need to air all subjects, no matter how controversial. Not at the dinner table, Miss Manners insists—unless there is a strict etiquette prevailing, which requires people to listen to one another respectfully and disagree without rancor. The dinner table (and by extension any social setting) is not the place to have highly emotional arguments that properly belong in political or academic forums.

Etiquette is against passing off as social conversation the stating of entrenched opinions that are known to be offensive to the listeners, when no true exchange of ideas is likely to result. It is against proselytizing of the sort that Miss Manners believes is known as in-your-face, whether it is to spread one's religious faith, political viewpoint, sexual practices or sexual restraints. Don't ruin everyone's supper when nothing is going to come of it, etiquette suggests.

That is the time to talk about—well, certainly not food. There used to be a ban on discussing that at the dinner table, too, on the grounds that the conversation was such an attraction that one hardly noticed what the cook had dished up. Miss Manners is reviving that ban, too. Nowadays, the subject of what is politically advisable, philosophically acceptable and sensibly healthy to eat is much too upsetting to be discussed at the table.

Offensive Objects

Dear Miss Manners,

A group of friends—mostly young childless couples with modest incomes—recently held a baby shower for a couple who announced that they were having a baby. The parents-to-be made it clear that while the baby was not sought after, it was warmly welcomed. The shower was delightful, except for one thing. The hostess gave the expectant couple a gift of condoms.

Was this merely tasteless, or offensive as well? I felt like a voyeur speculating about their bedroom activities. And I thought this suggested that the arrival of the baby was a misfortune we hoped they would have better luck avoiding next time. Finally, there was the chance that this couple, or some other guest, would find the idea of artificial contraception morally objectionable.

Gentle Reader,

You have provided Miss Manners with an interesting distinction between tastelessness and offensiveness, which, in a careless moment, she might have equated.

Tastelessness is what the prospective parents did in confiding that their child was originally not wanted. They expose themselves unpleasantly—or amusingly, depending on your attitude—but don't actually launch an offense at anyone else. (Of course, when the baby is born, and for the rest of the child's life, everyone will remember his or her being originally unwanted; it is just one of those pieces of information that sticks. So there is someone who is going to be mightily offended one day if told what everyone else knows.)

It was that tastelessness, providing others with a vivid look into these people's private habits and lapses, that prompted, but does not excuse, the teasing of their friends. Here we have genuine offensiveness, in that it is hardly possible that there won't be at least one person present at the party who will be bound to be offended. It is only too possible that the first of these will be the guests of honor themselves, who will find that what they considered a bit of charming frankness on their part is highly unamusing and intrusive when seized upon by others.

Words that Used to Be Scarce

When people who don't want to look prissy argue against the promiscuous use of profanity, they always state the case as follows: It's not that they mind strong language, of course. It certainly isn't that they are shocked by it—nothing of the sort, don't be silly. It's only that constant use of those standard curse words demonstrates a poverty of language skills. All that swearing is terrible because it just goes to show that people don't know how to express themselves forcefully.

This implies that if only the swearers would make more of an effort, they could think of all kinds of vivid and imaginative ways to insult the world and offend everyone in it. Miss Manners wishes to disassociate herself from this argument. It seems to her that people who go around cursing do express their feelings rather successfully.

Not that she is defending bad language. Goodness, gracious, no. She is just not afraid to say that the reason she objects to it is that it is plain nasty. Fortunately, Miss Manners has no objection whatever to looking prissy. On the contrary. Before she ventures forth in the morning, she makes a last minute check in the hall mirror to make sure that she is up to the prissiness standard. How embarrassing it would be if she accidentally went out seeming to be with-it.

If even Miss Manners has to listen to so much bad language that she can no longer manage to raise an eyebrow over words that used to make nice people faint dead away, something has decidedly gone wrong. This certainly kills the argument, made by people who curse for socially minded reasons, that strong words are needed to shock people out of their complacency. When Miss Manners' complacency can no longer be budged by those weary words, you may be sure that nobody's can.

If swear words were reserved for extremes of fury and alarm, they would regain their shock value. As when Miss Manners stubs her little toe and exclaims, "Drat!"—thus shocking herself so much that she claps her hand over her mouth with such force that she forgets about the pain in the toe to deal with the one in her lip.

What does still shock Miss Manners is the argument that vulgarity should be acceptable because it is the authentic language of poor people or of minorities. She can hardly think of anything more patronizing and cruel than the declaration that street talk should be the sole discourse of the poor, who would be violating their culture to learn the more sophisticated talk going on above the streets, where people make good money. Or that the ability to practice formal speech is more suitable to one race than to another, for whom it would not be "authentic."

She acknowledges that different venues, groups and occasions require different levels of talk, and what is offensive in some groups may be considered comradely in others. It is therefore necessary to be able to speak in different ways, if one wants admission to more than one type of work or social life. It is vicious to encourage others, especially children, to avoid acquiring the keys to such opportunities.

The Common Usage Argument

DEAR MISS MANNERS,

I will never, ever get used to the "F" word. It offends and sickens me. Yet when I comment on this, it seems that "it's everywhere" is the excuse to keep it going. Last year, while we were dining out at a nice waterfront restaurant, my husband had to get up and go over to a neighboring table where a group of businessmen (obviously having had too much to drink) were polluting our air with filthy language, and address the issue. They were stunned and, mercifully, quiet until we left.

GENTLE READER,

Which word is that? Never mind. Miss Manners doesn't want to hear it either. Unless we refuse to get used to it, the "it's everywhere" argument will be justified. Common usage is a powerful factor in language (although Miss Manners has been known to disallow it in etiquette, which by definition cannot incorporate crudeness) and a standard to which nobody objects may be defined as acceptable. She is therefore pleased that your husband addressed the issue, presuming he did so with polite restraint—along the lines of "I beg your pardon, but your language is shocking and offending my wife and me." To indulge in outright rudeness, even to the rude, is one of those common forms of crudeness that Miss Manners will not permit.

Euphemisms

If she can think of a delicate way to put it, Miss Manners would like to defend euphemisms. Delicacy is required because the very mention of euphemisms drives the righteous to distraction.

It always has. Dear Booth Tarkington once wrote about the fact that Victorians who were being attacked by their jaunty juniors, the Edwardians, were inevitably charged with the high crime of calling legs "limbs." It seemed to be unforgivable, even though, as he pointed out, "limbs" was generally used to refer collectively to both arms and legs. The explanation of the next generation's outrage was that Victorians found legs, even piano legs, so immediately suggestive of raw sex as to be socially unmentionable.

Miss Manners would have thought that children of a jaded age, when even the most blatant sexuality has become banal, would have only admiration for people so highly sexed as to have to protect themselves from the public excitement of hearing about piano legs. But no—euphemism itself came to be considered a sin.

Etiquette cannot do without euphemism. Society becomes less palatable when people who leave the table describe exactly what it is they are leaving to do. Even "I'm going to the bathroom" is a euphemism for what occurs in that room. (It is true that "Excuse me" is a sufficient statement of intent in this case, but Miss Manners feels sorry for gentlemen because they do not have the explanation available of absenting themselves to powder their noses. "Making a telephone call" is useless nowadays, when someone present is sure to whip a telephone out of a bag and offer it for the purpose.) How would we manage without euphemisms for being busy, so as to avoid the scrupulously honest "I'm hoping something better will turn up" or "Not if you were the last person on earth"? Neither of those explanations helps preserve the harmony of our lives. Personally, Miss Manners rather favors "That's the day I have to see a man about a horse."

We keep having to invent new euphemisms. "I'm not available right now" is now the standard euphemism on answering machines for either "You're probably a thief and I'm not going to tell you whether or not I'm at home," or "I'm not going to pick this up until I can figure out who you are from my callers' identification gadget."

Oddly enough, etiquette is on the record as being in favor of saying things in the simplest way possible. It intensely dislikes names that seem to inflate an object—"mansion" for "house," "limousine" for "car"—no matter how gross in size (or taste) the objects to which they actually refer. This is why people are apt to say that etiquette always favors direct speech. No, it doesn't. Think about it. (The common use of that very word you thought of, without regard to its actual meaning, but as a sort of reverse euphemism for "bad," is something that has always puzzled Miss Manners.)

Actually, it is one of etiquette's major missions to disguise what people mean. Not the kindly impulses, of course, but those that are likely to sicken, insult or otherwise offend others if they are not covered with a bit of polite foliage. It believes that people who go around voicing sorrow that others happen to be misinformed cause fewer etiquette problems (and live longer) than people who call one another liars.

When etiquette opposes translating "That was a good party" into "That was an elegant affair," it is trying to avoid the double etiquette problem of snootiness and the etiquette consequences of people getting a very wrong idea of what went on. A good euphemism, one that avoids letting people in on too much of an unappetizing or shocking fact, is something Miss Manners endorses heartily—after which she asks to be excused.

CAMBRIDGE, MASS.—A student who hung the Confederate flag at Harvard College's Cabot House, whipping up a storm of controversy, told the *New York Times* "that the treatment he had received at the hands of other students—including hate letters and obscene telephone calls—had gone beyond free expression."

An Example

DEAR MISS MANNERS,

Like you, I grew up in an age when underwear was worn under other clothing. I can remember my first girlfriend explaining to me that if you were in a mixed group and you noticed that one of the girls had a length of light-colored fabric depending from the hem of her basic black dress, you didn't blurt out, "Your slip's showing!" Instead, when you caught her eye, you said in as offhand a manner as you could muster, "It's snowing down south."

Not the height of sophistication, perhaps, but I like to think that my girlfriend was teaching me a lesson in manners: One does not heedlessly or needlessly embarrass somebody else.

Gentle Reader,

Unsophisticated? That you learned to think before you spoke? That you actually employed a euphemism instead of blurting out the obvious?

Ah, you make Miss Manners nostalgic for the days when such an accomplishment was not the height of sophistication.

Vulgarity as Humor

It is not Miss Manners' responsibility to instruct people in the various forms for exhibiting bad taste. This ought be one area where they could be trusted to do quite well enough on their own. But there seems to be such an interest in using bad taste as a source of comedy—and of even less entertaining forms of social commentary—and the results are so very dismal. Perhaps she had better run over the whole subject.

The number one attempted joke nowadays, among both professional humorists and amateurs, seems to be the surprise burst of vulgarity. Blatant rudeness, crude references to bodily functions (both purposeful and accidental ones) and undisguised meanness are being used constantly to jar the complacent and amuse the startled.

That is exactly why they no longer work. What is said or done in contrast to what is expected is no longer unexpected, nor is it in contrast with ordinary behavior. Mentioning the unmentionable is only possible when it customarily goes unmentioned. Overexposure has killed the joke.

Miss Manners is sorry to be forever bringing out her own agenda, but the fact is that you cannot have bad taste without good taste, so that is what people will have to relearn. There has to be a standard of taste for violating that standard to be possible, let alone amusing.

Overuse of bad taste has not only dulled people to the thrill of exposure to it but, as with profanity, created a new, lower, standard. Gauged by this standard, violations of the old standard no longer count as violations. We have been in such a downward spiral for some time now, although Miss Manners hesitates to suggest that we have reached the absolute bottom. She doesn't want to issue challenges.

What is worse, the very concept of taste, in the sense of knowing what is acceptable where and when, and of agreeing not to do or say what is offensive, is being questioned. People who do not believe that they should ever curb themselves, unless the law forces them to do so, see the mere idea of taste as threatening to liberty. What? NOT say or do something just because it might upset someone else?

What they do not take into account is that liberty is also threatened when there are no restraints of taste. Vulgarity is intrusive and people who do not wish to be exposed to it should not have to be. Not even Miss Manners would deny like-minded people the fun of having themselves a high old time, provided they are not spoiling the fun of others. This is why locker-room manners are different from drawing room manners. Long ago, there was even a distinction between the clothing properly worn in a locker room and that worn in a drawing room, but Miss Manners can hardly expect anyone to remember that.

Here, then, is a guide to the chief areas of taste, so that those who wish to violate the rules will have something to violate. There are three categories: Disgusting, Dirty and Mean. Do not bother pointing out to Miss Manners that all of these things are natural. Yes they are. The hope that we can do better than natural is what keeps her going.

The first category is where you will find bodily functions pertaining to the ingestion and elimination of food. Almost nobody wants to observe the former too closely or the latter at all. You really have to be new to bodily functions (which is to say, two years old) to find it a panic to allow things to fall out of your mouth or to explain what you are going to do on the potty. Even then, the joke depends on revealing a supposed secret, so it is first necessary to learn that it is not proper to do this all the time. Dogs using the sidewalk are not funny.

The second category has all that stuff that is beautiful to those who are actively participating. It is complicated by the fact that lovers (or individuals revealing body parts where they are not customarily aired) always believe that anyone who claims or seems to be offended is really excited and envious. The hope of exciting envy in others serves, in turn, to get them all aquiver. But cats in the alley (just to spread the comparisons around) are more apt to be amusing than exciting. The egocentrism of lovers mercifully prevents them from knowing how often the idea of doing what they are doing, with them in particular, has the opposite effect. In any case, audiences are supposed to have a choice about what they watch.

Finally, there is the category that attempts to cover viciousness with the sheep's clothing of honesty or humor. Meanness is always mean, and Miss Manners always deplores it. It depends on a general standard of kindness to be effective.

Taste—practicing self-restraint in order to shield others from seeing or hearing that which they find offensive—is essential to having a felicitous and agreeable society. For those who don't care about that as long as they are amused, Miss Manners adds that maintaining self-restraint is also the only way to allow bad taste to get an occasional laugh.

A Reply

DEAR MISS MANNERS,

Let's talk about meanness. Saying "cats in the alley are more apt to be amusing than exciting" is mean and discourteous to animal lovers and those who respect the rights of others to have animals when they themselves do not. How do you know what cats do in an alley? How do you know that it is more amusing than exciting? I know that I have more important things to do than watch cats in an alley and, frankly, someone who gets entertainment from that is "sick." Perhaps the courteous statement would have been "sex in an alley . . ."

GENTLE READER,

Good gracious! What goes on in your alley? And why aren't you doing good works instead of watching?

Miss Manners is afraid that picking quarrels with people who obviously do not mean a shred of harm to any of the world's creatures does not count as good works. It is the sort of thing that has given political correctness—which Miss Manners herself has just been busy defending as a struggle against real bigotry—a bad name.

BIGOTRY AS HUMOR

Some of the meanest social conversation there is surrounds the apparently innocent question, "Can't you take a joke?" Miss Manners is puzzled as to why those so queried seem incapable of replying, "Well, no, thank you very much anyway." Obviously, "Of course I can," no matter how resentfully murmured, constitutes permission to resume the taunting.

It seems to Miss Manners that the least you can do when your tormentor briefly suspends offensive activity in order to obtain your permission is to refuse it. To preserve a reputation for being jolly and playful, is it necessary to rollick with laughter over the idea that your own kind are stupid?

Etiquette does not require swallowing insults. Miss Manners will now deal with those who claim that she cannot have a sense of humor because restrictions on insults are killing all the possible subjects. The answer to that is: Well, pooh.

Not all humor requires skewering someone, but that which does has only two appropriate targets: oneself, and those who are positively not present. "Oneself" includes making jokes about groups to which everyone present belongs. Making jokes about people who are not present is a riskier business, as many a politician whose career went down in laughter can tell you. Someone present is bound to turn out to be a member of the targeted group, or married to one. If the joke is offensive enough, it will get repeated around, with the teller's name attached, until it gets to the ear of someone who is.

Looking for a group that doesn't mind being insulted is a silly quest, as the search for targets of dumb jokes will show. Once known as "moron jokes," these have made the ethnic rounds until they are now known as "blonde jokes," under the assumption that anyone who is blonde is so busy being happy about it as not to notice attacks. But some ladies have noticed that these jokes tend to be about blonde ladies. Anti-female jokes are not popular with ladies nowadays, in case the non-ladies have not noticed. Or rather, fewer ladies are being intimidated into being what the jokesters insist on calling "good sports," by pretending not to mind being ridiculed.

Gentlemen would be well advised to remember the nice old rule about not telling dirty jokes in mixed company unless they know the mixed part of the company well enough to be positive that there will be no offense.

In the workplace, the telling of dirty jokes must be banned entirely, as it takes on an extra offensiveness. As such jokes were traditionally told in non-mixed company, telling them in the workplace becomes a way of demonstrating—often to ladies—that the workplace is a male environment where females are outsiders. By herself accepting and even participating in this activity, the female worker acknowledges that her own workplace is rightfully male territory. Miss Manners is far from being the only lady whom this does not amuse.

Radical Bigotry

DEAR MISS MANNERS,

I am of a minority that is not usually born to wealth. I was born to a family of migrant laborers; we traveled a lot and worked out in the fields to earn our living. Despite this, we all managed to get an education and the family is well off now. My sister is a nurse, both of my brothers have responsible positions with large firms (one is

#2 man in this state for one of the better-known computer firms, if I may be allowed to brag a bit).

We all live well and our parents, who are retired, have their own home. We dress well, although not ostentatiously. All of us have positions that require a conservative appearance and so business suits are the usual wear in the day, and casual wear is on for the evenings. Except for our names and skin color, we are no different from most of the people you would meet in the course of the day.

Many people feel this is inappropriate. We are often told that we have "betrayed our heritage." Most who say that are, oddly enough, Anglos. Most have radical politics and apparently feel we should not dress well or live well if we are to have any ethnic identity.

We feel we have earned the life we have. Most of those people do not seem to know how important it can be after a day at hard labor to wash, put on clean clothes and eat a pleasant meal with the rest of the family. If they choose to be unkempt and live an unstructured lifestyle, that is their choice, but how can we tell them, in polite words, to mind their own business?

GENTLE READER,

In Miss Manners' opinion, some pretty strong words are called for. Your radical friends need to have it explained to them that poverty is not your ethnic identity. It is an insult to your heritage to assume that misfortune is its legitimate cultural expression.

Whatever political effort they wish to make ought to be devoted to helping others achieve the satisfactions and comforts that you have attained, rather than to prevent you from enjoying these. Disparaging such things is a particularly snobbish bigotry, born of the assurance that one takes them so much for granted that one can afford to despise them.

PROPER RESPONSES TO BIGOTRY

Taking Control

DEAR MISS MANNERS,

You're a rising star, black, Ivy League, at a private corporate party at the president's home, cocktail attire, with senior executives. The chief financial officer has everyone gather round and tells an off-color racial joke. After it's told, everyone turns to you and your wife standing by . . .

GENTLE READER,

. . . and you look unsmilingly around the room, finally allowing your eyes to rest on the person who told the joke. The room goes silent. Slowly, and in a conversational tone, you ask, "Do you find that amusing?" Then you allow your eyes to travel back around the room.

Here's what Miss Manners promises will happen: One person will become unfrozen and declare, "No, I don't, as a matter of fact." Immediately, the rest of the guests will fall all over themselves to show that they didn't like it, either.

Before the teller of the joke can recover enough to attempt self-defense, you say, "But I'm sure Brian didn't mean any harm by it." Then you turn to him and engage him in innocent social conversation that has nothing to do with what just happened. Against his will, he will feel grateful to you for having rescued him. The senior executives will register that you are not to be trifled with.

NORTHAMPTON, MASS.—"It's very hard to change the stereotypes that underlie prejudice. It's better to focus instead on discouraging racist acts," a Smith College psychologist told the *New York Times*.

The president will observe that you know how to be simultaneously smooth and firmly in charge. Miss Manners can't imagine that anyone could hope to get anything more out of an office party.

Taking Offense

DEAR MISS MANNERS,

I don't know how to respond to accusations concerning America's obvious racial and social inequities without condoning or excusing them. Would it be rude to ask how Turks, Algerians or whoever, are treated in the accusers' own countries, or should I be silent and graciously accept characterizations of America as the Great Satan?

GENTLE READER,

We Americans are in something of an etiquette bind when listening to complaints about America from people who, as both you and Miss Manners suspect, would declare war if we even seemed to question the perfection of their own societies. The difficulty is that our fair-mindedness, openness and good nature are major points of

American pride. Thus to claim that everything here is perfect, or to refuse to listen to criticism, or to go into a high fury over it, would be . . . well, sort of un-American. It is much more our style to admit that we have problems, while bringing into the discussion—politely and purely for the sake of fairness—the universality of such problems and the compensating virtues that we do have.

However, good manners have never required accepting outright bigotry. If the conversation is not a reasonable discussion, but an excuse for invectives, you would do well to announce that you will not allow your country to be insulted.

Responding Defensively

DEAR MISS MANNERS,

Upon return from vacation, I went grocery shopping to replenish the family cupboard. I decided to use the remaining traveler's checks to pay the bill and, to speed things up at the check-out line, signed them ahead of time. Behind me in line was a retirement-age woman who became impatient and said loudly, "What's the hold-up here?" She and her younger male companion became fixated on the amount of food I was buying and made loud comments—"Wow! Look at that!" "Well, I guess that's why she needs so many checks"—and finally he said, "Be glad that's not your order—it came to almost $200!"

She replied gruffly, "Well, you know, THEY get more than I do." He replied sheepishly, "Well, you know, you gotta eat."

Did I fail to mention that I am a young African-American woman and the people behind me were white? It suddenly occurred to me that they assumed that I was using food stamps to buy (heaven forbid!) a whole lot of food. Unable to restrain myself, I turned and said frostily, "I work very hard to make the money that I get." They were silent for the remaining time it took to complete the transaction. I thanked the cashier profusely for her hard work, bid her a nice day, and then turned to the people behind me and said, "And you have a nice day, too." My regret is that I may have implied that people who are eligible for food stamps do not work hard. Did I overreact or did I do the right thing?

GENTLE READER,

You remained within the bounds of politeness while allowing some appalling people to know that their rudeness is not without consequences. So Miss Manners finds herself in basic approval of your action.

Yet she shares your misgivings about your statement to them and has other misgivings of her own. By defending yourself, you not only inadvertently slurred those who do use food stamps, but you accepted the basic premise of the offender: that she had reason to be annoyed and to voice her annoyance. What food you buy and how you pay for it is so thoroughly not the business of the person in line behind you (presuming you were not in the express lane with eleven items) that to defend yourself is to agree that you need a defense. Also, it assumes that you can appeal to prejudiced people through reason, which is unlikely. Such a bigot could discover that you were the mayor of the city and still salvage her malevolence by telling herself you only got your job through unfair advantage.

Nevertheless, Miss Manners cannot but admire your success and the polite way you capped it off. She would have been more grateful to the cashier had that person coldly (yet also within the bounds of politeness) inquired of those next in line whether they had any objection to her checking out the customers' purchases in proper order.

Responding Softly

DEAR MISS MANNERS,

As a customer service representative for a distribution company, I deal with my customers by telephone only. While waiting for some information on an account, I stalled for time with small talk, asking this woman how she liked where she lived. She said she had lived there all her life, 60 years, but that it was being taken over. I of course asked by who, and she replied, "by wetbacks."

Shock was my first reaction. I am half Mexican on my mother's side and my self-respect, as well as my respect for my mother's heritage, could have made me react in a number of ways. But I chose to ask innocent, subtle questions: "Oh, really? Have they taken a lot of jobs away from the area?"

She replied, "Oh, mostly farm jobs, because they're willing to work for the cheapest wages."

I reiterated, in a neutral tone, "Oh, and does that take away a large part of the job market from your community?"

She then transformed the topic into one of welfare and jobs and her racial comment faded into the woodwork.

After I hung up, I felt disgust for this woman—not for her obvious ignorance, but for her negligence in not thinking of who she might be speaking to. I'm not telling her how to think and feel, just who she shares her opinions with. She had no idea who I was. Some co-workers said they would have belittled her by mentioning I was Mexican. I, however, was only thinking about the fact that regardless of my feelings, she was still a customer, therefore I didn't feel that I was in a position to do that.

GENTLE READER,

Although everyone would appreciate your feelings in reaction to such bigotry, fewer people would appreciate, as Miss Manners does, the delicacy of your feeling that you could not humiliate a customer. Whatever small talk you engage in should be neutral and you strictly observed the limits even when your customer outrageously violated them.

Yes Miss Manners is no more satisfied than you with letting such an insult pass. Her suggestion is to maintain the professional role while nevertheless mentioning your ancestry—something along the lines of "Well, we Mexican-Americans try to do our jobs well and I hope you feel I am doing mine." While it would not belittle the customer, Miss Manners feels it would, at the least, prevent her from repeating her mistake and might actually lead her to question her prejudices.

Responding in a Saintly Fashion

DEAR MISS MANNERS,

When I was young and foolish (over 21, but still foolish) I said to a man of another race something—just what, I have forgotten—ignorant and embarrassingly racist, and I said it loud and clear.

He said, exactly as a man whose mind has just wandered, "What?"

Foolish me, I repeated what I'd said.

He said, "I'm sorry, I still didn't get that," still with positive interest and attention in his voice, as if he really wanted to hear this important thing.

As I was about to repeat it again, I heard what I was saying and said something like "Oh, nothing," and the whole incident never came up again, which was good because with a mutual friend the three of us were just heading out on an all-day fishing trip.

This polite man, instead of attacking me, putting me down or rising to the defense of his race, allowed us to have a beautiful day together. What he did was take the attitude of: I like you, you like me, you have interesting things to say, it sounded like you said something awful, but that's way beneath who you are, so I must have mis-understood you, so what actually was this fine remark you were making—no, that's what I thought I heard before, that still can't be it, so what is it? Well, he thought better of it, I'll let it go.

I've never made as awkward a remark since. He just showed me the standard he would have me at, and waited till I got to it. Now that's manners.

I agree with you that you shouldn't say, "Shut up, you lousy lunk," but your freezing politeness sounds more similar to that than distinct. They are both intended to make the other person feel bad. They both say, "You are of lower social status than myself." They are both going to make future relaxed, friendly conversation difficult. They both have revenge at heart. How can revenge be good manners?

Gentle Reader,

In spite of your gentle rebuke, Miss Manners is flattered that you consider manners to be the saintly refusal to respond to extreme provocation. The example you give is a model of wise restraint, and it worked. She would be delighted to hear of others following it. One can hardly ask for anything better than that. However, she has been concentrating on pleading for just something better than the worst behavior. Frankly, she would be happy if people would only stop striking back, literally or rudely, even to mild or accidental provocation.

Manners do permit defending one's own dignity and the chilling response you condemn is within correct bounds. It does not require someone who is insulted to take upon himself the burden of cajoling the rude person into better behavior—although it admires those who do. Miss Manners begs to differ with you about the importance of how one says something unflattering. For example, your letter to her is faultlessly polite, although its meaning at heart, as you would say, is no different than if you had written, "Hey, you don't know what you're talking about."

Teaching Children How to React

Dear Miss Manners,

When my wife and I visit some of our relatives, we are put off by their prejudices, which border on bigotry. We know everyone has prejudices, as we do. We have learned to manage and control our own. We want our children to grow up with as few prejudices as possible. We are afraid that upon hearing our relatives, whom we teach our children to respect, they will adopt their prejudices. Our children are young and do not understand why people act as they do.

Is it right to ask them to refrain from the espousing of prejudiced and bigoted views and, in some cases, profanity while we are guests at their home? We are careful to have our children leave the room if the conversation turns, shall we say, sour. But it seems ridiculous to go through this.

GENTLE READER,

Nobody ever said that child-rearing was easy, and Miss Manners would like to remind you that the teaching of ethics is one of its most complex tasks. We all begin with simple rules, only to discover that almost any rules can have valid exceptions, or be in conflict with another, equally valid rule.

"Like the violence they resemble, racial epithets are not a legitimate part of the discourse at a university. They promote inarticulate rage or, worse, crushed silence, rather than free exchange or open debate," wrote a Stanford University law professor in a letter to the editor of the *New York Times*.

Take "respect your elders." Does that mean that a child should obey the commands of a strange adult? Or "Don't lie"—does that mean that a child can deliver honestly held but deeply wounding opinions to others? As much as Miss Manners admires your objectives, she does not believe that you can successfully protect your children from hearing repugnant ideas from others. So what do we do with a perplexing situation in which two moral imperatives are in conflict?

We call it a learning experience. You need to have a talk with your children about the unfortunate prejudices of others and how one sometimes has to learn to value people for their virtues in spite of their failings. Because bigotry in non-relatives is enough to condemn people, it will be a complicated lesson. A lot of explaining, and a lot of repetition, will be required. But, then, nobody ever said . . .

RUDENESS IN THE NAME OF DIVERSITY

It's amazing how many different etiquette traditions there are in the world, all of which are designed to allow the person practicing them to ride roughshod over the feelings of others. Miss Manners knows this because every time she slams a widespread practice for being greedy, inconsiderate or vulgar, she is told she is culturally insensitive.

"You don't understand," she will be told. "Among my people, it is traditional to shake down the guests." Or "We have a proud custom of pilfering from our hosts." Well, no, they don't quite put it that way. But ringing defenses of methods for collecting money in return for hospitality, and plundering food and flowers during parties for later use are routinely offered in the name of multiculturalism.

Then there is the Spring Break Defense (which grown-ups in otherwise disciplined professions, such as the military and the police, have also been known to invoke), which is used to explain the time-honored custom of being a public menace: "That's just the way we've always let off steam—going totally wild that week, doing fun stuff like mooning, groping, throwing up, destroying property. It's a tradition."

Even criminal behavior has been cited as an expression of cultural authenticity. (Miss Manners isn't responsible for those awful expressions.) A student who committed armed robbery in his hometown during vacation pleaded that he did it to prove that despite attending an Ivy League school, he was still loyal to his roots. Public drunkenness that culminated in a neighborhood riot was defended as valid within the tradition of the immigrants involved, although the detail that it is not tolerated in their countries of origin, nor by these traditionalists' own wives and children, was omitted.

Because etiquette is wildly fond of tradition, all these arguments are supposed to stab Miss Manners to the heart. They miss.

These people don't know their own cultural traditions or professional regulations. The customs they are trying to dignify turn out to be pesky habits or major nuisances that their own people have been trying for years to stamp out. What an insult it is to any society to claim that it has an obnoxious cultural heritage requiring some of its members to disregard the interests of some of its other members.

Such a thing is not totally unknown, Miss Manners admits. "Sure, we've always pinched women in the streets. They love it. If they didn't, why would they go out of the house?" Well, if people have been behaving disgustingly for centuries, then it's time they changed. It is a miscalculation to count on etiquette's being mindlessly mired in the past to the point of considering everything ancient to be hallowed. Miss Manners isn't quite so tradition-bedazzled that she can't tell a valid ritual from a history of having gotten away with murder.

All this not only defies etiquette and defiles rugs, but obscures legitimate multicultural questions: Which genuine tradition of etiquette should be followed by whom and when? Why should Americans, with their varied backgrounds, follow an English-based etiquette rather than their family heritage?

The answer is that both have claims and it is possible to honor both. Many Americans speak both English and their ancestral language. No society can operate without a common language of etiquette. Being able to interpret the intentions of strangers and to follow patterns that they will recognize is an essential skill of civilized life. Aren't there enough people running around asking suspiciously, "And just what did you mean by that?"

We use the English-based system, as we speak English, for historical reasons. It should not be overlooked, however, that the American version has its own highly honorable history. The same people who wrote our Constitution did a lot of work altering the prevailing etiquette so that it would better express American egalitarianism. Equal respect—for example, the custom of using the same honorific for the highest dignitaries as for every other citizen—was a decidedly novel touch.

Society-wide etiquette is only the beginning. Everybody knows other traditions—regional customs, generational ones, special occasion ones, job expectations and the little rituals of one's own family. Those who also know the customs of their ancestors are especially well endowed. The overriding requirements of a polite person from any culture or subculture are:

- To have the sense to use the appropriate forms at the appropriate time and occasion.
- To have the delicacy to avoid using specialized customs—whether hoity-toity or high school—to embarrass or confuse people who can't be expected to know them.
- Not to have the gall to try to pass off nasty tricks as cultural tradition, especially not to Miss Manners.

MULTICULTURAL MUDDLES

Misidentification

DEAR MISS MANNERS,

My problem seems to have its roots in a clash between African-American culture and the South Asian traditions of my ancestry. I was born in Washington, D.C., but my parents came from Sri Lanka, so I am as dark as most African-Americans and speak fluent English.

There appears to be an unwritten rule, at least at my place of work, that all African-Americans are expected to acknowledge other African-Americans, whether friend or complete stranger, when they pass through the halls. This structure does not appear to apply to white people or East Asians. Colored persons who do not walk around saying "Hi" and "How're you doing" nonstop are labeled as either "acting white" or stuck up, or both.

By nature, as well as by culture and training, I am rather reserved and was taught that it was impolite to speak to strangers unless one is spoken to. Besides, I enjoy walking through the halls thinking my own thoughts, instead of engaging in active social intercourse. If a complete stranger jerks me out of my reverie, I give them a quick mechanical smile and a quick "Hi" back, but I do not initiate the conversation and I make no effort to prolong it. The feedback I have gotten from my African-American friends and co-workers (whom I do acknowledge, since after all, I know them) is that I am considered quite rude by other African-Americans—but not by these friends, or by the white people in my work place.

GENTLE READER,

Removed from its racial and ethnic implications, your question would simply be "Some people in my office building are in the habit of greeting strangers in the hallways and when I don't banter with people I don't know, I'm considered snobbish."

Miss Manners realizes that she has removed the main thesis of your question, which is seething with racial and ethnic implications. Bear with her for a minute and she'll get back to that. The answer to the problem, the way Miss Manners posed it, is that it won't kill you to exchange friendly greetings. These people are not total strangers, whose overtures might seem threatening—they work in the same building and you must keep seeing the same faces over and over. How nice that they are acknowledging others courteously. All right, they are breaking into your reverie. But if you got the day off and went up a mountain in order to think your thoughts in peace, you would encounter the hiking etiquette by which strangers greet one another in passing. This is an old custom that does not seem to destroy the relative solitude and serenity.

Now let's get back to your account of the problem, by which you were racially misidentified, and then unfairly taxed with not following the etiquette of a social subgroup, when to do so would actually violate your own cultural heritage. That's a far nastier problem, isn't it?

BETHESDA, MD.—A Korean youth was severely beaten after describing a disfigured older Korean in what the older man considered disrespectful and insulting terms. The youth had apparently been hunted down by the disfigured man and two others in what police told the *Washington Post* they believe was an effort to teach the young man to respect his elders, an important tenet of Korean culture.

That's why Miss Manners wants to avoid it. It's also why she thinks everyone else ought to be able to avoid such problems. There are a number of them around and they create enormous amounts of ill will and hostility. America houses many cultures and many mixtures within those cultures. One could postulate your question on behalf of someone who had one Sri Lankan grandparent, one African-American one, one native American, and one Irish one, who was also Jewish. But this person was brought up in Mexico and later attended a British university. What etiquette should she follow?

The answer, if the person is in the United States, is that she can follow whichever she likes when strictly among people who share and understand it. In the greater society, she follows the overriding American etiquette. Similarly, many an American speaks another language at home, but uses English for everyday life in the outside world.

In American etiquette, a friendly greeting in a common hallway is reciprocated in a friendly way. That is what you should do. Should you fall into conversation with some of these people, all the better. When they learn that you are not African-American and are therefore responding to American friendliness rather than to an in-group signal, they, too, may come to reflect that courtesy contributes more to a pleasant atmosphere than daily heritage-identification.

By the way, "How're you doing?" Miss Manners takes the liberty of breaking into your thoughts with this inquiry on the grounds that she was born in Washington, too.

Identification Questions

DEAR MISS MANNERS,

Is it acceptable to use race or ethnic group as a form of physical identification?

A friend was telling me (a white woman doing undergraduate work in a field where women are rare and non-Caucasians of either sex are even rarer) which of the 48 women in the college she had been studying with. She described her height, weight, hairstyle, typical clothing and so on, but I continued to be confused.

Finally I asked, "Do you mean the [only] black woman?"

My friend (a white woman) said yes, but averted her eyes, as if I had committed a faux pas. Since we were not saying anything bad nor stereotypical about this woman, I could see nothing wrong with using as identification her most obvious physical distinction from the rest. Is there any reason not to use it?

GENTLE READER,

Your field may not be history or anthropology, but you may be interested, anyway, to learn that apparently illogical customs become less baffling when one knows their history. (Or you may not be. Miss Manners is always left out of the fun when innocent moderns have a terrific giggle over Victorian circumlocutions, because she unfortunately understands their original purpose.)

Not all that long ago, a habit opposite to the one you describe was common. Race, color and gender were used as the first and often only means of identification, any deviation from the presumed normality of being white and male being considered amazingly conspicuous. The implication was that this person stood out because he or she was really rather out of place.

This way of talking—"See that black gal up front?" "You mean the presiding judge?"—was so racist in its presumption that society finally got around to recognizing how rude it was.

You may well argue that avoiding any such mention, when it obviously is a conspicuous identifying characteristic, is also racist. If race weren't so much on your friend's mind, she wouldn't be going that far out of her way to avoid mentioning it when offering a physical description.

Presumably, if she came looking for you among all those male colleagues, she wouldn't ask a passerby if he had seen "the student in the checked shirt and black jeans" without supplying the clue that you were also the only female there.

But at least her intention was to steer herself away from exhibiting racism. Miss Manners is a lot more lenient on the stiltedness of people with good motivations than she is on the relaxed rudeness of people who don't care.

One of these days, the world may get used to the fact that there is a wide variety of people around. It's been an awfully long time in coming and personally Miss Manners can't wait.

The Prevailing Etiquette

DEAR MISS MANNERS,

When I encounter the manners of Japanese friends, I feel like an Ugly American in my own country! For example, I found out that Japanese courtesy requires that an invitation be declined three times before being accepted. I think I damaged my friendship with a Japanese woman (living here temporarily) by jumping at her gracious invitations and never persuading her to accept mine.

Also, my Japanese friends find ways to give me gifts when they visit me. The timing and selection of these gifts are mysteries to me. Should I continue in my luggish Western ways or try to reciprocate in kind? How about when I visit people in Japan (in-laws and friends)?

GENTLE READER,

It is not only because she is a pedant that Miss Manners reminds you that the title character of *The Ugly American* was a wonderful man who only sought to help the foreigners among whom he lived. The nickname inspired by his appearance has been used ever since to describe Americans who behave arrogantly overseas, which is the opposite of what he did.

Miss Manners' point is that one need not be ashamed of American behavior, which, at its best, is free, generous and dignified. Japanese manners are more elaborate than American, but Miss Manners does not concede that they (still less aristocratic European manners, which too many Americans admire excessively) are better. In any case, this is not a contest. Your Japanese friends and in-laws understand that there is a cultural difference and should be as interested in understanding our manners as you should be in understanding theirs.

The manners of the country one is in generally prevail, although neither you nor your friends will be able to mimic the other country's behavior perfectly. An attempt to learn what is proper, including asking questions, is considered sufficient evidence of good will. Incidentally, Miss Manners is counting on you tactfully to tell your friend here, before she finds herself in social isolation, that urging invitations after they have been declined is considered intrusive in America and quick acceptance is flattering.

The Prevailing Language

DEAR MISS MANNERS,

Is there any rule of etiquette that, if you're from a foreign country, you have to learn to speak the language of the nation you live in? I have lived in Chicago for 36 years and seen my neighborhood change. Not that the neighbors who moved in have not taken care of their property—they do. It's still a quiet place to live.

My problem is that none of them speak English. I am a friendly person. I like to know my neighbors and help when needed. I don't speak any other language. I don't feel I should have to. This is America and English is our language. I feel like a stranger in my neighborhood. I mean no harm, but isn't it considered good manners to speak English in front of others?

Years ago, my friend spoke her native language only at home, or when all of the people spoke that language, but spoke English where there was a person who spoke only English. They were considerate. What ever happened?

GENTLE READER,

A good thing happened, in that people began to take pride in their backgrounds instead of being ashamed of being immigrants. Then a typically American thing happened: They got so excited with a novel social idea that they went tearing off after it, leaving everything else behind and not looking where they were going.

What has been lost in this dash is that people also have to be able to understand those among whom they live or they will suffer the unpleasant and dangerous consequences of misunderstanding one another. Your case is a poignant one. You only want to be friendly and helpful to your neighbors, but you can't talk to them.

Miss Manners is not going to tell you, as some enthusiasts might, what a rich opportunity it is for you to learn their languages. She does not think it an unimportant point that you all happen to be living in the United States. Politeness, for you as the native—or, for all Miss Manners knows, a less recent arrival—consists of your interest and receptivity to being friends.

You are quite right that etiquette requires people to attempt to speak the language of the country they are in. Even short-term tourists are expected to muster a few words. Immigrants are politely accorded lots of tolerance—time to learn, patient attempts to understand their efforts, exceptions for the very elderly—but they are expected to try.

Other Languages

DEAR MISS MANNERS,

I am becoming annoyed at people who whilst in my company wish to start speaking another language to a third party when I know the third party speaks English.

The other day I was in a bank whose neighborhood was predominantly of Chinese-speaking people. Everyone in that bank was speaking Chinese, even staff to staff. Who ever said that racism is a thing that only white people do?

GENTLE READER,

It can't be a language problem, but Miss Manners is afraid she doesn't understand you. How could it be racist for people to speak another language among themselves if they are not either addressing you or deliberately excluding you from a conversation?

When Miss Manners argues for the need of a society to have a common language (she is usually referring to a common language of behavior), she never meant to discourage multilingualism. Please don't burst in and break up Miss Manners' Italian class. People speaking among themselves may speak whatever they wish, no matter how many languages they have available. It only becomes insulting when there is someone who ought to be a party to the conversation but can't because of the language barrier. Had your bank teller addressed you in Chinese, it would have been a violation of etiquette. If you are overhearing the bank staff talking to one another, the etiquette error is eavesdropping.

RELIGIOUS DIFFERENCES

Christmas and Hanukkah

How do you politely disassociate yourself from someone else's holiday merrymaking? The immediate question came up in connection with Hanukkah. One of Miss Manners' Gentle Readers, who identifies himself as the only non-Jewish employee at a small, family-run company, is troubled about how to handle the Hanukkah wishes, cards and presents he has been receiving from clients.

"Should I return the gifts and explain that I am not Jewish? Should I just remain quiet? Was I incorrect in not indicating that I wasn't Jewish when I was first told 'Happy Hanukkah,' etc.? I didn't, because I would have felt awkward stating my religious background to business acquaintances. Were the customers incorrect in assuming what my faith was without making inquiries? Is it appropriate to inquire about a business or casual acquaintance's religion?"

This is a reversal of a problem common to all Jews and others, non-Christian and Christian, who do not celebrate Christmas. How do you refrain from appearing to participate in a religion not your own while not seeming to reject the spirit that motivates holiday wishes and gestures? A number of Miss Manners' Gentle Readers have pointed out that the etiquette error lies in the promiscuous, nearly universal—and therefore often inappropriate—offering of Christmas greetings, cards, inquiries and presents.

"How can I remind the store clerks, receptionists, etc., who wish me a Merry Christmas that America is not a Christian country—without destroying the good will they intend?" asks another Gentle Reader. "I have tried saying, 'I don't celebrate Christmas,' and found that I get a confused or sour look that makes me feel mean-spirited. Answering 'Happy Hanukkah to you' seems petty."

Another Gentle Reader reports, "To some—friends, co-workers, acquaintances, neighbors, merchants—who inquire as to my Christmas plans, I truthfully and simply reply that not being Christian, I don't celebrate Christmas, but I hope that their holiday will be joyful—to which I often get a sympathetic, close-to-pitying look, and in one instance, disbelief."

Still another writes: "When co-workers ask such questions as 'Are your kids getting excited about Christmas?' or 'Have you finished your Christmas shopping yet?,' I don't want to embarrass them by indicating that I don't celebrate the holiday, which causes them to think that my feelings might have been hurt. But I don't want to suggest, 'No, my kids are getting excited about Hanukkah,' because Hanukkah is not a substitute for Christmas, just a holiday that occurs about the same time."

Miss Manners is pleased to note that each of these complaints contains a wish to spare the feelings of those who, carelessly but not unkindly, caused the problem. The Inquisition attitude of being mean to others as an act of devotion has never appealed to her.

Many of the traditions that have grown up around Christmas are, at best, tenuously related to religion. The exchange of presents and invitations among business acquaintances, in which good will is so heavily laced with the hope for commercial advantage as to be nearly unrecognizable, does not strike Miss Manners as religiously motivated. Simple greetings or inquiries seem to her to be no more related to religious affirmations or inquiries than "How are you?" is to a medical examination.

American Jews have a wide variety of approaches to the fact that Christmas celebrations are nearly ubiquitous in this country, from total nonparticipation to partial participation in the nonreligious aspects, to the adaptation of Christmas customs to Hanukkah (such as the sending of Hanukkah cards). The separate-but-equal approach of attaching the Christmas customs to Hanukkah is not, in Miss Manners' opinion, a solution. The customs could be easily separated from any religious implications, as they are in cards that offer greetings of the season, or inquiries that treat the holidays as vacation or family time.

Even when the connection to Christmas or Hanukkah is stated, it seems obvious that wishes and tokens from strangers are merely conventional expressions of good will. It is hardly necessary to reject them; letting them pass, with an ecumenical return wish, is all that is called for. This is an approximation of the rule about correct practice when a foreign national anthem is played: Stand, but don't sing.

People with whom one has personal ties are something else. Then a gracious acceptance of the good wishes should be supplemented with an explanation that this is not actually one of your holidays. Rather than being deflated, someone with an interest in you should be pleased and flattered to be learning more about you.

Dietary Laws

DEAR MISS MANNERS,

When I was invited out to lunch by my boss and his wife, a fairly rare occasion, I ordered the ham. Shortly afterwards, I wondered if I'd committed a faux pas. See, my boss and his wife are Jewish, and never eat pork of any kind. I thanked them for lunch, but I feel as though that might not be enough. Was what I did wrong? If so, how can I atone for my actions?

Gentle Reader,

What exactly is it you feel guilty about? You are presumably not Jewish, or if you are, you do not believe in keeping kosher, and yet you are looking for atonement because you ate ham?

Wait just a minute while Miss Manners tries to find you the name of a good Talmudic scholar.

If the question is only whether you have insulted your boss and his wife by eating ham in their presence, the answer is no. Had you tried to serve them ham, it would have been offensive, but at a restaurant, you are not required to follow the dietary laws observed by your companions. If that is your only problem, Miss Manners can handle it alone.

Saying Grace

Dear Miss Manners,

Is it appropriate to have grace said at a dinner party where the guests are of mixed faiths? I say it should be reserved for family or religious occasions. Could you enlighten us?

Gentle Reader,

There is nothing wrong with saying grace at any meal, provided one does not follow it by a sermon. Those of another faith or custom may merely observe a respectful silence.

Proselytizing

Dear Miss Manners,

I am not a religious person—I simply do not believe in any traditional definition of God—but I have relatives and friends who often refer to their religious practices and beliefs in letters and personal conversation. I simply keep silent and let them have their say.

That works until someone asks me if I agree with them, or what I believe personally. In an effort to be politely "neutral" and to close further discussion, I usually reply, "I believe differently" or, more bluntly, "I am not religious." What do I say when these responses do not end the discussion?

Gentle Reader,

That the discussion has come to an end anyway. No one is obliged to open personal beliefs for debate, and the attempt seems to offend as many people who are religious as who are not.

Miss Manners has noticed an increasing failure in general to pick up on polite conversation-enders. No matter how many times you say on the telephone, "Well, it was great talking to you," some people go right on talking. So although your remarks ought to have done the job, you will have to move to the next level.

Try "Oh, it's not something I ever discuss. Did you watch the game yesterday?" This is a double—not only the outright statement that you will not discuss the topic, but the insistence on a new topic, if friendly conversation is to continue. If it doesn't work, come back. Miss Manners has several such levels, in the hope that no one will be driven off the politeness scale entirely to saying "Mind your own business."

Discreet Prayer

Dear Miss Manners,

It is my custom to kneel and pray each morning and evening. This very personal activity gives me a great deal of comfort. When traveling and sharing a hotel room, how should I go about my daily prayer routine? It is not that I am embarrassed by my beliefs—I ask out of concern so as not to make my companion uncomfortable.

Gentle Reader,

It would indeed be tactful to mention when you will be saying your prayers, so that your hotel roommate can avoid inadvertent intrusion. Miss Manners is, however, puzzled that you thought she might take your wanting privacy as embarrassment about your beliefs. Real embarrassment is asking "What?" only to discover that the person you thought had addressed you was addressing God.

Chapter Twelve

THE UNAUTHORIZED REINVENTION
OF ETIQUETTE

Why don't all those people who oppose and ridicule etiquette just stop practicing it? That's what they claim they want. Miss Manners would prefer that they practice good manners, but she would be willing to settle for a compromise. Here's the deal: If only they would stop practicing bad manners, she would absolve them from having to practice good ones.

They have refused to accept her terms. The catch is that they have to move out back, to the hermitage, and never reappear, even for a visit.

Sweet-tempered Miss Manners is not being vengeful. It is just that it is impossible to live among other people without using the language of social behavior. Like dear Molière's Monsieur Jourdain, who discovered that he had been speaking prose for forty years without knowing it, the opponents of etiquette have been practicing a form of etiquette, if disastrously, because they cannot get along without doing so.

Miss Manners would feel vindicated when people who have tried to live without etiquette go to the trouble of reinventing etiquette, if she didn't have to spend so much of her time cleaning up the messes they make. They may not intend to make trouble, but omitting the duties of etiquette or improvising their own etiquette keeps causing trouble. Most have not thought through the consequences of what they are saying and doing, but even the finest idiosyncratic system would be subject to constant misinterpretation. She apologizes for being so peevish about it, but reinvented etiquette is not going over with those on whom it is practiced.

THREE BAD MODELS FOR REINVENTING ETIQUETTE

I. THERAPY

Consider all the professional help now available for an ever-expanding definition of psychological trouble, the plethora of support groups for increasingly specialized emotional injuries and the number of freelance proselytizers available everywhere to tout new therapies at the first declaration of emotional faltering. So—does everyone have a comfy shoulder to cry on?

Miss Manners gathers not. The professionalization of sympathy does not seem to have stilled the cries of complaint. Far from being comforted to the point of subsiding back into the normal state in which most of us accept, more or less with equanimity, the vicissitudes of life, the complainers sound worse off than ever. How often does one meet anyone nowadays who doesn't voice some sort of a grudge against life?

If Miss Manners were cynical, she would suspect that everyone concerned is making a career of misery, victims as well as helpers. She does not harbor such a rude thought. She is willing to believe that people have problems and others are trying to help them. The difficulty, she is beginning to believe, is exactly that trained assistance of one kind or another has driven the amateur comforter off the scene.

Amateurs would say soothing things such as: "That really was tough luck." "Is there anything I can do to help?" "You found a rotten apple, but they're not all like that." And best of all, "There, there." Nobody knew what any of this meant, but it sounded comforting.

One doesn't hear that sort of thing much anymore. Even traditional comfort-givers—relatives and intimate friends—are apt to say, "Give yourself permission to be angry" and "You have to stop trying to please everyone else and learn to satisfy the child within."

It is not as much of a comfort as it might seem to bring one's troubles to someone who takes the position of knowing all the answers to the eternal problems of life, with which humanity has struggled since the world began. Some people so blessed with knowing the answers have even been known to employ rude, bullying tactics to encourage confessions and the beliefs and changes they endorse. When the paraprofessional providers of cold comfort get annoyed by finding that it doesn't immediately perk up the afflicted, they recommend professional help or support groups. However kindly intended, this could also be interpreted to mean: "Oh, stop bothering me; go get someone who is paid to listen, or who is just as badly off as you are."

Miss Manners sees three dangers in turning over to specialists etiquette's everyday job of giving out consolation, whether those specialists are professionals or amateurs who have picked up the lingo.

One is that a problem has to be of some importance before one can justify spending great quantities of time and money for expertise in solving it. There is therefore a temptation to inflate a minor affliction to make it worthy of such attention. One can end up convincing oneself that things are worse than they are.

The second is that the cures, which are developed to confront major barriers to normality, almost invariably involve the anti-etiquette habit of focusing on the self. The troubled person is then advised to "work it through" by coming up with an unfortunate habit, which is harder to deal with than isolated examples of bad luck. Scant attention is given to the best-known folk cure for the blues—focusing on the troubles of others.

This brings Miss Manners to the third and worst aspect of the situation. In the medical model, the troubled person is excused on grounds of inability from trying to help others. In a polite world such exemptions should be given only in acknowledgment of severe handicaps. The rest of us who are experiencing the human plight should be helping one another, not by giving advice so much as by expressing sympathy.

Unfortunate Side-Effects

Making Friendship Impossible

Dear Miss Manners,

Two former friends would still be friends were it not for their pseudo-psychoanalytical approach to friendship. They remain friends with each other, which is nice for them. Any time conflict or problems arose, each would confront me in a so-called honest manner in order, they would each claim, to resolve the problem openly. (The husband of one of them claims this approach is merely an excuse to say whatever one pleases!) When I tried this method on them, each interpreted my openness and honesty as hostility—quite correctly.

I would like to extend tolerance for friends' human foibles, but I find it difficult to be tolerant when I am questioned for doing the same thing. I also resent not being allowed the time-honored custom they call "distancing"—stepping back for a while and letting time callous the rough spots in a friendship—without being expected to say why in great and gory detail. No face-saving excuse was ever permitted with these two.

I am not against sincerity and honesty, and I do think that psychoanalysis is one of the great advances of the 20th century. I object, however, to the application of its style, best left on the couch, by practitioners who were (and are) patients, not professionals. It is a shame to cut off friendships so coldly. I find the whole thing an object lesson in the social value of repression—another psychological term!

Following a *New York Times Magazine* article about a restaurant chain accused of racism and discrimination against customers, a letter to the editor commented on a new requirement that employees of the chain watch a 16-minute videotape about diversity and that managers must attend sensitivity seminars. This "perfectly illustrates how the therapeutic mentality infests everything nowadays. It would be more effective and less presumptuous . . . to enforce clear policies against racist behavior rather than to invade the psychic privacy of employees by requiring them to attend sensitivity seminars."

Gentle Reader,

Miss Manners hopes that your erstwhile friends will recover, not only from whatever afflictions sent them into psychoanalysis in the first place, but from the common side-effect you describe. The belief that undergoing treatment entitles one to practice the healing arts while skipping such preliminaries as education, certification and the formal establishment of the doctor-patient relationship, has become a social menace of epidemic proportions.

As you have sadly discovered, it is impossible to be friends with someone who only wants to play doctor. Miss Manners is afraid that the technique of putting a friendship on hold, without making accusations that would lead to a formal break—what they call "distancing"—is exactly what is necessary.

Discouraging Romance

Dear Miss Manners,

A bachelor's life is never dull in today's society, when polite conversation is turned upside down on a first date. I accepted a dinner invitation from a woman who works with some of my business associates. I had only spoken to her briefly at two business-related gatherings, so I really was not prepared to hear all about her numerous personal problems on our first date. I soon learned that she has led a most disturbing life but things were going to be better in the near future, as she had signed up at a weight reduction center. She went into great detail about her weight problem but unless she wears some kind of new miracle girdle to hide her girth, she did not appear to be overweight.

I tried to change the subject by praising her commitment to tackling personal challenges, but that opened a Pandora's box and out popped sad anecdotes about her broken family, her financial woes and other matters which most people save for talks with ministers or therapists. Please, Miss Manners, can you recommend any tactics to steer first date conversations in the direction of such subjects as films, books and hobbies? Although I will not be dating this woman again, this might come in handy for her next conquest.

Gentle Reader,

Lean forward, look deep into her eyes, and say, "But enough about me—tell me about yourself." Miss Manners offers this suggestion with the desperate hope that it might stun the lady into momentary confusion, during which she will be blessedly quiet. There is little hope of effecting a longer cure for a determined bore.

And a bore, plain and simple, is what this lady is. Promiscuous whining is more widespread than it used to be but bores have always been with us, even though they were more inclined to brag and go for admiration, rather than pity. The effect is the same. People who talk incessantly about themselves are no fun. Miss Manners congratulates you for not harboring the kindly but mistaken belief that being the victim of such a bore somehow serves the cause of mental health.

Discouraging Churchgoing

Dear Miss Manners,

A form of "instant intimacy" I find annoying is the hugging and kissing which goes on in most churches when they pass the peace. This action has driven my husband and children out of the church. This form of intimacy is reserved for my family and occasionally for a good friend I haven't seen in a while. It is interesting to note that the parishioners I'm best acquainted with only shake my hand. The ministry believes this action will break down the barriers between people, that it is impossible to remain unacquainted with people you hug. Nuts! If I want to know someone, I will get acquainted with conversation. Just stay out of my space.

GENTLE READER,

Miss Manners wonders if clergy who espouse this belief follow it to its logical conclusion. Do they really mean that physical manifestations of affection should precede the actual feelings? Nevertheless, she hates to think that you and others may be driven out of church by this issue. Surely you can arrange to explain to the ministry your dignified views on reserving intimacy.

An Antidote: Discretion

DEAR MISS MANNERS,

I have participated in a number of jargon-laden seminars and support groups over the years and it's sometimes a barrier to re-entering polite society. I think it rude (even in California) to expect others to follow my somewhat erratic path of ideas and enthusiasms and I do wish to keep up with my friends. Also, it would be nice to introduce friends from different groups to one another, without provoking war.

What I am looking for is a clear statement of some underlying principles for the transition between wild-eyed enthusiasm and a more sustainable social life. I suspect it's in the same old rules I've been told a few thousand times, but if they could be restated in this context, I would be grateful.

GENTLE READER,

As you point out, the behavior that is practiced in such groups, however useful it may be for the matter at hand, is sharply at variance with the etiquette of everyday life. You are not the first to write Miss Manners of the socially disastrous consequences of bringing one to the other, but you are the first to do so from the support group side.

Miss Manners confesses to having wondered why those who pride themselves on their understanding are generally so curiously inattentive to this nicety. As you have guessed, there is a relevant old principle underlying social etiquette. While Miss Manners would like to dress it up by calling it The Use of Social Distance to Demonstrate Respect, it is popularly known as Minding One's Own Business.

Specific rules include:

Don't probe. Polite society has ways of showing interest in others without grilling them to extract their secrets.

Don't offer unsolicited advice, even if you are persuaded that your own insightful wisdom would be of inestimable value. Miss Manners herself practices this rule every day of her life.

Don't proselytize, even if you have found the true and only way to live.

Finally: Don't hug people you don't know really well. What may be considered a show of love and support in one situation is considered an unpardonable liberty, if not outright molestation, in ordinary life.

UNFORTUNATE PHRASES

Replacing "How Do You Do?" with "How Do You Feel?"

The currently most annoying social question is "How does that make you feel?" Miss Manners is appalled at herself for being so surly as to be bothered by this. What more polite inquiry could there be than one about someone else's feelings, particularly in acknowledgment of an important event in that person's life?

It is one of the missions of Miss Manners' life to impress upon a me-first world that the feelings of others should be considered in determining their own behavior. Is it not progress that so many people are taking the trouble to find out what the feelings of their fellow creatures are? She should not quibble because the progress was made on that well-traveled road from psychotherapy to television babble to daily conversation.

Isn't it charming to offer another person a chance to talk about the matters that most concern her or him? Come to think of it, doesn't etiquette actually mandate a similar question, in different degrees of formality: "How do you do?" "How are

WASHINGTON, D.C.—The Department of Transportation offered training courses in management skills and diversity awareness during which blacks and whites were encouraged to exchange epithets, men were groped and women wept. "The training consisted of three days of psychological abuse," one department employee (who took early retirement because of the stress the sessions caused) told the *New York Times*.

you?" or "Hey, how's it going?" Surely a more probing version that is not merely a convention repeated by rote, but a genuine inquiry, asked with a soulful look and with the apparent desire to get a frank answer, has to be even better.

Even if it is just offered routinely, it should be protected by Miss Manners. Expressions of conventional pleasantry, which aren't supposed to mean anything other than a pledge of good will, are a staple of etiquette. Are people driven to irritability and impatience (two conditions not conducive to the practice of etiquette) by being asked "How does this make you feel?" any less tiresome than those who complain that "How do you do?" does not always indicate a sincere interest in the malfunctioning of their innards?

It is hardly Miss Manners' job to squash that which is benevolently intended. No matter how tempted, she is not going to declare the present habit rude. She would be satisfied to curb its misuses and excesses.

The New Age form of this age-old question may arise in response to good news or bad, a trivial event in a person's life or a major one. If you are newly married or newly bereaved, if you lost a game or won the lottery, had a haircut or had a disappointment—sooner rather than later someone is going to look you deep in the eyes and ask solicitously how that makes you feel.

If you brush it off by saying, "Great!" or "I'm getting along fine," don't think that's going to be the end of it. You may still be pressed with, "But how are you, *really?*" If that doesn't bring on a more responsive answer, suggestions may be made as to how you "must" feel—terrible, excited, nervous, whatever. Unaccountably, the suggestion will usually be on the bad side, even if the event itself is pleasant. One is supposed to feel "ambiguous," if not actually "threatened," by happiness these days. Parrying the question may bring on the insinuation that you are crushed under psychological barriers that ought to be overcome for your own mental health, and that you should dispense with the cover-up of equanimity.

Miss Manners wishes to point out some of the difficulties this creates. To begin with, this question rarely permits a satisfactory answer. We can all recall being asked, on one birthday after another, "So how does it feel to be ten [eleven, twelve, thirty, forty, a hundred] years old?" No one has ever yet come up with a clever response, or even one that was anything but foolish.

Next, such questions may be an invasion of privacy. The current belief that people always feel better when they talk about their emotions fails to take into account that this depends on the people to whom they talk, and the prevailing conditions.

Victims of tragedy who are grabbed on the scene and asked on television how they feel about it do not look noticeably relieved at the opportunity to talk. Those who are willing to serve others in the valuable office of confidant and sounding board need to establish a history of sympathetic but nonintrusive interest in them, and their own ability to keep a secret. There is no substitute, Miss Manners is afraid to say, for building a friendship, learning to interpret the feelings of others from their behavior and using imagination and experience to develop empathy. Some things are just not available on demand.

Finally, Miss Manners' most serious objection is that this line of questioning encourages the idea that it is improper to have any mismatch between one's inner feelings and what one expresses socially. In its many guises, this notion is the enemy of courtesy. The therapy version is that it promotes mental health to tell everybody everything, in which case we should have a mighty well adjusted society by now.

Etiquette does not forbid the relief of emotional disclosure, but it does require such disclosures to be voluntary. Polite people will not brag about good fortune or burden others with secrets and sensible ones won't turn over intimate information to anyone not bound by professional ethics or deep friendship. Miss Manners will permit "How do you feel?" to be used as a conventional pleasantry only if those who use it stop acting as if they are conferring some tremendous act of charity toward the afflicted. There is no cause for smug self-congratulation. They get credit for politeness, but not great humanitarianism.

They must also agree to accept conventional answers—"Fine, thank you, how do *you* feel?" for example.

Encouraging Negative Feelings

DEAR MISS MANNERS,

I have a "friend" who has the annoying habit of always asking, "How do you feel about that?" She never asks how I feel about getting a raise or any positive aspects of my life; only the negative, e.g., "How do you feel about your daughter dropping out of school?" "How do you feel about your husband's layoff?" My close friends are empathetic enough to know how I feel. Anyone who has to ask is not close enough to deserve to know. Please suggest a way I can evade her questions and guard my private feelings without sounding too defensive. I am tempted to tell her to mind her own business.

Gentle Reader,

While your friend was watching too much television, she has failed to notice how inane and uninformative the answers always are to such impertinent questions. The polite social way to let people know that you are prepared to sympathize with them, should they care to explain their feelings, is by greeting bad news with a concerned "Oh, dear, I'm so sorry." This gives them the choice of unburdening themselves if they wish. The way to avoid discussion is to say firmly, "Thank you, but I'm fine now" as often as it takes for your interrogator to get discouraged.

Replacing "I'm Sorry" with "I Know How You Feel"

"I know just how you feel," announce people who couldn't possibly know, never having been in a remotely similar situation.

"You'll feel better if you cry," they declare to someone who had been managing to hold up under difficult circumstances. If that person doesn't quite manage to hold up, they'll command, "Smile!" If a smile is actually produced, they denounce the attempt as a failure with that cheery favorite that could ruin even the happiest mood: "Come on, tell me what's the matter—you really look terrible."

Miss Manners does not wish to discourage empathy. It is still the best key we have to treating others humanely. She merely cautions that it has to be applied with a modicum of judgment. Putting oneself in another person's place means imagining that person's point of view, not just what you, with your ideas, would do in the other person's situation. In situations that no one who has not had the same experience could imagine, sympathy, and not empathy, is the kind thing to offer. For someone who has never suffered a loss to presume to understand what it is like to be the victim of a tragedy trivializes the emotions. It should be a simple matter of humility to substitute "I feel for you" for "I know how you feel."

Even common situations can produce a complexity of reactions, encompassing a wide range of feeling. It is arrogant to tell people which emotions you expect them to feel.

"I suppose you must feel guilty" is an impertinence. Worse is ascribing to someone an emotion of which that person might be totally innocent—or might be fighting—as in "You must be jealous."

Miss Manners is especially suspicious of any assessment of another person's feelings that begins with "You should give yourself permission to . . ." or "It's perfectly normal to . . ." This is a tip-off that the advice isn't based on shared feelings at all, but on a glib knowledge of pop psychology. To recognize someone else's feelings is comforting. To claim to know all about them and how to handle them is unbearable.

. . . Or "I Told You So"

"Why didn't you watch what you were doing?"
"Didn't I tell you this would happen?"
"I knew this would happen, I knew it."
"You should have been more careful."

Miss Manners has never succeeded in devising polite responses to these questions and observations, which are kindly prompted by the mistakes and misfortunes of those who are not as wise as the speakers. Possibly this is because she has had a hard time classifying these statements. Surely any comment uttered by a well-meaning person to one who has encountered trouble must be intended as sympathy. In that case, the reply should be, "Oh, thank you." That this somehow doesn't quite fit has tipped Miss Manners off that there is something wrong with the phrasing.

Even when the recipient is sufficiently chastened by adversity to reply, "All right, all right, you were right," it does not become a satisfactory exchange. The afflicted person isn't comforted and the sympathizer (for lack of a better term) doesn't quit. The next exchange is likely to wander farther and farther from politeness to "Of course I was right," and "Oh, let me alone."

Miss Manners wants to stop this progression. The correct response to other people's mishaps is not difficult: "I'm sorry," "That's too bad," "I hope everything will be all right," and, of course, "What can I do to help?" Adverbs and urgency are piled on with increased seriousness of the misfortune. Yet many people prefer to issue retroactive advice and postdated warnings. Miss Manners wonders what they have in mind.

They are operating, she has concluded, from an underlying belief that life is totally within each person's control and that therefore accidents indicate where the victim went wrong. Punitive consolation assumes that the suffering could always have been unilaterally avoided and, what's more, the healer knows exactly how. Never having made a blunder, he or she sees no excuse for the misfortunes of others.

Now, if anyone understands the burden of being perfect, it is Miss Manners. The hardest etiquette lesson, for those who have learned all the rest, is that targeting individuals—other than one's own minor children—for unsolicited advice is one of the major rudenesses. If anything is worse, it is doing so retroactively. Suppose the unfortunate person did know better, would have avoided the mistake and perhaps was warned against it. This still leaves Miss Manners wondering why the adviser would consider it helpful to point all this out again. Probably it is part of the general but erroneous belief that we are all mad for constructive criticism, even when it is of no practical use. (In this usage, the word "constructive" stands for "I can say whatever I want to you, no matter how derogatory, and if you don't like it, you're a poor sport.")

The companion justification for getting a person who is down is that it will make an impression then and act as a precautionary message should a similar situation occur. Colloquially, this is known as "rubbing it in." It is not a pleasant action, but those who practice it believe that it safeguards the future. Miss Manners doubts even that. Even if the same situation did recur, and the person to whom it had happened before recognized it the second time around, it is probably not because being scolded the first time made an impression. Defeat does not put one in a receptive mood for being scolded.

An Antidote: Constructive Silence

A lady of Miss Manners' acquaintance sought the legal advice of a relative before entering into a financial transaction as a favor to a friend.

"Don't do it," said the lawyer, explaining the dangers of introducing a money angle into a social situation.

"But this is different," protested the lady, who marched right ahead—and slunk right back, some time later, when the lawyer's dire prediction came true.

Her relative not only sympathized about her plight but set about minimizing the consequences of her folly. Grateful as she was, she found herself unable to bear what seemed the suspense before the recrimination. "Why don't you say 'I told you so'?" she demanded. "Why don't you say, 'If you'd done what I told you, you wouldn't be in this mess'?"

"Because it's obvious. And it wouldn't do any good."

Miss Manners points this out not only as a lesson in the exquisite manners of restraint, but for its effectiveness. What is not said, but hangs there in the air ready, makes a stronger impression than what is. The lady never made that mistake again.

MAKING THINGS WORSE

Misdiagnosing (Psychotherapy)

DEAR MISS MANNERS,

I was so fed up with the same people mooching the snacks I keep at work for my own consumption (I believe we should provide for our own vices) that I needed drastic measures. Asking them to repay and replace didn't stop them. I purchased a bag full of goodies, stopped by everyone who has the illness and asked them if they would like their favorite goody, and then gave them the following letter:

> *Dear Constant Moocher,*
>
> *I hope you accept this gift as a token in good faith. It has come to my attention that this mooching has become a habit of yours. I had hoped that you would realize your addiction and seek help for it.*
>
> *I can say now without remorse that you are a constant moocher. I hope that this offends you to the point that you will seek professional help.*
>
> *This will be my last gift to you. Please take heed and remember that I did not take you to raise, and that I am not a grocery store.*

This cured the sickness. I can now keep what I want where I want.

GENTLE READER,

Congratulations, doctor. But however successful your practice of medicine, your practice of etiquette is too unorthodox. Miss Manners is reporting you to the Etiquette Council.

Admittedly, the device you are wielding is a valid one, although now in undeserved ill repute. Euphemism is a handy tool etiquette uses to make harsh points while providing a face-saving excuse for the target. The classic example begins, "I'm sure you didn't mean to hurt my feelings, but . . ."

Unfortunately, you have not got it right. "Moocher," although it aptly describes the behavior, is neither a medical term nor one approved for etiquette use. When you euphemistically define rudeness as illness, you can't then go on to humiliate your patients. There is no shame attached to illness; the victims cannot help themselves and deserve sympathy instead. That explains why Miss Manners has never cared for the illness model being applied to rudeness—it lets rude people off the hook.

You would have gotten the effect you wanted by politely passing around those goodies and saying regretfully, "I'm afraid this is my last treat—the things I keep on my desk are for my own use." That way, you would not have shown yourself to have become infected by their illness—ah, rudeness.

Misdiagnosing (General Practice)

DEAR MISS MANNERS,

A close friend has lupus, affecting her skin and connective tissues. Lately it has manifested itself in large reddish-purple blotches on her arms and legs, which resemble blood bruises.

Total strangers draw her aside from her husband while the two of them are grocery-shopping in order to inquire if she needs help getting out of "that monster's clutches." While waiting in line at the bakery, she noticed a man staring intently at her and grew increasingly nervous. Finally he departed, brushing past her and thrusting a crumpled bit of paper into her hand—it offered a name, address and phone number where she was advised to seek "nutritional counseling."

She finds these experiences unpleasant and embarrassing. One wants to do all one can to help, but one frequently gets the feeling that misguided altruism causes more problems than it solves. Can you give us some guidelines for tactfully offering assistance to the disabled—or perhaps more to the point, for judging whether or not any help is needed? Likewise, how about some tips for those who are constantly on the receiving end on ways to handle such offers graciously and how to refuse them, if no help is wanted?

GENTLE READER,

Miss Manners really must stop going around saying that the most interesting conflicts in life are not between good and evil but between competing goods. Intellectually, this is true, but practically good *v.* good problems are ever so much harder to solve. This is an interesting case in point, where we have two virtuous imperatives:

1. Rush to the aid of strangers in danger.
2. Mind your own business.

That the first is a rule of morals does not automatically give it precedence over manners. This is not just trade loyalty on Miss Manners' part. The hope of doing moral good has encouraged many people to go around making others, such as your friend and her husband, miserable.

Miss Manners does believe that, for those who can provide real help, imminent danger overrides the need to respect other people's sovereignty and privacy. She just insists on strict definitions of "danger" and "help" before etiquette is sacrificed. People who are being beaten or mugged or are teetering on the edge of cliffs or stranded in the ocean are clearly in immediate physical danger and ought to be rescued by anyone able to do so. If one cannot help them, then the etiquette rule of minding one's own business prevails. Someone who sees the victim of an accident lying on the street but receiving professional medical attention ought to turn away instead of hanging around to gape, even if assuming a sympathetic expression.

What about less clearly imminent danger? What about people who might be purposely endangering themselves? Are outsiders likely to be able to tell them something that they don't already know *and* that they would be influenced by hearing?

For that matter, what about people who look depressed? Can you tell the difference, on a strange face, between looking depressed and looking sad? Or looking sad and looking thoughtful? Even if you could accurately spot serious depression, what real help can a stranger provide?

Miss Manners brings all this up to demonstrate the perils of making easy assumptions about people, especially strangers, being in danger—and even glibber assumptions that providing obvious suggestions is enough of a help to compensate for the certain damage caused by embarrassing interference. Had those would-be helpers you describe observed a lady being struck, they would be right, even heroic, to interfere. It's an awfully big leap from that to diagnosing bruises—which could have any of a number of causes—as definitively being malnutrition or evidence of her being beaten by her husband, and then to declare an emergency that justifies humiliating them both.

Miss Manners admits that it is not an easy call. Just because she deplores self-righteous busybodyness does not mean she does not also have a horror of the callousness that used to be known as "not wanting to become involved" in the obvious emergencies of others.

The response to mistaken altruism should be firm enough to discourage further inquiry. Your friend should say clearly, "Thank you, but I'm afraid you have seriously misunderstood the situation," take her husband's arm and turn away. Should her would-be helper attempt to run after her and offer the diagnosis that she is in denial, she will know that he is no altruist but a classic busybody.

Probing Emotional Wounds

DEAR MISS MANNERS,

Not knowing where to begin, I will say simply that my father has been arrested on charges which involve not only the local authorities, but also the United States Government. The stories have hit the local papers with a fair amount of spectacle. Our entire family has been devastated by the news, but it is nothing compared to the humiliation we feel when asked, by supposedly well-meaning neighbors and associates, questions that are, at best, horrendously rude.

"Is he really guilty?" "What did he actually do?" "Do you have a good lawyer?" "So, did you put up the money for his bail, or was it put up by mobsters?" "How much time do you think he'll do?"

Miss Manners, I know it seems contradictory, but although I had absolutely no idea what my father's activities over the last few years were and although I could never approve of what he is charged with doing, I've still put up every liquid dime I have to bail my father from jail and hire an attorney for him. I have no idea whether my father is innocent or guilty—that is a personal situation that I will have to work out for myself.

What I'm having trouble with is casual acquaintances, personal and business associates, even those not-terribly-close friends who feel that, since they know me, no matter how incidentally, they should be privy to my most intimate feelings. In all candor, there are a few people—in fact, three—to whom I have spoken frankly about this matter, and my personal feelings concerning it. It isn't easy for me, even to them. But it is so very uncomfortable for me when I am pressed for details by non-intimates. I can fantasize saying all sorts of clever, sarcastic things in answer to their impertinent questions, although in reality, the best I can summon is "Please, really, I'm just not up to that just now." In truth, I don't really want to be rude; I just want to be left alone regarding this.

GENTLE READER,

Miss Manners assures you that these people are not only snooping but congratulating themselves that they are doing you a favor. "It's healthier to get her talking about it," they are thinking while trampling on your feelings. It has not occurred to them that it is your choice whether you care to discuss the matter outside of the family and your privilege to choose your confidantes.

Naturally, Miss Manners agrees that you must not be rude, but you are not required to conceal how stunned you are by their rudeness. You need only say firmly, "That is my father you are talking about!"

Probing Physical Wounds

DEAR MISS MANNERS,

While I was working late, I was violently attacked by a robber who broke into the computer room of the school where I teach. I was severely injured—he had a knife—and so traumatized by the experience that I won't return to teaching for several months.

In order not to frighten the students and also to spare me the pain of discussing the incident, we have not made public what happened. The school simply said that I was ill. I am now faced with two types of nosy questions—those from people who want to know what was wrong and those from people who know about the incident and want details.

My lower arms are scarred from the knife attack, and some of the scars are too deep for the plastic surgery I have scheduled. People who see them have no qualms about asking, "Where did these come from?" or "What happened to you?" I don't want to have to wear long sleeves for the rest of my life! But the experience was so terrifying that I don't want to have to relive it by talking about it to people, some of whom I hardly know. I want to get on with my life.

Can you suggest a polite way to avoid these inquiries? Some of those who ask questions are people that I have to continue to get along with, such as a senior colleague's wife, and students whom I shall teach and my colleagues themselves. I don't want to be rude or appear to reject genuine sympathy, but I really cannot bear to talk to all those people about what happened.

GENTLE READER,

With all the sympathy in the world and complete support for you in your desire not to discuss this event, Miss Manners has to take exception to the way this tragedy was handled. By putting out an obviously unbelievable explanation, the school has left both your well-wishers and those who might be worried about their own security feeling that they need to find out what happened because there might be something that they can do for your comfort or their protection.

It would have been better had a representative of the school admitted that a robbery had taken place, but that you are fortunately recovering and that measures have been taken (Miss Manners trusts) to see that such a thing cannot happen again. That person might add that you do not wish to discuss it. At any rate, when anyone makes inquiries of you, you must say kindly and firmly, "I very much appreciate your concern, but I prefer not to talk about it."

Sabotaging Treatment

DEAR MISS MANNERS,

I got beaten up by a man I had dated for a year. I was hurt, shocked and angered. I pressed charges and had him arrested, and won the court trial. Even if I had lost, I would still feel that I was justified in pressing charges. No one has a right to beat, or even hit, another person. It is wrong. I felt that this violated me and his violence was deviant. If I hadn't pressed charges, then perhaps another woman would be subjected to his outrage in the future.

My actions were surprisingly criticized by some people—even close friends. I was shocked by their "Why bother?" attitude—why put my personal life on trial, why "hang the man" when he only beat me up once (as if it takes a couple of beatings or murder before one brings a man to trial for domestic violence). Others commented that my pressing charges would impact on his career (as if I should care) and my future life (as if being bruised and bleeding wasn't impact enough on my mental outlook on life and relationships). Some people asked me if he had been drinking when he beat me, as if alcohol would be a logical excuse for his actions.

Is it proper and polite and ladylike for women to keep their mouths shut when they are beaten up? Should I have just walked away and done nothing? Should I have made it seem as if his actions were correct and proper by not pressing charges?

GENTLE READER,

By asking whether a lady should endure criminal violence or social criticism, you have offered Miss Manners a false choice. She would never suggest that ladies should "keep their mouths shut" rather than bring their persecutors to justice. Neither does she condone an open-mouthed policy in which such personal matters are opened to general discussion (and therefore to the sort of unthinking and hurtful criticism you have received).

Miss Manners presumes that you did not go around asking your friends whether or not they approved of your decision. One should not invite comment on such matters—exactly because one might get it. Nevertheless, court action is a matter of public record and those comments come uninvited. What used to restrain people from jabbering about others' misfortunes was tact. The healthiness-helpfulness idea has resulted in such tactlessness that it even made you question if securing justice is worth it at that price.

Miss Manners urges you not to give up your fighting spirit. You must simply learn to say firmly, "I really don't care to discuss it," at the very first indication that someone wants to comment on your action.

CHICAGO, ILL.—The American Medical Association called for mandatory ratings for recorded music based "on the belief that violent lyrics are inciting children to violence, which adds more than $5.3 billion each year to the nation's health care spending," the *New York Times* reported.

Prescribing Rudeness

There is a school of thought that believes it is a wonderfully healthy thing for people to let loose with whatever anger they harbor, in all its natural force. Miss Manners need hardly mention that this is not an etiquette school.

According to the anti-etiquette school, kicking, screaming, swearing and breaking things provide a catharsis for the person who is, as they say, "acting out" his or her emotion. Audience reaction is not considered. Nor is the safety of the props.

In contrast, etiquette is accustomed to asking who and what else may be affected by any possibly intrusive form of behavior. Your anger rightly runs into trouble, etiquette believes, when the expression of it angers someone else.

Miss Manners realizes that this consideration has given etiquette a reputation as a genteel old wimp. If the only polite alternative to unleashing anger is swallowing all dissatisfaction, thus letting everyone else get away with murder, people are more than willing to forgo politeness.

Miss Manners hardly blames them. As it happens, there is something between the natural expression of anger and the unnatural suppression of it. Civilization has developed a variety of restrained but effective methods of showing anger, from the glare to the lawsuit, depending on whether you want to freeze the other person's blood or assets.

Even these measures are apparently too tame for the therapy-minded who believe anger to be an awesome force which, if blocked from spontaneous expression, will do internal damage. "Clear the air" is their battle cry. "Let it all out, and you'll feel better." Go ahead. Shout and carry on, all in good clean fun, and nobody will hold a grudge afterward. This is, of course, a credo that would apply to wife-beaters and child-batterers. Surely their actions are the natural outlet of their anger and may afford relief immediately afterward.

Etiquette would rather take its chances with problematical internal damage in order to prevent certain and obvious external damage. It therefore channels natural behavior with disastrous consequences into manageable forms. When limits are set, conflicts are expressed safely—and, incidentally, in ways that have more likelihood of resolution, since unforgivable behavior is, well, unforgivable.

Miss Manners was initially complacent about seeing her very own self described, in a long ago job action, as having had a "tantrum." Indeed, there had been a difference of opinion and she had said coldly, "Very well, if that's the way you feel, then perhaps I don't belong here"; that is her idea of a tantrum. Imagine her astonishment when she found the same source describing another lady as having had a "tantrum" that consisted of loudly screamed obscenities. If that is truly the definition of a tantrum, then tantrums are not in Miss Manners' vocabulary.

The strange thing is that a conflict can be just as strongly demonstrated and fought with delicate weapons as with crude ones. When Miss Manners discusses child-rearing, she is frequently asked her opinion about physical punishment. The answer to the simple statement that one cannot teach civilized behavior by hitting people is often a plea that it cannot be done any other way, either. Of course it can. Children can learn to register and dread a parent's displeasure by whatever signal the parent establishes. "I can do more with a raised eyebrow than you can do with a stick," Miss Manners brags when explaining nonviolent child-rearing.

Promoting Euthanasia

It is with great trepidation that Miss Manners pinpoints what seems to her to be the all time champion Etiquette Atrocity. If people feel moved to defend this example as humane, or report that it is common behavior, she dearly hopes that they

The death of an 11th-century Dogaressa of Venice is attributed by St. Peter Damian to her habit of eating with a fork, rather than to the fact that she had the Plague. This is the earliest known documentation of the belief that it is wicked to know which fork to use. The Fear of Forks plague rages to this day. That is why people who have no trouble programming their VCRs brag that the fork is far too complicated an instrument for them to master.

will spare her. She read it some years ago, in a newspaper account of a Georgetown dinner party given in honor of Bruno Bettelheim so that the distinguished psychologist, who had newly settled in Washington, could meet people.

The following dialogue was reported to have taken place:

GUEST: What's your excuse for being here?

DR. BETTELHEIM: I've just moved to this area.

GUEST: How do you like it?

DR. BETTELHEIM: I'm not happy.

GUEST: How old are you?

DR. BETTELHEIM: Eighty-six.

GUEST: Well, then, you might like to be introduced to my friends at the Society for the Right to Die. Or I could introduce you to my friends in the Hemlock Society.

At this point the hostess is reported to have changed the subject. As it turned out, Dr. Bettelheim, who committed suicide two weeks later, was already a member of the Hemlock Society. Miss Manners does not presume to analyze his reasons for doing so, much less to speculate that it had anything to do with the dinner party encounter. She acknowledges that he was known to have been a blunt talker and that he himself opened the question of his unhappiness.

And then she faints. One guest at a party suggested to another that he consider killing himself?

Miss Manners is already wary of sharing her shock, because the first person with whom she did so seemed to think that the etiquette problem here was that the guest "was not a close friend of his." Miss Manners had a relapse. "Oh?" she inquired when she came to. "Do you think it is all right to suggest to close friends that they kill themselves?"

We are not talking here about someone who has announced his desire to commit suicide and asked for advice or support. We are talking about someone who only admitted he was unhappy—to a stranger, who had no hesitation about suggesting a solution.

Miss Manners has long been aware that the society is full of people who think they know better how other people should live their lives than they do themselves. Apparently some feel they can also let them know when it is time to die.

II. SHOW BUSINESS

Let's hear a big round of applause for everyone—the entire society. Then let's quiet down and consider other methods of showing respect and appreciation.

Miss Manners has always known that America is a show business society. Birth is a spectator event. Everyone recognizes that the requirements for filming anything take precedence over the desires or convenience of all participants. The ability to entertain leads to the highest honors. The ability to "act natural" is the single skill most admired, unless it's the ability to act naturally on television. Not being willing to deliver public comments on any subject is classified as bad citizenship. Not being willing to sacrifice privacy to satisfy the curiosity of others is regarded as subversive.

The etiquette of show business—announcing the credits, casting roles for effect rather than by less visible qualifications and, especially, the kind gesture of rewarding all effort with applause—is practiced on all occasions. It is not uncommon to see the biographies and previous credits of bridal attendants listed on wedding programs and to know that they were chosen more for their height and similarity of appearance than for their degree of friendship with the bride or bridegroom. Bridal couples are applauded at the wedding ceremony and frequently at the reception— for dancing together, cutting the cake, or responding to requests to kiss each other for the entertainment of the guests.

Funerals, too, are merry with the sound of appreciative applause. It is still not customary to applaud the central figure for having, like the bride and bridegroom, achieved an important milestone, but services are often punctuated by applause for eulogists. Miss Manners once attended a funeral at which a United States Senator, in introducing other speakers, referred to himself as "your emcee." He and other political speakers were so robustly cheered for their efforts that when a member of the deceased's family got up to thank mourners for being there and wept, his sorrow, after everyone else had been entertained, seemed out of place.

Graduation ceremonies are so often punctuated with individual bursts of applause by the friends and relations of graduates that those presiding have to plead— generally in vain—that the applauding be kept for the class as a whole so that the ceremony can proceed. When time is not a problem, those who preside at ceremonies are frequently the ones to suggest rounds of applause.

At religious services, music is applauded, although sermons are not. Renditions of the National Anthem are followed by a round of applause by—and presumably for—those who sang it.

That all this applause is generously meant does not make it appropriate. Miss Manners is sorry to have to tell the fans, who used to be known as citizens, that not every effort made is made for audience approval and therefore that demonstrating approval is not always respectful.

Religious and patriotic rituals should never be applauded. Miss Manners is not as strict about banning applause at graduations as she is about weddings and funerals, where the necessity to express relief at obstacles overcome should not be present. People who preside at an event, even at a formal secular one such as a meeting, should never applaud. That job requires welcoming people at the beginning and thanking speakers or performers individually, using words.

However, for performers and speakers who do put forth their efforts purely for the benefit of those assembled in front of them, there is nothing like applause. Personally, Miss Manners likes it when this is followed by the audience's unhitching the horses on her carriage in order to pull it through the streets.

Clapping in Church

DEAR MISS MANNERS,

At my church, the congregation occasionally applauds following a particularly well-performed hymn or solo, but my mother says that she had always been told that applause was never to be given in church, excepting the times when small children sang on special occasions. When, if ever, is applause appropriate during the worship service?

GENTLE READER,

Having forgotten church manners, people are substituting those that would be proper for a performance. This drives Miss Manners wild. Hard as it may be to imagine, musicians in church are supposed to play or sing for the glory of God, not the pleasure of the congregation (whom people increasingly slip and call "the audience").

That is why there should be no applause for those who perform in church. Not even for small children, who particularly need to have the purpose of their performance explained to them. Miss Manners is not so hard-hearted as to disbar smiles, particularly parental ones that signal "You did splendidly," and favorable remarks after the services.

A Reply

DEAR MISS MANNERS,

Your statement that there should be no applause in church does not have Biblical justification:

Clapping to honor an awe-inspiring God (Psalm 47:1–2): "Oh, clap your hands, all ye peoples; shout unto God with the voice of triumph."

Clapping as commanded by God (Isaiah 55:11–12): "For you shall go out with joy, and be led forth with peace; the mountains and hills shall break forth before you into singing, and all the trees of the field shall clap their hands."

Clapping, a form of praise (Psalm 98): "Let the sea roar, and the fullness thereof; the world, and they that dwell therein. Let the floods clap their hands; let the hills be joyful together."

I am a member of one of the Reformed Churches of America, a very plain and traditional type of church which has a very traditional type of service. However, very often, the congregation is moved and led to clap because they are praising God, are honoring Him, and thanking Him for what He has done for each of us. Those are the times they clap in our church.

GENTLE READER,

Where is the Biblical reference by which God commands applause to honor musicians and newlyweds?

Miss Manners hopes she is not pressing too fine a point when she distinguishes between the clapping of hands as an expression of religious awe or joy and the clapping of hands to denote approval and appreciation for the achievements of one's fellow mortals. As you say, the former is a tradition of several churches. The latter is a tradition of secular entertainment. Commending human talent is a wonderful thing, but it should not be confused with the rituals of worship.

The Ceremony of the Talk Show

"I can see you're pretty nervous about this, but don't worry, we're all here with you. . . . Please hold your applause till the end. . . . There are still seats up front. . . . Please welcome. . . . When I was asked to be here today, I started wondering what I could say. . . . I've been asked to tell you to wait until the picture-taking is over before you go out. . . . Did you ever think you'd finally get to this day? . . . I'm reminded of the time when . . . I'm reminded of the joke about . . . There'll be food and drinks afterward in the other room. . . . Aren't they great? Let's give them a big round of applause. . . ."

On what occasion are you likely to hear these remarks? On every possible occasion, it seems to Miss Manners. Graduations, weddings, funerals, anniversaries, retirements, commemorations—all of these momentous events, each of which used to have its separate ritualistic form, have now taken on the same revered format.

It is that of the television talk show, complete with its warm-up routines, stage directions, backstage gossip, inside jokes, chatty confidences, immediate feedback, confessions of stage fright and reassurances and advice designed to relax the participants and cue the audience. The only difference seems to be that on a talk show, explanations and instructions about the mechanics of the event are obscured for the chief television audience at home by breaks for commercials. In private ceremonies, the chatter is incorporated into the event itself. The part about being gathered here today is given in the same tone as the part about clearing the aisles for the principals. There isn't even a break for the commercial. How to direct any contributions you may wish to make is announced by whoever occupies the host position.

Miss Manners understands that this new ceremonial format has been adopted in the belief that the culminating moment in modern life is an opportunity to talk about oneself to a national audience that will reaffirm one's existence by cheering. Perhaps the change in format is also connected with seeing attendance at ceremonies as an entertainment option rather than an obligation. People feel that the ceremony accepts an obligation to compete with the liveliness and revelations of the talk show. Or it could simply be that the talk show is now the only ritual with which people are familiar.

She suspects that it also derives from a notion that ceremony is no longer appropriate to our way of life. We are a people used to the improvisation of leisure and following any prescribed pattern of behavior seems alien. With its formality, ceremony makes people uncomfortable, the second most dreaded emotion of our time; with its predictability, it risks creating boredom, the number one dread.

Yet people crave ceremony. There is a longing to mark the major events of life by ritual, which has people continuing through the traditional motions even when the substance is absent. A student who has not completed graduation requirements will nevertheless march to accept a blank diploma. Renewals of vows, in the full style of formal first weddings, have become popular with couples for whom once is not enough.

Miss Manners understands this desire to take part in the traditional customs of the society, which have kept their spiritual meaning from long usage even when they no longer directly correspond to the circumstances. So people hold ceremonies—but then they undercut them by putting the emphasis on the natural feelings that underlie participation. The risk is that they thus destroy the wholehearted and undistracted participation in the ritual which is designed to produce rarer emotions.

Ceremonies are stiff and formal and produce an unfamiliar awe because they mark deep and important events. Dispelling that awe by focusing attention instead on the preparations and reactions to staging such an event only defeats the purpose.

It is also beginning to defeat its own purpose of holding people's attention. Miss Manners is probably not the only person who can be stimulated by the happiness, sadness, sentimentality or thoughtfulness evoked by ceremony, but who can't help nodding off the minute she hears the words, "I wondered what I could say today that would add . . ."

Filming Funerals

DEAR MISS MANNERS,

I recently attended a funeral which included a church service and a full honors burial ceremony. The deceased had died suddenly and the attendees' emotions were heightened by the suddenness as much as the actual passing. As I bent my head in prayer, the corner of my eye caught sight of a video camera. I and several other mourners were being filmed.

Being filmed at such a time was very disturbing and even more so when I later learned that copies would be sent to out-of-town relatives and friends who could not attend the services. What is your opinion of the use of tape recorders and video cameras to film funerals? Do you think the attendees have any rights when it comes to their most private emotions being captured on film?

GENTLE READER,

Once when Miss Manners was carrying on about the abuses of videotaping at weddings, she made the mistake of joking that the natural extension of it would be to videotape funerals. When will she ever learn?

Immediately afterward, in this case. Her Gentle Readers quickly informed her that this was already being done. While most voiced shock at the intrusion, one or two others declared how grateful they would be to have such souvenirs of the occasion.

That those who did not attend the funeral require an instant replay instead strikes Miss Manners as a revolting idea. It is no disgrace to be prevented by hardship from attending a funeral, but it does not require compensation afterward. If Miss Manners dared make another predictive joke, she would suggest that someday funerals will be attended only by the deceased, with family and friends merely watching the tape at their convenience.

How would they watch it? Alone and depressed? In a gathering in a recreation room? At an anniversary party for the "Celebration of Life" that took place on the deceased's death? Do they gather the descendants years later and say, "Let's look at Dad's funeral again?"

It is impossible to capture on film the solemnity of a funeral of assembled family and friends. It is also hard for Miss Manners to imagine the satisfaction that the bereaved who did attend might get from reliving the funeral. Surely it is seeing pictures of the person alive, and perhaps quietly rereading some of the eulogies, that they would treasure.

Miss Manners considers the funeral video as just another result of the historical approach that so many people take to the important events of their lives. In many cases, the wedding video has become the only souvenir of the marriage day, because the principals have little of the actual event to remember except being made to cooperate with the demands of picture-taking. To film weeping mourners is an appalling intrusion on their privacy, regardless of who commissioned the filming. Under the circumstances, Miss Manners would not have blamed you for rising, the moment you realized what was happening, and removing yourself to a secluded area.

Etiquette from Advertising

A proud shipping line advertises the magical luxury of its cruises with a photograph of a white ship in a turquoise sea. Beside that is a smaller picture in which a fine china cup and saucer and some delicate cookies evoke the leisurely pleasures of tea time.

There is a gilded spoon sticking awkwardly up out of the cup itself, rather than in its proper parking place on the saucer. Miss Manners had thought everyone knew that warts will grow on any hand that leaves a spoon in a cup, even for a second.

In another advertisement, the makers of high quality writing paper evoke the intimacy of letter-writing by picturing a bundle of aged letters lovingly tied with ribbon. One would imagine the lady to whom they are addressed rereading them, misty-eyed, after decades of blissful marriage to the gentleman who courted her by writing them. Modern lovers might be led to reflect that no one could ever similarly treasure While You Were Out notes or E-mail.

The envelope shows that the lady has been curtly addressed by her name alone, naked of any courtesy title. This would have been an insult in the era being suggested and it's not much better now. It is a graceless compromise, born of rough experience with the anger of ladies who are addressed as Miss when they prefer Ms., or vice versa, a hazard that telephone messages can neatly avoid.

Picky, picky, picky. Who besides fussy old Miss Manners even knows these details nowadays? Who else cares? Above all, who cares if advertisements are socially correct or not?

Actually, Miss Manners knows about these errors because she has received clippings in the mail from aggrieved Gentle Readers, with tisk-tisking notes about how ignorant such pretentious companies really are of the luxuries they handle. She has also received countless examples of silver, china and crystal advertisements, pointing out that the items are placed incorrectly on the table. It is not always high priced dry goods that offend. Gentle Readers report being offended by television advertising, particularly that which sells food, while ignoring the ordinary decencies such as saying "please," chewing with the mouth closed and not taking up a large percentage of the table space with one's upper body.

Surely some of the fussbudgets who complain had been targeted as customers. Miss Manners has also noticed that people who couldn't—or wouldn't bother to—single out such technical etiquette errors nevertheless know that something seems wrong and are left with vaguely unpleasant associations: If you go on a cruise, are your fellow passengers going to be slobs? If you order writing paper and write more letters, are you going to be on the giving and receiving end of petty conflicts? If you try to cook and eat nicely, are you going to be disgusted by the way others eat?

Not caring whether any of these goods are actually sold, Miss Manners is inclined to let advertisers sink in their own ignorance. She has argued, and will continue to, that it is foolish to look to commercial enterprises for one's etiquette guidance. Nevertheless, people often do—or at least they claim that they have a hard time teaching manners to children who produce popular counterexamples.

In the realms of etiquette not in their daily experience, they rely on salespeople to guide them to the correct. An opportunity is there for businesses to learn and to then set an example of high standards. If they don't want to do it for high-minded reasons, such as helping Miss Manners with her job, they might reflect that it would help them help themselves.

Etiquette Updates on Television

DEAR MISS MANNERS,

My mother always made me walk on the outside of the sidewalk, saying that an automobile could come by and splash water from the gutter and the gentleman would protect the lady. She also said pimps make their ladies walk on the outside to denote that they are for sale. I am only sixty-six years of age, yet I continue to practice this. Some younger ladies look at me askance. Is this an outdated custom? I noticed that on TV and in the movies, men walk on the inside or the outside, whatever is most convenient. But in movies made in the 30's and 40's, the gentlemen walk on the outside.

GENTLE READER,

Your mother told you about pimps and their ladies when you were only a lad? My, my, wasn't she ahead of her time. In agreeing with her lesson, however, Miss Manners does not endorse her explanations. Lots of stories grow up to justify, in practical terms, customs that may only be set arbitrarily and then followed out of habit that eventually turns into tradition. In the military, the gentleman walks on the lady's right to keep his sword hand free to protect her.

Miss Manners hopes you will not substitute the example of modern television for the teachings of your mother. The American civilian rule about gentlemen walking on the outside was never repealed, even though few ladies nowadays are acquainted with it, which accounts for the look of surprise on their faces as you gallantly leap about them.

III. FUND-RAISING (EVEN FOR A WORTHY CAUSE)

Offering hospitality is such a serious obligation of etiquette that it is mandated in the sacred literature and traditions of many religions. Just about everyone has been taught one version or another of the holy personage in disguise who was turned away by the uppity rich, but generously welcomed to share the humble home of the poor.

In case anyone misses the point, a vivid description was provided of how significantly the hospitality was reciprocated and its absence punished.

So how are we doing with this lesson? The question most frequently posed to Miss Manners these days concerns how to make money from one's guests, or at least how to make them pay for their own entertainment. Another question that has begun popping up concerns the efforts of hosts to enjoy a better standard of living than they are willing to share with their guests. Miss Manners suspects that these people are going to fry.

People with something personal to celebrate are full of ideas as to what their guests should contribute—money toward a trip or the mortgage on a house, the outright purchase of some other host-selected item, or that all-time favorite, no-strings-attached cash. None of them asks Miss Manners whether this dunning of guests is crass. The contribution these people want from her is some sort of delicate wording that gets the point across without offending the targets to the point where they refuse to ante up. "Where do we put 'Cost per person includes tax and gratuity'?" asks a blushing bride.

From the invitations that targeted donors have kindly passed on to Miss Manners because they could hardly bear to touch them, it seems that many hosts are ingenious enough without her help.

There was a sweet little card with pictures of balloons on it, an invitation to a child's ninth birthday party. Admittedly, nine is an age when the sentiment of purely disinterested friendship may not yet be fully developed. A successful birthday hostess of that age is one whose parents have rehearsed her so well that they do not have to follow her around during the party saying, "Say hello first, dear, and we'll worry about the present later. . . . Now what do you say when someone gives you something? . . . No, dear, the guest gets to keep the prize. . . . Yes, you blow out the candles, but then you have to make sure your guests get their cake and ice cream. . . . You can play with that later—come say good-bye to your guests who are leaving."

What was the little hostess's mother busy doing instead? She had written in the invitation, "Heather likes animals, not dolls. Gift ideas might be . . ." and supplied a list of the items wanted, complete with brand names. The invitation was passed on to Miss Manners by the mother of a bewildered little guest who had looked forward to the fun of selecting a present for her friend.

Even people who are *not* celebrating birthdays, weddings, housewarmings or the birth of children hope to get in on this scheme. Having calculated their own outlays to others, they declare that they deserve a return (plus overhead) and then they make up new occasions at which they solicit presents.

A Gentle Reader passed on an offer that she characterized as "a fund-raising letter from a supposed friend who is fully capable of getting a job to support herself." The idea, according to the hostess, was to have friends and family pay tuition and living expenses, and the inspiration was from "public TV and radio stations" to "take contributions and offer gifts in return. It's a way for people to own a piece of art while supporting a good cause! (Well, I think it's a good cause, but I do have to tell you I'm not tax-deductible)! All moneys will go toward rent, utilities and food or for tuition, fees and supplies."

A similar letter forwarded by another Gentle Reader was headed, "Hello Neighbor" and stated that the author was "finding it difficult to pay my rent" and, while not actually being acquainted with the neighbors (who were presumably living rent free with cash to spare), was inviting them "to come to a party and, if you can, bring $ or drink or food."

Some enterprising people have thought of dispensing with the presence of the guests altogether. Miss Manners has been sent several letters about showers "in absentia," instructing people to mail presents that the guest of honor could open at her leisure. She received one in which a previous giver of birthday parties (for herself) announced a "send me away" event at which friends were merely to send in money, in exchange for which she promised a postal card from the vacation she wanted them to sponsor.

Those still willing to endure their benefactors' presence at parties are particularly anxious that they not have to pay for whatever goes into the guests' mouths. So we have such charming additions to invitations as notification of the cash bar, the potluck assignment, or merely how much the bill will be for each so-called guest. The mother of a bride demands $30 of a bridesmaid so she "can pool our funds and purchase a nice gift for us to present to the bride at the bridesmaids' luncheon (in addition to shower and wedding gifts)." The father of a bridegroom asks everyone to sit down at the wedding supper so he can figure out how many people there are and how much each of them should give him—"even going so far as to ask his son who in the wedding party he was paying for."

Entertaining at home, one can at least restrict the guests from temporarily enjoying one's own standard of living. A Gentle Reader reports noticing that a friend with whom she frequently had coffee visits "usually had her coffee prepared, and mine would be poured on arrival, fresh from the pot. Time revealed that my friend prepared for herself a special 'gourmet' coffee, which was never offered to me. Of course, it was more expensive, and her 'special treat,' which she surely deserved.

"On another visit, to a household of tea drinkers, tea was prepared and served each morning. But then tea bags were laid out on the counter and we were to prepare our own. That was fine until one family member screamed in anguish that someone had taken her tea bag. It didn't occur to me that I should read labels on tabs attached to the tea bag string, and I was guilty of having taken the Earl Grey bag. Thereafter, I drank water, or tea only if it was prepared by someone else. I have been served ice cream, brand unknown, while a hostess served herself a special bar without the bat of an eye."

Another Gentle Reader passes on an invitation, sent to old friends, in which the hostess spells out what she calls "the no nos": "There is to be no cooking or use of MY kitchen or bath. That means no showers—or baths—just such spongings as you'd get from your own little sink. So many coffee shops and bakeries right downstairs—bring snacks in for your use in your quarters. . . . If you can keep to these confines, I'd be glad to have you. On the day of your arrival, there will be open house—thereafter, up goes the Berlin Wall!"

Or, as people used to say in simpler times, "Please consider that my house is your house."

The Gimme Party

DEAR MISS MANNERS,

We received an engraved invitation to an open house in honor of a young couple. There was no mention of an engagement or a marriage. In the lower right hand corner of the invitation were the words "silver, china, crystal." Is this the ultimate in tackiness and a major breach of etiquette? Also, shouldn't open houses be held after a couple marries and not before?

GENTLE READER,

Who says these people are getting married? As Miss Manners understands it, they are merely shopping for silver, china and crystal. You may cooperate with them in this enterprise or not, as you choose. There is such a thing as the legitimate open house party, not to be confused with a wedding reception. At an open house, often held to welcome friends to a new house, guests do not require their hosts to produce a marriage certificate. On the other hand, there is no legitimate social event at which hosts demand outright that guests furnish their houses. The traditional housewarming present is bread and salt, your friends will be disappointed to hear.

A Family Fund-raiser

Dear Miss Manners,

With an invitation from the children of close friends to their parents' wedding anniversary dinner, there was a line, next to the request for the number of people, with "$" and a space marked "signature." Is it to pay for our own dinner, or do they simply want money? Along with numerous other friends, I am from out of town, which adds travel expenses if I choose to attend. I feel this is in very poor taste. They are both successful professionals and do not appear to need financial help. I normally try to find special, meaningful gifts for such occasions.

Gentle Reader,

That they want money, there is no doubt. Whether they are graciously planning to spend it on you or are skimming a profit off the top, possibly as a present to their parents, is less clear.

Miss Manners is afraid that you will have to decide whether you want to pay admission, as well as travel expenses, to attend this event or whether you would prefer to honor your friends in a friendlier way on some other occasion. She cherishes the hope that they are innocent of their children's fund-raising schemes on their behalf.

SHOWERS

A mother writes that she would like to give a Going Away to College shower for her daughter. Although the lady had not actually heard of this being done, it struck her as a good idea because the high school graduation presents her daughter received did not include the sort of practical things needed for dormitory life. "With the cost of college," she notes, "the small things a shower could bring would be a great help."

The very mention of the word "shower," when it is intended to benefit anyone but the tomato plants, is enough to set Miss Manners off these days. That once charmingly frivolous gathering planned by intimate friends to surprise and delight the guest of honor, and to present her with amusing little tokens of a major change in her life, has become part of the greed-feast that has replaced honest hospitality.

While fewer people entertain, and those who do often seem to expect their guests to bring the very food they will eat, the concept of the personal fund-raiser is spreading uncontrollably. And the people doing the planning are less likely to be friends motivated by the hope of giving pleasure than the expected beneficiary herself. Brides have come to believe that no wedding is complete without such an event, preferably multiple showers with demands for specific, substantial presents. The baby shower has burgeoned, from a first-baby, one-time occasion to as regular a part of pregnancy as the visits to the doctor.

Miss Manners did not hear the mother of the new freshman saying, "Dear Danielle is so sad at leaving her high school friends that I thought I'd give one last party before she goes so they can all have a good time together before they separate." Nor did this lady seem to ask herself why her daughter's friends would want to help her furnish her college room when they have their own new ventures to finance.

So no, dear lady, Miss Manners is sorry to tell you that you can never properly give your daughter a shower, not for college, not for her wedding, not for her babies, not if she wins the Nobel Peace Prize. You may give parties in her honor on such occasions, but not showers; and your attention and hers at such parties must be directed toward pleasing your guests, not fleecing them.

The rules about showers are: They are never mandated; they originate voluntarily with intimate friends, not relatives, much less the guest of honor. Guests are only other intimate friends, not the entire list of credit card holders from the honoree's favorite stores. If someone is so fortunate as to have more than one circle of intimate friends, there may be more than one shower, but the guest lists should not overlap because that transforms good will into exasperation.

Presents should be inexpensive, as the serious presents from these intimate friends are sent as wedding presents or brought to the first formal call on the new baby. The charm of the presents is that they should be something that the honoree did not have need of before, such as kitchen gadgets or linens for someone who did not previously keep house or baby clothes for a first-time parent. This is why "cash" is not a proper shower theme.

The Shopping List Shower

DEAR MISS MANNERS,

I've been living on my own for 12 years now and have also been married before. I am about to get married and would like to know if you think it would be proper to enclose in both shower and wedding invitations a suggested gift list. I have most things and don't really need much.

GENTLE READER,

Well, whatever you do need, make yourself a nice list of it all. Then take it out and buy whatever is on the list. This is what shopping lists are for, Miss Manners feels obliged to inform you. They are not sent to other people.

ADMISSION FEES

How much are you willing to pay for friendship? And how much do you charge?

Miss Manners gloomily suspects that these questions are not as shocking as she intends them to be. Obviously, no respectable person, however lonely or poor, ever pays or charges for the warmth of human society. No matter how intimate a recreational activity may be, if money changes hands, it is a business. Bestowing hospitality, regardless of how humble it may be, is a privilege, and being offered it is an honor; neither of these can be bought or sold. Only how come Miss Manners seems to be the last person left who knows this?

Everybody else seems to be busy buying or selling tickets of admission to events they quaintly call parties, responding to holidays and milestones by forking over cash payments they oddly call gifts, and extorting such payments—or, more delicately, just farming out their shopping lists—by tactics they coyly refer to as helping others not to waste their money on things that won't be satisfactory to the extortionists.

The crowning touch is that they are all complaining to Miss Manners that others involved in checkbook society are straying from the traditional rules of impeccable social conduct. Miss Manners admits that she is highly receptive to wails of "Nobody answers invitations any more" or "We never even got a thank you note." She can always be counted upon to demand indignantly that anyone who receives an invitation must reply to it and that anyone who is entertained or given a present must express gratitude in writing.

Well, not always. She is not about to do this on behalf of commerce. She does not urge people to respond to invitations, no matter how prettily worded, to take advantage of a special sale. She neither requires salespeople to write thank you notes nor is charmed when they do so. (However, she did feel that there was something special about the clerk who sent her a note—"Thank you for giving us the opportunity to serve you. We appreciate your business and the confidence you have placed in us. Please contact me whenever I can be of further assistance"—and then, when Miss Manners called to say that the order hadn't arrived when it was supposed to, snapped, "Well, there's nothing I can do about it.")

The rules of social life are different from those connected with paid entertainment, even if many people have totally merged commerce with their carousing. They would find it useful for emotional, as well as etiquette, reasons to be able to tell the difference.

You may notice that your letter box is fuller than ever of what seem to be invitations, requesting the pleasure of your company at this and cordially inviting you to that. There seems to be no lack of receptions, cocktail parties, parties to honor prominent people, balls and birthday celebrations. Perhaps it makes you feel flatteringly sought after—right up to the moment of glimpsing the little enclosed card with the words "Make checks payable to . . ." At this point, Miss Manners—who believes that the obligations connected with a real invitation are sacred—would not bat an eye if you threw the thing right into the trash.

An event requiring an admission fee is not an act of hospitality. No matter how much the organizers of paid events wail that they, too, need to know how many people are attending, Miss Manners cannot see her way clear to demanding that one must formally decline solicitations. It would be like requiring anyone who received a store catalogue to write back saying, "I don't think I'll be buying anything, but thanks for offering."

The rule, therefore, is acceptances only. Let the committee know if you are planning to attend and with whom. This is the opposite of "Regrets only," that odd instruction by which cheeky hosts betray their assumption that anyone who declines will regret it.

In social life, only those who are invited are invited, but when tickets are sold, Miss Manners sees no harm in inquiring whether a substitute will do just as well, or if additional tickets may be purchased for others. Targeting individuals to buy tickets, no matter how snobbishly the committee stewed over the names, cannot be construed as the personal honor that a private invitation is. This means there should also not be complaints about being dropped from such a list, being seated in strict accordance with the amount of money paid, or being socially ignored by someone whose causes one has supported.

The proper wording on an invitation to buy a ticket is different from that on an invitation simply to attend. Even though certain people may generously do all the work, they are listed as a committee rather than as hosts. For example, a company that gives a testimonial dinner for one of its employees may, if it is doing the planning and paying, issue an invitation in the name of the officers as hosts. If, however, such a dinner is given by colleagues for one of their own, with the expectation that anyone attending will pay his or her own way, it is done with a letter and one is asked to be a participant, rather than invited to be a guest.

Loath as Miss Manners is to discourage thank you letters or reciprocal entertaining, they are not required for pay-your-own-way events. She does not object to these, but neither can the committee properly object to their omission. Thanks are, however, required for all presents above the level of logo-laden tokens distributed by businesses. The fastidious may politely decline inappropriate presents by following the thanks with the regretful explanation of a policy of returning presents from people with whom one does business, or the grateful admission that one has passed it on to a charitable institution.

What about the hybrid events—the party in someone's house that turns out to be a fund-raiser or a sale, the gala invitation from a friend that requests a check for admission, the present from a business acquaintance, the unsolicited guidance from a person for whom one really didn't know how to choose a present?

Bait-and-switch invitations from friends—events that appear to be purely social and then turn out to require some sort of purchase or donation—entitle people who have accepted them without knowing the financial angle to switch once this is revealed. The subsequent refusal is accompanied by a brief explanation and the assurance that one would like to see that person socially, as in "Oh, I'm so sorry, I know it's a worthy cause but I give what money I can to causes I'm involved with; let's get together some time just to catch up." No one who attends should feel pressured to buy anything at a supposed social event just to be polite, any more than one has to buy something when out shopping in order to avoid hurting the shopkeeper's feelings.

To make any financial demands on people invited to such private events as weddings or anniversary parties is outrageous. Miss Manners is amazed that people cooperate when asked to honor ersatz hosts who inform them that they will be paying their share or contributing to a fund.

Suggestions, whether from a charity or from an individual, made about what is anticipated in the way of a donation or present are always impertinent. Far from making her feel that she has to follow orders, such information is interpreted by Miss Manners as notice that no alternative present will be acceptable. She then respects the request not to trouble the person with anything else. If this encourages people not to volunteer their preferences unless they are specifically asked, well, good.

If it is costing you more to go to parties than to give them, Miss Manners believes that there is something wrong with your social life, and it is not that you're not charging your guests enough. If you are charging your guests at all, Miss Manners begs to inform you that you are not throwing (to say "giving" would be too ironic) parties. Pay-as-you-go social activity has, for many people, slyly replaced much of real social life. The trouble with your social life if you are paying for it is that you don't have one, any more than someone who pays for love can be said to be having a romance.

A Confused Guest

DEAR MISS MANNERS,

I was invited to a tea held by a volunteer group with which I am involved, but I was confused by the response card:

> The Etcetera Hospital Auxiliary Silver Tea
>> Please mark, sign and return.
>> __ I will attend
>> __ Guest(s) accompanying me.
>> __ I am unable to attend, but enclosed is my contribution for $____.
> Please make your check payable to the Etcetera Hospital Auxiliary.

There was no mention of a price for the tea in the invitation. As I am a student, I declined, fearing that to go without any contribution would defeat the purpose of any hidden fund-raising attempts. What is your interpretation of the card? Was I supposed to pay to attend when no admission fee was mentioned, or were they just giving their members a chance to be generous?

GENTLE READER,

Philanthropic organizations do not, if they are acting in good faith, give tea parties in order to spend on their workers the money that they raise for their cause. Although this tea does not specify an admission charge, Miss Manners takes it for granted that guests attending the tea would feel obligated to be, as you say, generous. Donations of effort should be valued even more than those of money and if you are a volunteer worker at the hospital, you need not feel odd about not being able to make financial contributions as well. The suggestion of an absentee donation is there because the organizers do not want to waste a perfectly good mailing.

Hurt Hosts

DEAR MISS MANNERS,

My husband and I were asked by a friend if we would open our home for an "Art Party." This is similar to a Tupperware party, where original art is shown with no obligation to buy, but hopefully to see some of the paintings. I called about 25 of my friends and/or acquaintances, and they said they would be "glad to come," so I sent out invitations. We went to a lot of time, trouble and expense for this, and on the night of the party a few showed up, a few called that they "couldn't make it," and the rest did not show up, nor did they even respond by telephone as to why. I am hurt by this lack of consideration, especially since most of them said they would attend. Is this the times, did they think they would be obligated to buy the art, or are people just brought up with no manners?

GENTLE READER,

Yes, to all three. It is perfectly true that there is a certain absence of manners these days and that a common manifestation of this is the failure to reply to social invitations. Nevertheless, Miss Manners refuses to admit your claim to be a victim of this state of affairs. You did not issue a social invitation, however much you tried to make it look like one.

Of course, the targeted people presumed that they would be expected to buy. That's why you gave the event, isn't it? The fact that you would probably let them safely out of your house without a purchase doesn't change the commercial nature of the situation. You can get through a department store without buying anything, too.

An Embarrassed Guest

DEAR MISS MANNERS,

I live in a closely-knit neighborhood and almost weekly I receive an invitation to some sort of craft selling party. It's awkward to leave these gatherings without purchasing, especially if the hostess is a friend.

What happens—as I'm sure you know if you've been forced to sit through one—is you walk in, the hostess hands you a check list and a catalogue, the guests sit while someone displays item after item, guests murmur "oohs" and "aahs" and then check off which items they will purchase, thereby supplying the displayer with an income and the hostess with some sort of free gift.

I cannot stand these events for several reasons:

1. I don't like baskets, knickknacks, expensive kitchen supplies, matching child/mother outfits, crystal, Halloween tennis shoes or hand-made crafts.
2. I don't have enough disposable income to buy many extras.
3. I prefer to spend my evenings with my husband and young children.

When I call to say I am sorry I will not be able to attend, the hostess usually waits silently for a reason. When one isn't forthcoming, there is an awkward silence.

To say "I don't like baskets" sounds churlish. To say "I have a meeting that evening" is a lie and also forces me to leave my home for the evening.

Also, when I say that I cannot attend, the hostess usually offers to let me look at a catalogue and purchase items before the party. This forces either a waste of both our time, an unwanted purchase or an admission from me that I don't like baskets, etc. Can you help me handle these invitations in a gracious manner?

GENTLE READER,

The awkwardness you feel at attending such a gathering without buying something, the embarrassment you feel when your hostess waits for an excuse and the discomfort you feel when she offers you the catalogue—all of these are false etiquette clues.

They are not to be mistaken for those nasty twinges Miss Manners sends you if you do something rude.

Shockingly, that is what these hostesses attempt to counterfeit in order to make you do something you do not have to do. Miss Manners detests this kind of blackmail, and hopes you do not succumb to it. Your dilemma is one reason that Miss Manners hates—hates, hates, hates!—such hybrid events. To invite one's friends to a party and then try to sell them things is unconscionable. It violates all the rules of hospitality.

Treat these overtures as if a neighbor had invited you to—for example—go on a skiing trip, which you could not afford and would not enjoy anyway. What you would say, to make it clear that avoiding the activity was not the same as avoiding the friendship, would be "No, thanks, count me out on that, I'm really not interested. But I'd love to see you on another occasion."

PRESENTS

A venerable concept of etiquette with which people seem to be having an inordinate amount of trouble these days is "It's the thought that counts." No, it isn't, they keep trying to tell Miss Manners: It's getting stuff.

What counts, they explain, is every opportunity to get something you really want, for free, without having to bother to shop for it. One way or another, you should be able to make other people understand exactly what your wishes are, so that they take the trouble to find and buy precisely what you would have gotten for yourself in order to surprise you.

The annoyance when other people bungle this mission is apparently well nigh intolerable, even when they get it only slightly wrong. But what can you possibly say when you receive something that is ugly and the wrong size and you already have one?

Miss Manners recommends "Thank you."

She goes so far as to insist that this obviously—and virtuously—hypocritical sentiment be conveyed with the appearance of gratitude, pleasure and sincerity. The difficulty of doing so is a powerful argument in favor of thank you letters, as they do not strain the facial muscles (or at least they wouldn't if you didn't twist your mouth like that with the tip of your tongue out the corner, as a way of concentrating while searching for words).

At a time of sharing, such as Christmas, lots of people seem to want to share their disappointment in their presents with the people who selected them. This is not only honest but educational, they point out. The offenders can see the actual results of their efforts and learn not to repeat their mistakes. If it's the thought that counts, these people should be taught to think more clearly.

The morose among us, whose numbers seem to Miss Manners to be depressingly on the upswing, so to speak, believe that the way to teach this is through projecting hurt feelings. Preferably these should be generalized until they stand for not just one unhappy holiday but a lifetime of deprivation and injustice. If you really cared, this act conveys, you would have known all my tastes, wishes, thoughts and inventory. But nobody ever does, probably because they're all so self-centered.

A different but also popular approach is taken by those who disdain pitifulness in favor of taking charge. After a frank explanation of how the present missed its mark of pleasing, they demand to know where it was bought so they can return it.

And those are the more considerate people who harbor this point of view. The truly practical shove the unwanted presents back to their donors and demand that they perform the exchange.

None of this spreads joy. The sulkers resolve never to expect anything again from a cruel world, and the irate vow never again to expect anything to be done right without their explicit orders. The present-givers are indeed learning never to make these mistakes again. It occurs to many of them that the surest way of doing that is never to give anybody anything. Others decide it would be better to show their sensitivity to the hidden wishes of others by shoving cash at them and saying, "Here, you never like anything—*you* get something."

Of course, Miss Manners' method, while gracious, doesn't correct the problem, either. Its only results are that the present-giver feels a glow of pleasure in having created pleasure (which might possibly be a consideration to the sentimentally inclined) and the receiver has something unwanted. What can a polite person do then?

The nicest thing would be to learn to love it, or at least to tolerate it, because it is a symbol of the effort to please. That is what is truly meant by counting the thought. Fortunately, etiquette has other remedies available. You may also:

Do some discreet detective work to find out where it comes from and exchange it for something else.
Donate it to charity.
Give it to someone who might like it.
Throw it into a yard sale.

Etiquette only demands that you never let the giver know that you didn't like it. Not only does this mean expressing thanks and not inquiring where to return it, but it means choosing a charity, recipient or yard sale that the original donor will never know about. This requires some thought. But then, as Miss Manners pointed out, thought counts.

The Self-Selected Present

DEAR MISS MANNERS,

This summer I have chosen to drive across America to learn something about my country that a textbook cannot offer. I also see it as a reward to myself for having survived four years of Catholic high school.

My parents are not willing to help in the area of finances. My mother states that she is spending time and money on a graduation party as it is. And my father holds fast to the fact that he is already covered by having bought me a car. Two very hard arguments to go up against. Of course I have a savings account of my own, but I'm beginning to realize how expensive a venture this is going to be. What should I do? Acknowledge gifts with written thank you notes and then try to return them for the money, or pre-state a need for cash to undertake a vacation?

GENTLE READER,

Allow Miss Manners to summarize your plight:

Your parents have given you a car. They are planning a graduation party in your honor. You have suggested to them that they could do more and they were not receptive. Nevertheless, you have picked up the idea that adult affection and good will can be turned into sponsorship for whatever plans you devise for yourself. You are now casting your eye further afield to see what the graduation party guests might do for you along these lines.

Do not expect Miss Manners to help you. She believes you should accept with gratitude any presents people happen to offer you, after which you can do with them whatever you wish.

The Money Tree

DEAR MISS MANNERS,

I might give my sister a 70th birthday party—I say might, because we argue a lot, and when the time comes, we could be on one of our non-speaking cycles. If I do,

I know people will want to bring gifts and there is little or nothing she needs and less than that she ever finds satisfactory.

All she really needs, and all that would make her happy, is money. She will soon have to quit her job and will be totally dependent on Social Security and her children, who are less than willing to offer any help, especially the kind that involves $$$$. I'd like to add at the bottom of the invite, "A money tree will be available."

Tacky or not? A second sister says Nix. By simply stating it will be available, wouldn't I just be telling them it will be there if they want to add to it—not particularly that that is what they should do? I get at least two invitations a year with that notation, so it can't be all bad.

GENTLE READER,

How do you know people will want to bring your sister presents? By your own account, she is quite unpleasant about receiving them. You're not even sure you want to give her a party. Not a lady to inspire outpourings of generosity, Miss Manners would think.

In any case, it is improper—tacky is hardly the word—to prime this pump. Please do not come to Miss Manners with the argument that something must be all right because other people do it. If you want to use examples of bad behavior as a model, you will have no trouble finding them without her assistance.

People who have generous impulses do not have to be told that generosity would be welcome. As invitations customarily contain instructions—as to when and where the party will take place—"suggestions" are not interpreted as merely providing options.

The Hint

DEAR MISS MANNERS,

My daughter is an accomplished violinist and has been working hard, saving her money to buy the violin she really needs. She has an event coming up this spring, unrelated to her music, but where gift-giving is traditional. Her father's family is planning to give her expensive gifts, but what she really needs is contributions to her violin fund. She is a sweet, well-mannered girl and will receive the gifts in the spirit they are given, but I know how much a new violin would mean to her. Any suggestions?

GENTLE READER,

A sweet, well-mannered girl does not solicit cash from her relatives, no matter how worthy the cause. But if a sweet, well-mannered girl were to chatter artlessly to her family about her love of music in general and her love in particular for a special violin, it would come under the heading of charming family news.

If asked about what would please her, she should say, "No, no, I really have everything I could possibly want—except my new violin, which you must let me play for you when I've saved up enough to buy it." The important part is that one must trust others to put together the different parts: 1. She wants that violin; 2. I want to give her a present; 3. I could give her a present that would help her obtain that violin.

BAD MANNERS FOR GOOD CAUSES

Lady Bountiful has fallen on hard times. She may not be down and out herself, dragging her tattered glories in the gutter in the company of those she used to pity. Aside from a moan or two about declining real estate values, she may even still be as rich in resources as in the desire to use them for the benefit of others. But nobody likes her any more. Or Lord Bountiful either, for that matter.

Miss Manners understands that people who indulge in luxuries without a thought for those less fortunate should be unpopular. It is less understandable that people who show concern for the needs of others, and who engage in efforts to help them, may end up as figures of ridicule. The problem seems to arise from errors of taste and etiquette committed in the very name of charity. Most contemporary philanthropists are careful not to be overbearing toward the objects of their charity—but they may fail to recognize that the rule against violating the sovereignty of others applies to rich and poor alike.

That it is arrogant to tell other people how to behave is a rule that applies to potential donors, as well as receivers, of charity. Spiritual ostentation is as ill-mannered as material ostentation.

Let us consider how the Christmas charity into which Marmee led her daughters might be practiced nowadays. (Note to ignorant gentlemen: Marmee is the mother of Meg, Jo, Beth and Amy March, the Little Women of Louisa May Alcott's novel, on which proper young ladies are still brought up, so that they can learn to eschew exaggerations of domesticity, passivity and selfishness in favor of warm and energetic self-reliance. The lady you love thinks of herself as Jo. Don't ask Miss Manners how she happens to know that.)

As written, Marmee asked her children to refrain from exchanging presents within the family "because it is going to be a hard winter for everyone" and "we ought not to spend money for pleasure, when our men are suffering so" in the Civil War. At the last minute, she asked them to give the Christmas breakfast they were about to eat to the poor family she had just discovered in the neighborhood.

The March sisters more or less went along with these ideas, which they came to appreciate as being in the true spirit of Christmas. (Note to children: No, Miss Manners is sorry to disappoint you, but Marmee's behavior is called child-rearing, and thus cannot be condemned as interfering with the dignity of others.)

But suppose, instead, Marmee March had suggested that they:

1. Give a sumptuous Christmas brunch, with loads of food and a cash bar for Bloody Marys, and charge admission—with the leftover money going to charity and the leftover eggs Benedict and cheesecake to a kitchen for the homeless.

2. Announce to Mr. Laurence and their other friends that they were not going to send them any Christmas greetings this year because they were going to donate that money to charity; and announce to Aunt March and their other relatives that they were going to give them presents in the form of donations of money to charities in their names.

3. Instruct friends and relatives to remember the needy and to take the money they might (or might not) have been planning to spend on presents for the Marches and give that to charity.

In Miss Manners' opinion, something of the spirit of the occasion might have been lost. While these acts are laudably beneficial, charity should not require the showy and dictatorial bad manners that make the Bountiful family ridiculous.

One should not deliberately juxtapose luxury with poverty. Miss Manners realizes that such a belief

"Many engaged couples who experience a twinge of conscience along with pangs of true love are asking for donations to a favorite cause in lieu of gifts," the *New York Times* reported, citing examples where wedding guests were asked to donate money to the homeless and to an animal shelter and to bring used winter clothing to the wedding to be donated to an emergency program.

would kill the entire charity benefit circuit, which raises much money for good causes, but she is not the only person to notice how vulgar it is to claim philanthropic credit for partying. This is not to say that all partying must cease until misery has been erased from the earth. It is just that indulging oneself and helping others are two separate activities.

It is bad enough to brag about one's philanthropies without doing it at the expense of others. Miss Manners has no objection to the curtailing of cards or presents—only to the practice of extracting self-credit from the perhaps disappointed expectations of others. The gravest charge against Lady Bountiful has always been that she is patronizing. Patronizing the poor, in the sense of believing that giving them money buys the right to instruct them on how to be virtuous, is now generally recognized as being offensive, but it is also offensive to patronize people from whom one hopes to extract charitable donations. Marmee would not have allowed it.

A Philanthropist's Present

DEAR MISS MANNERS,

I am a single mother with a son who grew two feet in less than two years' time. The cost of clothing and feeding this young man is astronomical and I have just received a notification from the court that states that because he is now 18, my $300 per month child support is finished. We didn't have any money at Christmas time, but we did manage to buy a coffeemaker for my sister.

I received from her a certificate that she had made a donation to the Humane Society in my and my son's names. She loves the society and it is the beneficiary of her will. Wasn't that an insulting present? I can't return it. I certainly would not choose it—we are next to homeless and she spends money on something that we can't use!

How can someone be so out of touch with reality? There are no other family members and my sister has tons of money. Am I an ungrateful wretch for thinking like this, or am I right in thinking that this is an example of bad manners? I thought I might give a contribution to the KKK in her name—not that I like the KKK! Please don't get me wrong—I would make one up to look real.

GENTLE READER,

Your sister is one of many people nowadays who try to claim double virtue for their philanthropy. It is generous of her to support an organization in which she believes. It would also be generous of her to give a Christmas present to her sister and nephew, even aside from the question of aiding them in their time of need. If she makes only the one gesture, Miss Manners does not recognize her apparent belief that she has performed two acts of generosity.

A Cause's Crudeness

DEAR MISS MANNERS,

I seem to have received more boxes of Christmas cards this year than usual. I know the people who run these charities are desperate for money and I don't fault them for that, but I object to printing advertising for the charity on the back of the cards. One box was really lovely and I would have like to have mailed the cards to friends, except that the message on the back read, "The sender of this card has made a sizable contribution to" the charity. It was too blatant. Cards from missions are more discreet, with three small letters identifying them. Paralyzed veterans have only the logo of a man in a wheelchair. Am I being too sensitive about this?

GENTLE READER,

Let us say that there is a fine line between a charity's putting its name or logo on a card and the statement you found, which seems to congratulate the sender on munificence that no fastidious person would want to advertise in social correspondence. Miss Manners congratulates you for making this distinction; but she also wishes to point out that you could simply draw a line through it and use the card.

The Committee's Obligation

DEAR MISS MANNERS,

I decided to respond to an invitation by writing the committee that it is "yet another invitation to a splendid event to raise money for an organization which I would love to support. But I am single and have never been quite sure where I fit into this scene. I suggest you might make up a few more tables if you included a third option on your seating request card, along with 'My guest(s) will be_____' and 'Please seat me with_____' and 'I would like to be seated at a table with other singles.' I hope this suggestion is not presumptuous. I think it will raise money by expanding the scope of those attending beyond the couple oriented social scene. It would make some rather lonely people feel at home and give a chance for single people to meet with others of similar backgrounds. I think it is the way of the future, innovative and hospitable."

Gentle Reader,

This is a splendid idea, but Miss Manners has to tell you that being hospitable to guests is not a new invention. What is of modern origin is calling people guests when they are obliged to pay their own way and no one makes any attempt to socialize with them. As far as Miss Manners has been able to observe, there are only three reasons for going to these charity parties:

> *To give money to the charity, minus the cost of an evening.*
> *To feel fashionable, both by taking advantage of a rare opportunity to dress up and by being present at an event with pillars of the community.*
> *To do both while entertaining yourselves or your own pre-selected party, treating the event as a public accommodation.*

To a great many people, this does not add up. Missing from the list is the greatest attraction of any party—the opportunity to make new friends. Not only singles miss this attention. Couples can, and often do, calculate how much cheaper it would be to stay home if they are only going to talk to each other and to entertain elsewhere the friends they already have.

Charity committees are often so clever about the other arrangements for their events that Miss Manners would like to see them turn their attention and imagination to the task of treating their guests more like guests. It doesn't take much to introduce people at parties—it doesn't even take knowing them oneself. Anyone doing host duty need only circulate, introducing himself or herself to whoever is nearby, but especially to those who look lost, and then grabbing the next handy person and introducing the person just met. Designated people who would do this with enthusiasm and charm would add an enormous attraction to such an event. They might even make some new friends themselves, instead of hanging around with all those people they see at meetings all the time, anyway.

A Well-Meant Bad Idea

Dear Miss Manners,

I hope to celebrate my sixtieth birthday in a socially significant manner. I mean I'd like to plan a celebration and invite friends to honor me by making a donation to a specific nonprofit community organization which I support with my time and energy. I realize that "no gifts" on an invitation is an offense to etiquette (you see, I do pay attention to Miss Manners' edicts), but is there any wording I can use to encourage voluntary contributions to an important cause without seeming presumptuous?

GENTLE READER,

Miss Manners wishes you a socially significant birthday. She regrets to inform you that it is always presumptuous to direct people to honor you with their money.

A Well-Meant Suggestion

DEAR MISS MANNERS,

What would you think of a national registry for nonprofit organizations?

I am a firm supporter of your point of view that it is rude to mention presents when you are inviting people to a social event (as in "No gifts, please" on a birthday or wedding invitation), but there are times when the person(s) to be honored really would prefer that their guests be directed toward more useful avenues than another glass bowl.

One would register at the nonprofit registry just as at a department store, listing one's preferred nonprofits, where one's guests could make donations. Of course, guests could always purchase a normal gift or not give at all, as per the current socially acceptable method.

How would one communicate this registry to one's guests? (How is it properly done for registries at department stores now? It has been too long since my own wedding to remember these details). How would one communicate this in the case of large celebrations of birthdays, anniversaries, graduations, etc.?

GENTLE READER,

Gift registries exist only to answer guests' inquiries. A guest of honor never, never, never volunteers any suggestions about presents, even negative ones, because that would indicate that presents were expected. Nice people do not expect presents. They are overwhelmed with surprise, as well as gratitude, when they receive any.

Presuming that you understand that (or accept it even if you have reservations), Miss Manners finds your suggestion a splendid one. Never having had the silly notion that the only proper wedding presents were china, crystal and silver (whether or not the couple already had them, and in spite of their announced plans to live aboard a submarine), she is delighted to hear of a proper way to suggest directing spontaneous generosity toward the needy.

Begging

Dare Miss Manners bring up the topic of etiquette between beggars and those from whom they beg? The superficially sensitive will recoil from the idea. Isn't it decadent and disgusting even to think of such a frill when hunger and destitution are involved?

Yet their own behavior toward beggars is determined not by a policy of how best to use charity to help compensate for misfortune but in reaction to etiquette pressure. To some people, it seems rude to turn away from any request. To others, the fact of the request itself seems so rude that they feel justified in responding rudely. Those who give sporadically tend to make their choices in terms of an etiquette assessment of the beggar's behavior toward them—aggressive, humble, defiant or pathetic.

Miss Manners denies, of course, that etiquette is a frill. The more desperate the situation, the more civilizing forces are needed. There are civilized and uncivilized ways of soliciting money, whether on one's own behalf or for others; and there are civilized and uncivilized ways of responding, both for those who wish to comply with the request and for those who do not. The encounter is a sufficiently delicate one that it should not be left to chance.

Like Judge Leonard B. Sand of the United States District Court in Manhattan, Miss Manners lumps those who seek charity for others with those who ask help for themselves. In ruling against a total ban on panhandling in the New York subways, Judge Sand defined charitable solicitation as including fund-raising for major philanthropic organizations as well as asking for change from passersby. This seems reasonable to Miss Manners, except that she has seen representatives of chic causes employ techniques that are more ruthlessly intended to embarrass people into giving money—in the hope that the importuners will think well of them or just plain go away—than any panhandler would stoop to use.

She assumes that every citizen with enough to live on has worked out his or her own moral policy on philanthropy. Whether giving to individuals provides immediate relief or encourages destructive vices; which organizations are the most effective or deal with the problems that seem the most crucial, or the most solvable; how much one can afford to give—Miss Manners does not presume to answer such difficult questions for anyone but herself. Once these questions are answered and a policy is determined, etiquette does not require that one be swayed to violate it. Techniques designed to make people feel that it is rude not to give—or not to give more—are an illegitimate use of etiquette. (Appealing to charitable impulsiveness is something else. Being able to present a cause so as to make it deeply compelling as an object of philanthropy—whether this is done by eloquent volunteers or by beggars—is a rewarding talent.)

The polite positive response is to hand over the money pleasantly, not to fling it or accompany it with censuring words. The polite negative response to a plea for money is an unelaborated "No, I'm sorry." Of course there should be thanks for the former, but the latter should never inspire unpleasantness. Development officers and other beggars should realize that it takes a moment for an unexpected solicitation to register. Many a person has walked on a few steps, only to think better of it and turn back.

Declining to Donate

Dear Miss Manners,

My husband and I are not rich by any stretch of the imagination, but we take pride in choosing our own causes to support, as each choice is well researched. We donate to local charities with less overhead than national societies with CEOs on expensive junkets. We have been approached four times in the last month by close neighbors asking us to donate to a variety of causes—American Cancer, Lung Association, Heart Association, etc. We have had a person stand at our door waiting for a donation, one who left an envelope to send a check to her and a bevy of other uncomfortable approaches.

We admit we have difficulty saying no, especially since we are new to the neighborhood and do not wish to be alienated, as this is the place we would like to raise a family. We have given almost $100 to neighbors and we CANNOT afford to continue to donate to every approaching cause. An affordable donation for us would be $5 per cause. Would an amount that low be rude? Is there a polite minimum? Better yet, we are seeking an extraordinarily polite way to say that we cannot afford it.

Gentle Reader,

No, what you need is to learn to say no politely. People who lack that skill get themselves into all kinds of fixes, such as pleading poverty to their neighbors, who will then look with suspicion on every new purchase that comes into the house or is parked out front.

Miss Manners has no desire to discourage philanthropy, but she does want to safeguard people against the misuse of etiquette. The reason neighbors canvass neighbors is that charities regularly look for what they call the personal touch, in order to embarrass people into making donations they would not otherwise make. Some very good people get caught on both sides of this unfortunate scheme.

The way to say no is with polite regret. "Why, hello, nice to see you. You're good to be doing this. I'll let you know if we decide to make a donation." No explanation is necessary, but among friends you might say, as you did to Miss Manners, that you support other causes that you have carefully chosen. As long as you cast no aspersions on another person's favorite charity, you can talk up the ones you admire. If neighbors who have different philanthropic interests cannot get along, Miss Manners cannot imagine what charity could mean.

Donating Friends' Secrets

DEAR MISS MANNERS,

I was invited to an alumni meeting purporting to "evaluate availability of future financial resources" to my university. I was given a medium-fancy lunch and provided with a computer printout of all the students and friends I might have known in my college years. A videotape of the university was shown and then someone I can only describe as a "sales type" took over and began explaining the procedure.

At first, I couldn't believe what I was hearing, but the "presentrix" got into explaining ways of assessing an individual's net worth. It turned out that the group assembled was to rate each known alumnus on the list on a dollar-value potential capacity to give to the university. I realized that I was being asked to violate the privacy and degrade the trust of classmates and friends.

I made apologies to my neighbors at the table and walked out, leaving a "This is disgusting!" note on my folder. The idea offended me to the bottom of my soul. I have therefore written to the leader of the group and to the Board of Trustees of the university expressing my outrage—and sending a check to cover luncheon costs. Am I naive, or is giving information (guesses) about friends' and classmates' financial status to a fund-raising effort accepted practice nowadays? Is this or is it not a hideous trespass upon traditional decency and courtesy?

GENTLE READER,

It is, indeed. Miss Manners, too, has long been offended to the bottom of her soul by such tactics. Bullying and embarrassing people to donate money by trading on knowledge of their private finances is, she regrets to say, the routine way in which funds are raised for nearly all charitable endeavors. Protests bring on the even more outrageous assertion that the worthiness of the cause makes it virtuous to toss aside the privacy of individuals and the loyalties of friendship.

Miss Manners had a valuable lesson in this when she donated a handsome sum anonymously to a favorite cause and then endured shameless attempts to shame her by the very fund-raisers who were, by her wish, excluded from knowledge of such a private decision. She was torn between wanting to quit the interests of the cause altogether or to keep giving anonymous donations so that there would be a sizable listing of anonymous donors that could shelter other badgered targets. In the end, she prefers not to penalize a good cause just because vulgar people support it. Your action is much more impressive and Miss Manners deeply wishes that it will encourage people to go about their charity work in a more charitable spirit.

Refusing Embarrassment

DEAR MISS MANNERS,

Like other pedestrians, I'm constantly approached by the homeless (some of whom I've seen off and on for years) for money when I walk in the city for exercise. I take the safer, more heavily populated thoroughfares rather than deserted side streets, and during a recent Sunday walk I was approached by over 30 solicitors.

While I do give to charities, I no longer give money to those on the street. I realize there is no way to curb the constant encroachment of panhandlers (who also think nothing of interrupting a conversation when one is with a friend), but I wonder if there is anything that can be said to them in response to the comments some make when I don't readily dip into my pockets. These range from a sarcastically delivered "Thanks for caring!" (from a teenager with a gold ring in her nose), to "I hope YOU have to live on the street someday," to vulgar name-calling. I usually say nothing in reply, but last Sunday, after I returned home, I felt like the passive victim at a whipping post and it made me angry.

GENTLE READER,

It may be the least of the misfortunes of those who live on the street that they sometimes lack manners.

Then again, it may not be the least. Absence of the social control and skills that manners require—the will and understanding needed to have pleasant and successful give-and-take with other people—may be very closely related to their other problems. There are many other possible causes, Miss Manners hastens to acknowledge, and quite a few homeless people who do have manners. Have you never been asked for money with a gentle "please" or been told "thank you, anyway, and have a nice day" by someone to whom you did not give money? Miss Manners has, and she notices, without surprise, that such people tend to be more successful at panhandling. She suspects they are also more likely to return to normal life because they are better prepared.

As unpleasant as it is to be subjected to bad manners, you are as correct as you are wise to ignore rude people on the street. There is no more facile cure for their inability or unwillingness to behave properly than there is for their other problems.

Soliciting Favors

Dear Miss Manners,

I am a volunteer who puts up posters in stores that I frequent to promote causes. This work involves time and money. Thus, I explain to the manager that I don't leave these posters in public places to be discarded. I request an assent with some cooperation so that these efforts won't be wasted and property destroyed.

Recently I visited a store where I had put up a poster four days previously. The poster was missing. When I asked the clerk about it, he said that it had been up for weeks. I disagreed. Then he said that the date had expired. I replied that nothing had been said about dates. When I requested the return of the poster and a talk with the manager, I was told neither was available. Would you bother to talk to the manager?

Gentle Reader,

Miss Manners would first take the time to calm down. To treat the manager (as you did the clerk) as someone who has reneged on a business agreement is a bad idea. No money was involved here; it was a favor. It is unfortunate that the favor was not carried out as promised and that false excuses were offered when you pointed this out. Nevertheless, the manners connected with nudging people to do favors are different from tactics connected with enforcing contracts.

Any thought that manners can be omitted when one is doing good works is a practical as well as an ideological mistake. You depend on the good will of the merchants, which Miss Manners promises you will not be forthcoming if you subject them to indignation. Try this: "I really appreciate your letting me put up a poster. As you know, it's a good cause—and people tell me they tend to favor stores where it looks as if the owners care about more than just taking their money. But we can't afford to put up a poster for just a few days. They're too expensive. You understand that. Could you let me know ahead of time how long you're willing to keep a poster up?"

Soliciting

Dear Miss Manners,

My parents are of a religious denomination that believes strongly in evangelization and proselytizing converts. I prefer a more orthodox approach to Christianity and try to extend to my parents and their friends the same tolerance I expect from them to me. The other evening, my parents introduced me to a charming young lady from their church. We hit it off rather well and made plans to meet for dinner in a couple of weeks.

Three days later, I received a form letter written in the first person, telling me of how God's goodness had enabled this young woman to attend this Bible school and that religious conference, etc. The letter ended with an outright request for both prayer and financial support so that this young woman might be able to go on a missionary endeavor to the Bahamas for two weeks. Written by hand on the letter was her name and the words, "I thought you might be interested in this."

I am most emphatically not interested in that. I am embarrassed by the letter and inclined not to pursue seeing this person again. Still, I do not wish to be hurtful or rude. Should I honor the still unconfirmed dinner date? Should I ignore the letter, express my disappointment in being considered a source of money, or send a contribution? All of the above seem in poor taste, as does even mentioning the circumstance.

Gentle Reader,

Poor taste? A young lady has one date with a gentleman and suggests that he contribute to her support—and he is worried that *he* might be guilty of poor taste? Miss Manners is shocked.

There is nothing rude about simply throwing out mail solicitations for money. If there were, polite people would probably die out, as they would spend all their time corresponding with shops, foundations, charities and get-rich-quick schemes. Yet Miss

Manners hates to kill off a possible romance so quickly. Suppose you wrote back saying that much as you would like to go off to the Bahamas with her, you are saving yourself for marriage; that you had thought she was so nice, but that you know that no nice girl would allow a man to support her; and that you are afraid you are simply not *that* kind of boy. Not only will you have made your point, but you'll find out if she has a sense of humor. If not, Miss Manners won't mind so much your dropping her.

GOING ABOUT IT PROPERLY

In Recent History

Pleas that Miss Manners occasionally issues for assistance in the glorious task of rescuing and spreading the noble cause of etiquette do not always attract the sort of support she had in mind. First to volunteer are always the avengers. They get Miss Manners' hopes up by deploring rudeness and then divulge their own plans for being rude back. Right behind them are the snobs. They seduce Miss Manners into what seem like benevolent discussions of the finer points of civilized behavior, only to make it clear that their interest is not to make life more pleasant for everyone, but to learn esoteric points that they imagine will allow them to parade their superiority over people with less money or fewer social opportunities.

So when people who understand the true purposes of etiquette show up in force to fight the good fight, Miss Manners is ecstatic. She was delighted to welcome to the etiquette honor roll a group of American soldiers who studied an aspect of the subject that they correctly suppose had hitherto escaped her attention.

Miss Manners' worthy helpers identified themselves as "desert-wise soldiers" who were stationed in Saudi Arabia. "As such," they wrote, "we are deeply concerned that military units may not know proper desert etiquette. Realizing someone with your sensitivities may not have been exposed to the harsh conditions, we have taken the liberty to provide you a list of important desert etiquette rules. We sincerely hope this will help new soldiers in a transition to the desert way of life." Here is their proclamation.

TEN SIMPLE RULES OF MILITARY DESERT ETIQUETTE
1. Don't leave half drunk, open water bottles. Finish them.
2. Don't leave dip cups (spittoons) lying around. Empty them.
3. Never separate a soldier from his cot.

4. Rinse out the washbasin after use. No one wants your soap scum and beard hairs.

5. Don't flatulate in closed tents. A professional steps outside.

6. Never open a new case of MREs just because you don't like any of the meals left in the open box.

7. Never relieve yourself in the presence of female soldiers. If by accident this happens, always apologize.

8. Never hog the shower water. Always turn the shower off until you need to rinse.

9. Always drive on the down dust side of pedestrians. It is very improper to "dust" walking soldiers.

10. Be cautious when playing volleyball in boxer shorts.

There, now. Miss Manners could hardly have put it better herself.

For the Future

The very first time Miss Manners mistook "delete" for "save" (whoops!) and had to accost the nearest small child to plead for help, she sensed doom. (She looked it, too.) The child was polite and accommodating, and used soothing words as well as rapid-fire key-tapping to haul both her and her work out of the abyss. But the natural order of the universe was obviously gone.

Adults are supposed to know more than children. Suppose that superiority to their elders at computers and other household technology should make children think that they also possessed greater wisdom in such traditional areas as moral values, driver education or—etiquette? What would happen to the transmission of civilization, as prefaced by "When I was young," "Well, in my day" and "Because it just so happens I've been around a while longer than you"?

It is now some years since that nearly fatal keyboard misstep. While Miss Manners is no less in need of juvenile computer counseling, that early generation of young know-it-alls (she uses the term respectfully) has come of age. To her amazement, it turns out that they do know more about etiquette than their parents' generation.

Oh, not more than Miss Manners, of course. They're only human. They may be lacking fine points, which their parents neglected to teach them and now resent their not knowing. But in contrast to people who are now of middle age, they recognize the legitimacy of etiquette as an essential factor in community life. This is a huge step forward. The old folks had thrown etiquette into crisis in the 1960s and 70s, not by changing the rules—which is the normal progression, no matter how much it might upset previous generations—but by declaring etiquette obsolete. Today's young adults rediscovered the value of etiquette when they started forming new types of communities—on the Internet.

Cyberspace communities fascinate Miss Manners because they lack what used to be considered the basic features that defined community. Social relationships are now established by people who have never met and probably never will meet. The vocabulary of nonverbal signals we ordinarily use and interpret—facial expressions, appearance, tone—are absent. Common backgrounds cannot be assumed, not even to the extent of agreeing on what constitutes basically acceptable behavior. Nobody has a reputation at stake, because real names are not required. As there are no introductions by third parties, what is known about one's cyberspace companions is only whatever they choose to tell. Inventing fictional histories is not only easily possible, but may be one of the attractions. Anonymity, which has always brought out the worst in people, has never been so thoroughly possible.

The result is freedom, as in no other community. So why should anyone worry about etiquette? Their elders (who have been safely parked elsewhere, with instructions not to try to operate their VCRs themselves—you remember what happened last time, Dad) would tell them not to worry about silly rules, but just to be themselves or, at most, to exhibit some nonspecific civility. But the computer literate do worry because they quickly discovered that communities need more than generalized good will; they need specific rules. So they have been calling for etiquette, by name. Or at least by the clever name of "netiquette," which is close enough for Miss Manners.

Anyone who wants to participate in a particular community or activity is supposed to learn its standards of appropriateness and taste. Ideas of what is fitting cannot be assumed. As there is a huge variety of different communities available on the Internet, local etiquette is required for each one.

How much preparation is one expected to do beforehand so that others are not bothered with being asked to repeat themselves? How much is it polite to contribute to the conversation before one makes oneself a bore? When is it all right to change the subject and by how much should any digression deviate from the announced topic? When can or should two people go off to continue their conversation in private?

Is shouting (which is to say, writing in upper case) permitted? Is angling for professional advancement (inserting any form of advertising) tolerated? How can salacious exchanges be contained so that they do not offend non-participants? What protection is there against offensive propositions? Where is the line between joking and vulgarity? Between friendliness and prying? Between teasing and flaming?

These problems are far from solved, but at least the acknowledgment has been made that only strict rules of etiquette will prevent individuals from spoiling Internet colloquy for the rest of the community. When violations occur, there has been little hesitation to issue warnings; repeated violations result in the ultimate social weapon of ostracism. There are attempts to bring in the law, but the hopelessness of policing this new community is obvious to those in it. Nowadays it is only the fuddy-duddies who fail to understand the relevance of etiquette to truly modern society.

As more and more computer users tap into the Internet, the level of incivility has increased to the point where some Internet pioneers are abandoning cyberspace, the *Wall Street Journal* reports. The paper said some newcomers are "taking a hostile, abusive attitude to anyone they disagree with" and a Harvard University physics professor told the *Journal* about so-called "flame wars"—name-calling exchanges—over whether the theory of special relativity is correct.

A California consultant explained to the *Journal* that when the Internet started in the 1970s, access was limited to a privileged few and "it was a fairly monolithic population where customs were enforced through a culture, and people were relatively polite." One academic told the paper: "The bigger the network community gets, the more it behaves like society as a whole."

Chapter Thirteen

TRADITION MOVES AHEAD

People seem to harbor the quaint notion that etiquette is a static set of rules fixed, back in the mists of time, by a council consisting of Miss Manners, her old chum Queen Victoria and each council member's very own less-favorite grandmother—not the grandmother who whispered, "Come here, I have a special treat for you," but the one who hissed, "Cahn't that chi-ild pul-eeze sit still, even for one minute?"

This trio is even yet lying in wait for the otherwise happy-go-lucky (the belief persists). Unless you vehemently reject their authority, they will spring out and humiliate you for violating a rickety and trivial rule no sensible person even knows.

Miss Manners tries to encourage this fantasy. She finds the notion of such power flattering—no, thrilling, if you want to know the truth. She also finds it more attractive than those tedious anti-etiquette arguments also currently floating about: that one individual's rudeness is another person's individuality, or that one culture's rudeness is another culture's tradition. By thus defining rudeness out of existence, this line of thinking declares all standards of behavior illegitimate and invalidates the complaints of those who are being treated badly.

All the same, people who claim that they are merely exercising their individuality keep right on disappointing, inconveniencing and offending everybody when they ignore the rules of etiquette. Whole cultures are cruelly insulted when such universally condemned behavior as public drunkenness, sexual harassment and intimidation are explained by saying, "Oh, but that's part of their culture." We can't have that, now, can we?

Neither can Miss Manners, in good faith, deny that etiquette requires individual judgment, is culturally based and, far from being a Victorian invention, has been evolving since civilization began and will continue to do so. Confidentially, she helps it along by giving it a discreet shove forward herself now and then. Every once in a while, society makes a technological leap that must be tamed with etiquette rules and now and again it even advances the cause of human dignity by including some previously maltreated group, and Miss Manners rushes to custom-tailor some old customs to make it feel welcome.

Does anybody want to help?

Why do the same people always volunteer—the ones who haven't done their homework?

It is with affection and exasperation (a combination that occurs frequently in nature, as anyone who has lived in a family can tell you) that Miss Manners contemplates those she thinks of as Miss Manners' Loyal Opposition.

These are people who are always making up their own rules of etiquette, or violating existing rules, because they think it would be more deeply polite than doing the obvious. Bless their souls, they drive us all crazy by giving etiquette too much thought. Rather than follow the common procedures, they analyze each situation and then do what they personally believe ought to be best for everyone.

This might mean guessing that people who have begged that they not be brought food when they entertain don't really mean it and would be hurt if their express instructions were followed, thus embarrassing everybody else at the party who obeyed. Or it could mean assuming that people who have sent a formal wedding invitation don't really understand that it requires a formal reply and would therefore think they were being ridiculed if they were, in turn, addressed in the third person.

It is impossible not to believe in the good will of Miss Manners' Loyal Opposition, as opposed to the Disloyal Opposition, who fight the sacred cause with arguments ranging from "But I don't feel like being polite" to "Because I don't feel like it, it would be hypocritical, and thus morally wrong, to act as if I do." Miss Manners is not fond of those people. She tries to be tolerant, but it is difficult; their own relatives and friends don't seem to care for them. In contrast, members of the Loyal Opposition are not only genuinely devoted to the principles of manners and aware of the specific rules of etiquette, but prepared to put a great deal of effort into getting the latter to serve the former.

This is what Miss Manners herself and all polite people must do. It is never enough simply to mean well, without following the particular rules that define politeness for a specific society. Nobody is going to appreciate the fact that your heart is overflowing with kindness if your mouth is overflowing as well. Nor is it acceptable to follow the rules while defying the spirit for which they were designed. You do not insist that food be served from the left if you know that the person to whom the platter is being presented is left-handed.

Being polite therefore requires constant judgments. Normally polite people check, while routinely following the rules of etiquette, that there are not some special circumstances that require suspending these. Not the Loyal Opposition, which approaches each case as a challenge, resorting to conventional behavior only when other possibilities have been exhausted. The guiding spirit is not "What is the common thing to do in this case?" but "What can I work out that would express what I assume that other people would prefer?" This sounds terribly considerate, and it is certainly more work. The Loyal Opposition will not accept either the standard practices of the society or the stated positions of individuals, but must go beyond them.

Even if the possibility of error were not enormous, it is audacious to be peeping constantly into people's souls and unflattering to assume that you know better what they mean than they do, either because they don't understand themselves or they don't understand the forms of etiquette they are practicing. Under ordinary circumstances, respect demands taking people at face value. Politeness requires presuming that they know what they are doing.

Giving the accepted response—practicing standard forms of courteous behavior—when there is not an obvious reason to do otherwise, has the advantages of being safe and intelligible. It minimizes offensiveness, because any discomfiting action is interpreted as being merely conventional, not custom-designed to the wrong fit. The Loyal Opposition, with its original approach, leaves itself open to being drastically misunderstood by those less aware than Miss Manners of its kindly intent. If they really wish to help—and Miss Manners and the world need all the help they can get with this—they must study the principles, techniques and roots of manners and etiquette so that they can effect change properly.

Looking Backwards

DEAR MISS MANNERS,

I see in you a tendency to romanticize the past and monsterize the present. Have people changed that much? Surely our world has changed dramatically and all of us need more awareness of the manner of how we treat one another, but all we have is now—this present moment. Greed, selfishness, pride, etc., are a part of all of us, now and in the past. I find the lamenting over how things used to be tiresome and a rose-colored view of the past.

GENTLE READER,

Have you been paying such close attention to Miss Manners' hairdo that you missed what she has been saying? Wild horses could not drag her back to live in the past. For one thing, she has too clear a memory of what perfectly agreeable tame horses, who kindly provided public transportation in a previous era, left in the streets. There are too many things she could not live without, such as air conditioning and feminism.

This does not mean that she doesn't also appreciate antiques. It is true that etiquette, like law, is deeply connected to tradition and Miss Manners refuses to discard tradition unless there is a compelling reason to do so—which there often is. One of her main tasks is to alter traditions so that they fit modern conditions.

Nobody is more aware than Miss Manners (who is beginning to sound defensive and really must stop) that many people erroneously believe that change is always for the worse. Grown-ups have always lamented the appalling manners of younger generations. It would be cheating the young of a source of satisfaction if they did not. There are also great improvements in traditional behavior—the egalitarian spread of respect, for example—and nobody champions them more than she does.

Nevertheless, there really is something different and seriously wrong—although not unprecedented—about the present era. Every two hundred years or so—MM has lost count—the idea resurfaces that natural behavior is the best and we should not just change manners, but do away with them altogether and use only the law to control behavior. This is a perfectly terrible idea that produces both a high level of friction and intense attempts at repression.

If only the society would recognize that the gentler, freer, extralegal system of etiquette cannot be abandoned, we could get peacefully back to sensible discussions of how people might like to change it.

A REVIEW

Etiquette, despite its simplistic reputation of being "just a matter of common sense" or "always making other people feel comfortable," is a complicated discipline. Even common sense can get you into etiquette trouble if you try to interpret convention (such as the statement "Call me any time") at face value. There are occasions when good people are obliged to make others—for example, people expressing bigotry—feel uncomfortable.

The prevailing etiquette in any culture is a mixture of tradition and practicality. Often something that "makes sense" does so merely because that is the arbitrary way it has always been done. In a field rich with symbolism and ritual, not everything can be deduced from first principles.

Why the rules should be followed, and when they are due for a change, is by no means obvious. There are universal ideals underlying the body of rules, such as respect for others, but the connection between that and when to wear a hat may be difficult for the casual observer to fathom; and what one generation interprets as respectful deference toward the weak, the next may interpret as disrespectful condescension.

Within the general rules of the society, there are special rules that subgroups—defined by such factors as age, occupation, background, geography or habits—use for their own pleasure and cultural identity. One has to know when they should be used and when the standard of the greater society should prevail.

Context and motivation must be judged in the application of any given rule. When two rules conflict, one has to judge which to follow. It is even possible to imagine a situation where proper etiquette would dictate violating a rule of etiquette.

As complicated as all this may sound, any child can learn etiquette successfully, just as any child can learn a language, regardless of how complicated a linguistics expert can make it sound.

Etiquette in Action: An Example

Let us go back to that troublesome "fork" question, which is always being pointed at Miss Manners' throat. Those who sneer at etiquette as being "a matter of which fork to use" fancy that they have skewered the entire complex subject for being silly and mean. However, setting out lots of forks violates the etiquette rule against showing off and remarking that someone else chose the wrong one violates the etiquette rule against criticizing others. Paradoxically (considering that no one is supposed to be monitoring, much less criticizing, anyone else), eating according to the rules of one's community is probably the deepest ritual of respect there is, even more strictly observed in primitive than in technologically advanced cultures.

Ordinarily, someone who violates a rule will be considered disrespectful of the company or the culture, especially if this seems to come from willful ignorance or indifference. If the lapses can be accounted for by an inability to comply (because one is ill or too young or a stranger to the community), the onus of making the mistake *seem* undetected falls on those who knew better. Because these rules have changed with time, Miss Manners is the only one allowed to set her table with such booby traps as bacon forks, bird forks, anchovy forks, lemon forks and ramekin forks. In anyone else, it would be a violation of current rules to go by the mid-Victorian variety.

WORKSHOP TOPICS

RESPECT

Authorized Change: Overdue recognition that even servants and passersby are human beings has required that they no longer be treated as furniture.

Continuing Problem: There are so many opportunities to recognize humanity that nobody has any peace anymore.

Examples:

Total Interaction

Do we really have to interact with everyone? Telephone solicitors? Former spouses? Doorbell ringers with a cause? Chatty people sharing mass transit? Criminals who have been rehabilitated through celebrityhood?

It was a noble advance in etiquette, Miss Manners admits, when everyone was required to acknowledge that all those other people in the world are human beings, regardless of the circumstances under which one encounters them. Before that humanistic breakthrough, polite people were allowed, even required, to pretend that most of the people they clearly saw were invisible. Servants were considered to be robots who should not be recognized in any way except for three jolly minutes at

Christmas. Things simply got done or didn't get done or appeared on the table or crashed in the kitchen, without any apparent realization that human effort was involved. In turn, the polite servant was supposed to stifle any animation in order to appear as much of a robot as possible.

Even people in the same social circles were not to be approached if a proper introduction had not been performed. Those who met accidentally while visiting the same friend were able to presume on that chance encounter for later socializing. Ladies had the option of consenting or refusing to be introduced to gentlemen who showed an interest in meeting them. They had the further option of appearing not to "see" gentlemen they did know when they ran across one another in public, meaning that so long as they kept a plausible distance, they could refuse to stop and chat with them without being insulting. However, if one *wanted* to be insulting, the practice of pretending not to see someone, under circumstances where it was obviously impossible not to, was a severe social weapon. To "look right through" someone whom one knew was to signify dignified outrage, the consequence of either a personal affront or extreme disapproval of someone one considered to be in disgrace.

As mean as this system was, Miss Manners feels obliged to mention that it had its advantages. The servants whose presence the masters forgot through the habit of ignoring them made a fortune from repeating or agreeing not to repeat what they had plainly seen or heard. Ladies didn't have to tell certain gentlemen that they had to wash their hair every night of the week. After being out in public, they could save themselves the trouble of having to explain to their other friends why they were where they were, or with whom. People who were perfectly furious at one another did not have to engage in shouting or shooting matches to make their disapproval clear.

Miss Manners is not suggesting that these advantages would be worth reviving the habit of ignoring people. Yet she has some sympathy for the increasing exasperation on the part of people who simply cannot hold full social amenities with everyone who importunes them and still go on with their own lives. If every chance encounter opens the possibility of acquaintanceship, and anyone who wants to approach the public for commercial, political or personal reasons is free to do so everywhere, there have got to be polite ways to decline these opportunities.

The skill of civilly acknowledging having been approached, followed by a firm return to one's privacy, is essential if people are to be allowed to run their own lives rather than always react to the wishes of others. A quick but uninviting smile, a "No, I'm sorry," or a "Thank you, but I'm afraid I'm not interested," is all that is required toward a well-behaved stranger on the street or one who rings a door or telephone bell. Excuses are superfluous, because the encounter being proposed was never accepted. People who perform services, or their clients, should be cheerfully recognized and thanked, with the recognition that attempts at more intense socializing invade their privacy. Serving the public should not open one to the public's nosiness or flirtatiousness.

The total refusal of recognition—the Cut Direct, as it was called—is still appropriate for strangers who make obscene remarks, or former acquaintances whom one has judged to have otherwise overstepped the bounds of civilized behavior.

As for the merely inconvenient encounter, Miss Manners misses the 18th century Venetian custom of wearing masks. They may or may not have concealed one's identity, but they obliged everyone else to pretend that they did.

A Poor Solution

DEAR MISS MANNERS,

I am a professional telemarketer who spends a great deal of time on the phone speaking with the public. My colleagues and I agree that we are not at all offended by a firm but polite "No, thanks, we are not interested." We do, however, take issue with those individuals who feel the need to verbally abuse us over the phone simply for doing our jobs. Realizing that we do, at times, call at indelicate moments, that our calls do occasionally constitute an invasion of privacy, it is not our intention to do so.

GENTLE READER,

By no means excusing the rudeness you encounter, Miss Manners fears that she must gently point out that you cannot reasonably expect people to separate the personal motivation of a stranger from the task he is doing.

What you are doing is rude. Never mind arguing that you need to earn a living, that you personally do not intend to break into people's lives and that many people must be grateful for the opportunity your employer offers for you, or telemarketing would not be profitable.

When the telephone rings and a stranger begins a sales pitch, the object of it has been caught in the privacy of his or her own home and forced, however momentarily, to drop everything and listen. Although those called should know that they can politely cut the call short as you suggest, many react as if a stranger has broken into the house, as indeed one has. Miss Manners is sorry to tell you that she hopes such techniques will not be permitted and that you are able to earn a more acceptable living in another manner. Angering large numbers of people is not good business.

In the meantime, she suggests at least beginning with an apology. You might bring to your employer's attention the idea that if you open with a polite "I'm terribly sorry to bother you," perhaps you could encourage more polite, and even more productive, responses.

A Better Solution

DEAR MISS MANNERS,

My wife chided me a few evenings ago. It's not the first time, but I'm still struggling to recover. Our family had just been seated to enjoy the evening meal when there was a knock at the front door. I went to the door, accompanied by my two daughters. Upon seeing through the window two young men with whom I was not acquainted, I sought to set an example of caution for my children, so rather than opening the door I asked them through the window how I might be of assistance.

They responded that they had a petition on some environmental issue upon which they wished me to place my signature. Now, you must understand, Miss Manners, I am a champion of environmental causes. I compost grass clippings and recycle newspapers. But I was hungry, my dinner was quickly becoming cold and I didn't want to chat about acid rain. I therefore responded—with a disappointed half smile, as you suggest—"I don't believe we'll be interested."

The young man responded in a scolding tone, "Is there a reason?"

I answered "Yes," and returned to the table to eat. My wife believes I set an example of rudeness for my children.

GENTLE READER,

Miss Manners trusts that your wife didn't chide you in front of your children, thus setting them a bad example about respect. As for the rest of the incident, she is almost entirely on your side. The lesson you have taught your children is not only not to open doors to strangers, but not to allow unauthorized intrusions to disrupt your private life. Not answering the telephone or the doorbell, or making short work of those interruptions, teaches that family time is more important than the non-emergency demands of others.

That you couldn't resist a smartsy reply at the intruder's persistence is the source of Miss Manners' tiny reservation. You might have merely said a firm "Excuse me, please," and returned to the table. It is a minor point. Miss Manners just doesn't want to encourage other smartsy remarks from people claiming that the plight of the environment is an emergency, thus justifying the disruption. It is a fine cause but so is the perilous state of family life.

MAKING FRIENDS

Authorized Change: Because young people refuse to stick around until their parents have found them proper mates and social circles, work is now considered a proper venue for meeting new people.

Continuing Problem: You never know whom you will meet and whether they want to be friends.

Examples:

The Lineup

DEAR MISS MANNERS,

I have recently begun employment in the records section of a police department. Because I fit the general description of a suspect, I was asked to participate in a lineup. Four of us knew each other, as we all work together here. The fifth (the suspect) was not acquainted with us. We were not introduced and the four of us kind of thoughtlessly left her out of our conversation which was, for the most part, joking about being in the lineup. She wasn't a suspected murderer, just a suspected forger, so we had no reason, I feel, to shun her. Please let me know what is the correct etiquette for a lineup. I am sure this is right up your alley.

GENTLE READER,

Indeed. It is also the kind of letter that inspires otherwise polite people to suspect Miss Manners of making these problems up. She begs to assure them that it came on police department stationery, so we are dealing with one character or another in this story—if not the police employee, then the suspected forger.

Even allowing for the fact that the newcomer is under your roof, so to speak, and is to be considered innocent because she has not been proven guilty, this is not a social occasion. Miss Manners assures you that although politeness is required (as much, by the way, to a suspected murderer as to a suspected forger), making one feel at home and at ease is not.

The Cafeteria

DEAR MISS MANNERS,

I'm a new employee and would like to meet and get to know people. But in the cafeteria, people often discuss business or need time alone. How could I approach people politely to invite an honest answer? I've tried, "Excuse me, are you discussing business, or may I join you?" I get, "We are, but please sit down." Sometimes I learn more about the company and sometimes I sit like a dummy, wishing I could read my book.

GENTLE READER,

It seems to Miss Manners that the fault is neither in the way you put the question nor in the way the people you approached put the answer. It was in the fact that after the exchange, you sat down.

You must realize that there was no polite way for these people to say, "Yes, go away." Had they wanted to chat at that time, they would have said simply, "Please sit down," to indicate that whatever they were discussing before, they were now open to conversation with you. The answer they did give was a polite refusal meaning, "There is a conversation in progress that we plan to continue," but making it clear that they were neither rejecting your company in general nor holding a conversation that they wanted kept secret from other employees.

Had you said cheerfully, "Oh, well then I'll catch you some other time" and moved on, you would not only have allowed them to continue as they wished, but would have given a friendly indication that you wanted to get to know them, which they would probably respond to at a more convenient time.

PRECEDENCE

Authorized Change: From Ladies First system among strangers to one based on age and need.

Continuing Problem: Nobody can figure out which system we're on, and they're clogging up the bus aisles so Miss Manners missed her stop.

Examples:

Changing Systems

DEAR MISS MANNERS,

If you have two males or two females coming to a door from opposite directions and both are being rude by trying to go through the door at the same time, who has the right of way—the person who's going into or out of the building, or the person who opened the door first? Even if the door is opened from the inside or outside of the building.

GENTLE READER,

Miss Manners notices that you specify that both people are rude. Therefore, the person who goes through the door first is going to be the one who is bigger.

Etiquette is the system that tries to replace this Might Makes Right system with something kinder. The person who opens the door should hold it open so that the other may pass through first, and that person should offer thanks. But that is presuming two polite people, which is, Miss Manners admits, something of a stretch.

Changing Seats and Systems

DEAR MISS MANNERS,

Is it proper for a young healthy female (age 27) to give up her seat on the bus to an older or elderly gentleman?

GENTLE READER,

As you may have noticed, we are changing our precedence system. Miss Manners has noticed that many people are stuck at that in-between stage, where they have kindly dropped the gender system but forgotten to start the need system. That people would rather keep their seats while they give up any claim to being polite strikes Miss Manners as indeed a sorry state of affairs.

This is a time for both systems to be used and for expressions of gratitude for either. That is to say, the young lady should offer the seat, the gentleman should thank the young lady and take it; but a young lady offered a seat by an older gentleman should also accept and thank.

A Poor Solution

DEAR MISS MANNERS,

My problem is one that many older women might think they'd like to have, but it troubles me. I am in my mid-60's and I assume I look it, because recently men have started offering me a seat on the subway. It doesn't happen every day but probably a couple of times a month. Sometimes I have taken the seat, with a warm smile and a gracious "thank you," but I don't feel right about it. I'm perfectly healthy and able to stand. What is more significant, I'm out there in the working world, competing with men—I hold what until recently was considered "a man's job"—and don't feel entitled to any special courtesies on the sole ground that I am a woman. Furthermore, I think that women who expect the courtesies but also expect equal treatment in the job market are helping to perpetuate male resistance to women's equality.

For these reasons, I have generally refused the offer of a seat, also with a warm smile and, I hope, a most gracious manner. Sometimes I try to explain my reason; sometimes I just say something like "I'm okay standing, thanks." Neither response feels adequate and I worry that the gentleman will feel like a fool and will never again take the risk of showing a courtesy to an older woman.

GENTLE READER,

Miss Manners admires your argument, although she disagrees with your action. As you point out, your refusal—not to mention the threat of giving a lecture on equality to someone who is only trying to be nice on the bus—would make the gentleman resolve to control such impulses in the future. Some frail, pregnant or overburdened lady will suffer the consequences.

"Ladies first" is not the only possible system of precedence, even in this case. Before your claim that it was on "the sole ground that I am a woman," you mentioned your age and the fact that it is only recently that you have been receiving such offers. Do you really wish to extend the competition of the workplace to all facets of life? It is true that age often counts for nothing in the job world—it is likely to count against one. Do you wish to extend this to private life, erasing the tradition of respect the young were supposed to show to their elders?

A sure way to do that is to reject courtesies on the grounds that you do not find them philosophically correct.

Another Poor Solution

DEAR MISS MANNERS,

The cast:

Me, a gray-haired woman, strong and healthy.

Well-intentioned Person, who doesn't just walk through the entrance, holding the door for me to follow, but who opens the doors, steps aside, and gestures me to enter first, thereby placing me in line first.

The question:

Although annoyed at this behavior, I smile and offer my thanks because the motive is sincere. Once inside, do I insist that the door-holder take a place in front of me in line, or assume that if it's perceived that opening a door is not easy for me, perhaps standing in line also is not?

GENTLE READER,

How nice that you want to use your strength and health to knock out the pitifully few remnants of courtesy we have left. Of all the annoyances reported to Miss Manners, you get the prize for being subjected to having a door held open for you.

What makes you think that courtesy is only a patronizing sop extended to the helpless? To civilized people, the gesture you spurn represents human kindness, respect and grace. Miss Manners is at least grateful that you smiled, pretended to be pleased and suggested offering a return courtesy, which is a good idea. She just wants to make sure you don't go around spoiling things for those of us who hope to live to be not as strong as you are now.

NOMENCLATURE

Authorized Change: From a system by which wives automatically took the names of their husbands, causing them to have to check their drivers' licenses to ascertain their identity, to allowing those who wish to keep their original names or to make up original names.

Continuing Problem: All terms of respect for everyone are being dropped and still nobody knows how to address any lady without running the risk of angering her.

Examples:

Honorifics

DEAR MISS MANNERS,

I thought everything was all cleared up about name usage in addressing letters—until I went to write my graduation thank you notes. First, I decided to address my grandparents by what you recommend—Mr. Grandpa and Ms. Grandma. I thought they wouldn't care which name was first.

But then I hit a bump with my aunt and uncle. The husband of my dad's sister has always been kind of domineering and he would probably not like it very much to see a woman's name before his own. Nonetheless, I decided to address the letter to "Mr. and Mrs. Smith" because I could only think that the "and" would make them equal. But that doesn't sound right at all. And last, I came across my other aunt and uncle, whom we've always called "Mary and John" (wife first) because I guess it just sounded right. But isn't John being left out? Maybe you can set this straight and you won't have to be bothered any more by the "rationale of name usage."

GENTLE READER,

Miss Manners certainly hopes so. Having to puzzle out which part of a couple is more egotistical than the other is not a fit occupation for anyone, and Miss Manners does not want to see it used as an excuse for delaying thank you letters.

Conventional address exists exactly to spare writers the necessity of figuring out what "sounds right" for each letter and to prevent the recipients from taking idiotic insult. The trouble now is that we have more than one conventional form. In the absence of absolute knowledge about individuals' preferences, one must guess which is more agreeable to them.

The traditional usage is "Mr. and Mrs. Grandpa Teddybear" (not "Mr. Grandpa" and "Ms. Grandma"). Married ladies who do not use their husbands' surnames, or who use professional titles socially, are "Dr. Grandma Kitten/Mr. Grandpa Teddybear" on two lines. If you can't find out what each one prefers, choose one or the other for each couple and hope for the best. Fortunately, there are no special designations for the domineering or the self-effacing.

A Poor Solution

DEAR MISS MANNERS,

One result of the push for male-female sameness is the practice of many newspapers of referring to a woman by her last name. After an introductory reference "Mary

Jones" becomes simply "Jones." Since surnames historically have been passed along the male line, this can turn out to be ridiculous, as well as crude. One comes across examples like "Stockman gave birth to her baby," "Beard likes her beauty make-over," or "Peterson feels her identity as a woman . . ."

The reverse mix-up can also occur when a man happens to have a first name like Joyce or Rose. One way to avoid this neutering of the species is to use titles.

Obviously, the women's movement intended to honor equal treatment and courtesy both, by coming up with the designation "Ms." I don't like it myself. It looks and sounds like a linguistic mutant. Personally, like you, I choose "Miss," a title that can connote a lively professionalism, even glamour. We are living through a spasm of conflicts as to what innate sexual identity is. In the same printed document, I have come across the designations, "Mrs. Richard Smith, Chairperson," and "Ms. Helen White, Vice Chairman."

GENTLE READER,

Before Miss Manners voices her agreement with your distaste for abandoning titles, she feels obliged to point out that you are the cause of the problem of which this is an unfortunate solution. (And you thought you and she were on the same side, two nice misses together.)

Oh, maybe not you personally. It is the habit you share with the rest of modern society of analyzing what ought to be a simple convention until it becomes a dangerous minefield that has caused newspapers, and a lot of individuals, simply to give up using courtesy titles. By unilaterally vetoing the sensible solution of "Ms." and ignoring the conventional interpretation of "Miss," you are suggesting that your idiosyncratic preferences be forced on everyone. (Nor is your claim historically accurate. Although revived by 20th century feminists, "Ms." has been around since at least the 17th century as an abbreviation for the honorific "Mistress," which applied to both married and unmarried ladies and from which both "Miss" and "Mrs." derive.)

You would infuriate those who feel that "Miss" conveys unglamorous spinsterhood, those who prefer the traditional married form and those who do not want their marital status defined in a way that is not done for gentlemen. That's a lot of angry people. It is precisely in order to avoid this tedious furor that courtesy titles are disappearing. Those who compile such lists as you mention are making the polite decision that addressing people as they wish is more important than uniformity.

Yes, there should be a standard system. It is probably Miss Manners' obligation to devise one. One of these days—when *she* feels she can stand all that tedious furor—

she will. In the meantime, a lady should be addressed by the courtesy title she prefers, if it is known, and as "Ms." if it is not known. For all her sternness, Miss Manners agrees with you that abandoning touches of courtesy, in a world already desperately lacking in it, is a horrible solution.

A Worse Solution

DEAR MISS MANNERS,

My friend refers to her clients, in their absence, as "ladies," while I say that they should be called "women." Please enlighten us; a dinner is at stake.

PITTSBURGH, PA.—A Federal Judge apologized to a lawyer after he threatened her with jail when she insisted on using her maiden name and the honorific "Ms." in court. The Judge told her in front of the jury that he was going to call her "Mrs." followed by her husband's last name and at one point during the trial he had said, "What if I call you sweetie?"

GENTLE READER,

"Guys." Two or more female persons are now addressed to their faces as "You guys," Miss Manners has observed, and in their absence as "Those guys." Does she get the dinner? No?

Perhaps you would prefer to take each other out. You are right that they should be called "women" in their absence, although your friend is right if she calls them "ladies" to their faces. Except for Miss Manners, one uses the term "ladies" socially and "women" otherwise. Those who want to ban the term "ladies" altogether, on the grounds that it perpetuates denying them any other role than a social one, are going about reform in the wrong way. The way to improve matters is not to strip female persons of courtesy words, but to insist that usage always be parallel to that of those whom we will generously call gentlemen.

A Poor Example

When Miss Manners' dear college informed her it had named a new president, she was both pleased and curious. Who was it? Diana. Not even President Diana; just Diana.

For a wild moment, Miss Manners put together her knowledge of what sort of people traditionally use only their first names in official life, with the evidence that there is currently a tenuously employed princess by that name who might welcome a sensible job. Could it be . . . ?

Well, no. When Miss Manners went back and read more carefully the official announcement from the college's chair of the board of trustees, she discovered that the new president did have a surname. Two, in fact. But these were only used in first mention, while all subsequent references used her first name alone. (Miss Manners does not wish to dwell on the relationship between her hasty reading and her academic record, except to say that the college is certainly not to blame for that.)

Was it for this that the alumnae fought for the dignity of being referred to as women rather than girls? That it took decades to get across the idea that women should be addressed, in professional life, with honorifics other than "Honey"? As a general in the battle against the invasion of false familiarity, Miss Manners thought she had known the extent of the territory the enemy had conquered. But for the forces of instant intimacy to have captured a college president was an amazing feat.

What reasoning could have been involved here eludes Miss Manners. She is familiar with the rationale of the opposing forces and cannot understand which argument proved to be overpowering. The most usual explanation given by adults who want strangers and children to call them by their first names is that it makes them seem young. How would that apply in this case? Is it really an advantage for a college president to appear callow?

The next most popular argument is that it seems friendly. Indeed, many professors have succumbed to the odd notion that students should feel personally attached to and on an equal level with their teachers. Why anyone would tolerate friends who grade them and make them write papers is a question that springs to mind. As for those personal attachments initiated by teachers, the less said the better.

Besides, who would want a college president who is on the same level with the students? Okay, students would. But what about rich people who are careful not to turn over large sums of money even to their very own children until those children are able to convince them that they are mature?

GREETINGS

Authorized change: Strict formality has been loosened in favor of pleasantness and warmth.

Continuing problem: Some of those people bearing greetings are scary, and some of them are sloppy.

Examples:

"Why, hello there."

"Hi."

"How y'doing?"

What could be more innocent than such greetings, even when they are offered to passersby by people previously unknown to them? Surely only a petty stickler for manners (and we know who that is) could object to obvious manifestations of pure friendliness in this otherwise cold world.

Etiquette, after all, depends for its existence on the very feelings of sociability that inspire people to extend courtesies to others. Stern discipline that it is, it also recognizes that good motives may cancel out the fault of violating its own technical rules. In fact, it considers that to rebuff what are obviously intended as courtesies is a much worse form of rudeness than slipping up on the details. But . . . what motives are obvious?

Let us suppose that a lady is hurrying home after dark, approaching her car, which is parked on a suddenly quiet street. Out of the isolation and silence, she hears an unknown masculine voice close at hand, breathing a friendly greeting into her ear.

Or a child out playing is approached by an unknown adult, all smiles, and warm greetings.

Eeeeek!

It may be found, on strict examination of the individuals proffering these greetings, that they were both kindly people hoping to bring a bit of pleasantness into the lives of others without any sinister plans. Indeed, it has been vehemently argued in the past that ladies actually enjoy receiving acknowledgment of their attractiveness from strangers on the street. Only one hears that less now that the ladies' point of view has been aired in no uncertain terms.

It is easy to find instances when the greetings of strangers may be judged to be well meant. Miss Manners does not bar the customary greetings of mountain climbers passing on a path, or the spontaneous recognition following having often seen the same person in one's neighborhood. Nor does she suggest that those who are overcome by the charm of children be arrested for saying, "My what a cute baby," or that people confined in a train or airplane be forbidden to attempt conversation.

But passing greetings must be greetings and they must be made in passing. In other words, "Lookin' good" is not good, as it is not a greeting; and passing means that the greeter passes on, without lingering for conversation.

Handshakes

DEAR MISS MANNERS,

I have three objections to the fact that when I meet a man for the first time, he invariably extends his hand for a shake.

1. The handshake is an anachronistic, male-originated custom, started as a peace sign proving there were no weapons in the hand.
2. The custom is that only the female may initiate the handshake.
3. As a physician, I can assure you that it is needlessly transmitting germs.

You may imagine my discomfiture at assaying a decline to such a friendly gesture. Most of the time I yield to the social pressure but occasionally I get away with either pretending not to notice or giving a wave. One man was so insistent that I gathered up my courage and said, "I do not like to shake hands," to which he responded as if I had just bitten him.

Being the pessimist, I am anticipating Miss Manners' rebuff: Oh, my, you are making such a fuss over this trivial little nicety and yes, those men don't know their etiquette about ladies' initiating, etc. I really don't want a lecture. Someone starts a tradition and someone can begin the slow process of changing it. How do I go about this least painfully?

GENTLE READER,

Don't worry about the lecture. You already know the etiquette you wish to violate and Miss Manners has no desire to quarrel with a physician about germs—or anyone about the philosophical trade-off between symbolizing peace and maleness.

All you have to do is to refrain from lecturing the gentlemen as well, which would be another etiquette violation. The one who looked bitten naturally assumed that you didn't want to shake hands with him in particular. A friendly smile and the quick comment, "Oh, I'm so sorry, I can't shake hands" would excuse you from the gesture you disdain.

The way to change people's thinking is not to get them miffed when you first meet them but to engage them in conversation after, when they do not feel you have threatened their dignity. A physician who goes around saying that handshaking promotes illness will probably attract quite a bit of interest. Miss Manners expects to hear from you again when some enthusiastic convert gives you a big old grateful hug.

Hugging and Kissing

DEAR MISS MANNERS,

Some people are uncomfortable with hugging and kissing as greetings, now a widespread practice, and prefer a more traditional form such as a handshake or a pleasant exchange of words. What is a sensible way to fend off those who launch themselves with outstretched arms and puckered lips?

The rules for shaking hands in both business and social situations have become somewhat blurred. Please review traditional practices of shaking hands when an older person and a younger person are introduced to each other and when a male and female are introduced.

GENTLE READER,

Miss Manners supposes that the target of this human missile of the outstretched arms and puckered lips could just step out of the way and let it crash into the nearest wall. The next time, it would probably stick out a cautious hand to feel its way and that hand could be grabbed and shaken.

A method less harsh on the plastering is to put out a hand first, serving the dual purpose of indicating friendliness and protecting the face from friendly assault.

The first move is the privilege of the lady, the older person and the higher ranking business person or government or religious official. When these attributes all converge on the same person, this is simple. When they do not—for example, when an elderly male governor meets a young female rabbi—things do get blurry. When in doubt, Miss Manners suggests a big smile and two steps backwards.

CAUTION

Authorized Change: The increase in crime has required people to develop ways of protecting themselves.

Continuing Problem: People are being considered guilty until proven innocent.
Examples:

Etiquette has always urged caution. Introductions were not invented simply to embarrass people who hadn't memorized whether a female bishop married to a second lieutenant should be presented to a MacArthur Foundation genius of indeterminate gender, or vice versa.

The view that hug-everybody movements never met the standards of etiquette was a bit of standoffishness that gave etiquette a bad reputation. Given the choice between being thought prissy and being thought available to being felt up by strangers, etiquette decided it could live with prissiness.

The sensible need to distinguish between friends and strangers does not, however, absolve people of the obligation to be polite to strangers. It seems to Miss Manners that fear of crime is increasingly being used to excuse the omission of such basic courtesies as giving directions and other forms of assistance in harmless situations. However, the courtesy of making sure that every lady is offered a protective escort after dark is back in effect. The requirement for not unduly scaring people now includes keeping a formal distance between oneself and, for example, the person ahead who is using a banking machine.

The problem Miss Manners finds most heartbreaking comes from people who feel that they are being regarded as criminals, not because of anything they do but because of race, gender or age. A seventh grader complains that the candy stop on the way home from school has become unpleasant because he is obviously under suspicion. "I can understand how the store might be concerned about teenagers stealing candy," he concedes, "but I have no intention of doing so. What would be a polite way to get the message across that I'm not going to grab some Snickers and run? I don't want to say something like 'Get off my back!' or get upset, nor do I want to growl at them under my breath."

A father reports that mother-to-mother invitations for their daughter's play dates are "received with enthusiasm—until my wife happens to mention that Dad would be looking after the kids. I am as protective of children as any of these parents and at least as aware of the prevalence of abuse in these times. I don't mind meeting parents and talking with them prior to picking up their kids for a play date. I'm already well known to the children and teachers at my daughter's school, having carved pumpkins in her classroom, given a presentation there and carpooled."

While trying not to take it personally, he confesses "despair that involved and loving fathers like myself are doomed to suffer many more such indignities in the future. And my wife and I wonder how to behave. May we communicate our dismay without being rude ourselves? Should we (gasp) confront the parent by asking what s/he is afraid of?"

Miss Manners doesn't need to tell these generous-minded people that fear, not meanness, prompts these unpleasant encounters and ask them to refrain from being rude back. She can only hope that they will derive some satisfaction from politely addressing the concerns so crudely shown—the youngster by saying pointedly but pleasantly, "Hello, I'm one of your regular customers," and the father by making the date directly and saying, "I don't believe I've seen you around school, but our daughters are friends and perhaps you'd like to come by with her. I'm sure you understand that we prefer to know the other parents."

What Miss Manners obviously does need to tell the fearful is that they cannot therefore dispense with the apparent presumption of innocence that is due to the dignity of someone who is behaving properly. She may not be able to change their assumptions, but she can point out that making them clear to those they suspect is rude. The clerk who says "May I help you, sir?" to the young customer, or the mother who says she always likes to meet her child's friends' parents, may be just as frightened and vigilant—but has decently covered it.

A Sensible Solution

DEAR MISS MANNERS,

Some gated front courtyards have doorbells, intercoms and electronic locks that the hostess controls from in the house, while others just have regular gates. Once admitted electronically through the gate, does the guest ring the front door bell, or should the hostess be waiting there, after previously talking to the guest when she buzzed him through?

How should the hostess answer the intercom to a caller that she can't see? What about leaving? Does the hostess walk the guest to the door or the gate?

Some of these gates are for security, privacy or to limit liability of small pools, etc., but aren't they a bit rude? Do you have any suggestions on how to make them more welcoming and friendly?

Gentle Reader,

If etiquette were in the habit of disparaging security measures as rude, it would have killed off its clientele long ago. Miss Manners prefers to acknowledge the necessities of the day and work politely around them.

The buzzer is answered, like a home telephone, with "Hello?" Giving one's name, or a free welcome, to any passing stranger would rather defeat the device's purpose.

Unfortunately, the reply from friends is always, "Hi, it's me!" or the occasional, "It's I." The polite but doubtful hostess will then say, "Sorry! Can't hear you—who is it?" to obtain a name.

Once identity has been established and the guest admitted through the gate, it is rude, Miss Manners agrees, to pretend to be surprised that this person actually shows up at the door. The front door is still the official point of entry—it is not necessary to fetch or return a guest to the gate, unless a host accompanies a lady for reasons of security, gallantry or both—but the hostess should be stationed by it, sparing the guest from having to petition for entry a second time.

An Awkward Solution

Dear Miss Manners,

Some of us are in professions in which we must carry a gun discreetly, mingling with others who may or may not also be armed but more often are not. While every effort is made to honor the adage "Out of sight, out of mind," occasionally a social misfortune occurs: One's gun tumbles to the floor with a loud clank or clatter. This normally is noticed by those in the vicinity, who usually stop their conversations to watch, sometimes a bit shocked. One scoops up and replaces the gun as swiftly and gracefully as circumstances permit. However, what does one say? The silence is embarrassing, and at times can deepen, to one's social disadvantage or business hardship if not eased.

Gentle Reader,

Well, yes, there is something about the sudden appearance of a gun that cuts out the chatter. Miss Manners supposes you are lucky that your friends and associates don't go diving under the nearest furniture, refusing to leave until you are gone. To restore calm, the first thing you should say is, "Excuse me, I'm terribly sorry." Beyond being the standard apology for an accident, this establishes the idea that notwithstanding the evidence of raw power, you consider yourself firmly bound by the polite restraints of civilization. Then it would be nice to add, "Sorry, I'm afraid I'm required to carry a legal weapon." Never mind the details of this. Miss Manners assures you that everyone in your vicinity will deeply appreciate knowing that you respect the law.

NATURALNESS

Change: People are behaving more naturally and openly than they used to, and frankly following the dictates of their urges and feelings.

Problem: Miss Manners would never authorize this in a million years.

A Terrible Example:

DEAR MISS MANNERS,

As I recently came out of a business office and walked into the parking lot, I encountered a young male street person urinating behind a tall shrub. I pretended not to notice him and continued walking toward my car. But as he turned and hurried past me, he said, "Excuse me." Now I felt committed to my original plan and pretended not to hear him. Should I have acknowledged his apology? If so, what could have been an appropriate response? As you have commented many times, changes in our society are constantly presenting us with new problems.

GENTLE READER,

They sure are, and Miss Manners wishes she could walk right past this one, pretending she didn't see it. That this should never have happened goes without saying. The offering and acceptance of excuses applies to matters that, however unfortunate, are not beyond civilized behavior, as this is.

Yes, Miss Manners is aware that what happened is a natural occurrence. Redirecting the promptings of nature is a basic skill of civilization. A commitment to this principle does not, however, prevent Miss Manners from noticing that in this particular case there are two ways of interpreting the offering of the excuse. One is that it was intended to pardon an unpardonable offense. The other is that the offender genuinely wished to express shame for an unavoidable accident. Still, your acceptance of the apology would kick the act back into the first category, even if it arose from the second. What a good time to practice the habit of not involving oneself in exchanges with strangers.

An Even Worse Example

Dear Miss Manners,

Is it really proper for tourists to attend a funeral "to observe local custom"? I live in a picturesque community, a tremendously beautiful area near a national park where an annual chili cook-off brings many tourists through. I live in one of those "Ghost Towns" in a home built onto an historic remain and people drive by slowly and video our houses and us while we cook or enjoy outside. I am learning to wave as they drive past the "No Trespassing" signs at the highway and pass the "Private Drive" sign, which should clearly let anyone know that this is not an exhibit. Surely this is some kind of odd compliment.

What has me so rankled is an article in a travel magazine which invites tourists, "by all means" if there is "a real burial" here to "delay your plans and attend this event steeped in local custom." I consulted an etiquette reference, which states that anyone may attend a funeral. However, I would appreciate your thoughts. I have had some experience with grief. I had the unfortunate adult responsibility of arranging and attending the funeral for my mother and simply attended the one for my father, as I was but 16. Thank goodness I knew the people in attendance. Such a personal thing is mourning, I feel.

It could happen that you might be just traveling through here someday; and just by chance, my friends might be burying me, or my ashes, that day. If you wanted to come that would be all right with me, as I feel I know you somewhat and feel that you have respect for life, but the odds of its being you are not so good. See what I mean?

Gentle Reader,

Let us hope that day is far, far off. Miss Manners would grieve to lose someone who understands the underlying principles of manners so well; she needs all the help she can get to reform others.

Apparently, we also need to rewrite some of those etiquette rules so that concepts that could once be taken for granted are made explicit for people from whom one can take nothing for granted. Sure, the books have said that anyone can attend a funeral. It just never occurred to the writers that they needed to rule out people who were simply wandering around the area looking for amusement. It was assumed that "anyone" meant anyone who wished to show respect for the deceased, whether friend or admirer from afar. It also assumed that everyone present knew how to behave at a funeral, which precludes those who go to gape at local custom, as well as those who go to make a show of their own. (Here, Miss Manners is thinking of examples she has been given of unseemly competition for the role of the most closely bereaved.)

COUPLES AND SINGLES

Authorized Change: From assuming that adults must all be married, we have stopped monitoring their private legal and social arrangements.

Continuing Problem: To avoid slurring unmarried couples and other single people, we have removed the assumption of respectability from the married. Also, all the terms being used for and by unmarried couples for their relationships are foolish.

Examples:

Spouses

"I am not Ann Guest," exclaimed a lady of long-standing respectability. "I'm the man's wife. We've been married for forty years and they all know it. So why can't my husband's office invite us as 'Mr. and Mrs.'? It's always 'Mr. . . . and Guest,' even from people we see all the time. Are they afraid the marriage isn't going to last another two weeks until the party? And that he'll be furious they didn't anticipate his bringing someone he's picked up since?"

"I refuse to be anybody's Domestic Partner," roared a redoubtable gentleman. "Quaint as it may seem, my wife and I happen to be married. The last I checked that made me her husband. I may have had to learn to help with the housework in ways I didn't anticipate when I made the arrangement but, by God, that's still not my primary function in this union."

"What should I have said?" asked a bewildered matron. "A lady I met at a party asked me if I were 'involved' with one of the men there. I suppose I made a fool of myself, because I blurted out, 'Oh, good heavens, no! We're married, and we have three grown-up children.' "

Miss Manners understands that these sputterings can be seen to be the dated protests of people who are used to having lives, rather than lifestyles. She could, of course, explain to the married that more general terms—guest, partner, involvement—are used nowadays in order to include the comparatively recent social acceptance of couples who, while not legally married, have nevertheless gone public and expect to be treated as a social unit. By using more inclusive language, rather than terms exclusively reserved for the married, the hope is to offend fewer people.

After all, the hosts are not interested in checking licenses over who is attending a party with whom. As a matron of Miss Manners' acquaintance was told when she explained that her husband was out of town but that she would like to bring her brother, "You can bring anyone you like, and you can call him whatever you like."

Miss Manners could also point out that people are understandably wary of making presumptions about any sort of couplings. The polite inquiry, "How's the family?" may set off all kinds of emotional explosions in those who have dissolved their families since the last inquiry. Nobody wants to overassume anything.

Still and all, Miss Manners sympathizes with the indignation exhibited by ordinary people who see their conventional arrangements treated as special cases. There is something not quite nice about the assumption that married people are exceptions to the rule and that marriages are so fragile that anyone who hasn't checked in the last week should not treat one as being intact. It leads to the chilling terminology now ubiquitous among the young who are embarking upon marriage. "This is a first wedding," today's blushing bride will confess. "It's the first marriage for both of us," the bridegroom will say manfully.

"Oh," one feels like replying, "only the first time. Well, come back and tell me when you're getting married for the final time." The proper wording, you idealistic young things, is "We're getting married." The event is referred to as "our wedding" without putting a number on it.

The proper term for a guest is that person's name. If you don't know whether the person you intend to invite is married, you must ask; and you could use the opportunity to find out if the couple uses "Mr. and Mrs." or other honorifics and the same or different surnames. If you intend a person to bring someone else, you must ask that person's name. Dignity demands that wives and husbands should be acknowledged as such, aside from whatever other terms are used for other pairings. And there is no dignity at all in anyone's being addressed as "and guest" or "escort."

Single Parents

DEAR MISS MANNERS,

I would like to know your definition of a single parent, a term you often use but which, to my mind, brings up the question of their offspring. My encyclopedia defines children conceived by unmarried parents as illegitimate and calls them bastards. But such names don't seem to affect people, or at least it doesn't mean anything that their offspring could be called that. I am from a time when that word would be very degrading, but I realize the current mode of living is entirely different and morals have changed considerably.

Gentle Reader,

Miss Manners is a nice lady who doesn't use that word to describe anyone, not even the people who steal potted flowers from the porch, and certainly not innocent children.

By "single parent" she means anyone who is a sole parent, remembering that it is a condition commonly arising from divorce, death or, more happily, adoption, and not just from what the delicate among us used to call waywardness. In any case, Miss Manners concerns herself with whatever problems such parents care to present to her without probing into their pasts. As it happens, nobody has ever asked her permission to become pregnant.

Nevertheless, your implication that etiquette is involved in the change of morals, if not responsible for it, is a valid one. She didn't mean to worm out of that one by prissily defending her own impeccable manners. Social disapproval used to be a formidable force against unmarried mothers and their children. Perhaps it discouraged some such births; certainly it encouraged people to disguise the ones that did occur through hasty marriages, secret adoptions and tangled cover-up stories.

Miss Manners would not go so far as to say that chastity reigned until etiquette stopped looking shocked. She does admit that the dramatic drop in community condemnation made life easier for those reproducing out of what was sternly called wedlock.

You mustn't think that happened because etiquette was falling down on the job. It happened because there was a conscious feeling, which Miss Manners shares, that the people who suffered most from this technique of shaming were the children. The technique of being mean to children in the hope of getting at their mothers—while the fathers have no share at all in the shame—is simply not just. Miss Manners does not oppose the use of social pressure to encourage stable family life. She only insists that it take a less cruel form.

The Search for a Good Descriptive Term

Ever since the fun went out of scandal and the nice old-fashioned term scandalous couples used about themselves—a huffy "We're just good friends"—was appropriated by people who really were just disappointingly good friends, a term has been needed for the openly unmarried couple.

Miss Manners attacks this issue periodically, it being the only problem she can't solve, but it has been a while since she's held open forum. Frankly, this is because she finds it convenient to be able to have something to trot out when asked if she has ever been stumped. It is so unappealing to have to admit to knowing everything.

Meanwhile, however, the suggestions have piled up. And if there is one thing Miss Manners loves almost as much as duty, it is a clean desk.

Aside from terms that are either naughty or nasty, the ones that have multiple advocates are "consort," "co-vivant," and "spouse equivalent." Miss Manners is not crazy about any of them and not only because the first might embarrass dear Prince Albert, who had witnesses to his being legally married. Should one of them achieve vast popular support, however, she would not stand in the way of its success.

She is even less enthusiastic about the variations on mates ("freemate," "space-mate," "comate" "home mate" and its nickname "homate,") and domestics ("domestic partner," "domestic associate," "domestic accomplice" and a suggested nickname, "doma"). Mating and cleaning up afterward—the latter being what domestics used to do and the former, too, for all Miss Manners knows—are indisputably part of the deal. But Miss Manners does not know that they need be drawn to other people's attention.

She has therefore turned to the more imaginative entries sent in by Gentle Readers:

" *'Nuance.' In my case, I would be referring to my ex nuance. I will not go into sound and sense compatibility, which makes the term so easily recognizable. Words that work, work of themselves. Try it out. You may be pleasantly surprised.* "

" *'Helpmeet' or 'helpmate,' an existing English word with an appropriate meaning and no other meanings to confuse people, even has the King James Bible in its background to ensure respectability. In fact, its use to describe Eve as a helpmeet for Adam describes just such a relationship as we are looking to describe, with everything a marriage has except the 'piece of paper.' *"

" *'Tally'—to live in concubinage. 'Tally-husband' or 'tallyman'—a man living thus, from the 1870s. 'Tally-wife' or 'tallywoman,' a woman living thus, early 1860s and late 1880s.* "

CHERRY HILLS VILLAGE, COLO.—A three-year dispute between those who want to pump water from a local creek to their country club golf course and those who want to protect the creek has been characterized by quiet civility, according to the *Denver Post*, which noted that water disputes in the West are usually loud and acrimonious. The *Post* reported that the adversaries have thus far confined themselves to letter-writing and telephone calls and that one group decided against picketing the country club because it was undignified.

"I find that 'coheart' works quite nicely, drawing in the pleasant connotations of 'cohort,' but sweetening it with the 'heart.' "

" 'Co-hab,' much easier than habitant, and very 21st century."

" 'Symbiont,' an organism that lives in a state of symbiosis, the living together of two dissimilar organisms in close association or union, especially where this is advantageous to both. Or 'commensal,' an animal or plant living with another for support or sometimes for mutual advantage, but not as a parasite."

" 'Duo'—a combining form meaning two. When used with an address (Duo John Doe and Sally Smith, Duo John Doe and Tom Smith, Duo Sally Smith and Jane Doe), it would indicate living together."

" 'Swalah': Someone Who Acts Like a Husband. 'Swalaw': Someone Who Acts Like a Wife. Both words are pronounced the same."

"My wife and I put our thinking caps on and came up with 'Palse,' from pal, which has gained status in the courts, and spouse, which everyone knows."

"I do not know whether there is a male name to go with 'concubine,' but perhaps 'concubor' or 'concubinor' would be appropriate."

" 'Counterpart.' "

" 'Quasi.' As in, 'The other day, my quasi said . . .' Try it, you'll like it."

Others have suggested foreign terms in actual use, or foreign-ish ones they did some work on:

"As you could guess, the perfect word is Greek, 'syzon,' from the prefix 'syn,' meaning together, and the verb 'zo,' which means to live. This is used in modern Greek to describe persons living together and intimately involved emotionally as well as sexually. The word is the same for both genders, and the lover can be a person of the opposite sex or, for that matter, of the same sex."

"A German gentleman supplied me with the answer that has been used in his country— *'mitleben,' which simply means 'live with.' "*

"In Sweden, the word 'sambo' is employed as naturally as we would use 'wife.' "

"I would suggest borrowing from romantically versatile Italian. Why not 'live-inamorata' (f.), 'live-inamorato' (m.), and even 'live-inamorati' (pl.)?"

"As a grandmother who often meets today's couples who share both love and finances, I use the term 'sharee.' I believe the French 'chéri(e),' meaning 'loved one,' is related to the verb 'to cherish.' "

"Appropriate the French 'copain.' This will nearly always be literally accurate."

Miss Manners thanks all these kind people for their help. She would appreciate it if they would keep trying.

A Star Pupil (A-Minus)

Dear Miss Manners,

You've heard the argument until it's nauseating: Manners are arbitrary social convention. I feel that manners are a good thing, but this is not enough. I need proof.

I've been able to argue back that manners are intended to recognize and protect demonstrable values, like secrecy, earned position and femininity; that manners establish predictable behavior, like traffic rules do, some specifics of which are optional (which side of the road one drives on) but whose principle has value and should be implemented (at a proper table, one does not have to waste any effort on where the fork is); that manners introduce order into behavior as a sort of art: dance is beautiful partly because, though its motions are natural (often), and because nothing is unintended, in the same way the behavior, motions and conversation of a graceful woman are all in place, nothing is accidental.

Gentle Reader,

It seems to Miss Manners that you are doing an excellent job of defending the holy subject of etiquette against those who think they have trounced it when they point out that it is arbitrary social convention. Of course it is. That is where the analysis of etiquette should begin, not end. As you so aptly point out, such conventions can be manifestations of moral values (although Miss Manners might have said privacy rather than secrecy, and dignity rather than femininity). They make routine behavior predictable and orderly. They provide an aesthetic dimension, especially to the ceremonial side of life.

You want proof, do you? Miss Manners regrets to say that there are plenty of examples available of what happens when etiquette is omitted. The conventional ways of showing respect for one's fellow human beings are often bypassed, as a result of which people are constantly taking offense from one another's behavior, even when no ill was intended. The convention of etiquette that is supposed to control perfectly natural curiosity is commonly ignored and privacy is under assault as everyone feels free to pry and ask nosy questions.

Generous people never know whether their guests will appear or their presents have arrived because their benefactors ignore the conventions of replying and thanking. Ceremonial occasions turn ugly as the convention inhibiting people from exhibiting their greed at weddings, birthdays and anniversaries is loosened and traditions are trashed.

You can surely think of such examples from your own experience, or extract them from that of your scoffing friends. Sadly, there is no end of proof that raw human impulse requires the civilizing influence of arbitrary convention.

Miss Manners's Parting Shot

DEAR MISS MANNERS,

Is it ever possible to be too polite?

GENTLE READER,

When politeness is used to show up other people, it is reclassified as rudeness. Thus it is technically impossible to be too polite.

Index